PRAISE FOR *SALOON MAN* BY/ ABOUT ROBERT MUGGE

One of our best and savviest documentarians about American culture brings his keen social insight and richly expansive vision to his family history. And what history! *Saloon Man* melds meticulous research with relentless narrative energy in bringing to vivid life Mugge's great-grandfather and namesake. The elder Robert Mugge, making his way in a turn-of-20th century America rife with both endless possibility and embedded bigotry, is shown throughout to be highly alert to injustice and just as inventive in his means of circumventing it. The lively and diverse supporting cast, from Black entertainers and radical activists to rapacious businessmen and intransigent prudes, enriches this tale of a life well-lived through both travail and triumph.

—GENE SEYMOUR worked 18 years at *Newsday* as film critic and jazz columnist

Robert Mugge steps out from behind the camera and proves himself a first-rate historian, part David McCullough, part Carl Hiaasen. Bursting with the cinematic flair of one of the country's greatest documentary filmmakers, *Saloon Man* tells the riveting story of Tampa's Gilded Age original buccaneer, the visionary saloon magnate and civil libertarian who "tapped" Tampa's untapped potential.

—AIDAN LEVY is the author of *Saxophone Colossus: The Life and Music of Sonny Rollins*

A great American immigration saga that takes as many dramatic twists and turns as an epic film. Author Mugge takes us along with his great-grandfather Robert Mugge, as the German immigrant turns himself into a Florida businessman of imagination, skill, and shrewdness. Along the way, *Saloon Man* shows its subject to be an American Everyman battling entrenched power, racism, and corruption.

—KEN TUCKER is an author, editor, and cultural critic for *Entertainment Weekly*, NPR's *Fresh Air*, and other publications

In *Saloon Man*, acclaimed filmmaker Robert Mugge turns a documentarian lens onto his own family, bringing the same attentive detail and storytelling acumen to this compelling and carefully researched biography that he has to countless musical luminaries. A fascinating and ever enjoyable portrait of the American entrepreneurial spirit, *Saloon Man* is a rollick of a read that reminds us how the immigrant experience has long shaped our country and national identity.

—WILLIAM LEE ELLIS is a singer-songwriter, journalist, historian, Professor of Music, and Chair of Fine Arts at Saint Michael's College

Saloon Man: A German Immigrant Battles the Limits of Liberty, 1870 to 1915 chronicles both the struggle and the success of the "saloon magnate of Tampa." The book is written by Mugge's great-grandson, also named Robert Mugge, who eloquently describes the life of his ancestor, who inspired his own distinguished career as a documentary filmmaker. Clearly, the apple did not fall far from the tree.

—WILLIAM REYNOLDS FERRIS, Ph.D. is a folklorist, former National Endowment for the Humanities Chair, and Joel R. Williamson Professor of History Emeritus at U. of North Carolina, Chapel Hill

Anyone is lucky to become a grandparent, and even more so to be a great-grandparent. But imagine having a great-grandchild who not only bears your name, but also devotes their time and gifts to writing a book about you. That is a loving memorial of the highest order.

Robert Mugge, the principal character of *Saloon Man*, fully deserves the biographical treatment that Bob Mugge has delivered. The book offers much of value to readers across the spectrum of interests, because of the way that the younger Mugge has connected rich, meaningful stories to the remarkable life of his German-born great-grandfather.

Saloon Man is more than just a biography, but it must be noted that, as an example of that genre, it remains clear-eyed about its protagonist—remarkably so, considering the relationship between the writer and his subject. The two Robert Mugges never met, but the senior of the two was such a larger-than-life figure that his influence has endured among his descendants. The *Urgroßvater* was keen of intellect, ambitious, fearless, entrepreneurial, and contentious, to name a few of the personal characteristics that emerge from this narrative. He left his native Germany on the eve of Bismarck's war of national unification and brought those gifts and traits with him to the United States on the eve of its centennial. On arrival, he adopted his new country with the zeal of a convert.

The story of Robert Mugge is immigrant history, urban history, and a revealing story about race in Tampa, Florida—a southern seaport city in what was formerly the Confederacy. It documents the bitterly divisive culture war of the 19th and early 20th centuries that resulted in Prohibition. *Saloon Man* is a rich resource for the political history of Tampa and Florida, and helps illustrate what complicated places those were during the years just before their growth exploded.

The younger Mugge is fortunate to have family memoirs and anecdotes on which to build his narrative. He leveraged those as he mined the published literature on Tampa and the South. His good fortune continued though, in that his namesake was not only newsworthy in his time, but a prolific writer of letters to the editors of his local newspaper—indeed, the senior Mugge maintained a lively public correspondence that survives in the records of Tampa's print media.

Read *Saloon Man* for a fascinating glimpse of a time and a life on which modern Tampa stands.

—ALAN BLISS, Ph.D is CEO of the Jacksonville History Center

In *Saloon Man*, Robert Mugge does a deep dive into the life of his namesake and emerges with a detailed rendering of a man, a city and a country. The man is Mugge's great-grandfather, an immigrant from Germany who arrived in the U.S. in 1870 with nothing and, through hard work and an almost superhuman resiliency, went on to build a business, a family and a fortune. His is a rags to riches story, but it is so much more. Every opportunity and obstacle on his road to success is rendered in great detail through newspaper articles, journals, business records, census entries, maps, etc., drawing us into a time when the American dream had to be honed from the hard rock of racism, class warfare, disease and corruption. This is the story of a man who faced his chosen country's contradictions head on and who, in the end, emerged bruised but victorious.

This is also a story that would, like most stories, have been lost to history except for the enormous effort of Robert's great-grandson who shares his name and resilient nature. Bob Mugge's life as a documentary filmmaker has provided him with the skills necessary to edit thousands of details, gathered over years, into a full, overarching story. And like Mugge's many films, *Saloon Man* is a work that never fails to intrigue, surprise and ultimately enlighten.

—DAVID APPLEBY is a Peabody, duPont-Columbia, and Erik Barnouw Award-winning historical filmmaker & Professor Emeritus of Film & Video at the University of Memphis

Mugge tributes his great-grandfather, a prominent developer of the fledgling city of Tampa, Florida. In 1870, 17-year-old Wilhelm August Robert Mugge, apprentice jeweler and watchmaker, fled Germany immediately after the outbreak of the Franco-Prussian War. He made his way to Henderson, Kentucky, where his cousin Augusta lived. Two years later he moved to the larger city of Terre Haute, Indiana. In October of 1876, Robert...move[d] to Tampa, Florida, a small hamlet with a population of only a few hundred ("Tampa was little more than a settlement"). Restless and ambitious, Robert became involved in a variety of business ventures—he built a bottling plant for his soda business, later converted into a beer distributorship, leading to his position as the saloon kingpin in Tampa. Mugge intertwines Robert's biography with an extensively detailed history of Tampa's development. The story describes a complex dance consisting of a man and the historical events of which he was a part, each impacting the other. The narrative is rich in material that should be of interest to aspiring historians. And Mugge introduces a wide variety of unique individuals, the most humorous and captivating being a Russian Nihilist, Dr. Frederick Nicholas Weightnovel, who was said to have escaped from a Siberian prison camp by swimming to safety. An intriguing, challenging read, packed with historical and familial minutia.

—*KIRKUS REVIEWS*

PRAISE FOR ROBERT MUGGE'S MEMOIR, *NOTES FROM THE ROAD: A FILMMAKER'S JOURNEY THROUGH AMERICAN MUSIC**

*Named to Kirkus Review's List of
"The Best Indie Books of 2023"

A documentarian revisits the funkiest musical byways in this scintillating memoir. Mugge's vivid prose mixes piquant sketches of musicians with atmospheric evocations of the music. The book is also a master class on the director's craft. A vibrant, entertaining panorama of music-making and the picaresque struggle to capture it on film.

—*KIRKUS REVIEWS* (starred review)

The stories he tells go well beyond anecdotes about musicians. He opens us up to the whole world of documentary filmmaking. *Notes from the Road* is the best thing I've read about what it's like to direct films since Sidney Lumet's 1996 classic, *Making Movies*.

—KEN TUCKER, NPR's *Fresh Air* w/Terry Gross

The overriding takeaway from the book is Mugge's genuine love for the music and all the cultural aspects that surround it. To call him an American treasure is not an overstatement.

—JIM HYNES, *Making a Scene*

Anyone unfortunate enough not to have seen any of his 30-plus films can get a comprehensive view of Mugge's magnificent cinematic legacy through his new volume *Notes from the Road*.

—RON WYNN, *Nashville Scene*

MORE BOOKS FROM THE SAGER GROUP

The Swamp: Deceit and Corruption in the CIA
An Elizabeth Petrov Thriller (Book 1)
by Jeff Grant

Chains of Nobility: Brotherhood of the Mamluks (Book 1-3)
by Brad Graft

Meeting Mozart: A Novel Drawn from the Secret Diaries of Lorenzo Da Ponte

by Howard Jay Smith

Death Came Swiftly: Novel About the Tay Bridge Disaster of 1879
by Bill Abrams

A Boy and His Dog in Hell: And Other Stories
by Mike Sager

Miss Havilland: A Novel
by Gay Daly

The Orphan's Daughter: A Novel
by Jan Cherubin

Lifeboat No. 8: Surviving the Titanic
by Elizabeth Kaye

Into the River of Angels: A Novel
by George R. Wolfe

See our entire library at TheSagerGroup.net

Saloon Man

By/About
ROBERT MUGGE
A German Immigrant Battles the Limits of Liberty, 1870 to 1915

Published in the United States of America.

Cover and Interior Designed by Siori Kitajima, PatternBased.com

Cataloging-in-Publication data for this book is available from the Library of Congress
ISBN-13:
eBook: 978-1-958861-35-6
Paperback: 978-1-958861-36-3
Hardcover: 978-1-958861-37-0

The Sager Group takes no responsibility for the interior content of this book. All editing was done personally by author at his request.

Published by The Sager Group LLC
(TheSagerGroup.net)

Saloon Man

By/About

ROBERT MUGGE

A German Immigrant Battles the Limits
of Liberty, 1870 to 1915

THE SAGER GROUP

Artifex Te Adiuva

Robert Mugge
Saloon Magnate
1853-1915

CONTENTS

Foreword

What are the instances in which our personal histories meet world history? How do larger movements and events shape us, and when do we have the opportunities to shape them? Where are the meeting points and what are the results?

For those of us whose lives span the end of the twentieth century and the beginning of the twenty-first, where in our personal scrapbooks do we place international wars, struggles for civil rights, a changing climate, threats to individual freedoms and challenges to democracy? When that scrapbook is completed, how will history's bright sunshine and darkened shadows fall upon the faces seen in its pages?

These are questions that filmmaker and author Robert Mugge invites us to consider as we read his majestic accounting of the life of immigrant, entrepreneur and saloon-keeper Robert Mugge.

Our Robert Mugge is great-grandson to the saloon-keeper. He never met his great-grandfather, and in my experience, emotional ties fray a bit once you get past two generations. Yet the story he tells is a deeply felt one. As I read, I found myself wondering why I was rooting so hard for the Florida businessman to prevail.

One reason: His challenges are shown to be our challenges.

Again and again, we see Mugge encounter and try to persevere over the forces of history. His friendships and business associations—and a possible love interest—cross a hardening color line. He and his family experience the duality of being both German and American in the years leading to the First World War. And he apparently had a sit-down in 1908 with the crusading prohibitionist Carrie Nation. Speculating about their conversation about women's suffrage and temperance provides one of this book's most intriguing passages.

The author of this book is, of course, best known for his documentaries, especially those about music and musicians. For a full fifty years, he has told the stories of artists working in traditions as diverse as blues, soul, zydeco, jazz, bluegrass, Hawaiian hula, and more. Many of his subjects are larger-than-life figures—think Sun Ra, Gil Scott-Heron, Rubén Blades, Al Green and Sonny Rollins. Mugge never brings these artists down to size. Instead, he transports his audience up to a level from which we can closely encounter the subject. A hallmark of any Mugge film is that it is both a documentary and a celebration of lives that are lived with staggering amounts of creativity. It is in this tradition that *Saloon Man* might be best understood. "In truth," Mugge writes in his preface, "he created businesses the way others compose music, paint pictures, or write books: as an extension of his inner self."

Mugge the writer—just like Mugge the filmmaker—gets to this inner self by deep immersion in the world of his subject. Just as a musician develops mastery of an instrument, our early twentieth century saloon-keeper has to master water works and fire safety and electricity and roads and rivers—all the while contending with personal tragedies and public prejudices. Musicians in Mugge's films are seen and heard re-inventing their genre with every performance. Writes Mugge: "Robert, too, was an artist at heart—one who adored dreaming big dreams and working out fixes for the most staggering problems."

We encounter both horrors and pleasures along the way, each written about with detail and candor. Mugge unflinchingly portrays a world in which public violence is an acceptable tool for maintaining white supremacy. Yet he also keeps his literary camera rolling when the most extravagant characters walk into frame. Mugge the storyteller knows a gift when he sees one. This is certainly the case with the wondrously named Dr. Frederick Nicholas Weightnovel, an exiled Russian doctor and capital-N Nihilist who, among other pursuits, staged a "Free Love" parade in Tampa. To give more details would be to risk spoiling Mugge's story, but like much else in this book, the fate of Weightnovel provides an invaluable perspective on roiling controversies of our time.

By book's end, the city of Tampa is built, and saloon-keeper Robert Mugge passes. Some of his contributions to history have been previously acknowledged, while others are being introduced here for the first time. Few of us will be granted a chronicler who will bring such rigor and compassion to our lives—but all of us can benefit that this German-born saloon man and city builder ended up with a great-grandson who was born to tell the tale.

Even Carrie Nation might drink to that.

—Michael Tisserand

Michael Tisserand's books include *Krazy: George Herriman, A Life in Black and White; Sugarcane Academy; The Kingdom of Zydeco;* and most recently, *My Father When Young,* a collection of Jerry Tisserand's lost photographs from the 1950s, published with The Sager Group.

Preface and Acknowledgements

This book is about a time in American history when a small minority of white Americans owned the majority of wealth, when monopolies controlled the marketplace, when the best health care was restricted to those who could afford it, when African Americans were targeted by white police and racist mobs, when women had to struggle for acceptance in the workplace, when Spanish-speaking immigrants were demonized, when high courts issued decisions split along ideological lines, when efforts were made to prevent minorities from voting or serving in government, when many politicians were corrupt, when the Southern states voted as a conservative block, when unions were crushed, and when the religious right (or progressive left) struggled for decades to impose its own moral views on the nation. Although that may sound uncomfortably familiar, the period in question stretched from the late nineteenth into the early twentieth centuries.

This is also a book about a man who inhabited that era. He was an imperfect person, as are we all. But he stood head and shoulders above the time and place in which he lived. His name was Robert Mugge, and he was a German immigrant who came to the United States in 1870 at the age of seventeen. Once here, he identified with the Founders' values, becoming a living expression of their revolutionary dream.

Robert Mugge would, in many respects, become the chief builder, visionary, and celebrity businessman of greater Tampa, all while generating unwanted controversy as the dominant liquor dealer of South Florida or, as one friend dubbed him in a revealing book inscription, "The Philosopher of the 'Everglades.'" In truth, he created businesses the way others compose music, paint pictures, or write books: as an extension of his inner self. It was American liberty that made it all possible, and it was that ideal for which he never stopped fighting.

Robert Mugge also happens to have been my great-grandfather, which is how I came to have his name, which I also share with my father and elder son. I have no more right to his legacy than do hundreds of others who are, and have been, part of the Mugge diaspora. However, for more than four decades, I have been a documentary filmmaker, and therefore a professional storyteller. As such, I feel uniquely equipped to tell his story.

In taking on this project, I was aided enormously by the memoirs of my grandfather, August B. Mugge, as later edited, introduced, and shared by my parents, Dr. Robert H. and A. Elizabeth Mugge, as well as by books, documents, and photographs collected, saved, and passed along by the three of them. Significant additional assistance came from my first cousin, Patricia Mugge Andrews, former President of the Board of the Jacksonville Historical Society, and keeper of the photo albums and journals of Martha Washington Mugge; from Pat's parents, Richard A. and Jeanette L. Mugge, who spent years collecting bottles produced by the Robert Mugge bottleworks; from Gretchen Petri Harrington, the last surviving grandchild of Robert and Caroline Mugge, who offered firsthand recollections of Caroline and her children; from two other of Robert and Caroline Mugge's granddaughters, the late Patricia M. Reams, who researched family heritage at two German churches, and Margaret Regener Hurner, who built upon the work of my grandfather; from my father's first cousin, Dr. Ernest Reiner, who researched the Robert Mugge beach house and acquired correspondence between Robert Mugge and Adolphus Busch; from sister and brother Bertha Ann and Karl "Moose" Hartung, who chronicled the Kiefer and Hartung families of Henderson, Kentucky; and from David Byron McCullough and his son John Lindsey McCullough, two descendants of the family of Robert Mugge's first wife, Alice Janthe McCullough, who provided priceless information from their nineteenth century family Bible. Family members offering further assistance included my second cousins Joe and Stephen Reams and Dr. Christopher D. Reiner, cousin-in-law Dr. Fred Lambrou, and Kentucky cousin (a few times removed) Lorna Cooper Snow.

Next, I must thank a host of historians, archivists, and genealogical librarians at multiple institutions. Those include Rodney Kite-Powell, Heather Culligan, and C. J. Roberts at the Tampa Bay History Center; Andrew Huse with Special Collections at the University of South Florida Libraries in Tampa; Dan Perez at historical website tampapix.com; the genealogical staff at the Vigo County Public Library in Terre Haute, Indiana; Nancy Voyles and Kristy Vanderpool at the Henderson County Public Library in Henderson, Kentucky; June Dunning at the Alexandrian Public Library in Mount Vernon, Indiana; Tracy Lauer, intrepid Manager and Curator of Collections for the Anheuser-Busch Companies in St. Louis, Missouri; and the late Tony Pizzo, who pulled together remarkable photos, documents, and artifacts and entrusted them to archives he knew would preserve them. Special thanks as well to my author friend Michael Tisserand for his narrative inspiration, book business advice, and brilliant foreword; to Herbert McKee Jr., Clerk of the Henderson County Circuit Court for access to his archives; to Roxanne Kesner of the City of Terre Haute Board of Cemetery Records for helping me to locate the unmarked gravesite of my great-great-grandfather, Ludwig/Louis Mugge; and to author and publisher Mike Sager and team for their generous presentation of my work.

Perhaps my greatest thanks goes to Diana F. Zelman, my filmmaking partner since 2005, my wife since 2012, my biggest supporter in the writing of this book, and the uncontested love of my life. But finally, my enduring thanks and love to my parents, Bob and Liz Mugge, and to our dear friend, Marvin R. A. Johnson, FAIA, who, together, convinced my siblings and me that we were descended from giants, even if no one remembered a great deal about them. Everyone deserves such a family.

In closing, two key points remain: one is that, in late nineteenth and early twentieth century America, word usage and spelling were often different than today, and I acknowledge that difference; the other is that, too much turn-of-the-century press, regardless of region, embodied the overt racism of its time. For both reasons, this book's commentary will utilize current terms such as "African American," "Black," and "mixed race" for "people of color," whereas quotes from period publications will include dated words such as "Negro," "colored," "mulatto," and in the context of Black minstrel shows and vaudeville, the word "coon," which has long been thought offensive. Therefore, I appreciate your forbearance as we visit a time which, in too many ways, resembles our own.

Introduction

In 1873, Mark Twain and Charles Dudley Warner published their collaborative novel, *The Gilded Age: A Tale of Today*. With its title, they named an era of American history which they saw beginning in the late 1860s (the years of well-intentioned but quickly undermined Reconstruction following the Civil War) and which would later be seen as running through the end of the century. It was a time in America of vast economic growth, technological innovation, often booming employment, and expanding immigration, yet also systemic corruption, consolidation of wealth, exploitation of workers, repressive moral crusades, and the renewed oppression of racial and ethnic minorities. In other words, when Twain and Warner wrote of a "gilded age," they envisioned a shiny gold surface, but with unchecked evil underneath.

Just three years before, Robert Mugge (pronounced "muggy"), a seventeen-year-old German immigrant, fled the newly declared Franco-Prussian War in pursuit of unlimited American opportunity. Once in the US, he sought out a cousin in Henderson, Kentucky; opened a store and found a wife in Terre Haute, Indiana; and after six years in the Midwest, set sail with her to semi-tropical Tampa, Florida, then merely a settlement in the Deep South, but with untapped potential to be a great American city. In the years that followed, he embodied the rags-to-riches narrative of juvenile novelist Horatio Alger, employing ambition, self-confidence, quick wit, and a capacity for hard work in creating his own business empire, while helping as well to build a city around him. And yet, as a latter-day American pioneer, he also suffered continuing heartache and devastating loss.

Although Robert's successful ventures included an ice factory, an electric company, a bottling company, a shipping line, an insurance company, restaurants, retail stores, hotels, rental properties, vaudeville theaters, bowling alleys, a machine shop, a saw mill, two large farms, a corporation manufacturing gas lamps, a partnership manufacturing printing presses, and more, his core companies were alcohol-related, from his wholesale liquor business, to the state's first legal distillery, to his South Florida distribution of Anheuser-Busch products, to his scores of well-equipped saloons. Of course, even as Robert amassed wealth and fame as the undisputed "saloon magnate of Tampa," the inexorable rise of temperance forces meant increasing challenges as well.

In many respects, Robert Mugge was typical of the hard-driving, self-made men of his day. In fact, as one example of his trademark ingenuity, when he learned in the spring of 1898 that American troops would encamp in Tampa during the Spanish-American War, he spent just twenty-four hours building a saloon with an eighty-foot bar and pool tables on the edge of the encampment, while also convincing Anheuser-Busch to send him a trainload of beer. By the time the increasingly restless troops had shipped off to Cuba, he had sold all the beer, made an enormous profit, and played a supporting role in momentous historical events.

Robert also was a fervent believer in the personal and professional liberties that all Americans (at least those initially enfranchised) had been promised in the Bill of Rights, and therefore, he was the first to respond to what he considered unfair regulation, punitive taxation, and crooked governance or law enforcement. For instance, after years of paying exorbitant city, county, and state license fees for the operation of his many saloons, only to have city police and county sheriff's deputies harass his resorts (as they were called at the time) while also accepting bribes to overlook illegal liquor sales by so-called "blind tigers" (mostly unlicensed drug stores, restaurants, gambling houses, and brothels), he not only fought them in court and in front of the City Council and County Commissioners, but in August of 1912 took out a prominent newspaper ad declaring the following: "According to my opinion, when it comes to crime, vice and corruption New York City is but a sleepy Sunday school village as compared to the lawlessness existing in Tampa, and the sheriff's office and the police department are responsible for ninety per cent of it." Naturally, the two groups took exception to the ad and found numerous occasions in which to take their revenge.

Finally, although living and working deep in the Jim Crow South, and forced to abide by many of its laws, Robert refused to participate in the subjugation of his African American friends and associates. Instead, he purchased land to construct an African American neighborhood in what became the heart of the city, hired a large number of Black workers for his assorted businesses, paid off the mortgage of a Black church which was founded by former slaves, constructed a three-story African American hotel containing seventy-two guest rooms and eight stores (at a time when most Southern cities offered no provision at all, save for private homes, for traveling persons of color), and took out government licenses for saloons, many of which he leased to Black entrepreneurs who would never have been granted licenses on their own. Through the years, Robert's support of the Black community, and the positioning of some of his key businesses within it, so infuriated many white citizens that, in 1903, during a four-month period when several African American men were lynched, castrated, or both by white mobs (with the quiet collusion of law enforcement), anonymous letters were sent to Robert Mugge promising similar treatment if he continued such support. In response, Robert announced in local papers that he had purchased a weapon of his own and would greet any mob with at least as much violence as they directed at him.

The story of Robert Mugge offers revealing glimpses into America of the late nineteenth and early twentieth centuries, not only because his ambitions, achievements, and character made him the equal of his first-generation peers, but also because, like Twain and Warner before him, he was drawn to the glitter of opportunity, while fully rejecting the rot and rust hidden beneath, the most serious examples of which were corruption, inequality, and oppression. In the Gilded Age, as in America today, freedom was widely promised, yet too often denied. Therefore, the battle for liberty—as well as for equality and the pursuit of happiness—was, and is, never-ending. And with that understood, the story begins.

Chapter One

Heartland

obert Mugge was not always the "Saloon Magnate of Tampa."[1] Neither was he always an American. And neither was he always known simply as Robert Mugge, much less the more formal and succinct R. Mugge with which he conducted business.

He was born Wilhelm August Robert Mügge on January 5, 1853. For generations, his family had lived in the German village of Badenhausen in the southern Harz Mountains. But Robert's father, Johann Heinrich Ludwig Mügge, moved to the nearby town of Lauterberg (now called Bad Lauterberg), met and married Christiane Luise Wenzel, and proceeded to father three children, the other two being Bertha, born in 1846, and Louis, born in 1857.[2] Both Badenhausen and (Bad) Lauterberg were, and still are, in the orbit of Hanover, the capital city of the German state of Lower Saxony. (Note: "Bad"—literally meaning "bath"—has been added to the names of German towns that offer thermal spring spas meeting strict government standards. It is considered a term of distinction for these municipalities.)[3]

Over the years, Ludwig earned the title of *schneidermeister* (master tailor), a designation meaning he could take on apprentices. Much of his renown came from the fact that, periodically, he would travel to London and Paris to acquire the latest fashions in men's clothing.[4] The notion that a merchant could lay down roots in a small community, while also having a global perspective, would not be lost on Ludwig's ambitious middle child.

Encouraged to adopt a trade of his own, the tall, blond-haired, and blue-eyed Robert, like his father, spent his youth as an apprentice, in his case learning all that was needed to be a jeweler and watchmaker.[5] But this was a trade he would not long practice in his native country. Instead, it gave him essential survival skills transferrable to any future destination.

On July 19, 1870, provoked by Prussian Chancellor Otto von Bismarck, French forces invaded German territory, which permitted Bismarck to unite the various German states into a new German Empire in order to defeat the professional French army.[6] Prussia's own military relied on conscription, and all German males, aged twenty to twenty-eight, were expected to serve three years in the regular army, followed by four years in the reserves.[7] Although Robert was seventeen at the time, no one knew how long the war would last, or what would become of those asked to fight it. For many young men of his age and older, it was a time to consider their options.

Across the ocean, just two years before, the United States of America had adopted the Fourteenth Amendment to the Constitution which, conceivably, could have caught Robert's attention. Section One of the amendment states as follows: "All persons born or naturalized in the United States, and subject to the jurisdiction thereof, are citizens of the United States and of the State wherein they reside. No State shall make or enforce any law which shall abridge the privileges or immunities of citizens of the United States; nor shall any State deprive any person of life, liberty, or property without due process of law; nor deny to any person within its jurisdiction the equal protection of the laws."[8] To quote author and historian T. J. Stiles, writing in *The New York Times* on July 26, 2018 (as the amendment turned 150): "Before the 14th Amendment, the Bill of Rights protected almost no one ... [This amendment] established birthright citizenship, required 'due process' and 'equal protection' of the law for everyone, and put the federal government in the business of policing liberty. It removed race and ethnicity from the legal definition of American identity ... If it did not invent freedom, it transformed and strengthened it, codifying a universal definition of individual rights and national identity that has been an example to the world." And though he freely admitted that, again and again, Americans have failed to uphold those standards, he still asserted that "Americans of 150 years ago created something greater than their own limitations ... a broad reimagining of individual rights and federal power."[9]

As for Robert Mugge, considering his diminished prospects at home, and his lifelong concern with personal liberty which was just then beginning to stir, these words would have offered genuine promise. And as it happened, Robert's first cousin, Augusta Friedrika Römermann, the daughter of his father's sister, the former Christina Wilhelmina Mügge,[10] had already found her way to Henderson, Kentucky, a small city in the American heartland, and married into a German American family there.

Augustus Kiefer, a shoemaker from the German province of Baden, had lived a life not unusual for immigrants of that time. Six weeks after the birth of his second son, Albert, in 1843, he buried his first wife in his homeland. Eventually, he would marry again, have additional children, and in 1854, would move on his own to Mount Vernon, Indiana to prepare a new home for them. In due course, he was able to send for them, but cholera broke out on the ship which was transporting them to New Orleans. Tragically, when Augustus met the ship in New Orleans, only three members of his family were still alive: Albert, now ten; Edward, now twelve; and their younger sister Ida, now seven. His second wife and their infant child had both been stricken and, as was the custom on sailing vessels at the time, their bodies tossed overboard.[11] Three years later, Augustus would marry his third wife, Catherine Newfelder, eighteen years his junior, and a native of Bavaria, and they would have five additional children together before he buried her as well.[12]

In 1862, when Albert was nineteen and Edward twenty, they joined the Union Army, each of them serving for three years, then returning to Mount Vernon. In March of 1867, Albert married Augusta Römermann who, like him, had been born in Germany in

1843.[13] The two of them immediately moved up the Ohio River to the larger city of Henderson, Kentucky, built a house at 1012 Main Street, and then enlarged it as each of their five children was born. Albert initially worked as a tailor but, in time, opened a neighborhood grocery store at Ninth and Elm Streets, which he would operate for many years.[14]

Noting that America's Civil War was now over, whereas Germany's war with France was just beginning, Robert decided this would be an ideal time to visit Augusta, his Kentucky cousin, and meet her growing family. And so, booking a ticket in steerage on the Steamship Iowa, Robert set sail from Bremen, stopping in Glasgow, Scotland, and arriving at New York City's Castle Garden immigration processing center (the predecessor to Ellis Island) on September 19, 1870, two months to the day after the start of the Franco-Prussian War.[15] According to the Library of Congress, Robert was one of more than five million persons who entered the United States from Germany during the nineteenth century, a majority of them settling in the so-called "German Triangle," which was bounded by Cincinnati, Milwaukee, and St. Louis.[16] [17]

In a 1902 publication titled *Memoirs of Florida*, author Roland H. Rerick created a portrait of Robert Mugge based on Robert's own recollections of his early years in America and all that he had accomplished since. For instance, Robert recalled that he had arrived in New York City with only twenty dollars to his name, but immediately went to work as a watchmaker, earning enough money to travel to Henderson, Kentucky two months later.[18] From New York, he likely took a train to Pittsburgh, then followed the Ohio River all the way to Henderson. This is a safe assumption in that, throughout his life, circumstances permitting, Robert would always travel by water, because journeys by horse-drawn wagon were brutal, and railroads were only available between larger population centers.

Welcomed by Albert and Augusta Kiefer, Robert spent the next two years in Henderson, perfecting his English, studying American culture, and continuing to earn a living by repairing clocks and watches. Apparently, word of his success convinced his older sister Bertha and her husband Wilhelm Mahn to join him there in

September of 1871,[19] followed by his father Ludwig, mother Luise, and younger brother Louis in November of 1872.[20] Yet, no sooner had his parents arrived than Robert decided that Terre Haute, Indiana, a larger and more cosmopolitan city than Henderson, offered greater potential than Henderson, and his family members agreed.

Inasmuch as Terre Haute is perched on the banks of the Wabash River, just as Henderson and Mount Vernon overlook the Ohio, Robert and family were able to travel there by steamship, first sailing west on the Ohio, then north on the Wabash. Upon their arrival, Robert likely sought work in one of the half-dozen jewelry stores huddled together in a couple-block area of downtown Terre Haute. But with a strong work ethic and a longing to succeed, he may also have accepted part-time or short-term physical labor to pay his bills while becoming established in his chosen field.[21]

One such opportunity almost surely was assisting John McCullough with his cooperage business; coopers being men who built and repaired the casks and barrels widely used for transporting goods. Since such containers were used especially for shipping cargo by boat, coopers tended to congregate in cities adjacent to rivers, and this is why John had brought his wife Mary Ann, daughter Alice Janthe, and son David to Terre Haute. Alice, though in her mid-teens when Robert first met her, was training to be a milliner, which is someone who designs, constructs, sells, and repairs hats, as well as a professional dressmaker. Her brother David, a year younger than Alice, was already helping in his father's business.[22]

Another Terre Haute resident whom Robert befriended, though no record exists of their working together, was William Patrick,[23] a prominent local nurseryman.[24] He had started out as a Terre Haute house painter but eventually acquired acres of land on which he grew and tended large numbers of fruit trees and flowering ornamental trees for sale to his neighbors and to customers at a distance.[25] He must have been quite successful, because around the time Robert started establishing himself in the city, William was promoting large shipments of his trees while also building himself and his family what the *Terre Haute Daily Gazette* termed "a handsome, roomy and substantial two story dwelling house, south of the blast furnace, on his extensive nursery grounds."[26]

Ludwig (now Louis) Mügge and Wilhelm (now William) Mahn were both tailors, and as they too arrived in the city, each found a way to practice his trade. Louis apparently worked from home, while William was hired by Erlanger's, an established men's clothier with a shop in the beautiful Terre Haute opera house. Louis's younger son, who shared his name, though only fifteen when they arrived in America had already been trained as a clerk, and he soon found a position with Riddle, which was Terre Haute's largest and most aggressively advertised jewelry, watch, and clock store.[27] Yet it was Robert who most quickly and successfully integrated himself into the life of the city.

By at least 1873, Robert added his own jewelry store to the group of them coexisting downtown. This is documented by a voluminous "Watchmakers & Jewelers Hand Book," written entirely in florid English script (perhaps translated, in part, from a similar handbook he had used in Germany) and signed, "Robert Mugge Terre Haute, Ind July 22d 1874."[28] His place of business was at 321 Main Street, on the south side of the block between Third and Fourth Avenues.[29] Later, the street name was changed to Wabash Avenue, and the U.S. Postal Service revamped the address numbering system at least twice over the years. But there is still no mistaking the south side of the street between Third and Fourth.

Additional changes included Robert dropping the umlaut (two dots) over the "u" in "Mügge," as did the rest of his family. Although other German Americans, when dropping an umlaut from a letter in their names, would then follow that letter with an "e," Robert and his family did not. That may be because the family had only begun using the umlaut a few generations before, so perhaps they were not as wedded to it.[30]

The growing visibility of Robert's store meant an increasing role for him in the political, cultural, and social life of the city. For instance, an ad in the *Saturday Evening Mail* for a political event at the Republican Wigwam listed "Robt. Mugge" as one of perhaps a hundred people inviting others to attend.[31] (Note: The Republican

Wigwam of Terre Haute was a gathering place for the public exchange of political views, patterned after the Chicago Convention Center where Abraham Lincoln was nominated for president in 1860 and named after the domed dwellings of Native American people that were used for ceremonial purposes.) In another ad in the *Evening Gazette*, it was announced that anyone wishing to acquire tickets for the Turner's Centennial Masquerade Ball, a New Year's Eve event slated for the city's Turner Hall, could do so from three individuals, one of whom was Robert Mugge.[32] And in another issue of the *Evening Gazette*, members of the Union Band wished to announce that they were under new leadership and that "engagements will be taken at Mugge's jewelry store."[33] In none of these ads did Robert's name include an umlaut.

Speaking of engagements, other changes in Robert's situation had nothing to do with his business. For perhaps the first time in his life, he was deeply in love. The object of his affections was the same Alice Janthe McCullough who had caught his eye a few years before, and who was finally thought old enough to be courted. No, she was not as worldly as he, having grown up largely in Indiana, and if anyone should doubt that fact, they could note her complete lack of accent, a sign that she was a product of the Midwest. But no less obvious were the facts that she was smart, a fast learner, a tireless worker, strikingly creative, bubbling over with youthful energy, and a dark-haired, hazel-eyed natural beauty. In fact, in Robert's own mind, and certainly in his heart, his feelings for Alice had merged with his passion for this new land, for his new life, and for the American ideals that had made them all possible. When he embraced this remarkable young woman, he was also embracing his adopted country, and as he did, he was fully and irrevocably transformed.[34]

On Tuesday, September 14, 1875,[35] at the home of John and Mary Ann McCullough, their daughter, Alice Janthe McCullough, recently turned sixteen, married Wilhelm August Robert Mügge, now all of twenty-two.[36] From that day forward, she would adopt Robert's surname as her own, and he would abandon his first two given names as a needless encumbrance of his former self. A whole new world was opening for them now, and they would make of it what they chose; because that was the promise of the Fourteenth Amendment, and of the people and places Robert had come to love.

Chapter Two
River of Styx

I n the winter of 1876, while visiting Florida, Terre Haute nurseryman William Patrick purchased a grove outside of Tampa, and hoping to grow acres of orange trees and others bearing semi-tropical fruit, he resolved to move his family there by the coming fall.[37] Meanwhile, John McCullough was in his second year of working for a cooperage firm called A. B. Mattox when, in mid-August, all of the coopers in Terre Haute suddenly went on strike, and the eight coopers of A. B. Mattox were said to be the ringleaders. The strike was an honest response to citywide rates being lowered from twelve cents to eleven cents per completed barrel, a rate that would leave them struggling to make just nine dollars per week, an amount on which it would be impossible to support a family.[38] But as the strike stretched from one month into two, with John McCullough earning no income at all and suspecting that, even when it ended, the wrath of the owners would be taken out against the A. B. Mattox coopers, the idea of his family accompanying William Patrick's to Florida sounded better and better. After all, Tampa stood beside the Hillsborough River which, itself, flowed into Tampa Bay, an estuary along the Gulf of Mexico. So, one could imagine it having plenty of demand for coopers. And with that in mind, and the agreement of Mary Ann and David, John informed William that his family would relocate as well.

Naturally, this was welcome news for William, but a cause of concern for Alice Janthe. By the early fall, she was heavily pregnant and expecting to give birth in November. For a seventeen-year-old girl facing her first childbirth, the thought of her mother not being present was likely unbearable.[39] Happily, though, when she took her concerns to Robert, he was fully accommodating. One reason is that he had long suffered from asthma and bronchitis, and Florida was said to have an agreeable climate, totally free of rough, Midwestern winters.[40] But the other reason was that, even though his jewelry store was doing well, the downtown competition was fierce, and he had been thinking that, perhaps he would do better in a community not yet so established.

With all three families—the Patricks, the McCulloughs, and Robert and Alice Mugge—committed to travel in mid-October, everyone still had business to wind down, possessions to pack, and other arrangements to make. But each of them did what was needed, and after tearful goodbyes to Robert's family, he and Alice set out with the others. William had sent his family ahead with plans to meet along the way, while the rest of them made a leisurely stop in Henderson, Kentucky, so Robert could bid the Kiefers farewell. It was during that visit that Robert—perhaps on a whim, but more likely with forethought—dropped by the Circuit Court building of Henderson County and applied for citizenship.[41] Appropriately enough, John McCullough and William Patrick bore witness to his good character and time spent in the country.[42]

After a few days, their group set sale on another steamship, this time heading west down the Ohio River, then taking the Mississippi all the way south to New Orleans. It was not until the May 25, 1913 issue of the *Tampa Morning Tribune* that Robert would describe that last leg of their trip to Tampa: "In '76 the small side wheel steamer 'Emily' plied between Cedar Keys and Key West, acting also as lighter [a barge used in loading and unloading ships offshore] for the New Orleans-Havana S. S. line. In that way, I happened to get on the 'Emily.' The captain, in talking to me, said, 'I understand that you intend to settle in Tampa. It's a good little town; I used to live there myself, but I tell you now, it will never be worth a d____ till after they have had a dozen first class funerals.'"[43]

As Robert and company quickly learned, at that time, Tampa was little more than a settlement. It had grown out of an 1830 military reservation called Fort Brooke, which was, itself, named after Colonel George Marshall Brooke, who had led the first troops there. According to *The Blue Book and History of Pioneers, Tampa, Fla., 1914*, written by Mrs. Pauline Browne-Hazen and published that year by the Tribune Publishing Company, the post provided "protection for white settlers against the Indians, and Tampa was headquarters for the outlying military posts: Fort Dade, Fort Myers, Fort Meade, and others." In the words of the author, Fort Brooke's military role continued for "half a century," and the original tract "comprised one hundred and sixty acres, which the government turned over to Tampa."

In the beginning, Washington Street was the primary street for business, later replaced by Franklin Street, and teams of mules and oxen were the only means of traveling and hauling around the village or through the dense countryside. Meanwhile, settlers came there from as far away as twenty-five miles to secure their mail and provisions, families accompanied some of the soldiers who were stationed there, and "civilians immigrated from time to time, until the village grew slowly ... into a city."

Military personnel based at Fort Brooke fought against the Native American Seminole tribe in the war of 1835-42, then fought with the Confederates in the War Between the States of 1861-65. However, "the original military reservation of sixteen square miles was reduced by executive orders as war troubles ceased, until in 1878 only a comparatively small portion remained. On January 8, 1883, the reservation was relinquished and was transferred by the Secretary of War to the Interior Department. The land was restored to public domain under the law then in force, and was open to homestead claims."[44]

By 1914, when Browne-Hazen was writing, Tampa was a greatly developed city of more than fifty-five thousand, with thousands more on its outskirts. But again, at the time Robert and Alice first saw it, probably in late October of 1876, Tampa was a hamlet containing several hundred people. After the group's arrival, William Patrick took his family to their new farm five miles northeast of the city, and the others apparently joined them there while getting their bearings. Then, for fifty dollars, half of the money he and Alice had brought with them, Robert purchased a quarter block of property at the corner of Marion and Jackson Streets in "downtown" Tampa and proceeded to build a small house where he and Alice could start their family.[45] Alice did give birth on November 17, 1876 but, sadly, the baby, whom they named Louis Mugge, in tribute to Robert's Americanized father, died just ten days later on November 27.[46]

Without doubt, this woeful event was followed by a period of family grieving, as Alice Janthe also worked to regain her strength. But grieving or not, Robert spared no time in completing their first small Tampa house, including a section where Alice could carry on her millinery and dressmaking business. By March of 1877, he also began placing classified ads in the small, weekly *Sunland Tribune* newspaper, announcing that "R. Mugge's Jewelry Shop"[47] was now based within the large general store operated by another ambitious young entrepreneur named William W. Wall.[48] Since Mr. Wall was then 42, and Robert 25, it is easy to picture the slightly older businessman serving as a mentor for the younger one. Nevertheless, those announcements were soon followed by another on May 5, 1877 stating that "R. Mugge has been called home to Terre Haute by the death of his father and will be gone about three weeks," with Mr. Wall promising, in the interim, to look after his business.[49]

During Robert's time away, reversing the route he had taken to Florida, he consoled his family and helped to settle his father's affairs. But upon his return to Tampa, having now lost a major link to his past, plus one to his potential future, he recommitted himself to his family, his business, and his new American home. At the same time, he must have been deeply affected by his trip because, in the years to come, he developed myriad sayings which he would repeat when apropos. One was that "a day should consist of 48 hours instead of 24" which, of course, would allow him to accomplish twice as much. But another was that, once you have left a place you liked, never return, because "you will be disappointed."[50] For the rest of his life, he never again returned to Terre Haute, to Henderson, or even to Lauterberg; henceforth, he would only move forward.

Weeks later, at the end of June, Robert initiated a series of classified ads in the *Sunland Tribune* that painted a detailed portrait of his, his wife's, and his father-in-law's budding business efforts in the city. For instance, on June 30, 1877, this ad appeared: "Mrs. R. Mugge will open a Millinery and Dressmakers Establishment at her residence on the corner of Jackson and Marion Sts. next Tuesday. She has a good stock of Millinery Goods on hand and will dispose of them at low prices. She will cut and make dresses and all kinds of Ladies' wear to order. A large stock of notions and jewelry will be added in two or three weeks."[51] A week after that, in the July 7, 1877 issue, the *Tribune* editor wrote the following: "Mrs. R. Mugge opened her shop on Tuesday last, and from what we can learn the ladies are much pleased. The stock is entirely new, and Mrs. Mugge seems to understand her business thoroughly. No more excuse for fathers and husbands saying it is impossible to get a stylish hat or bonnet. We on our part welcome any enterprise and wish Mrs. Mugge good success."[52]

For his part, Robert mostly repeated an occasional ad stating the following: "Mr. R. Mugge—a first class jeweler—can be found at Mr. Wall's store, where he will do good honest work in his line on the most reasonable terms."[53] But as of the July 7 issue of the *Sunland Tribune*, it was clear that he was not content simply to sell jewelry and repair watches. On that date, the *Tribune* editor wrote the following: "How can we obtain cool water? Mr. R. Mugge has given the best answer to this question so far. He bought a so called drove pump. He gets his water 14 feet below surface water, all of those who tasted it proclaimed the coolest water in town, it is carried so far as 5 and 6 squares. The cost of these pumps is not larger than the riffing of one of our old fashioned wells and the annual expense of repairs can be saved."[54]

In the same issue of the *Tribune*, Robert apparently placed an ad on behalf of his father-in-law, John McCullough. In it, John announced that, "about five miles from here," which likely meant on

William Patrick's property, he had discovered lime rock and, upon "trying to burn it into lime, [he had] found it to be of the very best quality and pure white." As a result, he made it known that he was "putting up kilns" and planned to sell lime "for building purposes ... at about half of what we have been paying for shell lime," which he declared was inferior to "lime made from rock."[55]

Late the following month, John McCullough submitted a letter to the editor outlining again what he was offering in terms of lime rock as a building material.[56] But what was most notable about that issue were indications that Robert, himself, was continuing to make a stir among his fellow residents. For instance, the editor published the following observation: "As an industrious and enterprising citizen we can not speak too highly of Mr. R. Mugge. This gentleman purchased a lot in one of the lowest and wettest places in town, on which he built a small and comfortable house. He went to work at once and filled the lot up, and is now engaged in securing its being well drained in the future. To do this, he has intersected the lot with narrow ditches, which he is going to partly fill with shell, and then cement the bottoms and side. Many of the older citizens were disposed to laugh at Mr. Mugge when he commenced improving his place, but he has certainly set them an example of enterprise, and we cannot but wish that many more such as he would settle in our town."[57]

The same issue featured a somewhat concerning classified ad: "Mrs. R. Mugge will reopen her Establishment on Monday next. She is fully recovered from a severe spell of sickness, and is now ready to return to former duties. Several cases of new goods have arrived and others are on the way."[58] For reasons that will later become obvious, it seems possible her so-called "spell of sickness" may have resulted from a stillbirth.

In the September 22, 1877 issue of the local paper, Robert Mugge placed two long ads in which he made it clear that he, himself, was now making concrete bricks, the dimensions of which were 12 x 6 x 6, and that he would soon begin filling orders.[59] Next, in the October 6, 1877 issue, Alice ran the following ad: "Mrs. R. Mugge is a practical Milliner. She learned the trade with some of the best Milliners in

Indiana, and therefore suits the taste of every body in that line."[60] As Christmas approached, she submitted additional ads touting products that would make for good holiday gifts.

Then, on November 13, 1877, in seeming contrast to the coming holidays, Robert purchased lot number 59 in Tampa's Oaklawn Cemetery.[61] Presumably, this plot would be a final resting place for the child who had died the year before, and perhaps another that, more recently, had failed to be born. And yet, having learned that the mysteries of life and death are equally unknowable, he must have surmised that simply owning such a plot gave him zero control over who would yet fill it, much less when.

For now, of course, Robert's and Alice's businesses continued apace. But little was heard of them again in the paper until the following spring. In the *Sunland Tribune* of April 6, 1878, Alice advertised the assorted spring and summer hats and other lines of merchandise she had received and urged potential buyers to come and see.[62] Then, on April 22, 1878, Robert suffered another blow when his friend and fellow Tampa merchant, William W. Wall, died at age forty-three.[63] Thirty-five years later, in the *Morning Tribune*, Robert would write, "Tampa lost some very good men ... the prince of all was W. W. Wall."[64]

Robert apparently knew Mr. Wall's health had declined to this extent because, in the April 13, 1878 issue of the *Sunland Tribune*, Robert announced that he was moving his jewelry shop from the W. W. Wall & Co.'s store to his own premises at the corner of Jackson and Marion Streets, where he was "preparing to build a shop."[65] Although Mr. Wall's partners kept his store going for some time after the passing of Wall himself, Robert apparently saw this death, almost exactly a year after that of his father, as a sign that his own businesses should be fully autonomous.

Perhaps the most surprising project Robert initiated during that time involved his emulating what had already been done by older businessman Bartholomew C. Leonardy (later spelled Leonardi). In 1871, Mr. Leonardy had purchased eight acres of land owned by African American landowner Thomas Jackson, along the northwestern edge of Tampa at that time, and created what scholars Dr.

Larry Eugene Rivers and Dr. Canter Brown Jr. call "Tampa's first African American suburb." In what became known as Leonardy's Addition, the developer created a ten-block grid, donating two lots to the African Methodist Episcopal Church, and selling the rest to assorted African American families. Then, in 1877, former Civil War blockade runner and merchant Samuel Mitchell decided to subdivide property of his own facing the town's northeastern side, creating what would be termed Mitchell's Addition. And finally, in 1878, Robert Mugge and Rev. A. F. Bernier claimed the core of what was called the Scrub lands and subdivided them for sale to African Americans. To quote Dr. Rivers and Dr. Brown: "'Mugge's Subdivision' established twelve blocks in four tiers limited by Nebraska Avenue on the west, Nassau Street on the east, and Short Emery on the north ... Following Leonardy's lead, Mugge attracted purchasers by deeding a lot for church construction, in this case to the African Methodist Episcopal Zion Church."[66]

With the church at the center of this section, other buyers could settle around it, creating one of Tampa's first genuine African American communities. No doubt, Robert took on this project as another means of supporting his family. Yet, he did it in such a way as to initiate progress for some of the region's most neglected residents, and thereby also helped to diversify the city for decades to come.[67]

As Alice continued to conduct business from their residence throughout 1878, she also became pregnant again. However, that particular year turned out to be a poor time to have a weakened immune system, even due to pregnancy, the reason being that, in 1878, a yellow fever epidemic, which was centered in the Mississippi River Valley, killed an estimated 20,000 people across the American South. In the August 17, 1878 issue of the *Sunland Tribune*, Tampa Mayor Thomas Edward Jackson published twin proclamations stating that, due to the preponderance of yellow fever cases in both New Orleans, Louisiana and Key West, Florida, no one from Tampa must have any communication, whether direct or indirect, with either of those cities.[68] Then, a month later in the same paper, one article announced the following: "The yellow fever still continues its ravages unabated in the stricken cities in the valley of the Mississippi. Last week, three cases and one death were reported in Key West." A Second article in that issue went on to report that, "during the present epidemic," seven physicians had died in Grenada, Mississippi; two in Vicksburg, Mississippi; two in Canton, Mississippi; one in New Orleans, Louisiana; and eight in Memphis, Tennessee.[69]

On December 10, 1878, Alice Janthe Mugge gave birth to Walter William Mugge, perhaps at least partially named after Robert's late merchant friend William W. Wall, his brother-in-law William (formerly Wilhelm) Mahn, and his nurseryman friend William Patrick. But exactly two months later, on February 10, 1879, Alice died of yellow fever. The announcement in the *Sunland Tribune* read as follows: "Died.—On the 10th, at the residence of her father, Mr. John McCullough, Alice, wife of Mr. R. Mugge, after a protracted illness."[70] Her death marked the end of Robert's first great romance, but also the partnership of two vital young entrepreneurs who pooled their resources, their energies, and their aspirations.

Just over a month later, on March 21, 1879, three-month-old Walter William died as well. A grave marker at Tampa's Oaklawn Cemetery reads as follows: "Alice M. Mugge—and 3 sons—died February 1879," implying that three sons were buried with her. Mugge and McCullough family records do not mention the birth and death of a third son, yet the marker was placed there decades later by Robert's grandson, Richard A. Mugge, presumably based on information from aging relatives or cemetery records. One logical assumption, as has already been mentioned, is that perhaps another son was stillborn in 1877, which would have placed his appearance midway between that of the two sons whose brief lives were recorded in the McCullough family Bible, probably in hope of keeping them close to God. Nonetheless, as the death toll continued to rise, Robert saw his well-made plans slipping away.[71]

On April 30, 1879, while experiencing his worst grief yet, Robert was declared a citizen of the United States. The Hillsborough County, Florida paperwork refers to his earlier application in Henderson County, Kentucky, in what must have felt a lifetime before, even though it had been only two and a half years.[72] The deaths predicted by the captain of the steamer that brought their party the final distance into Tampa were now coming to pass, yet still more lay ahead. On November 17 of that year, Alice's mother, Mary Ann McCullough, who had nursed her daughter and both grandsons through their final weeks of life, also died, conceivably one final victim of yellow fever, but surely also of a broken heart.[73]

Apparently, Mary's death was as much as her husband John and son David could take. And so, soon thereafter, the two of them relocated to Louisiana, where rice farmers were said to be doing well. David took to farming and went on to raise his own family in rural Louisiana. But John grew restless on the farm, returned to New Orleans to renew his coopering business, and eventually died there alone.[74] As for Robert, he, too, was now very much on his own.

At some point in 1879, Robert's mother Louise (formerly Luise), and his younger brother Louis, decided to return to Germany, and both would remain there until their deaths. Louise would die in 1892 and be buried in their hometown of Lauterberg, but not before finding Robert a second wife.[75] For his part, William Mahn, Robert's brother-in-law, seemed to be doing well in his employment with Erlanger's, because on May 31, 1879, Bertha, William's wife and Robert's sister, was able to travel to Germany for an extended period. Surely, the purpose of her trip was to help Louise become settled there again.[76]

At around the same time, Robert started urging William to come to Tampa and go into business with him. Robert had lost his wife and infant children, of course, but his businesses had done well, gaining him increasing security. And as he watched his new city taking root, he envisioned fresh opportunities for them both. One can imagine William, who was ten years Robert's senior, being reluctant to quit the solid situation he had secured in Terre Haute, and perhaps even fearful of succumbing to the next Southern epidemic. Yet he too was seduced by the thought of new adventures and of being his own boss.

Also during this period, Robert must have been introduced to a Mrs. Vaughn, a milliner who had recently moved to Tampa with her husband, and convinced her to ply her trade in Alice's former shop.[77] By then, Robert had built at least the one store at his residence, creating a more expansive space in which Alice could make and sell hats and dresses, and where he himself could sell jewelry and repair watches. Moreover, Alice no doubt had left the tools of her trade and a good deal of merchandise, so having Mrs. Vaughn take over the business would have benefitted Robert as well.

Then, on December 18, 1879, the *Terre Haute Weekly Gazette* carried the following notice in the "Personals" column: "Mr. Wm. Mahn of Erlanger's shop, left last night for Tampa, Florida, on a health trip, and to visit his brother-in-law, Mr. Mugge."[78] Perhaps William still had not made up his mind about permanent relocation to Tampa, or maybe this talk of a family visit and a trip for health were so that Erlanger's would hold his position, at least until he could examine Robert's new situation. However, by early 1880, he clearly was making the move. In late January, Mrs. Vaughn moved her millinery and dressmaking store from Robert Mugge's lot to "Kennedy corner opposite the court house."[79] Following that, Robert announced he had leased the location of Bartholomew C. Leonardy's one-time general store on the east side of Franklin Street, just above Jackson, where he would sell and repair clocks, watches, and jewelry, and soon open a grocery store.[80] This was a property he would use for one business or another for the rest of his life.

By April, the rest of the plan was revealed. In a series of *Sunland Tribune* classified ads, Robert and William proclaimed their joint operation of the new grocery store,[81] offering "dry goods, groceries, and notions,"[82] as well as garden seeds.[83] In addition, Robert would continue with his clock, watch, and jewelry business, and William would sell men's clothing. According to one of their ads in the *Sunland Tribune*, "Wm. Mahn, the tailor, has a fine variety of samples of gent's cloth. Have your measure taken for a suit and keep up appearances."[84]

For Robert, 1880 was a year of recuperation and rebuilding. No doubt it gave him comfort to have his German brother-in-law working by his side. And then, in early October, his sister Bertha sailed back to New York from Germany and joined the two of them in Tampa.[85] As a result, for the second time since he had come to America, Robert's original German family was sharing his new life.

Soon enough, the grocery store would offer many products that were not food-related, making it more of what was then known as a general store. For instance, as the Christmas seasons of 1880, 1881, and 1882 approached, William Mahn advertised "the largest Stock of Toys ever in Tampa," including "5,000 dolls of all sizes and kinds."[86] Meanwhile, on the property at Marion and Jackson Streets, Robert erected a two-story wooden building intended to house their grocery store, William's tailor shop, and his own jewelry and watchmaking business.[87] Behind that, he constructed a second two-story building as a family residence, and presumably developed new businesses for their Franklin Street location.[88]

Still, coexisting with such opportunities for gain in South Florida was the continuing potential for loss there. As if the three original families who moved to Tampa together in October of 1876 had not suffered enough, on November 16, 1880, William Patrick died at his tropical fruit grove outside of the city. He had earlier sent his wife and children back to Terre Haute, probably due to fear of the recent yellow fever epidemic. This is known, because the 1880 US Census showed that, as of June of that year, the entire Patrick family, aside from its patriarch, was living back at William's Terre Haute nursery.[89] And as a final reminder of how the fates of the Mugge, McCullough, and Patrick families were intertwined, when William's English-born widow, Hannah Jane Patrick, returned to Tampa to deal with probate, "surety" was provided by one R. Mugge.[90]

In 1882, after Robert had spent three years grieving the tragic loss of his wife and sons, his father, his mother-in-law, and two older friends, his mother, Louise, suggested from Germany that he correspond with a young lady friend of hers named Caroline Rautenstrauch. Caroline, a dark-haired beauty born in 1861, had been orphaned young and, along with her brother George, been raised, not always happily, by foster parents August and Melanie Bremer of Goslar, Germany. In their increasingly intimate correspondence, Robert eventually broached the idea of marriage, and Caroline was not averse to the idea. So, they agreed to meet. At his suggestion, Caroline took a steamer, which ultimately brought her to Fernandina, a small coastal town a few miles north of Jacksonville,

Florida, while Robert sailed from Tampa to Fernandina on a ship owned and operated by his friend, Captain Ernest Hausmann. Later, Captain Hausmann would sell "bar fixtures, pool tables and bowling alleys," all of which would interest Robert in the future; but on this day, he had one focus and one focus only.[91]

Robert arrived in time to meet Caroline, and as arranged, wore a red carnation in his lapel. He had instructed her to look him over and, if she did not like what she saw, to take the next boat back to Germany. Clearly, that was not a problem, because they were married in Fernandina on October 12, 1882, then sailed back to Tampa together in Captain Hausmann's best cabin.[92] At this point, Robert was 29, and Caroline was approximately 21.

By now, Robert's tragic losses were approaching those of his cousin's father-in-law, Augustus Kiefer. He did not want to lose another wife, and very much hoped that all his future children would survive. He likely had come to recognize that expecting Alice Janthe to work full-time while also pregnant and keeping house had perhaps weakened her enough to make her susceptible to the yellow fever that killed her. Then again, perhaps Midwestern women were as fragile and as vulnerable as the liberties outlined in the Bill of Rights. This time, he would place his bets on a German wife, who perhaps would be stronger, and he would do everything in his power to protect her from the dangers of a semi-settled nation and a semi-tropical climate. If she wanted to work as well, that was fine. But he would see she wanted for nothing, and all the options were her own.

As it turned out, Caroline was indeed strong, but she also was a gentle soul, easily able to thrive in the orbit of her force-of-nature husband. She missed friends and family in her homeland, but she wrote to them often. In fact, one of the only times she would become upset was when the postman failed to bring her a response, at which point she would call out, "Alte fool!" (*alte* meaning "old" in German), to the amusement of all around. But mostly, Caroline was a warm and loving spirit who prepared German dishes—among them, *Kartoffelpfannkucken* (potato pancakes), *Eierpfannkuchen* (egg pancakes), and *Kaffeekuchen* (coffee cake)—which Robert loved and which, over time, added heft to his youthful physique.[93]

It had now been seven years since the steamer captain ferrying Robert, his friends, and his family members into Tampa foretold that many would die before the city could fully take root. So, by 1883, Robert must have felt their American curse had run its course. Sadly, though, on the ironic date of July 4, 1883, during a visit to Germany, William Mahn, Bertha Mahn's husband and Robert Mugge's business partner, died at the age of forty, leaving Robert on his own in business once again.

Probate did not take place in Tampa until February 22, 1884, but Robert assisted Bertha with the process.[94] Fortunately, during this same period, new life arrived as well when, on November 14, 1883, Caroline gave birth to a daughter named Louise Melanie Mugge, clearly named after Robert's mother Louise and Caroline's foster mother Melanie.[95] Both Caroline and her daughter proved to be as strong as Robert had hoped, and balance was restored at last.

Chapter Three

New Foundations

I n many ways, the mid 1880s were when modern Tampa was born. In 1883, phosphate was discovered in southeast Tampa, creating new industries for the mining of this important mineral and shipping it around the world. Shortly thereafter, Henry B. Plant completed a railway line west across the center of the state to connect Tampa to his railroad network, thereby opening the city to greater transport of cargo and passengers than ever before. And in 1885, the Tampa Board of Trade helped Vincente Martinez-Ybor move his cigar manufacturing company from Key West to Tampa. Ybor's relocation, followed by other manufacturers after a catastrophic fire in Key West, brought thousands of primarily Cuban cigar workers to a newly developed settlement called Ybor City, which was annexed by the City of Tampa in 1887 and eventually made Tampa the capital of US cigar making.[96]

As for Robert Mugge, in the 1906 book, *Twenty Four Years In the Woods, On the Waters, and In the Cities of Florida,* Judge Harry A. Peeples reminisced about arriving in Tampa in 1887 when it was "a hamlet of about eight hundred inhabitants, with little crude wooden buildings, and the only fire protection, as was proven in the fire of 1887, was a nine-foot hose owned by R. Mugge."[97] Of course, Judge Peeples likely arrived earlier in the decade, because his description of the town, the fire, and his first meeting with Robert Mugge do not match up with Tampa as late as 1887. In addition, others from that era remember Robert having a twenty-foot hose,[98] which would be far more practical for fighting fires than one reaching only nine feet. Still, the details of his first meeting with Robert have the ring of truth, even if the year stated is almost surely incorrect:

> My watch got out of order one day, and I was inquiring for a jeweler, when Archie Ross told me to go to the corner of Marion and Jackson Streets. I found the jeweler at his work table, near the east window of a little grocery store. He examined my watch, and then went right to work on it. We got into conversation, and he soon found out I had lived in Hernando county. He told me he had never been there himself, but had met a very amusing sailor or sea captain from there, and that his name was Jake May, and that May had made a most wonderful voyage with an old steam gauge for a compass, and had been to him to have it repaired.
>
> On telling him I knew Jake May, he asked me, please, when I saw him again, to send him around. "I will do so," said I, "but who are you?" "Oh," said he, "my name is Robert Mugge, and if you are keeping house here I will be glad to sell you your groceries. I haven't a great deal, but I can guarantee them cheap and for cash." He gave me my watch and I paid him, and walked around to the court house, to talk with Sheriff Jim Martin on a little matter. I incidentally asked him who Robert Mugge was, or in other words, what was he? "Why, he is a German," said Jim Martin, "and he, Henry Kruse and a few others are the only ones of that nationality that can speak English, and anything that had one-eighth German blood in him they made vote for me, and landed me in office for a second term."[99]

As someone who had grown up in Germany, possibly accompanied his father, Ludwig, on trips to European capitals in search of fabric for Ludwig's tailoring business, spent time in the American Midwest, and was extremely well-read, Robert must sometimes have hungered for more worldly companionship than was available in Tampa in the 1880s. For that reason, it is not surprising he would have been drawn, at least initially, to Dr. Frederick Nicholas Weightnovel, a newly arrived Russian doctor who reportedly had been banished from Moscow to Siberia because of his Nihilist political activities, then fled from Siberia to the United States, eventually ending up living near Tampa. It was said he had escaped Russia through some spectacular feat of swimming, but it was unclear whether he was supposed to have swum the fifty-five miles across the Bering Strait to Alaska, which the U.S. had purchased from Russia in 1867, or perhaps to have swum down a river into Mongolia.

The Nihilists were a prominent Russian revolutionary group at the time, and Dr. F. N. Weightnovel certainly shared their contempt for established laws and institutions. Since the movement culminated in the assassination of Tsar Alexander II in March of 1881, leading to the group itself being crushed by the Russian government, it figures that Frederick Weightnovel could have shown his face in the Tampa area a couple of years after that. In his memoirs, Robert and Caroline's fourth child, August Mugge, later shared his mother Caroline's recollections of how his father and the doctor first became friends.

According to Caroline, via August, not long after her 1882 arrival in Tampa—probably in 1883—Robert made the acquaintance of this self-proclaimed Nihilist who had escaped from Russia and now was living in the country (actually, in an orange grove near Seffner, approximately thirteen miles from downtown Tampa). Dr. Weightnovel suggested that Robert and his wife come for a visit. So, one Sunday afternoon—the traditional time for social visits—Robert bundled Caroline into their horse-drawn carriage, and the two of them took a hot and dusty ride to Seffner.

After their arrival, Dr. Weightnovel killed a chicken and invited them to join him for dinner. Robert happily agreed. But the more proper Caroline, noting the "filthy bed linen" Weightnovel used as a tablecloth, opted to wait in the buggy while the two men ate their "hearty meal." According to August's own recollections of the Russian doctor, "In later years, he moved to Tampa and for a time flourished as a practicing physician. He would strut up and down Franklin Street, dressed always in white, carried a parasol and wore ladies' shoes. He was a handsome man with long hair and well-kept beard."[100]

In fact, when Dr. Weightnovel first arrived in Tampa, he was not supposed to practice medicine, because he could not produce his medical degree, which he said had been stolen. So, initially, he found other ways to make a living, draw attention to himself, and practice his Nihilist beliefs. Decades later, former *Tampa Times* editor Donald B. McKay recalled him as being incredibly fit, with broad shoulders and hair that hung to them. Mr. McKay went on to describe how, on Sunday afternoons, people would flock to the Atlantic Coast Line's docks to watch the ship arriving from Havana and to enjoy Picnic Island south of the docks. Typically, Dr. Weightnovel would be present among them, exhibiting his abilities as a swimmer, including the endurance which had enabled him to escape Siberia. "He would float on his back and eat his dinner from a plate on his chest and after his dinner would smoke a cigarette and read a newspaper even in rough water."

Reportedly, after this display drew a crowd, Dr. Weightnovel would swim to shore and sell bottles of his self-manufactured "hair tonic, picturing on the label his own heavy growth as an example of the crop his tonic would produce." Yet, as Mr. McKay also remembered, it was the doctor's hair tonic that almost proved his undoing. One day, he was riding in an open-air car of one of the "dummy line" trains running between Ybor City and downtown Tampa when a boy seated behind him applied a match to his "oil-soaked hair" and jumped off the car. Fortunately, other passengers were able to smother the flames before he was seriously injured.

In the same column, the veteran editor described the most notorious of Dr. Weightnovel's early exploits in Tampa, which involved "a parade and banquet of a 'Free Love' society he had organized, composed largely of young men of questionable character." One morning, Weightnovel and a group of followers, all of whom wore sashes printed with the name of their group, rode horses from Twenty-Second Street, which was the eastern end of Ybor City, down Seventh Avenue to Nebraska Avenue. Although the paraders were jeered along the way, they soon reached their destination, then backtracked to Hotel de la Habana at Fifteenth Street and Seventh Avenue. There, they sought to enjoy a lavish banquet served by fully naked African American women. However, thanks to the restaurant's large exterior windows, the entire scene was visible to a growing crowd in the street, which surely was the doctor's intention.[101] Much like later events staged by radical European writers, artists, composers, and choreographers—for instance, the 1913 Stravinsky-Diaghilev-Nijinski-Roerich Ballets Russes premiere of "The Rite of Spring" in Paris, which was designed to inflame and did incite a riot, of sorts[102]—this Russian event, too, was meant to provoke, and it quickly achieved its goal. As the banquet was barely beginning, police and sheriff's deputies hauled Tampa's first-ever performance artist and his roomful of co-conspirators to jail.

Admittedly, even without a diploma and license in hand, Dr. Weightnovel found ways to practice medicine on the sly. As just one bit of evidence, in the fall of 1887, a syndicated newspaper article about a conference in Washington, DC made humorous mention of his presence and even included an illustration of him. The piece described The World's Medical Congress as attended by five thousand doctors and divided into eighteen sections, each of which offered two sessions per day. And yet, even at an event of that size, Tampa's most colorful citizen stood out: "A notable figure everywhere at the meetings of the Congress is the Russian Doctor Weightnovel, with his tremendous shock of black hair. He is one of the best-educated physicians in the Congress, but has been barred admission because he violated the ethics of the profession by putting his portrait on his calling cards."[103] However, another syndicated article, appearing thirteen days before, proclaimed the real reasons for excluding him from conference sessions were his "peculiar kid gloves" and his "very dark complexion [probably a tan from working all summer in his

Florida orange grove], long kinky hair and shaggy eyebrows," which caused Southern doctors to allege he was "a negro" and state that admitting him "would set a bad precedent."[104] Although nearly all Northern doctors came to his defense, it appears that the Southern doctors won out, perhaps with his controversial calling card proving the face-saving excuse for excluding him.

A second indication that Dr. Weightnovel was quietly practicing medicine, and with Robert Mugge's help, was printed on the calling card in question. While one side featured a handsome and hairy photo, the other side listed him as an "accoucheur" (essentially an obstetrician), physician, and surgeon who was available for "treatment personally or by correspondence." More specifically, he was said to consult with patients on Sundays at his residence, "Felicity Home," which was three miles south of Seffner, Florida, and Tuesdays "at the Mugge House, Jackson Street, Tampa, Florida." Presumably, Robert, often wary of authority himself, allowed his Russian friend use of one or two of the rooms he rented out at his home, and as August Mugge reported in his memoirs, even trusted Dr. Weightnovel with his family: "He was our house physician and delivered some of us."[105]

Throughout the 1880s, Robert's own unquenchable curiosity and restless spirit took him in many directions. Tampa and Jacksonville city directories of the period described him as an agent of general merchandise, but that hardly imparted all his interests. According to Karl H. Grismer's 1950 book, *Tampa: A History of the City of Tampa and the Tampa Bay Region of Florida*, "[Robert Mugge] first attracted attention in December 1884, when he put up the first street lights in town in front of his Jackson Street home and bottling plant. The lights burned oil. At that time he also laid the first concrete sidewalk. Said the *Tampa Tribune*: 'Mugge's example is one that many other good citizens would do well to follow.'"[106]

The bottling plant mentioned was a work in progress for some time, but it went into service in the mid 1880s and was almost continually in use for decades to come. Sanford fire maps were a means for fire insurance companies to assess their liabilities when downtown buildings caught fire around the country, and the 1887 map of the block in downtown Tampa surrounded by Jackson, Marion, Monroe, and Lafayette Streets revealed a "foundation" rising directly next to Robert's "general store." That foundation would soon underlie an ice plant which, in turn, would buttress his bottling works and other businesses yet to come.[107]

Speaking of fires, Karl Grismer's book of Tampa history also mentions that, prior to 1886, the city's firefighting tools consisted of "twenty buckets, two scaling ladders, and some axes," probably supported by Robert Mugge's famous hose. Then, on May 8 of that year, a terrible fire leveled nearly every building "in the block bounded by Franklin, Whiting, Tampa, and Washington," bringing it within a block of Robert's own businesses at Franklin and Jackson, and only two blocks from his home. This convinced the city to order its first fire engine, a horse-drawn hand-pumper that required the firemen themselves to pump water from the river and onto the flames. It arrived on July 30, complete with 350 feet of two-inch hose and a hose reel, and caused widespread excitement when firemen put it to an immediate test, throwing water "clear over the top of John T. Lesley's two-story building at Franklin and Washington."[108] According to a 1958 article on the "early days" of Tampa's fire department, Robert donated the entire $600 cost of the engine, after which it was known as the "Mugge pump."[109]

Grismer's book also recounted that, a month later, on August 30, 1886, the Tampa Fire Company was established, "with A. C. Wuerpel as president, Robert Mugge as secretary, and Herman Glogowski as treasurer." Reportedly, they and their multiethnic colleagues all "served without pay." And such information, gleaned from period newspapers, clearly shows that the dates given in the previously mentioned book by Judge Harry A. Peeples were at least a couple years off.[110]

Of course, even Robert (who guaranteed payment for the printing of the judge's book, then was forced to pay when Peeples defaulted) did not seem to mind the errors it contained. But then, many people of that time were not overly concerned with personal record-keeping, which is evident from the family birth, death, and immigration dates changing from one decade's Census records to the

next. Fortunately, though, Robert and Caroline kept track of important dates for their own family (with one exception, to be mentioned
later), which is why we know that, on May 17, 1886, Caroline gave
birth to Eugene George Mugge, her first son, and their second child
to survive.[111]

According to Roland Rerick, writing in his 1902 book, *Memoirs
of Florida*, Robert was a survivor as well: "When he first came to the
city he worked at this trade [watchmaking] for several years. In 1879,
he engaged in general merchandising and to these businesses gave
his attention until 1887, when he retired from both of them. He
took up the manufacture of soda and mineral water and from this
drifted into the liquor business and won a reputation for rare business ability."[112]

It would be four more years before Robert and Caroline's second
son, August Bremer Mugge, would be born. But again, it was August
who later wrote personal memoirs providing lucid recollections of
his father, his family, and his father's businesses. According to those
memoirs, Robert built his bottling plant close beside the family home
on Marion Street, with Caroline's garden sitting in between (after his
ice plant was moved elsewhere).[113] In fact, Robert's last surviving grand-
daughter, Gretchen Petri Harrington, remembers Caroline lining her
garden with Robert's discarded bottles, sticking them into the earth
upside down, with the larger bottom ends displayed in neat rows.[114]

August recalled further that, at the rear of the bottling works
was a large wooden tank which held water pumped from their well.
Inside the shop was a boiler room at one end, and a syrup room
at the other. In the latter, his father "concocted the various syrups
which were used in the manufacture of lemon, strawberry and sarsa-
parilla soda water." Robert also operated the primitive machinery
himself, filling each bottle individually while, in another corner sat
vats where the bottles were washed, sometimes by young August,
who had a propensity for falling headfirst into the dirty water. Of
course, August assisting with the washing of bottles, and his falling
headfirst into the vat, would not happen until well into the 1890s.[115]

The *Tampa Journal* of September 29, 1887 announced that Robert
Mugge had hired R. Merrown to take charge of his bottling works.

The two were proposing "to give us something new and delicious in the way of beverages. The bottling business is quite an industry in Tampa from which the whole of South Florida is supplied." Reportedly, Mr. Merrown had spent "seven years an employee with the famous firm of Cantrell & Cochrane," pioneers of carbonated drinks based in Belfast and Dublin, Ireland.[116] With that in mind, it was no surprise when, the following May, 1888, a new ad appeared in local newspapers: "Soda & Mineral Waters Made of Pure Artesian Water and the Finest Ingredients. Aromatic Belfast Ginger Ale a specialty. Live Agents wanted in every Town in South Florida. R. Mugge, Tampa, Fla."[117]

On September 9, 1888, Caroline gave birth to another healthy girl, Frances Bertha Mugge, who was the first of Robert's daughters named for American first ladies. In her case, Frances was named after Frances Clara Cleveland, the young and popular wife of US President Grover Cleveland, then serving the first of his two, nonsuccessive terms.[118]

Yet, as fast as Robert's family expanded, his businesses expanded faster. Confirmation could be seen in the 1889 Sanford fire map, which showed that the ice plant had been built on the previously outlined foundation; the two-story "mineral water factory" had been constructed just beyond; the once evident general store and tailor shop appeared to be vacant; and the building comprising the former shops was being converted into living space. Meanwhile, Monroe, one of the streets bordering the family block, had been renamed Florida Avenue. And as to the icehouse, although it did stand for several years on the Jackson and Marion property, it would eventually be replaced by a full-fledged ice factory on Central Avenue.[119]

Just a month after Frances was born, with a middle name paying tribute to her Aunt Bertha, Bertha, herself, got remarried on October 10, 1888. She married Dr. August Berger, a German physician who had served in the Ulanne medical corps during the 1870-71 Franco-Prussian War, then, immediately afterwards, immigrated to America with his wife and children. By the time he met and married Bertha, his first wife had died, his four children were grown, and he, himself, had become a pioneering researcher into Hansen's Disease, commonly known as leprosy, which he had uncovered on trips to Cuba and other islands in the Caribbean. According to recollections of *Tampa Times* editor Donald B. McKay, the doctor's acclaim was due to his having helped conceive methods for detecting and treating the disease, as well as helping found the Louisiana isolation leprosy colony.

For some reason, Robert had opposed the marriage. Was there tension between Dr. Berger and him, because the doctor had served in the Franco-Prussian War, whereas Robert, admittedly not yet old enough for conscription, had left for America? Did Robert feel protective of his sister's marriage to the late William Mahn, who had been Robert's business partner? Did Robert fear that the doctor's research could expose his family to disease? Or was Robert simply appalled by the doctor's fundraising techniques? As an example of the latter, in the same column, McKay recalled Dr. Berger entering the office of First National Bank President T. C. Taliaferro, pulling an "elaborate magnifying apparatus" from his medical bag, and saying, "I want to show you the leprosy bacillus and some scab samples." Reportedly, President Taliaferro leaped from his chair, escorted the doctor out of his office, and instructed a cashier to grant him a loan. But regardless, any antipathy between Robert and Doctor Berger was short-lived since, only three years later, on December 23, 1891, the doctor died in Long Island, Bahamas, the implicit victim of his zealous research.[120]

After the death of her second husband, and for the rest of her life, Bertha resided in upstairs rooms of the Mugge family home and lodging house. Reportedly, she mostly kept to herself, and she and Robert rarely spoke. In fact, Bertha also spent some of those years afflicted with a terminal illness, with Caroline nursing her through it.[121]

In 1890, much of the family took a trip back to Lauterberg, Germany. At the time, Caroline was pregnant again, but she managed the trip without problem. There, in Lauterberg, on June 6, 1890, two-year-old Frances was christened at the Mugge family church.[122] Then, after the family's return to Tampa, red-headed August Bremer Mugge was born on September 10 of that year,[123] allowing him to recount family history more than seven decades later. For instance, August pointed out that his father ultimately owned "an electric plant in conjunction with an ice manufacturing plant," both of which were "located on Central Avenue near Cass Street." It was August's understanding that, as his father had become an agent for the Anheuser-Busch Brewing Association in the late 1880s, an ice plant became essential. Yet, as he also established a wholesale and retail liquor business, with Anheuser-Busch providing much of the financing, he needed an even bigger plant: "He became the owner of saloons in all sections of Tampa, including St. Petersburg, Port Tampa City and Plant City. The 'Wholesale House' was located on Franklin Street, in the 300 block [first on one side of the street, and then on the other]."[124]

Although, again, August recalled his father's relationship with the Anheuser-Busch Brewing Association beginning in the late 1880s, the earliest available documentation is a color print ad from 1890 listing several Florida agents, one of whom was "R. Mugge," the representative for Tampa. Moreover, in later newspaper ads for his wholesale liquor business, Robert claimed 1890 as its year of founding. Yet, regardless, in very short order, Robert would be dubbed the Anheuser-Busch "distributor" for South Florida, and he would retain that title for the rest of his life, even as he branched into dozens of other businesses.

According to Karl Grismer's book of Tampa history, "In April, 1890, Mugge organized the Tampa Electrical Illuminating Company, installing a generator in his ice plant on Central Avenue, and started supplying electricity to the scrub district."[125] Actually, that date, too, may be a bit off because, according to the *Tampa Daily Journal* in March 1890, Robert already was erecting poles "on Lafayette Street below Franklin" and hanging wire for his electric company. Executives for a rival company, the Tampa Electric Light & Power Co., were up in arms and threatening to sue because they felt Robert's poles were interfering with their own.[126] Nonetheless, a month later, the same paper reported that the wife and children of Mr. C. C. Radabaugh had arrived from St. Louis the previous Saturday night, joining Mr. Radabaugh in "the Mugge cottage, next to the works of the Tampa Electrical Illuminating Co., of which Mr. Radabaugh is superintendent."[127] Finally, in October, the *Journal* reported Robert had been asked to move his electric plant to Key West, Florida, but his terms proved more than the city could handle.[128]

In his memoirs, August Mugge offered more details about his father's electric company. According to him, it operated from approximately 6:00 p.m. till midnight, and "often the lights were very dim, and then there were breakdowns." Of course, in the previously mentioned March issue of the *Journal*, Robert discussed similar limitations in the service of his rivals. But regardless of which company offered brighter or longer-lasting illumination, August recalled Robert's boilers burning wood hauled from his farm near Bloomingdale, then, later, burning oil stored in huge tanks in the ground.[129]

As August and others have reported, Robert also was instrumental in the building of an electric light plant in Port Tampa City. That is, in 1891, he sold them "the machinery and equipment adequate for a plant of sufficient power to serve the town, including 25 miles of wire at one-half of what it would have cost from the manufacturer." August added that, "There is a letter dated July 13, 1891 in existence to Captain J. W. Fitzgerald, General Superintendent of the P. & O. Steamship Company,"[130] in which Robert made the offer to sell.[131] The offer was accepted, and the plant was in operation for many years.

Naturally, as so many new Mugge ventures were being born, some of the older ones were pushed aside. For one, the Mugge grocery store (again, sometimes called a general store), originally created in partnership with William Mahn, simply faded away. For another, Robert's jewelry and watch repair business met a similar fate.[132] Of course, period watches were complex mechanical wonders, with hundreds of parts (wheels, gears, jewels, etc.) working in harmony to quantify time, and Robert's grasp of that process—its collective precision in motion—would have informed his design for a growing commercial empire. In fact, as one more sign of previously mentioned expansion and diversification, the 1892 Sanford fire map of the main Mugge lot showed the former general store and adjoining business areas now converted into a lodging house, featuring living quarters for the family and upstairs rooms for renting out.[133]

Still, as exciting as all this was, it must be said that the biggest event of 1891 in Tampa had little to do with Robert Mugge, though it would over time. That event was the opening of the Tampa Bay Hotel, and Robert's son, August B. Mugge, remembered not only how it began, but how it came to have a larger and larger part in the life of his family. The hotel, of course, was the brainchild of industrialist Henry B. Plant who built the first, all-important railroad down the west coast of Florida, and envisioned a wondrous hotel which would lure tourists to Florida in general, and to Tampa in particular. "This was a beautiful structure in the Moorish architecture on the west side of the Hillsborough River, and it was surrounded with beautiful gardens, and in addition a beautiful theatre, the Tampa Bay Casino [an entertainment area designed to be converted back and forth between a theatre and a swimming pool]." August went on to point out that the heyday of the hotel was the "Gay 90s," during which newly minted millionaires would hitch their luxurious private railroad cars to Henry Plant's trains and ride them to Plant's palatial hotel.

One such millionaire was Anheuser-Busch president and co-founder Adolphus Busch, who often vacationed there with his wife Lilly while the worst of winter was hitting St. Louis. It was during such trips that Robert and Adolphus developed a deep bond that had less to do with business and more to do with their shared German heritage. "Naturally, my father and my mother and some of us older children would go over to the hotel in the evenings and visit the Busches," August wrote. "They would shower us with presents, and at Christmas a huge box filled with toys would arrive from St. Louis for us."[134] The growing friendship was such that, once, informed that Mr. Busch would be visiting, Robert purchased a new suit for the occasion. Then, when the trip was unexpectedly canceled, Robert "sent him the bill from the tailor, with the remark, that since he had made it especially for his visit ... he felt that Mr. Busch should pay the bill."[135]

This quirky relationship would become the most important of Robert's career. As August already mentioned, after his father became South Florida distributor for the Anheuser-Busch Brewing

Association, he invested heavily in saloons, not only in Tampa proper, but also in West Tampa, Ybor City, Port Tampa City, Plant City, St. Petersburg, and elsewhere. He also helped pioneer an arrangement wherein, initially with financing from Anheuser-Busch, he would build, or else acquire and remodel, numerous saloons (initially ten at a time, and later twenty); purchase expensive annual city, county, and state liquor licenses for all of them; and then lease each saloon to an individual operator who would be responsible to acquire all product from Robert's wholesale liquor business, and to pass on a share of profits on a weekly basis. If the operator did well, then so did Robert, and so did Anheuser-Busch. But if the operator did poorly, then he eventually would be replaced. It was a business relationship later emulated by other budding liquor wholesalers, especially the successful Florida Brewing Company, probably best-known for creating Florida's first big brewery.[136]

One additional benefit to the operator was that, if he ran afoul of the law, Robert would bail him out and provide legal representation for his court appearances. Of course, the saloon's licenses would be in Robert's name, so often he would be the one arrested and expected to answer in court for whatever infractions allegedly had been committed. As a result, Robert became especially adept at courtroom matters, generally dictating the defense provided by his attorneys and working on his business accounting while they carried it out.[137]

Moreover, in case it is not yet clear, for most of the time Robert lived in Tampa and did business there, that city, like the rest of the Deep South, imposed legal separation of the races.[138] As was previously established, the original Fort Brooke, out of which Tampa grew, had been a Confederate military fort during the Civil War.[139] So, many of the city's pioneers, as well as other white Southerners who later flocked there for work, were, at best, dedicated segregationists.[140] Robert, whose roots were in Germany, cared nothing about that, and merely followed the law to the extent necessary. But he also maintained many of his businesses deep in the so-called Scrub, which was the primary Black section of town, and which he, himself, had helped to develop, shortly after his arrival in the city.

Over the years, Robert employed African Americans throughout his businesses as drivers of his ice and alcohol delivery wagons, as engineers, as porters, and more. But what especially irked city authorities was that he also took out licenses for saloons which he then leased to African American proprietors who, in turn, hired a Black staff and served a Black clientele. In addition, he would some-times create Black "annexes" for his white saloons, turning them over to African American personnel as well.[141] City politicians and police, reflecting popular white sentiment, did not want the Black community having saloons at all, fearing whatever behavior could result and extend out into the streets of the city. But Robert created this workaround which benefitted him just as much as it benefitted his African American partners, employees, and patrons, even as it created resentment in much of the white community, where he was increasingly labeled "immoral."

It should also be noted that, for all the sins of segregation, in Tampa as well as in other Southern cities, it did encourage the creation of a robust, alternative, African American economy which was built upon the efforts of innovative Black merchants, educators, attorneys, and church leaders. Such developments have been beauti-fully addressed by scholars Dr. Larry Eugene Rivers and Dr. Canter Brown Jr. in their 2018 essay, "'The Negroes are There to Stay': The Development of Tampa's African American Community, 1891-1916." As they point out, much of the African American business activity was focused around Tampa's Central Avenue,[142] which was also an enduring center for Robert Mugge's own business concerns. In fact, an interesting story was told by August Mugge in his memoirs, as well as by former longtime Tampa mayor and newspaper editor Donald B. McKay in two of his newspaper columns of historical reminiscence, about Robert assisting a Black church. In August Mugge's words: "He deeded part of his property on Central Avenue where the ice plant was located to a Negro church, and jokingly told the congregation that he would be their preacher! After the church was completed, he paid off the mortgage and also paid the preacher's salary for a long period, requiring him to drive a beer wagon on week days, for which he received the same pay as other employees."[143] Mayor

McKay clarified that Robert actually paid off the mortgage when he learned the mortgage-holder was foreclosing on the congregation.[144] [145] The church in question was probably Beulah Baptist Church, which was founded in 1865 by former slaves and, in 1881, moved to a lot on Harrison Street,[146] close by Robert Mugge's Central Avenue rental properties (plus, eventually, his ice factory, electric plant, distillery, Sunlight Manufacturing Company, Hillsborough Machine Shop, Grand Central Theatre, Central Saloon, and Central Hotel—all important parts of Robert's smartly wound and smoothly running collection of businesses).

Chapter Four

Taking Liberties

The mid-1890s saw an all-out expansion of Robert's businesses, and new technology played a part as well. Although a few Tampa companies secured telephone service as early as 1893 or 1894, most would not connect until the following year. As an illustration, between July 1 and August 25 of 1895, only twenty-two companies or government agencies signed up with the Tampa Telephone Exchange. However, two of those lines were acquired by businessman Robert Mugge, with phone number 201 going to his Marion Street home and bottling works, and number 202 going to his ice factory and electric company on Central Avenue.[147] The change would mean faster and better communication within the city and, as wire was slowly strung across the country, to other cities as well.

On the personal side, however, Robert experienced setbacks. On January 9, 1893, Caroline gave birth to Melanie Wilhelmina Mugge, affectionately known as Lanie. She proved to be physically healthy, but mentally ill. Although diagnosed as epileptic and retarded, descriptions from those who knew her indicate she may simply have been autistic, which would not have been understood at the time.

Whatever the case, the family adjusted, which included keeping her with them as much as possible but institutionalizing her when necessary.[148] [149]

Early in 1893, Robert also staged the first of many tax rebellions he would initiate through the years. On this occasion, he printed and distributed a circular which was addressed to his "Fellow Citizens and Taxpayers" and headlined by the words, "Fraud! Taxes! Swindle!" The gist of his proclamation was that city government was overtaxing small taxpayers to underwrite rampant corruption, while allowing wealthy citizens to pay little or nothing in support of critical city services. As just one example, he pointed out that Edward Manrara, a powerful founder of the local tobacco industry, paid no tax at all in Tampa, because his official place of residence was New York City. But he named others as well who failed to share any of their growing wealth with the city where they had earned it. In Robert's words, "They enjoy our water works, fire protection, street lighting, police protection, etc., and then pay taxes in New York instead of Tampa. At election time, they bribe enough voters (by paying their poll taxes) to keep in power and elect such officials as will allow the swindling to continue." In urging taxpayers to rally against the "vampires and leeches," he cited the example of a farmer who raises two or three crops on a piece of land, but never uses fertilizer, then, as the land becomes less and less productive, "leaves it in disgust and tries the same thing on a new piece of land."[150]

Meanwhile, Robert Mugge's own business efforts were bearing fruit in extraordinary ways, while also receiving increasing press coverage. For example, beginning in the spring of 1894, and carrying through to the fall of 1895, his Central Avenue property alone was a source of continuing public interest: in March of 1894, the Hennig Cigar Factory moved into one of his Central Avenue buildings;[151] in November of 1894, he partnered with H. R. Myers of Cincinnati to open a wholesale rectifying plant;[152] in February of 1895, the Tampa Lumber Company cut 100,000 feet of lumber for use in building a large new home for Robert's electric plant;[153] in March of 1895, George King of the Sulzer-Vogt Machine Co. began installing Robert's new ice factory;[154] in May of 1895, the ice factory was connected with

Robert's electric plant, thereby reducing operating costs for both;[155] and in October of 1895, he was permitted to connect the water pipes of his ice factory with the sewer of the county jail.[156]

The importance of Robert's ice plant, in particular, could not be overstated, in that, as his son August suggested, it made many of his other businesses possible. In other words, without the ice his drivers delivered daily, the saloons and cafes he and others were opening across the region could not have kept beer and soda water cold for sale to the public. In addition, both consumers and assorted businesses needed deliveries for use in ice boxes, which were the freezers and refrigerators of their day.

One spot in need of ice was the New Parlor Theatre, a vaudeville house which Robert Mugge opened in February of 1895 in partnership with impresario and manager T. J. Keogh at Scott Street (also known as Rock Road) and Central Avenue.[157] Although Robert had presented vaudeville shows since at least 1882, when he collaborated on one with Dr. O. W. Crosby,[158] this was the first to receive major public attention. For instance, according to the *Morning Tribune*, because the New Parlor Theatre was located at the edge of the city and beyond the limits of public transportation, patrons were advised to take streetcars to Central Avenue, where "free [horse-drawn] busses" would meet every car.[159] In return for such effort, ads promised seven nights a week of first-class entertainment, new novelties and specialties, a top-notch restaurant, and the best brands available of wine, liquor, and cigars.[160]

Almost from the beginning, however, the New Parlor Theatre was a source of controversy, first due to rumors Mr. Keogh had left town, which he decidedly had not,[161] and then due to reports of a brawl erupting on March 11, which sadly were true. Among those arrested that night were Alberto Soreno, "who did the shooting at Mugge's Monday evening,"[162] and Chas. Hunnicut, "who knocked Officer Coleman down with a chair," and who later escaped for a time when Officer Timmerman failed to lock his cell.[163]

For whatever reasons, the partnership between Robert Mugge and T. J. Keogh lasted only a few months. However, an interview appearing in the *Morning Tribune* of August 10, 1895 demonstrated the range of Robert's current interests, and the intensity with which he applied himself in all directions:

> Robt. Mugge, the well-known bottling man, and owner of the variety theater at the corner of Scott street and Central avenue, was seen by a *Tribune* man in his place yesterday, surrounded by all the paraphernalia of his damp and steaming trade.
>
> "What about the new variety theatre, Mr. Mugge?" asked the reporter, trying to drown the terrific racket of a mysterious bottling machine the proprietor was manipulating.
>
> "Well," replied Mr. Mugge, deftly capsizing one filled bottle after another into the receptacle prepared for them. "T. B. Butler, the Thunderbolt man, writes me that he will open up about September 1st or before."
>
> "Is Butler the man who was burned out at Thunderbolt not long ago?" asked the reporter.
>
> "Yes," said Mr. Mugge, "but that don't cut any figure he says. He's going to open on the date mentioned with a first-class Vaudeville show, and that's all there is to it."
>
> And turning again to his popping, snorting little bottle machine, Mr. Mugge left the newspaper man to meditate upon the growing cosmopolitan character of Tampa as indicated by its amusements.[164]

To the surprise of all, "Butler, the Thunderbolt man" later tore up his contract, at which point Robert declared the theater closed through the winter.[165] Fortunately, though, Robert's wife Caroline—nicknamed Lena—was far more dependable. Since joining him in 1882, she had provided a happy home and growing family which, in turn, gave meaning to his work. For instance, Caroline's latest contribution, a handsome son named Thomas Paine Mugge, arrived on June 22, 1895,[166] and for the moment, he, too, was healthy. His name embodied what Robert valued most about the American contract, which were his rights to express himself, to engage in multiple forms of congress, and to seek to improve not only his own lot, but that of his family and community as well. Of course, the more Robert tried to exert such rights, the more local officials sought to hold him back.

This was never so true as the summer of 1895 when Tampa's City Council resolved that a growing city such as theirs needed more extensive regulations to keep its business community in line, while simultaneously raising the funds needed for wider city services. After all, the humble town of a few hundred people had, during the nearly two decades Robert had been living and working there, grown to a city of more than fifteen thousand, with thousands more living in the adjacent or nearby communities of Fort Brooke, West Tampa, East Tampa, and Port Tampa City, all of which would one day be incorporated into the city itself. Regardless, in September of 1895, with such goals in mind, city fathers passed the wide-ranging "Ordinance No. 112: An ordinance providing for the assessment and collection of revenue" as "ordained by the City Council of Tampa." Yet, the new law not only shifted the burden of taxation from individuals to businesses, which Robert supported, but also onto some businesses more than others, which Robert did not.

Annual licenses, which included fees of varying amounts, would now be required for those conducting nearly any sort of business within city limits, and that included operation of hotels and boarding houses, billiard and pool halls, bowling alleys, skating rinks, and shooting galleries. Fees would also be required for merchants, storekeepers, druggists, manufacturers of cigars and tobacco, distillers of spiritous liquors, brewers of malt liquors, and dealers in spiritous, vinous, or malt liquors. Of course, the highest fees, which tended to be hundreds of dollars in every instance, were reserved for companies making or selling alcohol, and Robert Mugge controlled more such companies than anyone else. In addition, separate fees were imposed on liquor-related firms by Hillsborough County and the State of Florida, creating the sense that all such assessments were biased and morally punitive. And yes, as prohibitionist sentiments gained wider currency, the amounts of such fees would continue to rise.[167]

Eleven months later, City Council would pass another major ordinance, the text of which was published in full in the *Morning*

Tribune of August 7, 1896. Titled Ordinance No. 175, it was the biggest sign yet that city government intended to restrict any citizen behavior which at least a portion of the public considered to be improper. Certainly, it was true that most American communities had, from the beginning, written and enforced laws against prostitution, but this ordinance brought the defining and punishing of allegedly immoral behavior to whole new extremes, and it was aimed primarily at women.

Not only did the ordinance outlaw brothels, as expected, but it also banned women considered to be of bad reputation from walking the city streets after 9:00 p.m., from visiting saloons or connected dance halls, from attending theaters, from being in any other public places, from using "lascivious" language or gestures, from being "indecently attired" in public, or from sitting in an open window or doorway. In addition, it outlawed anyone, of either gender, keeping company with such a person after 9:00 p.m., and that was later extended to keeping company with someone of another race.[168] In other words, if either sin or crime is in the eye of the beholder, the entirely white male City Council of Tampa was inviting the equally white male law enforcement agencies to see such behavior virtually everywhere they looked, while criminalizing not only prostitution, but also any female activity diverging from a highly repressive norm.

Regardless, efforts to restrict Robert Mugge's behavior in any way only led him to fight harder, and certainly to work harder. Over a several-month period in 1895 and 1896, he repeatedly ran a newspaper ad under the title, "To Those That Drink Beer." The upshot was that Robert Mugge, local agent for Anheuser-Busch, had received the following telegram from company headquarters in St. Louis: "Supreme Court of Washington, declared Anheuser-Busch Brewing Association rightful owners of the disputed highest award of the World's Columbian Exposition. Rejoice with us in complete and final overthrow of fraud and forgery. This proves that barley malt beers will always reign over corn and other adulterated beers."[169]

The actual story was that the World's Columbian Exposition of 1893—what later would be called a world's fair—had featured various competitions, one of which was among brewers.[170] The latter competition had been marred by corruption, which had led to a disputed outcome. It then had taken until 1895 for the matter to be adjudicated, with the case going all the way to the United States Supreme Court, and with Anheuser-Busch finally emerging victorious.[171] Yet, in running this ad, Robert was not merely showing he represented beers considered to be the best in the world; he likely also was giving repeated notice that he was a growing force in South Florida, that he had powerful friends, and that he would resist any efforts to restrict his rights as an American citizen and business owner—something he would demonstrate again and again in the coming years. And taking a cue from his friends at Anheuser-Busch, such battles would often be fought in the courtroom.

Mostly, though, Robert used the clout he derived from representing Anheuser-Busch to consolidate his position as the dominant saloon operator of Tampa, Florida and beyond—not only in fact, but also in image, and for the rest of his career. The *Morning Tribune* of April 23, 1896 acknowledged both under the punning headline, "A Corner on the Saloon Business." It opened with the words, "R. Mugge is determined to control the saloon business of Tampa, or at least a majority of it," then reported how, the day before, Robert had purchased two of the most important corner saloons in the city (and two he would go on to control for years to come). At 1:00 p.m., he had purchased the Missing Link Saloon at 902 Franklin Street, then immediately "went further up Franklin Street" and purchased Kirk's Place at 1102 Franklin. And yet, everyone knew this was only the beginning. "What he will do next is hard to tell," added the *Tribune*.[172] "From present appearances he means to carry the war clear into Africa."

In fact, under Robert's ownership (and new construction), the Missing Link became his Armory Saloon, and later his White House Saloon, while Kirk's Place became his Greater New York Sample Rooms and Billiard Hall, and later his longtime Crystal Saloon. However, just prior to these back-to-back acquisitions, Robert also had purchased the Parlor Wine Saloon (wine parlors being more formal alternatives to saloons, which at least some considered more appropriate for female attendance).[173] Unfortunately, that resort, as drinking establishments were called at the time, proved a disappointment, and he ran it for only a short time, demonstrating that not all his acquisitions paid off. Overall, though, his progress was unrelenting.

One of Robert's friends, the Russian Nihilist doctor, Frederick N. Weightnovel, also had a good run in the mid-1890s. In the spring of 1895, Imperial Moscow University agreed to send a certified copy of his 1863 medical degree to the Russian Legation in Washington, DC which, in turn, translated the original document "under the seal of their government" and passed it along to the Board of Medical Examiners for the 6th Judicial District in Tampa. As a result, Dr. Weightnovel was finally granted a medical license.[174]

Now able to practice openly, the doctor became prominent in local medical circles, at least for a time, and some of his exploits were covered in the local press. For example, in November of 1896, one edition showed him responding to a suicide,[175] and another showed him aiding a man whose head had been crushed when a scantling holding a hot-air balloon in place fell and hit him.[176] The latter happened at the amusement park Robert and a partner opened that year.

But right as Dr. Weightnovel was gaining new credibility with the press and the public, he fell into a scheme that threatened his image still again. And who better to set the stage for that than former *Tampa Times* editor Donald B. McKay, reminiscing in print some five decades later? According to Mr. McKay, not long after the Fort Brooke military reservation was at last transferred from the War Department to the Interior Department, the land stretching from Whiting Street to the bay front was thrown open to homesteading. Yet, even before 1893, when this happened officially, squatters had moved onto the land in anticipation of taking ownership, and many more would follow. "Among the horde was Dr. Weightnovel, who took with him a group of loafers and bums. They erected several shanties and attempted to incorporate a town under the name of Moscow."[177]

Aside from his obvious love of political theater, why would Dr. Weightnovel risk his improving reputation on such an effort? In his memoirs, August Mugge offered an explanation. Apparently, Dr. Weightnovel was in debt to August's father. So, when the property known as the Garrison, "south of the Seaboard out to the Bay," became available, the two of them devised a scheme: Robert would build a house for the doctor in one of the more attractive parts of the Garrison, and Dr. Weightnovel would live in it as long as necessary to claim squatter's rights; then, once the rights were granted, he would deed the property to Robert in return for money owed.[178]

Still, the doctor was a natural leader with an agile imagination. He enjoyed staging a kind of "beggar's opera" in this ersatz "Moscow" by the bay, being elected that city's mayor, and calling on his comrades to resist future evictions with force.[179] Yet, it was simply theater, because through it all, the respective claims of settlers were being denied in the courts, falling victim, one after another, to applications made earlier or more effectively by others.[180]

As the futility sank in, the rebellion slowly fizzled. And for any not yet aware, the *Weekly Tribune* of April 14, 1898 rang a death knell: "Capt. John McKay, deputy United States marshal, has finished serving eviction warrants upon the squatters on the Garrison reservation. Nearly all of the squatters have vacated."[181] Of course, thanks to the slow-moving efficiency of the legal process, the US Supreme Court's final decision about ownership would not be confirmed until the January 4, 1905 issue of the *Morning Tribune*. But by then, the game was long over, and all that was left was to reminisce: "With Weightnovel as their mayor, scores of squatters representing many nationalities, took possession of the property, living in hovels and huts that would have put a respectable dog kennel to shame. They were outed ... but not until one irate squatter of the feminine persuasion had chased a brawny deputy sheriff, who had come to dispossess her, into the bay with a ladle of hot soup as a weapon."[182]

Considering the money Robert had lost on this venture, he was unlikely to bet on the Russian again. And yet, if Dr. Weightnovel had proven anything, both in the original Moscow and in his newer one, it was that he should never be counted out. It was a trait the two men had in common.

In 1896, one of Robert Mugge's bigger projects involved collaborating with Bautista M. Balbontin, a Spanish cigar manufacturer and wine merchant, in the building and operation of the previously mentioned amusement park called the DeSoto Park Pleasure Co.[183] Although Robert's son August would have been only five-or-six-years-old when these efforts were beginning, they were the sort that a young child would remember, as he later did in his memoirs. According to his recollections, the amusement park was situated outside of city limits to the east. It included a dancing pavilion, a bar, bath houses, and other amusements. But the highlights were performances by the nationally known Forepaugh Family, whose shows were considered comparable to those of P. T. Barnum. They included clowns and trapeze artists and climaxed with a man doing stunts in a smoke-filled balloon as it ascended. Every Sunday afternoon, enthusiastic crowds would attend, including many members of the Cuban population.

Regrettably, whether influenced or not by the tragic, balloon-related accident treated by Dr. Weightnovel, the Mugge-Balbontin amusement park did not do well financially and was short-lived. However, as August Mugge recalled, the old pavilion they created at the heart of the park stood for many years, even after the park became city property.[184] And of course, this would not be the only setback during the period in question.

The fall of 1896 brought a downturn in business at fourteen saloons for which Robert Mugge, backed by Anheuser-Busch, had purchased annual licenses with the understanding that the operators of the saloons would pass along so much profit per week. When the operators could not pay what was owed, Robert and Anheuser-Busch were forced to shut them down through attachment.[185] For instance, Deputy Sheriff Mooney announced that the White Rose saloon was shut down, and that he was attaching its stock for Robert Mugge.[186]

In another case, however, Robert's approach was simply to make his establishment more appealing. That was evident when the *Morning Tribune* of October 16, 1896 proclaimed that he was converting his Saratoga Saloon "into quite a large and elaborate resort."[187] Then, exactly two months after that, the same paper reported that B. S.

Hankins had resigned his position at the Saratoga, making way for the popular Archie Cerf, whose "purpose is to put the place in thorough condition and run it in up-to-date style."[188] Yet, it would be two months more before anyone knew the true purpose of these upgrades.

In the meantime, the election of early November provided a welcome distraction from the ups and downs of saloon operators. Robert Mugge and fellow liquor wholesaler Max Caras even placed a bet on the election, and Mr. Caras lost.[189] Therefore, on November 9, 1896, a crowd gathered at the corner of Fifteenth Street and Seventh Avenue—an intersection known as Robert Mugge Corner, because of his prominent Golden Eagle Saloon and other businesses there—to see Mr. Caras "pay the wager." The two good friends, one of them from Germany and the other from Spain, each showed up in costume. Then, with a Cuban band leading the way, Mr. Caras used a decorated wheelbarrow to push Mr. Mugge all the way to Fourteenth Street. The cheering crowd was as big as it was largely because someone had spread the rumor that free beer would be available. However, as the *Morning Tribune* of the following day reported, "Mr. Mugge alone was the recipient of a bottle of Mumm's Best."[190]

As mentioned, the true purpose of changes to Robert's Saratoga Saloon did not hit home until February of the following year, when the *Morning Tribune* carried the following announcement: "Don't forget the grand opening tonight of May Cameron's London Gaiety Company at the Saratoga, corner of Franklin and Polk Streets, where through the enterprise of Proprietor R. Mugge, a thoroughly high-class Vaudeville entertainment will be furnished, gratis to his patrons until further notice. Constant change of program is promised."[191] That was accompanied by a series of ads stating that the company would appear nightly from 7:00 p.m. till 11:00 p.m., "introducing all the Latest Songs and Dances of the day."[192] And apparently, the show did extremely well because, by mid-March of 1897, a second series of ads said that May Cameron's Gaiety Girls were now performing at a larger theater, The Gaiety, specially constructed for them by proprietor Robert Mugge at the northwest corner of Franklin and Tyler, precisely two blocks north of the Saratoga. The reopened show was said to feature "New Songs and Dances, Living Pictures, and [a program titled] 'The Shadows of a Wicked City.'"[193]

Even as Robert expanded his latest foray into vaudeville, he also extended his saloon empire in more than one direction. According to the *Weekly Tribune* of April 1, 1897, Robert was completing his new building at Seventh Avenue and Twenty-Second Street, which soon would hold his Seminole Cafe, and later his Seminole Saloon. "Workmen are now putting on the wood finish over the plastering inside and painters are following close behind."[194] Then, in early June, he purchased a saloon at the corner of Franklin and Jackson Streets,[195] as well as the large storeroom next door.[196] The saloon, actually located at 302 Franklin, would become his Eureka Bar, and then his longtime Eureka Saloon, while the storeroom at 304 Franklin would house his wholesale liquor business.

Nowhere near finished, in early August, he purchased the African American Saulter & Eaves Saloon at 1332-34 Central Avenue, just north of his ice factory and electric plant, as well as the building in which it was established.[197] This would become, among other things, his longtime Central Saloon, complete with billiard room and dance hall. And yet, as was noted in the *Morning Tribune* of September 4, 1897, the more Robert acquired, the more he also gave back, as when he donated half of the prior day's receipts at his El Dorado Saloon in Port Tampa City to Francisco Valdez, "whose wife and daughter were burned to death" the previous Sunday afternoon, and whose hands were badly burned in the process of trying to save them.[198]

At this point in his life, there was no doubting Robert's own good fortune. As just one more example, on July 1, 1897, Robert's wife Caroline gave birth for a seventh time, this child being a daughter named Martha Washington Mugge.[199] In a 1969 issue of Jacksonville's *Florida Times-Union* (date uncertain), Martha enjoyed divulging that she was the "seventh child in the family and was born in the seventh month of a year that ended in seven." At the time, she also had seven godchildren, plus seventy grandnephews and grandnieces, had gone to work on the seventh floor of the Florida Theatre Building, and had sat at a desk there labeled with the number seven.[200] Of course, more pertinent to Robert was the fact that he had named her after the wife of President George Washington. Still, he had little time to enjoy her arrival, or to take advantage of all her "lucky sevens," before an unexpected pitfall.

According to the *Morning Tribune* of July 13, 1897, while walking down Franklin Street the day before, Robert Mugge "fell into an ugly washout in the street ... sustaining injuries which confined him to his bed yesterday." That unfortunate news was accompanied by a plea that the city "fill in such dangerous and unsightly holes" in Tampa's downtown streets.[201] The July 22, 1897 issue of the *Weekly Tribune* followed up, revealing that Robert was still suffering from the accident, even to the point of claiming to be considering selling off his business interests and returning to Germany. In response, the paper joked that his departure would offer big opportunities for those wishing to replace him.[202]

In the October 29, 1897 issue of the *Morning Tribune*, no doubt still reeling from his recent injury, Robert proposed how the "terrible streets" of Tampa could be improved without immediately paying for the high-quality pavement and accompanying sewers available in Jacksonville. The article opened: "Robert Mugge is one man in Tampa who has an enviable reputation for sound common sense and a fund of practical ideas that seem never to become exhausted." The point of Robert's proposal was: "Good pavements ... are impossible without good drainage." But inasmuch as it could be ten years before Tampa would be in the position to install sewers, his proposed alternative would "give us twelve feet of pebble phosphate roadway, surrounded on each side by a strip of dirt that will answer the purpose of a sewer, and slowly, but surely eliminate from the problem the drainage question altogether."[203]

Meanwhile, Robert continued to diversify his business holdings. According to the memoirs of his son August, at some point, Robert bought forty acres of land near Bloomingdale from "an old German named Klein," who walked with a bad limp. After the purchase, Klein would occasionally come to Tampa "to get his jug of whiskey," which he called his *kruke* (German for "stone jar"), the cost of which was applied to Robert's purchase of the forty acres. In return for all the whiskey he had drunk, Mr. Klein eventually gave Robert the deed,[204] and according to the *Sunday Morning Tribune* of September 25, 1897, Robert's initial plan was to grow a large crop of tobacco.[205] However, as his ambitions grew, he acquired more land, expanding his Bloomingdale holdings to 319 acres.[206]

Finally, in late December, Robert arranged to collaborate with F. M. Knight, "a producer of fine champagne wines and California fruit juice syrups for soda fountains." Reportedly, Robert would erect a plant for production of these products and then place them on the market.[207] Truthfully, little more is known of this project. But it was an upbeat ending to a challenging, yet productive period of several years, all of which were leading to one of the biggest of Robert's life.

Chapter Five

Center Stage

As everyone around him was quick to acknowledge, Robert Mugge was smart, highly adaptable, and forward-thinking as a businessman, yet also notoriously eccentric. Already one of the wealthier men in Tampa, he continued to see himself as a worker, and he dressed accordingly. In a studio photo taken in Germany in his teens, he was shown wearing a coat and tie, but looking distinctly ill-at-ease. In the later words of his son August: "Clad only with an undershirt, trousers, and shoes and coat, he would conduct his business, but on occasions such as collecting on Monday morning, he would don a white shirt but without collar. He calculated how much time it would take in the life of a man to put them on and take them off, and this he regarded as senseless waste. He wore blueish linen clothes, winter and summer the same, and these were purchased by the dozens. I remember that he wore a Panama hat, and later sort of a marine cap which some friends brought from Spain for him." Still, in another studio photo from 1899, at which point he would have been forty-six, he was shown brimming with confidence and wearing a handsome suit. So, he clearly knew how to dress when appropriate for social events, court appearances, or important business dealings.

Because August spent his youth with Robert, and later worked closely with him, he was given views of his father available to few others. For example, he described Robert's extraordinary memory, his quick wit, and his ability to hold conversations while writing letters or answering the phone, providing instant answers to every question. He also noted his father's "boundless energy," the fact that he routinely worked eighteen hours out of every twenty-four, that he wrote letters by hand, and that he neither employed a bookkeeper nor owned a typewriter or adding machine.

For many years, Robert maintained a small office in the center of his wholesale liquor business on Franklin Street, where he worked at a high desk with a similarly high stool, the two of them backed by a small table, an armchair, and an empty Budweiser barrel which he used as a waste basket. Next to his desk, attached to a column, was a box that served as his bank, with money inserted through a slot in the lid. On other occasions, he would work from the house, walking the two blocks between office and home with writing materials in a basket under his arm.

Sundays, at the wholesale house, Robert would write out bills to accompany his Monday morning collections, and did so surrounded by wisecracking friends. This was also his time for consulting with B. H. Davidson, the contractor who oversaw construction and remodeling of most of Robert's buildings (usually based on Robert's own drawings) along with the plumbers and electricians Mr. Davidson had hired.

But again, according to August, no matter how successful Robert became, and how many companies and employees he oversaw, he still identified with those who labored for a living. Unlike other business owners, for whom physical work was anathema, Robert would bottle his own soda water, truck beer into his warehouse, pack empty beer bottles into barrels, and more. In earlier years, August also remembered him driving a horse-drawn buggy to a dairy at four in the morning where he purchased milk at wholesale prices, then delivered it to his various saloons, as he also picked up receipts from the day before. Any additional milk was brought to the house for his family.

In fact, during most of the years Robert was in business, horses and mules were integral to daily life. As August pointed out, Anheuser-Busch had provided multiple wagons for the delivery of beer, and teams of horses and mules were kept in a stable near the ice factory, overseen by a former slave known as Uncle George. Robert also maintained a horse and buggy of his own, and carriages for the family. On Sundays, the family would go for rides, driven by another African American employee named Gus Wilson, or sometimes by Robert himself.

August went on to remark that, despite sometimes doing manual labor, Robert was always "spotlessly clean." Eventually, the city sewers proved too small to accept surplus water from the ice plant, which therefore had to be held in a large tank before being siphoned off. Robert's creative response was to construct "a swimming pool made of concrete with a cupola in wood overhead in lieu of the tank." This allowed him to take a daily swim, and August sometimes followed suit. Later, Robert built a concrete addition to his bottling works, in which he could shower with water streaming from all directions.

As is obvious from these recollections, by the end of the 1890s, despite Robert's growing number of businesses, buildings, and employees, he maintained a close watch over all of them himself. Occasionally, as with contractor B. H. Davidson and a series of top attorneys, he would entrust aspects of his operation to someone else with the necessary experience. But final decisions were always his.[208]

In the spring of 1898, the biggest topic of conversation in Tampa was the coming war with Spain, and the likelihood US troops would assemble in South Florida before embarking for Cuba. According to author Karl H. Grismer in his history of the city, "When Tampa was first mentioned as an embarkation point for troops, [Robert Mugge] wired the Anheuser Busch Company for a trainload of beer. The company wired back: 'There won't be a war and we don't sell beer by the trainload.' But there was a war and Mugge did get beer by the trainload—and he profited handsomely."[209]

Perhaps this exchange happened exactly as described; certainly, it has a poetic ring to it. However, the words quoted without attribution in Mr. Grismer's 1950 book strangely evoke the 1941 Orson Welles film, *Citizen Kane*, in which the lead character, Charles Foster Kane, is a stand-in for wealthy newspaper publisher William Randolph Hearst.

In one of the film's most quoted scenes, taking place just before the Spanish-American War, Kane is sent a cable from one of his reporters in the field. The cable reads, "Girls delightful in Cuba. Stop. Could send you prose poems about scenery, but don't feel right spending your money. Stop. There is no war in Cuba." Undeterred, young Kane wires back, "You provide the prose poems. I'll provide the war." Then, decades later, having just returned from Europe, an older "Citizen" Kane is asked about prospects for a second world war. His confident reply? "You can take my word for it. There will be no war."[210] Whether accurate reporting or a "prose poem," Mr. Grismer's tale was a good one. Fortunately, though, an actual witness recorded the rest.

August Mugge, Robert's son, was only seven during the war, which lasted from April 21, 1898 to August 13, 1898. Yet, in his memoirs, he was able to provide graphic descriptions of the war itself and of how his father responded. He remembered American troops arriving via Henry Plant's railroad, then marching up Franklin Street to the northern part of the city, creating their encampment "in the neighborhood of Michigan Avenue." In August's opinion, the soldiers, mostly volunteers from the West, were quite undisciplined. They were commanded by General Shafter, whose headquarters were at the Tampa Bay Hotel, and whose army included Lieutenant Colonel Theodore Roosevelt's Rough Riders, a cavalry regiment consisting of cowboys from the Southwestern US. (Note: Also included among the troops were four regiments of African American "Buffalo Soldiers.")[211] [212]

According to August, in Robert's capacity as the agent for Anheuser-Busch, he established a huge saloon in an orange grove near the military encampment. The aforementioned B. H. Davidson and crews built the entire structure, "including fixtures and ice-box," in a single day. The resulting saloon was named the Noah's Ark and operated around the clock, with eight bartenders tending an eighty-foot bar. It also featured pool tables, which had to be bolted to the floor, because the rowdy troops kept turning them over. The trainload of beer Robert received from St. Louis was utilized there, at his Green Goose Saloon in Port Tampa City, and at his other places of business.[213]

Not mentioned by August, but covered in the *Morning Tribune* of Wednesday, June 8, 1898, were the armed mobs of both white and

Black soldiers who spent all the previous Monday night invading saloons, cafes, and brothels throughout Fort Brooke, Ybor City, and the Scrub. Among them was Robert Mugge's Seminole Cafe at Seventh Avenue and Twenty-Second Street. Reportedly, shots were fired, businesses were ransacked, beer and whiskey were stolen, and Black and white prostitutes were raped at gunpoint, with local authorities mostly afraid to intervene.[214] In a second article titled "Inhuman Brutes" in the same issue, one apparently white soldier of the Ohio volunteers held a two-year-old African American child by its foot and called on another soldier to shoot at it. "The bullet from the pistol passed through the sleeve of the child's night dress, and grazed its arm. This satisfied the brutes and they returned the child to its mother."[215] The following morning, some drunken soldiers even smashed open doors of downtown saloons that were closed for Election Day and continued their unimpeded drinking and pillaging.

Little was done to restore order until Tuesday night when "large squads of volunteers, mostly from the Georgia regiment, patrolled the street," making arrests and exchanging gunfire with those still in revolt. Tampa's extremely shaken residents, now heavily armed themselves, warned clueless military leaders that, for their remaining time in the city, they were to keep their men in camp after 6:00 p.m. Although that would have been frustrating for the troops—especially those displaying good behavior—such a curfew at least benefitted Robert Mugge, in that his Noah's Ark Saloon, set up on the edge of the encampment, would perhaps have become their sole source of nighttime entertainment.

According to scholars Canter Brown Jr. and Larry Eugene Rivers, some of the Black troops declared their revolt was in direct response to the treatment they encountered in Tampa. Many were from parts of the country where a Black soldier—or indeed, any Black citizen—would not have been turned away from the best saloons, hotels, eating establishments, and even brothels; and being armed, and perhaps despairing for their futures, they responded with rebellion.[216]

Understandable or not, these expressions of rage did nothing to improve race relations in South Florida. To the contrary, although both white and Black troops had participated, the events left local

African Americans feeling less secure than before. Therefore, as one mammoth troop ship after another departed Port Tampa that summer, few in the city—and certainly not communities of color—were sorry to see them go.

Just weeks after the war ended, the *Morning Tribune* of September 8, 1898 reported tragic news closer to home: "Thomas Paine Mugge, the bright [three-year-old] son of Mr. and Mrs. Mugge of this city, died Tuesday night, and was buried yesterday [Wednesday, September 7]. His death was a great shock to his fond parents, whose many friends tender sincere sympathy in their sad affliction. The funeral was largely attended yesterday afternoon and during the day all of Mr. Mugge's places of business were closed."[217] Having lost his first two sons two decades before, Robert's pain would have been familiar, only that much more intense, in that Thomas had been a part of his life for three full years. And sharing this loss with Caroline, who had not yet lost a child, would have been even worse. According to Thomas's sister Martha, born in 1897, the cause of his death was typhoid fever.[218]

By comparison, what happened next was more a nuisance. But it offered closure to Robert's Spanish-American War adventure, while signaling a serious issue that would plague his saloon business for years to come. The November 24, 1898 edition of the *Weekly Tribune* explained: "Noah's Ark located near Florida on Michigan Avenue and formerly used by Robert Mugge as a resort for the bibulous inclined soldiers during the good old times of the war with Spain, was consumed by the maddened flames of the fiery fiend at a late hour last night." According to the paper, the fire apparently had been the work of an incendiary and, "owing to the heavy sand," Chief Harris and his department had been unable to reach the scene before the structure was fully destroyed. The building was not insured, and the loss was estimated to be $800.[219]

At least, as August would later observe, "The Noah's Ark was destroyed by fire, but little did my father care. He actually never knew how much money he had made in this venture."[220] However, in similar situations, he would soon care very much.

Chapter Six

Fire and Water

1899 began quietly, almost quaintly, as Robert Mugge, in the words of the *Morning Tribune* of January 5, presented Superintendent Dan Wiggins of the Tampa Bay Hotel grounds with: "a fine deer which will be placed in the hotel grounds so that it can be seen by all visitors. The deer is a healthful animal and Superintendent Wiggins is proud of his present." Robert, of course, was a devoted fan of the hotel's magnificent gardens, which included a small zoo, and his friend Adolphus Busch was equally fond of Henry Plant's creations. At the same time, the gift could have been in memory of his three-year-old son, Thomas, who had died four months before.[221]

This charming beginning for the year was duplicated a month later when the *Morning Tribune* gave thanks to Robert Mugge and Anheuser-Busch for a gift box containing a dozen bottles each of original Budweiser, Black and Tan, Faust, and Malt Nutrine. Reportedly, accompanying the bottles were "a beautiful tray, six fine glasses, and that necessary article, a corkscrew." *Tribune* editor Wallace F. Stovall was so grateful for the gift that he was moved to respond in verse, a portion of which follows.

> Let Germany and France unite
> To sing the praise of wine!
> While other poets whisky sing,
> Here's a brew that's more divine ...
> Hurrah! Hurrah for Anheuser-Busch!
> Hurrah for the golden brew!
> Let others praise inferior brands--
> A-B's the best for you.[222]

Although sweet, Mr. Stovall's response was also ironic, in that, Adolphus Busch, himself, was said to prefer wine to his own "barley malt brews." But drink choices aside, four days later, it was the press providing the hangover. That is, on March 11, 1899, the *Morning Tribune* reported that, the night before, two serious fires had broken out at Port Tampa City. The first hit the Sandana cigar factory, located near the southwestern part of town, and the second struck a saloon owned by Robert Mugge, which was destroyed.

The article ended with the supposition that: "The origin of both fires is a mystery."[223] Yet, it would have been easy to conclude the fire in the empty cigar factory was a diversion, allowing time and cover for the real target, Robert's saloon, to be set ablaze while firefighters busied themselves elsewhere. Lending credence to the theory? Five months later, a Robert Mugge saloon in Port Tampa City would once again burst into flames, this time under even more suspicious circumstances.

Regardless, five *days* later, almost as if an antidote to the first story, Robert Mugge announced establishment of a new schooner line called the Tampa and New Orleans Transportation Co., which, logically, would sail primarily between Tampa and New Orleans. The company had secured the large schooner Samuel T. Beacham, and according to the *Weekly Tribune* of March 16, the "fine schooner Estelle," also part of the line, was already on its way to Tampa "with a big cargo of merchandise." The article continued: "The proprietors of the enterprise are among Tampa's most successful business men. The prime movers are Robert Mugge, Capt. Fred Thompson, and [for the moment] Commodore Miller." The office was said to be at 304 Franklin Street, which was the address of Robert's wholesale liquor house.[224]

The prospects for such a company were great, and well deserving of the initial fanfare. Yet, the perils were great as well, as became clear just two and a half months later. The *Morning Tribune* of June 1, 1899 reported that Captain Fred H. Thompson was newly returned from the sinking of the schooner Anna M. Estelle at a point known to be one of the most dangerous along the Florida coast. He then had departed for Baltimore where he expected to purchase "another large schooner to take the place of the Estelle." An interview with Robert Mugge revealed the loss to be approximately $10,000, which would be shared equally by Robert and Captain Thompson.[225] However, better news came in the *Morning Tribune* of August 12, 1899, which announced that, the day before, the schooner Eva I. Shenton had departed for New Orleans with a cargo of empty casks belonging to Robert Mugge. No doubt, the casks would be filled in New Orleans and then returned to their home port. The paper noted this was one of the schooners of the Tampa and New Orleans Transportation Company, a line "rapidly building up large business under the able management of Mr. Mugge."[226]

Even as Robert was launching his shipping line, then struggling to keep it afloat, he was also preparing another business. The *Tampa Times* of May 22, 1929 reprinted the following story it had first published thirty years before: "Robert Mugge, that most enterprising of all Tampa citizens, now proposes to add a distillery to the city's numerous commercial interests. He has perfected all his plans and will have the building erected at once adjoining his big ice factory on Central Avenue. Mr. Mugge never goes into anything blind, and that he will make a success of this enterprise, as he does of all others launched by him, there is no doubt."[227] That was followed in July by news in the *Morning Tribune* that City Council had granted permission for him to lay a sidetrack "from the Plant System line, along Jefferson and Cass streets and Central avenue" up to his distillery. As a thank-you, he would "pave the streets along the tracks fifteen feet on each side," while also "building up an enterprise that promises to be one of the largest in the Southern States."[228] Later, he would agree to pave Harrison Street for free as well, effectively upgrading all the roads surrounding his key Central Avenue businesses.[229]

With everything now in place, only one more element was needed, and that was the October arrival of Mr. J. H. Villier of Louisville, Kentucky, an expert in operating distilleries. According to the *Sunday Tribune* of October 22, 1899, thanks to the first legally operated distillery in the state, Tampa would soon be enjoying "some of the most elegant sour mash ever manufactured in the South."[230]

Yet, for Robert, the pendulum still swung both ways. As reported in the *Morning Tribune* of August 29, 1899, arsonists once again struck his Port Tampa City saloon, compelling him to offer "liberal rewards" for information leading to "the arrest of the firebugs."[231] Then, in the issue of August 31, 1899, the *Tribune* followed up with an attack on those who would resort to such methods, hoping to drive Robert and his Green Goose Saloon out of Port Tampa City. The editorial went on to declare that, although the paper was not "especially in love" with the saloon business, it did believe that the law should afford the same protections to saloon owners as it did to anyone else.[232] Unfortunately, the arsonists were never identified.

In other news, the *Morning Tribune* of October 31, 1899 included a blurb suggesting how much Robert's Tampa Electrical Illuminating Company had grown: "The movement against the light service of the Consumers [a competitor] has its hotbed in Ybor City, where all merchants are using either kerosene, gas or electric light service."[233] Not mentioned was the fact that, from the beginning, Robert's company had made inroads into the Scrub as well, which is where it was based. However, Robert may not have known that, at this very time, the dominant Tampa Electric Co. was conspiring to put his company out of business. According to Leland Hawes in his *Tampa Tribune* column of January 7, 1990, West Tampa's "untiring researcher," Armando Mendez, aided by Arsenio Sanchez, had discovered evidence in the archives of Tampa's longtime dominant utility that such a conspiracy had taken place.

The basic idea was that, in 1899, as Tampa Electric was taking over Consumers Electric, which it saw as its primary competition, Robert was still running a small electric plant of his own on Central Avenue. George J. Baldwin of Stone and Webster, which had recently purchased a controlling interest in Tampa Electric, sent a letter to H. J. Bradley of Consumers Electric in which he expressed concern over Robert's intentions:

> "This man owns a small competing plant and has been preparing to change over ... to a more modern one, possibly with the view of extending his business.
>
> "All of his property is mortgaged to Anheuser-Busch Brewing Co., who control him entirely, and with whom I am now negotiating direct for this purpose of purchasing this plant and business, doing this unknown to Mugge.
>
> "He is rather an influential man in Tampa on account of his large ownership of beer saloons. Please keep me posted concerning any moves he may make in changing or extending his plant."[234]

Even if Mr. Baldwin had understood the relationship between Robert Mugge and Adolphus Busch, which he clearly did not, his conspiracy would have mattered little. At the time, what did matter was that a rough year ended as sweetly as it began, thanks to the birth on Christmas Eve of Nellie Busch Mugge, Robert and Caroline's final newborn of the outgoing century.[235] She was named after Nellie Busch Loeb, who was the second daughter of Adolphus and Lilly Busch, and she was healthy and strong. The Busches celebrated Nellie's arrival by giving her parents a beautiful vase.

Chapter Seven

Sign of the Times

The new century started for Robert Mugge with the frustrating news, reported in the *Morning Tribune* of January 18, 1900, that, somewhere between his ice factory and his Eureka Saloon, he had lost a bag containing $156.75.[236] However, that news was more than offset by the following notice in the same paper: "The two-masted schooner Eva Shenton ... entered port yesterday from New Orleans, and is tied up at Lucas Bros.' wharf. The Shenton is loaded with wines, whiskey, etc., for R. Mugge."[237] The latter good news was repeated exactly a month later when, despite inclement weather, the Eva Shenton successfully delivered another large load of merchandise.[238]

Yet, the pendulum swung to the negative again as, first, the *Morning Tribune* of March 1, 1900 announced Robert being confined to his room for what proved to be ten days, due to a severe case of rheumatism,[239] [240] and second, the issue of April 19, 1900 reported the third assault of an incendiary on one of his saloons in Port Tampa City. The news was that the floor and wall of the Eldorado Saloon building had been saturated with gasoline and then set afire. The wooden structure was owned by a Mr. Dombrowski of Tampa and included second-floor apartments occupied by twenty-five or thirty sleeping people who, once roused, came racing down the stairs, barely escaping with their lives. The article went on to say that, because Robert had previously closed his saloon in the building, at least no stock was lost. But overall, the losses were significant for all concerned.[241]

The next big news of the year, as related by the *Morning Tribune* of April 27, 1900, was that, "Captain McIntyre, of Jacksonville, chief store-keeper and gauger of the Mugge distillery, has arrived, and is making preparations to open the new plant for business on May 1."[242] This was long-awaited news, in that gaugers were agents of the US Bureau of Internal Revenue responsible for measuring whiskey production and collecting excise taxes, and whiskey barrels could not be accessed without their presence. A second article in the *Weekly Tribune* of May 24, 1900 clarified that Robert's distillery had been ready to go for four months, but that delays were caused by having to work out "certain details with the government." Reportedly, operations had finally begun the day before, with production initially limited to one barrel per day, but with plans to increase production as business warranted. The article closed with assurances that, "Mr. Mugge proposes to turn out only high-grade whiskeys."[243]

Turning to another Mugge business, the *Morning Tribune* of July 13, 1900 revealed that "The electric lighting plant of R. Mugge is being remodeled and enlarged under the direction of Expert Adolph M. Lang, of Cleveland, Ohio. The increased facilities will allow of 3,500 lights."[244] Robert may have disclosed this information to attract new customers, or he may have done so simply to annoy the rival Tampa Electric Co., which he knew would be concerned.

The city's population was growing as well, which was leading to new conflicts between personal liberty and government regulation. For instance, actions under consideration by City Council during July, August, and September of 1900 displayed increasing lunacy on the part of its members. To begin with, in July, one councilman reasonably suggested that Ordinance No. 175 be rewritten "to allow women to enter barrooms by side doors and to frequent dance halls, which the present ordinance strictly prohibits." But other councilmen thought the ordinance just fine, and one even felt that prostitutes should be given more opportunities "to get out on the streets," so that they could be arrested.[245]

Next, in August, in response to complaints in the newspaper from residents of the more exclusive Hyde Park section of the city that cows "are now allowed to run at large in that fashionable quarter," and that it is therefore "impossible to maintain any flower-yards while the bovines are given free rein,"[246] a new ordinance was designed that would prohibit "the running at large of cows, hogs, sheep, goats or asses on the streets of the city," would provide that the police should seize all such animals, and directed that fines be imposed on those who violated the ordinance.[247] Late in the month, the ordinance passed and became law.[248]

Also in August, the chairman "recommended that the northwest corner of Woodlawn cemetery be set aside for the use of colored citizens." The resolution passed, "with the proviso that the section allotted to the negroes be fenced off, and have separate entrances on the west and north,"[249] it going without saying that white and Black relatives of the dead should not be expected to mingle, or perhaps the prohibition was actually intended to prevent mingling among the deceased.

Finally, in September, City Councilman Elmo Ballard introduced an ordinance making it illegal to "spit or expectorate on any sidewalk, public building, or street car in the city."[250] It wasn't until March of the following year that the resulting ordinance was unveiled to immediate ridicule, as well as a series of warnings in the *Morning Tribune* of March 23, 1901 as to how seriously it would be taken by city police and judges.[251] However, a week later, the *Tribune* announced that Mayor Francis Lyman Wing would "exercise the veto power of the city's chief executive for the first time" with the Ballard anti-spitting ordinance. "I will not sign it," he said. "They may pass it over my veto, but they will certainly have that privilege."[252]

Of all the dubious ordinances passed by City Council during the summer and fall of 1900, only one received a direct response from Robert Mugge, and it was announced with great flourish in the *Morning Tribune* of August 19, 1900 under the primary head-lines, "Pull Down Your Signs—Swinging Ones Are Doomed." Councilman Elmo Ballard, the same man responsible for the anti-spitting ordinance, also introduced one meant to outlaw all swinging signs in front of businesses, as well as any others not meeting a strict set of guidelines. As reported by the *Tribune*, "The only signs now legal in Tampa are those parallel with the property line, and not over one foot therefrom, and those painted on awnings or show-windows." Despite estimates that the city contained no less than 8,000 offending signs, many of which could only be removed with great trouble and expense, the ordi-nance passed and became law.[253] And yet, one business owner was having none of it.

In the *Weekly Tribune* of August 30, 1900, Robert made known that he refused to remove the sign in front of the Saratoga Saloon, on the grounds that it was fixed and not swinging. As a result, he was placed under arrest.[254] However, seemingly, Robert was not alone in his disdain for the new law, because the *Morning Tribune* of the following day offered the final word on the matter: "The case against Robert Mugge, for refusing to pull down a sign, was heard in police court yesterday morning, and dismissed by Judge Peeples."[255]

Without doubt, in Tampa, the twentieth century began with legislative overreach, even if, on two occasions, the executive and judicial branches did reimpose at least a modicum of common sense. Still, that would not always be the case, and perhaps the reason was numerical, or even numerological.

Some do not believe new centuries begin in "double zero" years, like 1900. They believe centennials should start with "zero one," the idea being that you count to ten, or to one hundred, or to any multiple of ten, and only then do you start again.[256] But some people—most people—are simply in a hurry to celebrate, and to gain a new start.

That seems to have been the case with Tampa, because the city grew noticeably loony in 1900; while 1901 is the year it abandoned American values, fell into an ethical chasm, and lost its collective mind. It was a bad period for the whole country, but it was especially bad for Tampa. And Robert Mugge—that quietly moral, patriotic, no-nonsense, German immigrant—could see what was coming, and was filled with despair.

Moreover, some years begin with omens, and this year's were right on time. First, the *Morning Tribune* of Sunday, December 30, 1900 reported that a bay horse belonging to Robert Mugge had been stolen from his stable Saturday night, "with bridle on, 14 or 15 hands high."[257] Then, the *Morning Tribune* of Tuesday, January 1, 1901 (the paper not printing on Mondays back then) carried a notice from Robert that, "I will pay $25 reward for the return of my horse, which has been stolen."[258] Certainly, in any culture, a horse being out of its stable, or property being stolen, is not a good sign.

Second, it only took an additional month for Councilman Ballard and friends to engage in their first moralistic overreach of the year, passing what the *Morning Tribune* described in headlines as a "Goody-Goody" law that "Would Reform Tampa at One Fell Swoop." The point of the new ordinance was to ban all lotteries, games of chance, raffles, and prize-drawings, even going so far as to "stop merchants from issuing tickets to their customers for each certain amount spent in the store, and awarding a prize to that lucky ticket-holder," and "put an end to voting contests at so much per vote for the most popular young ladies, etc., such as are conducted at fairs and bazaars." And the penalties for violating this law? A fine as much as $2,000, or hard labor for as long as ninety days. As the Tribune writer (probably outspoken editor Wallace F. Stovall) noted, "It is the aim of Mr. Ballard's ordinance to make Tampa angelically good ...The ordinance will create fully as much commotion as the sign ordinance by the same author."[259]

As for Robert Mugge, he continued to go about his business, often inspiring resistance from city officials. For example, in late February, it was reported in the *Weekly Tribune* that Mugge was charged with violating "the conditions under which council had given him permission to erect [his electrical] poles on the street. Mr. Ballard moved that Mr. Mugge be notified to comply with the conditions or remove the poles. Carried."[260] And yet, almost surely behind such actions of City Council was a powerful hidden hand.

By 1901, George J. Baldwin who, two years before, had personally conspired to take over Robert Mugge's electric light company,
now was the president of Tampa Electric Co., and not merely part
of the holding company that controlled it. As researchers Armando
Mendez and Arsenio Sanchez discovered in the archives of Tampa
Electric, and as journalist-historian Leland Hawes laid out in the
Tampa Tribune in 1990, on February 11, 1901, Mr. Baldwin wrote the
following to H. H. Hunt, the manager of his company: "I notice
that Mr. Mugge wants permission to place poles on Harrison Street.
What does this mean? Is his business increasing? We should not let
Mr. Mugge build up a business, but must devise means to keeping
him at about the point he was when we purchased the property."[261]
If Tampa Electric would ask Anheuser-Busch to suppress Robert's
rights, it would certainly ask the same of local government, making
this but one of many occasions when his ambitions were subverted
by a corporate and governmental alliance.

So, could any of Robert Mugge's businesses avoid controversy?
Construction, perhaps? Not if the buildings were used in his liquor
business, as was described in an otherwise-innocuous article in the
Morning Tribune of March 20, 1901 under the headline, "Mugge Buys
A Brick Block": "Robert Mugge yesterday bought through Fulton
& Watson the Leonardi block [more precisely, 'group,' because it
was not the entire city block] of brick buildings, extending from
the Knight building, corner of Franklin and Lafayette streets, south,
along Franklin street 104 feet, and including five one-story stores.
Mr. Mugge intends to add a second story to the buildings, and use
them for his wholesale liquor business. One of the stores will be
converted into a retail bar. The buildings are now occupied by the Elk
barber shop, Hancock's saloon, and the sewing machine agency."[262]

Translated for anyone not residing in Tampa in 1901, the so-called
three-hundred block of Franklin Street had an eastern side and a
western side. The western side included Robert's Eureka Saloon at
302 Franklin, and his wholesale liquor business next door at 304
Franklin. What Robert had now purchased was on the eastern side of
the street where, in 1880, he and his brother-in-law, William Mahn,
had leased a Leonardy (later spelled Leonardi) building to house their

general store. Some twenty years later, Robert was acquiring the five original Leonardi buildings, was adding a second story to all five, and likely was breaking down walls in preparation for moving his wholesale liquor business into the three buildings at 305, 307, and 309 Franklin. Moreover, he was remodeling an adjacent building—311 Franklin—to contain his latest saloon, soon to be called the St. Louis Cafe. In short, when Robert was finished, he would have a large new center for his ever-expanding empire; it would be clearly and unashamedly built upon alcohol consumption; and, inevitably, this would inspire envy and resentment from assorted opponents.

Yet, controversial or not, Robert never shied away from debating his critics, as was confirmed in the *Morning Tribune* during late May of 1901. The paper described how Rev. Franklin M. Sprague, pastor of the Congregational church, had recently conducted a "Law and Order" campaign in which he had made Robert Mugge, "the most prominent saloon man in the city, besides being a wholesaler and distiller," one of his primary targets.[263] Ironically, this had led to "luminous and interesting correspondence" between the two, with each expressing his own views on "the subjects of the saloon, the gambling house and the brothel … the minister alleging many evils of the saloons and similar resorts, and the saloonist arguing that, properly conducted, the institutions were necessary."[264]

Conversely, Robert felt just as free to share his views when no one was looking to debate him. For instance, in the *Tampa Times* of June 17, 1901 (fortunately reprinted in the *Tribune* of the following day, or else it would have been lost), he declared Tampa in need of the following: "Two hundred miles of suburban street car lines; two market houses; an opera house; a Fourth of July celebration; a county fair; [and] someone to guide and entertain the strangers who visit our city." The *Tribune's* Wallace F. Stovall went on to concur with all those needs, while declaring, wrongly, that streetcar lines were unlikely and, rightly, that what they really needed were more "good roads in the rural districts and paved streets in the cities."[265] Two days after that, Mr. Stovall added, "All the good things he speaks of will come in time."[266]

On July 9, 1901, Robert purchased an ad in the *Morning Tribune* which touted his primary businesses of the moment, including his distillery and rectifying concerns, his wholesale liquor enterprise, his Anheuser-Busch dealership, his ice factory, his bottling works, and his electric company. Even more than his ad of six years before, when the beer he represented was legally ruled the best in the world, it was a declaration of his widening power and influence. In fact, the final line of his ad could have been intended simply to generate new customers, but just as likely was meant to taunt the Tampa Electric Co.: "Having greatly increased and improved the facilities at my electric lighting plant, I am now prepared to furnish first-class lighting service at reasonable rates."[267]

Yet, on July 26, 1901, all such business-as-usual suddenly ground to a halt in the city, pushed aside by a new citywide cigar workers strike. According to the *Morning Tribune* of the following day, the manufacturers would not accede to the demands of La Resistencia, a Cuban-dominated union, which included the expulsion from factories of all so-called "International Men," who were members of a more moderate national union, and the increasing of worker pay to "the highest scale allowed by the Havana federation." Therefore, what the strike leaders predicted was suddenly coming true: "Five thousand men and women will be idle. All the larger cigar factories of the city, except two, possibly three, will be shut down immediately."[268]

It is important to note that, by 1901, the economy of Tampa was heavily dependent on the welfare of the cigar manufacturers of Ybor City and West Tampa. So, as the strike dragged on for weeks, with most of the factories remaining unproductive, city fathers began to panic. And very soon, their alarm was exacerbated by none-too-subtle declarations from the cities of Jacksonville, Pensacola, and Key West that each would happily offer new homes to all of Tampa's factories.[269] Because of that panic, the strike is known not for its ideals, its job actions, or what it did or did not accomplish for the workers, but for the city's lawless responses.

In the *Tampa Tribune* of December 11, 1988, respected journalist-historian Leland Hawes referred to the book *Urban Vigilantes in the New South, Tampa, 1882-1936* by Professor Robert P. Ingalls when he wrote,

"Author Ingalls cites an 1887 agreement whereby Tampa's Board of Trade—forerunner of today's chamber of commerce—pledged to support and protect cigar manufacturers' 'lives and property by every legitimate means.'" Hawes then documented, as Ingalls had before him, how "a 'Citizen's Committee' of businessmen rounded up the cigar strikers, forced them aboard a chartered schooner and eventually stranded them on a deserted beach in Honduras." Both men reported that this international kidnapping took place on August 5, 1901, and Hawes, as a career newspaperman himself, was extremely critical of *Tampa Tribune* editor Wallace F. Stovall for writing so supportively about these actions, and even more so of *Tampa Times* editor Donald B. McKay, who not only wrote about the events, but also assisted with their planning and execution.

Mr. Hawes went on to reveal that, in addition to the Citizens' Committee "disappearing" the leaders of Resistencia (and one man named Cresenzio Gonzalez, who was mistakenly taken to Honduras with strike leaders but was later invited back), its raiding party dismantled the union newspaper's press, and other of its roving squads destroyed soup kitchens set up for strikers' families in Ybor City and in West Tampa." And just as reprehensible, Florida Governor William S. Jennings did little to investigate the kidnappings or other anti-strike efforts, and even members of some other unions praised what was done.[270]

All these decades later, it is fascinating to read W. F. Stovall's *Morning Tribune* reports written right as the extra-legal actions were being taken, with no interference whatsoever from law enforcement. For instance, in the August 7, 1901 issue, Stovall wrote as follows: "The forcible deportation of the cigar strike agitators had been practically accomplished up to last night at midnight, and the boat which is to bear them to other shores will probably sail early this morning ... They will be treated to an excursion which, while against their will, will be free from anything like violence or inhuman treatment." The story ended with the line, "The people generally approve the decisive plan of action adopted."[271]

Still, not everyone approved. The *Morning Tribune* of August 10, 1901 included a notice that, "Mr. Robert Mugge will give a Sunday

Coffee lunch to women belonging to families of the cigar makers of West Tampa."[272] Clearly, Robert had no involvement with these officially sanctioned acts of terror against striking cigar makers, but neither would it have been safe for him to speak out against the plotters, assuming the newspapers, which supported the terror, would even have printed his contrary statements. What he chose to do instead was more subtle: Knowing that the strikebreakers were attempting to starve the strikers and their families to a point where they would give in, he arranged a free lunch for the female members of the striking cigar makers, giving aid that was clearly humanitarian, and therefore designed to be less threatening than other forms of assistance. Perhaps he even provided this service more than once, and in more than one location. But the *Tribune* only printed one notice.

In weeks to come, the *Morning Tribune* found plenty of space to chronicle the shocking conclusion to the abduction which both major Tampa newspapers had supported from the start. For instance, on August 23, 1901, the *Tribune* noted the return, shortly before midnight, of the schooner Marie Cooper. It had departed for Honduras on August 7 with "thirteen deported agitators," arrived there August 13, and returned with "a cargo of cocoanuts" in place of its earlier human cargo. Also onboard were Captain A. C. LaPenotiere, his crew, and eight Tampa citizens who had guarded the prisoners on the voyage south. "The guards," clearly trying to conceal their identities, "hurried off the vessel as rapidly as possible, got into the first hacks [coaches, carriages, or taxis for hire] they found, and were driven hastily up town." As for Captain LaPenotiere, he was happy to discuss the "fair voyage to Honduras," and how the thirteen union officials had been deposited "on a desolate beach and furnished with sufficient food to last them a week, and all their personal baggage and effects."[273]

Editor Stovall and his staff possessed a singular ability to describe reprehensible behavior in terms that made it appear not simply normal, but praiseworthy. They did so again a day later when they turned the public hanging of James M. Mercer into what was then known as a "dime novel." In its massive Page One and Page

Two coverage, the *Tribune* described forty-year-old Mercer as "a junk dealer who went about the highways and byways, with a crippled horse and a shaky wagon, collecting rags, old iron, etc." But they claimed that, a few months previous, he had enticed nine-year-old Jessie Taylor, a "pretty, well-developed girl," into an unoccupied house a few blocks from the small grocery store run by her father. There, he allegedly offered her a dime to "yield to his lustful embraces," and she "innocently complied."

The case is interesting, if only because of the way it seemed to occupy the people of Tampa at the same time the strike was going on. And of course, considering the hysteria surrounding his case, Mercer was sentenced to a public hanging, and on the scaffold, he made the following declaration: "I want to say to all this great congregation, so that you all can hear me. I am an innocent man. I am clear of this thing, and my life is to be stole from me."[274]

To all of this can now be added the recollections of August Mugge, Robert's son, who was not quite eleven at the time, but in his seventies when he penned his memoirs. August remembered that, in preparation for the hanging, a scaffold had been built in the yard surrounding the County Jail, adjacent to Oaklawn Cemetery: "Being very young and inquisitive, I wandered to the Jail that morning, managed to climb the brick wall, and just as I reached the top, I saw Mercer fall though the trap and saw him hanging. I was horrified, and rushed home and told my parents tearfully what I had done. I think I slept with my aunt [Bertha] for several nights afterwards, since I was haunted by this terrible experience." Yet, the story does not end there. August added that, years later, the local sheriff (he did not specify which one) told him that, once Jessie Taylor was grown, she repudiated her original charge and claimed that Mercer had been an innocent man.[275]

One further by-product of the strike was its effect on many Tampa businesses not directly involved in the cigar business. As just one example, in mid-September, the *Morning Tribune* revealed that Robert Mugge had closed one of his West Tampa saloons because of the strike. Reportedly, the manager to whom Robert had entrusted the saloon was a supporter of La Resistencia and therefore would not serve members of the competing International union who had joined the strike. Therefore, the business was losing money.[276]

Eventually, all the illegal tactics used against the strikers took their toll. In the *Morning Tribune* of Sunday, November 24, 1901, editor W. F. Stovall announced that "the longest and most serious strike in the history of Tampa's cigar industry" had ended, and that men were returning to work. But they were returning under the terms set forth by the manufacturers, which meant that, for the immediate future, no unions would be recognized.[277]

Chapter Eight
Life Goes On (Partial Rewind)

Throughout 1901, while some of Tampa's most respected citizens were publicly conspiring to kidnap strike leaders, execute an accused rapist, and impose their own personal morality on others, Robert Mugge continued to plug along on his own, purchasing property, constructing buildings, expanding his businesses, and questioning government authority. Some of these activities were conducted quietly, outside of the public eye, while others were publicized in newspapers to win public support or patronage. In addition, he still managed to spend time with his family.

One impressive 1901 acquisition did not make the local papers—at least, any issues still available more than a century later—but was recorded by Robert Mugge's son August in his memoirs: "In 1901 my father purchased 560 acres from the State of Florida at Six Mile

Creek, six miles beyond Ybor City. It was bought for $560. This proved to be a wonderful investment ... He conceived the idea of starting a farm, and called it Schweinfurth. A house and two barns were built. Sugar cane was raised."[278] Not mentioned by August was the fact that much of this sugar cane likely was used in Robert's distilling of whiskey.

One family-related story *did* make the papers. According to the *Morning Tribune* of April 24, 1901, Robert and Caroline were packing off their two eldest children, seventeen-year-old Louise and fourteen-year-old Eugene, to Robert's home district of Hanover, where both would visit relatives and see the sights. Then, after a few months, Louise would return home, while Eugene would begin longtime schooling in the German city of Darmstadt.[279]

Rounding out 1901 for Robert were two more saloon-related acquisitions. First, he bought out the Tampa saloon business of retiring Villamil & Gonzalez, including their La Brisa Saloon and Cafe at the northeast corner of Water and Washington Streets.[280] Second, he tore down his old Missing Link Saloon at Franklin and Cass Streets, erected a new brick building in its place, and added furnishings from his former Saratoga Saloon.[281] [282] And with all that accomplished, the year was over at last.

The first big news of 1902 was the Valentine's Day (February 14) birth of Alice Roosevelt Mugge, who was the ninth and final child of Robert and Caroline Mugge.[283] Sadly, baby Alice died three days later—the morning of February 17—and was buried in the afternoon. The *Morning Tribune* of the following day closed its report of the loss with an offer of sympathy for "the heart broken parents."[284] But these events are worth noting as more than family tragedy.

Less than five months before, Vice President Theodore Roosevelt, a progressive Republican, had replaced the assassinated William McKinley as president. Then, as noted in the *Morning Tribune* of October 20, 1901, he had scandalized much of the country, and angered virtually all the South, by inviting his adviser, African American author, educator, and civil rights leader Booker T. Washington, to dine with him as an equal at the White House.[285] For Robert, a successful businessman of the Deep South, to pay Roosevelt indirect tribute at such a time was truly impressive.

Yet, perhaps Robert was doing more than honoring the current US president and that president's first wife. As it happened, Alice Roosevelt had died in 1884 after giving birth to her only child with Teddy Roosevelt,[286] while Robert's first wife, also named Alice, had died soon after giving birth to what would have been at least their second child together, had she and the boys lived. In other words, what Robert appears to have done is to pay tribute not only to a president he admired, and to that president's sadly deceased first wife, but also to his own first wife, and to the children they had lost. And as he did all of this, he and Caroline mourned a second death of their own.

Still, by 1902, despite recurring personal loss, Robert Mugge was considered a huge success. As Roland H. Rerick wrote in his 1902 book *Memoirs of Florida*:

> In 1876 he came to Tampa ... His worldly possessions at that time amounted to less than one hundred dollars, and today he is one of the wealthiest men in the city ... He has been during the twenty-five years of his residence in Tampa the busiest man in the city, doing more work than any three men, and he yet works as tirelessly as ever. He donates about eighteen or nineteen hours a day to various enterprises and attributes his fine health to incessant activity. Mr. Mugge has more varied enterprises than any other man in Tampa ... He transacts a business of a quarter of a million a year, yet does it without the assistance of a clerk or manager.

(Note: One business mentioned by Mr. Rerick, and not acknowledged anywhere else, was "a saw mill with a five-mile tram road."[287] Presumably, this was located at one of his farms and contributed to his constant building efforts throughout the region.)

Inevitably, increasing recognition brought requests that Robert run for office. On November 27, 1901, it was reported that the German American Club was pushing him for mayor.[288] But the same day, the *Morning Tribune* speculated that, although Robert could make a lively race, it was "doubtful he could spare the time."[289] Then, in December, the *Tribune* reprinted an editorial from the *Sanford Chronicle* stating that, "Robert Mugge would make the best mayor that town has ever had. Mugge is full of brains and cussedness."[290] Not surprisingly, Robert declined. However, he did allow his name to be placed in contention for a seat on the Board of Public Works, because that was a job where he could effect positive change for the city.

In so doing, of course, he must have known that his primary line of work would become an immediate topic of conversation and a source of controversy. For instance, the April 30, 1902 issue of the *Morning Tribune* reprinted an endorsement from a small paper called the *Tampa Advance-News*, which is excerpted here: "We are not the champion of Mr. Mugge, even if he needed such a thing, but we desire to be just to every man no matter what his business, nationality, or religion may be ... We are warranted in saying that he is a sober man. A man of good judgement and sound sense, and one who, for public spirit and progressiveness, has few equals. He is a large taxpayer; he is honest, and above all, he is just what he is; no deception nor trifling in any matter has ever marked him in anything ... With this conviction and positive belief, we shall give Mr. Mugge a hearty support."[291] Of course, such voices represented just one side of a very polarized electorate.

The coming election was centered around the newly formed Good Government ticket, which hoped to unseat the current administration of the Citizens League, which the former considered to be corrupt. The ticket was put together by party leader Colonel M. B. Macfarlane and included candidates for all city offices, the most important of which were mayor and City Council. It also was supported by the *Tampa Tribune* newspapers, which chronicled all aspects of the increasingly heated races.

For instance, in the *Morning Tribune's* issue of May 10, 1901, under the headline "More Campaign Lying," discussion was provided of a controversy which suddenly was surrounding the candidacy of Robert Mugge for a seat on the Board of Public Works. The article reported that advocates of the Citizens League candidates had, the day before, circulated a false report of what Colonel Macfarlane had said regarding saloon keepers at the Good Government rally the night before that. They claimed Col. Macfarlane had said, "I would rather trust the affairs of this city to a saloon-keeper than to any church member." But the *Tribune* reported what Col. Macfarlane had truly said about Robert Mugge's candidacy, which was as follows: "Men are not elected to the Board of Public Works to superintend a Sunday School or to preach from a pulpit. They are or should be chosen for their business qualifications and their ability to conduct public improvements. So far as Robert Mugge is concerned, everybody knows that he is an able and successful business man, and that he is honest. I had rather have Robert Mugge in charge of the paving of the streets of the city than any church-member that I know, or than any member of the Citizens League that I know.[292]

Five days later, the article was followed by a concurring *Morning Tribune* editorial in which editor Wallace F. Stovall pointed out that the Board of Public Works was a "purely business arm of the city government," the purpose of which was to spend money voted by the City Council for paving of streets and other civic improvements. Therefore, so long as a candidate possessed a business background, integrity, and an interest in building up the city, it mattered little if he happened to be a saloonkeeper.[293]

Yet, ironically, politics, religion, and the saloon business were merging into a single conversation, inspired, at least in part, by the fact that two prominent saloon owners, Robert Mugge and B. M. Balbontin, Robert's partner in the building and operation of an amusement park, were running for public office in Tampa. It therefore should have come as no surprise when, a few days later, the paper announced that the Clerks' Union, assisted by the city's ministers, had won a ruling from Judge Harry A. Peeples of the municipal court that, not only saloons, but also stores, fruit stands, soda water stands, and every other business except drug stores and restaurants, would now be forced to close on Sundays. Police had agreed "to keep a diligent watch and to arrest every saloon man who opens his doors for whatever purpose," with Judge Peeples promising a fine of $100 for any offender.[294]

Returning to the election, early the next month, the *Morning Tribune* announced that nearly the entire Good Government Club Ticket had been elected. Among the winners announced was Robert Mugge, elected to the First Ward seat on the Board of Public Works,[295] which began a whole new chapter of his life. August Mugge reflected on that chapter in his memoirs, first noting that, in 1902, James C. McKay had been elected Mayor of Tampa, and then revealing that his father had won a seat on the Board of Public Works, "defeating Minish, a butcher, by a large majority." According to August, Robert "never attended a rally, never made a speech, and did not contribute one dime toward the campaign." When asked why he had not promoted his own candidacy, "he answered that the people knew what he stood for, and if they did not want to vote for him, they could lump it."

August went on to relate two additional memories of his father's time in politics. In one case, Robert told his son how he had been offered a $10,000 bribe and responded by throwing the man "bodily out of his office." In the other, Robert explained why he had refused numerous requests to run for mayor. His reason was that the mayor of Chicago had been assassinated, "and he did not want to follow in his footsteps."[296] That would have been Carter Henry Harrison Sr., who was shot and killed in 1893, early in his fifth consecutive term as mayor, and two days before the end of the World's Columbian Exposition then being held in Chicago.

Chapter Nine
Division and Deadlock

Public office in Tampa, Florida was part-time, and in the case of members of the Board of Public Works, it was unpaid as well. Therefore, no one would have cared that, even as the election results were being announced, so, too, were more of Robert's business prospects, including one in the *St. Petersburg Times* of May 31, 1902. Reportedly, a local preacher and businessman (business and religion apparently mixing, the same as business and politics) named R. J. Morgan had invented the Simplex Printing Press, which he claimed would do the work of the "country cylinder press," but at a far lower cost. The *Times* appeared suitably impressed, taking for granted that his new product would "soon invade every country office in the land and make its inventor a millionaire." According to the paper, Morgan would now be partnering with Robert Mugge of Tampa, "and the firm will be known to fame and fortune as the Mugge-Morgan Press Company."[297]

Another of Robert's projects was revealed by the *Weekly Tribune* of July 3, 1902 in a notice headlined, "Oil Fuel Plant." In his memoirs, August Mugge mentioned how Robert eventually switched from wood to oil as the fuel used to power his electric plant and ice factory,[298] and this article captures the point when that happened. According to the *Tribune*, "Robert Mugge asked permission to lay an iron pipe, 2 1/2 inches in diameter, along Central avenue, from his distillery on Cass street to the Plant System [railroad] tracks on Polk street. He is making arrangements to install a system of oil fuel into the plant and wanted the pipe put down in order to have the oil carried from the cars to the distillery. The matter was referred to the committee on streets, alleys and buildings."[299]

At the same time, this and other aspects of Robert's primary business, the making and selling of alcohol, were under increasing threat from the temperance movement. As a start, movement leaders were pushing city and county officials to enforce laws banning the sale of alcohol on Sunday. This not only caused distress for saloon owners and operators who paid hefty city, county, and state licenses to be able to operate, and who, when forced to shut down for one full day per week, lost a seventh of their potential revenue; it also affected laboring men who worked Monday through Saturday, leaving only Sunday on which to socialize with their friends or meet with political and fraternal organizations. And yet, prohibitionists would never be satisfied with Sunday closures alone, or even with turning county after county "dry" through so-called "wet and dry" referendums. No, the ultimate goals of the temperance movement were, number one, to eliminate saloon culture nationwide, and number two, to end the production, importation, distribution, and sale of alcoholic beverages for all time. Equally dismaying was the fact that a growing number of newspapers, dominant voices for their communities, had come to support movement demands.

Conflicts of this sort, which only now were taking hold in South Florida, had appeared much sooner in regions with earlier development. For instance, in his book *Sam Patch, the famous jumper*, author Paul E. Johnson described what happened in the late 1820s when the swiftly established city of Rochester, New York—then known as the celebrated crossing point of the Genesee River and the Eerie Canal—spawned an aggressive middle class.

According to Johnson, the elite of Rochester were "small-town descendants of the Puritans" in central New York, now traveling west in search of a "new market economy" where they could thrive. Such people "valued domestic comfort over public display, work over idleness and leisure, sincerity over affectation, prayerful contemplation over gay sociability," and their view of the world came to be known as "respectable." None of this would have been a problem had they not also sought to "impose respectability on the town as a whole," by which they meant eliminating gambling, drunkenness, Sabbath-breaking, and cruder forms of entertainment.

Initially, these efforts failed, because "most Rochester workingmen—and more than a few in the new middle class—continued to drink and go to shows, and to elect local officials who would not try to stop them from living their lives." Seemingly, what the new elite could not grasp was that the so-called "sporting" types whom they considered "low vagabonds, sneak thieves, and drunkards" were actually "skilled craftsmen and small businessmen, many of them family men" who happened to enjoy "the company of other men, sipping alcohol, telling stories, planning hunting and fishing trips, and concocting broad practical jokes."[300] And yet, this defeat was short-term only, in that the battle for respectability was just beginning, both in Rochester and across the nation.

Some seventy years later, Tampa's primary Gulf Coast neighbor—St. Petersburg, Florida, just across the bay—tended to have two or three saloons, including one owned by Robert Mugge. The city's newspaper, the *St. Petersburg Times*, was comparable in quality to the *Tampa Tribune* and *Tampa Times*, though it was more aligned with temperance forces than were either of Tampa's key papers. For example, its issue of July 19, 1902 offered a glowing report of a union temperance meeting at the Congregational church with "attendance that overtaxed the building." The bulk of the piece was a series of resolutions endorsed by the group, one of which attacked Robert Mugge directly, asking that his current saloon license not be renewed, and that neither he nor anyone else be given a new one.[301]

By this point, of course, the saloons of Florida were patronized almost exclusively by men, it being thought necessary to protect the delicate female nature from demon alcohol, and to prevent said women from being preyed upon by intoxicated men. But this was not solely about shielding the "weaker sex." Local governments and law enforcement officials wanted women, as well, to know that their behavior was being watched. Toward that end, local newspapers would print occasional warnings, such as the one included in the *Morning Tribune* in early July: "Ordinance No. 175, which prohibits lewd women from being on the streets after 9:00 p.m., is being rigidly enforced by the police."[302]

Yes, this was Tampa's notorious law restricting women of "ill fame" from being on the street after 9:00, or from being in a range of public places at almost any time. It also is important to note that, early in that new century, women so branded could include women who were divorced, who remained unmarried, who engaged in sex outside of marriage, who gave birth outside of wedlock, who smoked or drank alcohol, who dressed or spoke in unconventional ways, who specifically dressed in clothing associated with men, who kept company with other women of poor reputation, or who were simply too outspoken or independent—all behavior which was less prone to condemnation in men, unless, of course, the male behavior was carried out in collaboration with such women, which also was covered by Ordinance No. 175. More on this shortly.

Meanwhile, in St. Petersburg, the temperance forces found Robert Mugge to be a convenient foil, especially since he lived in Tampa while owning a saloon in their mostly dry city. For example, on July 26 of 1902, an editorial in the *St. Petersburg Times* made allegations about Robert's business practices: "During the week Mayor Thomas has been taking some steps to ascertain whether St. Petersburg is really a self-governing community, or a sort of provincial tributary of the saloon magnates of Tampa." Allegedly the two saloons then functioning in St. Petersburg had been warned to stay closed on election day, but Manager Wickwire of the Winner Bar had remained open and, when caught, claimed he had done so under orders from Robert Mugge, the saloon's owner.[303] Although Robert had denied giving such instructions, now both the mayor's office and the local newspaper were on his case.

Driving home the paper's message was a political cartoon featuring a flattering portrait of the mayor wearing a tuxedo, smoking a pipe, carrying a mallet that said "Law," and facing a clownish beer barrel with arms, legs, a smiling face, a wooden belly inscribed with "Tampa Saloon Magnate," a cowboy hat labeled "R. Mugge," and a sign bragging that "I'll Sell in Petersburg Whenever I Dern Please. See?" Finally, below this insulting illustration was the mayor's response, which was the cowboy-like, "We'll see about that."[304]

At the same time, there were recurring attempts by law enforcement to bring saloon owners and operators to their knees, such as one chronicled in the *Morning Tribune* of August 1, 1902 (and reprinted in the *Weekly Tribune* of August 7). On this occasion, Robert was implicated in crimes allegedly committed by fellow amusement park owner, and now fellow member of the Board of Public Works, B. M. Balbontin. The *Tribune* mined a rich vein of humor in both cause and effect.

According to testimony, on Sunday May 4, a delegation of preachers had "descended upon DeSoto Park," intent on showing that, contrary to current law, both liquor and baseball tickets were being illegally sold on the Sabbath. In search of proof, the ministers moved back and forth between the park's saloon and its baseball field, with curious crowds trailing behind. "When the preachers 'lined up' at the bar, the scene beggared description; and great excitement attached to the arrest of Balbontin, [M.] Ferlita, and the several bartenders who came under ministerial observation."

At the subsequent trial, it was decided to try Balbontin and Ferlita first, since they were charged with being "proprietors of the resort." Only two of the half-dozen preachers alleging criminal behavior— Rev. John G. Anderson of the First Presbyterian Church, and Rev. F. M. Sprague of the First Congregational Church—appeared in court, and each was ordered to testify. They told the court that Balbontin had been in authority, and that Ferlita had sold tickets that could be exchanged for drinks. The problem came when the clergy present were asked to identify the drinks sold that day as being whiskey or beer but could not tell the difference. "Neither of them had tasted of the fluid that was red or the fluid that was amber, and neither could tell whether it was of the sort that 'biteth like a serpent.'" Yet perhaps the problem was less a lack of knowledge than a surfeit of fear, in that Rev. Anderson spoke of threats from members of the crowd that day, declaring, "he had gone there prepared to die, if need be, to accomplish his mission."

Among the others testifying were the tax collector who admitted to issuing Balbontin a license for selling beer, wine, and liquor at DeSoto Park, and Robert Mugge, who "confessed to furnishing Balbontin with beer in wholesale quantities." But attorney M. B. Macfarlane soon took charge of the proceedings, insisting that, due to their excitement, the preachers had not been accurate. "A preacher feels at home in his pulpit, where he belongs," said Colonel Macfarlane, "but, when he goes into a barroom, where he doesn't belong and has no business, he naturally gets excited and sees things that do not occur.

"The next time these ministers go to DeSoto Park or to any other barroom to get up a case for criminal court," he continued, "let them get more witnesses and fewer prisoners ... Their case must fail because they have no testimony to support it." And seemingly, half the jury agreed, because their group split three to three, which worked in favor of the defendants.[305] At a later retrial, the numbers changed, but not the verdict.

Chapter Ten

Scandalous

Florida's state abortion law was enacted in 1868 and stood for more than a century. As Abby Kaighen wrote in the *Tampa Times* of December 14, 1971, while the law was still in effect, abortions were "permitted only to save the mother's life." Like other laws written during the same period, the Florida law also included punishments both for the doctor offering the abortion and for the woman receiving it.[306]

Whether Dr. Frederick N. Weightnovel sympathized with the plight of women suffering from unwanted pregnancies, or whether he simply saw a business opportunity and, as a Nihilist, did not recognize the right of the state to regulate such matters, he opened what he termed a "maternity hospital" in his offices and residence at 210 Whiting Street, between Franklin and Tampa. Without doubt, he did assist women with childbirth, as well as with other medical issues, which were among his specialties. However, Wallace F. Stovall offered a harsher, retroactive judgement in the *Morning Tribune* issue of June 19, 1902: "He has advertised himself as a 'specialist in diseases of women' ... His establishment on Whiting Street has always been a subject of suspicion, and he has been generally regarded as a criminal practitioner, who was sharp enough to avoid the courts." The public may or may not have shared Mr. Stovall's view before the article in question, but it certainly would afterwards, as the piece also reported the death of an 18-year-old girl "under mysterious circumstances," and the resulting arrest of Dr. Weightnovel for "manslaughter."

The apparent facts were that, yes, among other services offered, the doctor's practice had become known as one where pregnancies could be urgently and discreetly terminated; where women from good families could find relief, and where women working in brothels could be assisted as well. And yes, that likely would have continued to be the case had not one woman's painful death alarmed not only Dr. Weightnovel's neighbors, but also the physicians he had responsibly called to help save her.[307]

The young woman, Irene Randall, had come to Tampa from Quincy, Florida, near Tallahassee, specifically to secure the assistance of Dr. Weightnovel, and letters showed that members of her family had both encouraged and assisted with the move.[308] Now, however, she was dead, and the legal system concluded that her apparent abortionist should be charged, not only with conducting illegal surgery, but with manslaughter, which could bring a sentence of ten to twenty years at hard labor, despite the doctor being in his mid-sixties. For W. F. Stovall, writing in the *Morning Tribune* of June 20, 1902, even that would not be commensurate retribution: "He is guilty of one of the most heinous crimes known and is none too good to stretch hemp, and the heart-broken parents of the poor murdered girl will never be sufficiently revenged until he and the girl's betrayer are both dangling side by side on a gallows."[309]

In view of such sentiments, it probably was best that Dr. Weightnovel did not manage to raise bail until he had been through the entire process, including delays, a guilty verdict, a sentence of six years at hard labor, and an eventual reversal from the State Supreme Court. By the time he finally was released in 1904, he had served nearly two years in the county jail, which seemed to satisfy anyone still paying attention.[310]

To Mr. Stovall's likely displeasure, the *Morning Tribune* of December 20, 1903 announced the State Supreme Court's ruling granting the doctor a new trial.[311] But since, as previously mentioned, the city no longer had the stomach to pursue the matter, he was released on bail a month later, even though charges against him were never officially dismissed.[312] From that day forward, Dr. Weightnovel disappeared from public view, probably sticking to his orange grove, Felicity Home, outside of the city. Perhaps it offered him a modicum of happiness, as the name implied, but the incarceration and vilification had left him shattered. Once again, he was exiled to Siberia, but this time, without the strength to swim away.

Two years later, the *Morning Tribune* of April 4, 1906 reported that he had been found, and it could not resist kicking him again: "At the Emergency Hospital, Dr. F. N. Weightnovel, at one time the most talked-of citizen of Tampa, is now reduced to penury and want. Suffering with heart disease, which may put an end to his career at any time, the doctor is also without funds or friends."[313]

This was followed by an equally cruel announcement in the *Morning Tribune* of May 20, 1906, which at least hinted at the social role he had played: "Dr. F. N. Weightnovel died at 10 a.m. yesterday at the Emergency Hospital, where he had been confined for some time, a helpless victim from a paralytic stroke ... Interment was made in Woodlawn Cemetery yesterday by J. L. Reed. There were few mourners and no religious service. It is said that, with this old man, died many secrets, which, made known, would shake the social fabric of Tampa."[314]

Whatever his faults, unlike Tampa's predatory newspapers, the city's most colorful character never betrayed the beleaguered women he served. And if any hint of resurrection followed this uniquely American crucifixion, perhaps it was revealed in the *Morning Tribune* of Sunday, November 3, 1907, which reprinted a story from the *Tarpon Springs News*: "The Peninsular Packing House will open its doors next week, preparatory to the shipping of oranges ... By the time operations have been fairly gotten under way in our packing houses, the fruit will be ripe and yellow ... The latest acquisition to their holdings is the big Weightnovel grove near Tampa, from which they will this year market a large amount of fruit."[315]

Meanwhile, Robert Mugge was involved in scandals of his own, though of an entirely different nature. The *Morning Tribune* of August 31, 1902 asked one question over and over in various parts of the paper: "Did the *Herald* ask Robert Mugge for $40 a week Blackmail?"

Their own immediate answer was, "The *Times* says so. The *Tribune* and the public wish to hear from the *Herald*." In other words, the *Morning Tribune* was reporting that the *Tampa Times* was reporting, that the *Herald*, the city's latest daily newspaper, had asked a prominent Florida businessman and commissioner of public works for a bribe.[316]

The *Morning Tribune* of September 6, 1902 carried forward this story of the *Herald* requesting a bribe from Robert Mugge. The key point was that, knowing how important it would be to Mugge for his saloons to be able to sell alcohol on Sundays, the *Herald* staff offered to stop crusading against such sales if Robert and others would purchase $40.00 per week of advertising. Included in the long piece were quoted sections of an interview which had appeared in the *Tampa Times* of the day before:

> "Mr. Mugge, it is current report that the *Tampa Herald* levied, or attempted to levy, blackmail from you as president of the Tampa Liquor Dealers' Association. The *Times* has charged this, and it would like to have a statement from you for publication. Is the report true?"
>
> "Yes, the report is substantially true. A. F. Lovering, who is announced as the advertising manager of the *Herald*, called on me some weeks ago and submitted such a proposition to me. He said great pressure was being brought to bear on the paper to attack the Sunday liquor selling business; that numerous communications had been received, and unless they got some compensation from the liquor dealers that they would publish the communications. His definite proposition was this: That the Florida Brewing Company and myself give him a page of advertisement for the Saturday issue, for which we were each to pay $20 per week. He said it would take this much to keep their mouths closed ...
>
> "I told him that I considered this the boldest piece of blackmailing I had ever heard of, and that is saying a great deal."

The article went on at great length, with Robert recalling feigning interest to convince the *Herald* to put everything in writing, the *Herald* refusing to do so, and Robert and associates telling the *Times* what had happened.[317]

Naturally, the *Herald* denied the story. Therefore, the *Tribune* organized a mock trial in which the management of the *Times* presented charges, the management of the *Herald* defended itself, and the management of the *Tribune* sat in judgement.[318] After nearly three weeks of coverage, the scandal faded from view, but not before the *Weekly Tribune* published a full "Proof of Charges" on September 11, 1902,[319] and a lengthy summary a week later.[320] Of course, to be fair, the *Herald* did have one ally, which was its fellow temperance-supporting paper, the *St. Petersburg Times.*[321]

Speaking of temperance and St. Petersburg, in a story sure to please Robert's critics there, he told the *Morning Tribune* of October 2, 1902 he had closed his St. Petersburg saloon known as the Peninsular (probably a new name for his Winner Saloon). He explained that business there had not been up to expectations, though he may simply have tired of pressure from local temperance organizations, and of being vilified by the St. Petersburg press.[322]

Otherwise, as much as Robert had enjoyed the moral high ground during the *Herald* blackmail story, familiar forces in Tampa ensured he would not hold it long. In late October, the *Morning Tribune* featured a short article under the primary headline, "Slot Machine Shown in Court." Suffused with sarcasm and a dollop of racism, the article began as follows: "The presence of a slot machine, two alleged chicken thieves, and a large number of members of the S.S.S. (Smart Scrub Set), added new life to the proceedings of the municipal matinee yesterday morning."

The article noted how literal slot machines had been a feature of every saloon in the city during the summer of 1901, but had disappeared after repeated fines from Judge W. S. Graham of the Criminal Court. Now sometimes taking their place was a handheld version which accepted nickels, and in return for the patron hitting a lucky number, offered complimentary drinks. One such handheld gadget "was found Sunday in one of Robert Mugge's Central avenue saloons, which was being managed by Eugene Gill. Patrolman Guy Middaugh saw a negro use it and lose, and at once placed Gill under arrest." Gill, one of Robert's African American managers, was convicted, but Robert's attorney for the occasion, Judge Harry A. Peeples, gave notice of an appeal.[323]

Chapter Eleven

Lawless

From 1895 until 1925, when West Tampa was annexed by Tampa, the former was an incorporated city, even if never entirely autonomous. In 1902, its part-time mayor was a charming, well-liked Italian named Francisco Milian, who was also employed as a so-called "reader" for a local cigar makers union. In his latter role, he represented the interests of union labor in its dealings with a particular factory for which its members worked. But the *Morning Tribune* of Sunday, November 2, 1902 shocked its readers with the following headline: "Mayor Is Missing ... Milian disappears."[324] As previously mentioned, the *Tribune* was not printed on Mondays. But by Tuesday, November 4, 1902, the paper was overflowing with hair-raising details.

Reportedly, officials at the Bustillo Brothers & Diaz cigar factory had suddenly decided Mayor Milian would no longer be allowed to make his "collections" inside the factory, or even at the front door, as was standard for union readers. Instead, he would only be allowed to conduct his business outside the factory where he felt he would be ineffective, plus subject to the elements, which could damage his health. As a result, the mayor sent union members a letter in which he informed them of the situation and, with obvious regret, resigned his position. At the same time, he urged them not to respond with any sort of provocative actions, yet the four hundred union members working at the factory immediately went on strike.

What happened next was never entirely explained. However, some in the community apparently blamed Mayor Milian for the strike, and they responded by forcing the mayor to sail to Key West, with his family expected to follow. At that point, cigar makers throughout the region threatened that, unless the mayor were allowed to return, they would strike all factories operated by the Cigar Manufacturers Association. In the process, they also pressed for long-needed changes.

The cigar workers "manifesto" contained many issues common for workers having disputes with management. They demanded, for instance, that readers be given appropriate conditions in which to serve their roles within the factory; that they be permitted a committee to represent their interests; that they be given regular updates on the size, thickness, and cost of the different cigars they were expected to make; that the firm supply them with drinking water in the work-place; and that the company take no actions against those attempting to represent the interests of fellow workers, with or without union involvement. In other words, nothing the slightest bit radical.[325]

As it happened, the deportation of Mayor Milian proved to be a step too far, even for Tampa businessmen who had quietly supported the abduction of alleged agitators during the cigar maker strike of the year before. In response, the *Morning Tribune* of November 8, 1902 reported widespread signing of the following letter of protest: "We, the undersigned, business and professional men, together with the different labor unions through their delegates assembled and central body, feel that the deportation of F. Milian was an unlawful act— an act which establishes a precedent by which private citizens are denied the right and liberties guaranteed them by the Constitution ... Therefore, we, the undersigned, request the return of F. Milian to his home and family." Among the businessmen signing was Robert Mugge, soon to be followed by professional men of the city, merchants of Ybor City, officers of the Building Trade Council, sixty-five members of the Painters' Union, and the officers of the Central Trades and Labor Assembly.[326]

Thanks to this massive show of support, plus pledges of protection, both noted in the *Morning Tribune* of November 12, 1902, Mayor

Milian promised to return, while also wiring the following: "Thank you for doing me justice in these times of trial for me. Thanks to the noble American people. Hurrah for liberty. Equal rights to all."[327] And yet, the following day, an editorial comment in the *Morning Tribune* showed that some lessons were not yet learned, at least by a paper that, just the year before, had actively supported the abduction of strike leaders: "Mayor Milian has returned. Now let us have no more of this high-handed business *unless there is occasion for it* [italics added]." Still, progress was being made.[328]

The following day, the *Morning Tribune* itself made that clear when announcing an emergency meeting to feature speeches by top political leaders. In the *Tribune's* own words, "To discuss the recent deportation of Mayor Milian, of West Tampa, and to express the condemnation of the people of Tampa upon such practices, a mass meeting of citizens has been called for tonight at the courthouse." In a second sign of progress, another piece in the same paper revealed that the strike had been settled, with the Bustillo Brothers & Diaz largely meeting the demands of striking workers.[329]

Of course, with Milian back in West Tampa, and strike issues settled, the city could return its focus to Robert Mugge. For example, the *Morning Tribune* of December 4, 1902 reported the second trial of African American saloon manager Eugene Gill, charged with operating an illegal gambling device in Robert Mugge's Central Saloon. In court, the police and prosecuting attorney insisted the "Game o' Skill Amusement Toy" was akin to a full-fledged slot machine, whereas Robert, who was the local agent for such devices, and in whose saloons they had been operated, "denied that it was a slot machine in the accepted sense of the term."

While the jury watched, a witness held up one of the offending devices and inserted a nickel. From there, the coin fell into one of eleven slots which revealed the player's success or failure. Six of the slots were blank, two paid five cents, two paid ten cents, and one paid fifteen cents, which meant that the player had six chances to lose, two to stay even, and three to win. Predictably, the witness lost four of the five nickels inserted, convincing the jury that the machine was meant for gambling, rather than an "incentive to business," as argued by the defense. Mr. Gill was found guilty, but his attorneys gave notice of still another appeal.[330]

That resolved, a second story in the *Tribune* was even more exciting, though not for everyone present. The issue of December 14, 1902 reported an explosion in Robert Mugge's wholesale establishment loud enough to draw a crowd, as well as the Fire Department. Said explosion resulted when a Mr. Jacqueman dropped a lighted match into a seemingly empty whiskey barrel, causing Jim Burgert, an African American employee, to be struck by a flying missile and nearly knocked unconscious. After that, the flames were quickly extinguished. But perhaps most surprising, as an anxious crowd entered the building, it found Robert, himself, seated at his desk and making out bills as if nothing had happened.[331]

Finally closing out the year, the *Morning Tribune* of December 21, 1902 announced the long-awaited reopening of his Eureka Saloon at the corner of Franklin and Jackson Streets. Over the past three months, Robert had installed "new floors, new furniture, new fixtures—everything up-too-date." In addition, adjoining the saloon, he had "equipped the finest pool and billiard room in the city," including three new billiard tables furnished with Monarch cushions, "the best ever brought to Tampa." According to the *Tribune*, the Eureka's George Green and Elmo Ceconi were "two of the most popular as well as the most expert mixologists in Tampa," and they invited all their old friends "to call in Monday and see the newest and best equipped saloon in Florida."[332]

Chapter Twelve

The Tampa Plan

Showing it to be a typical year for Robert Mugge, 1903 began with both good news and bad. The good news, announced in the *Tampa Times* sometime in January (and reprinted twenty years later), was that "Robert Mugge's schooner line to New Orleans is proving a great benefit to local merchants."[333] By contrast, the bad news came in more dramatic fashion in the *Morning Tribune* of January 27, proving, under the headline, "Heroic Battle," that Robert's fire and water dialectic was also still in effect.

At 1:10 the previous morning, a fire was discovered by an African American hackman (driver of a coach, carriage, or taxi for hire) at the intersection of Central Avenue and Scott Street in the Scrub. It had started in Robert Mugge's warehouse on the corner which had housed his New Parlor Theatre in 1895, also reportedly served as a vaudeville theater during the Spanish-American War encampment of 1898, and now "was unoccupied except as a storeroom for the printing presses manufactured by R. J. Morgan," as part of a partnership forged with Robert Mugge. The hackman who discovered the fire told police he saw flames in two parts of the building simultaneously, leading to suspicion of arson. Despite the fast response of Fire Stations One, Two, and Five, Robert's building was destroyed at a loss of $8,000, and a loss of $15,000 for the fire, overall, making it the most destructive blaze to hit Tampa in the past two years.[334]

That arsonists were rarely caught and prosecuted may have been at least partially due to a lack of interest from local police. This appeared evident in "A Brief Interview," featured in an issue of the *Morning Tribune* in mid-March: "'What are you giving up during Lent?' we asked every officer and patrolman we could find at police headquarters. The reply was the same in each case. Very solemnly, they said, 'Looking for the firebugs.'" Whether this was intended as serious journalism or satire, the point being made was the same.[335]

Meanwhile, on the personal front, Robert decided two more of his children (daughter Frances and son August) should join their older brother Eugene for schooling in Darmstadt, Germany. The *Morning Tribune* of May 10, 1903 announced their departure that evening,[336] and August, in his memoirs, mentioned how much of Tampa's German American community was at the P&O train station on Polk Street to see them off. Traveling with Frances and August were their mother, Caroline, and their two younger sisters, Martha and Nellie,[337] with only Robert, Louise, and Melanie staying behind. Considering Melanie's presumed mental illness, she either was being looked after by Robert's sister Bertha and eldest daughter Louise, or else this was a period when she was committed to what was then called the Georgia State Sanitarium in Milledgeville, Georgia.[338]

In recreating the group's journey, August began with their arrival in Jacksonville the morning of May 11, where Robert's friend, Captain Ernest Hausmann, showed them around the city. After that, once again traveling by train, they arrived in Baltimore on May 12, staying in the home of a Mr. and Mrs. Weber whom Louise had met on her own trip to Germany two years before.[339] Then, on May 13, they set sail on the SS Köln at 3:00 p.m.,[340] preparing for one of the long, transatlantic voyages typical of that time. According to August, "We had a very nice crossing, stormy at times, and it became extremely rough in the English Channel. We arrived in Bremerhaven on the 27th of May at midnight."

Once in Germany, they again proceeded by train. Along the way, they met up with August's brother Eugene, still studying in Darmstadt; Caroline's brother, George Rautenstrauch; Caroline's foster parents, August and Melanie Bremer (August Bremer, after whom August had partially been named, now wearing a long white beard); and Robert's brother Louis, who had returned to Germany with their mother years before. To quote August's memoirs, "We went to Lauterberg, the birthplace of my father. While there, we lived in the Hotel Kurpark, which was owned by my father's Uncle Wenzel and his daughter Friede. We visited my father's former home, where he was born, the church in which he was confirmed, and the grave of my grandmother [Robert's mother Luise, or Louise, who had died the year before]."

The group would travel around Germany through the end of July, when August and Frances were delivered to their respective educational situations in Darmstadt. In his memoirs, August continued, "My mother remained in Darmstadt through the end of August. She told us goodbye at the station, all of us were in tears, and I was heartbroken."

At this point, Frances, nearly fifteen, went to live with two sisters, Adelheid and Helene Streb, who ran a finishing school for young women. Like other such German schools of the time, it likely focused on foreign languages, literature, the arts, and more modest doses of math and science than were offered in schools for boys. August, almost thirteen, moved into a *pensionat* (French for boardinghouse) for young males run by a Professor Gustav Stammler and his wife, was tutored for a time by several professors, and then, after being tested, was admitted to a higher end *oberrealschule* (German secondary school) where, according to August's memoirs, "modern languages, Mathematics, Physics, and Chemistry were given," in preparation for his later college studies in engineering and architecture.

For years to come, Frances and August would not see their father, their mother, or most of their siblings. Both parents wrote to them faithfully, and Robert sent money for all their needs, as he did with Eugene. But for a painfully long period, they were on their own in a city of 80,000 people. Fortunately, whenever August wished to visit, the Streb sisters, who ran Frances's finishing school, welcomed him into their home, allowing brother and sister to retain a sense of family throughout their lonely years together in Germany.[341] [342]

Back in Tampa, in the *Morning Tribune* of June 7, 1903, Wallace F. Stovall wrote an editorial about the need of more watering places for horses used for transportation and hauling around the city: "R. Mugge, of the Board of Public Works, reminded us today that, in addition to the two watering places for stock mentioned by us yesterday, there is the Seminole [Robert's saloon at Seventh Avenue and Twenty-Second Street], and that all of them were furnished by whisky men."[343] After that, on June 25, 1903, the *Tribune* followed up by stating that Robert once again had "presented the city with a handsome fountain," which would be placed at one of the city's prominent corners.[344]

Then, in the latter part of July, and continuing through much of August, Tampa went crazy again, kicking off one of its worst periods of mob violence aimed at African Americans. It started with rumors that a "negro hackman" named George Houston had been enticing a "half-witted" fourteen-year-old white girl named Nellie Groover to his house for the purpose of "criminal intimacy." As reported in the *Morning Tribune* of Friday, July 31, 1903, two patrolmen followed the girl to Houston's house and "got to a window in time to see the negro and the child together on the bed, the negro's black arms around her."

Both Houston and the girl were taken to the police station where they were questioned. According to the *Tribune*, when the story had circulated, "great indignation resulted among white citizens." Supposedly, Houston had bragged for some time about his conquests of white women, to the point where, "He had been warned repeat-edly by people of his own race that his talk and habits would get him into serious trouble." Whether intentionally or not, the article read as a none-too-subtle call to action.

At 7:00 that night, the police decided to move Houston to the county jail, and City Detective Frank Bell was assigned to transport him. Securing "a closed carriage ... with a negro driver," Detective Bell took Houston down Lafayette Street to Pierce, which he anticipated having little traffic. But as they turned onto the latter road, a mob of a few dozen men appeared, fired shots, grabbed Houston, gagged him, and placed a black cap over his head. Then, as the crowd grew to perhaps 100 men, they carried him "to the gun club grounds in the Garrison, where they were joined by others, swelling the crowd considerably." There, they thoroughly castrated Houston, at least working "to prevent the negro bleeding to death," but leaving him there, unattended.

A short time later, the police located Houston, still lying there on the ground. Determining he was not dead, as they had expected, they summoned a patrol wagon which drove him "hurriedly to the colored hospital, where surgical attention was at once given him."[345]

The following day, August 1, 1903, the *Morning Tribune* featured the second story of a mob attack on a local Black man, making it sound almost like entertainment. "The George Houston affair of Thursday night had an exciting sequel last night, when M. M. Wadkins, a well-known negro tailor, was waited upon by a small but determined mob and shot twice as he fled from his would-be persecutors." Described as "a light mulatto" who had frequently been "mistaken" as white, Wadkins owned a newly erected small building at the corner of Franklin and Fortune Streets, to the rear of the home of prominent businessman Colonel A. J. Knight, in which he both lived and conducted his tailoring business. Opening a business and residence in a mainstream section of Tampa would already have placed an African American man in potential jeopardy, but apparently, he, too, was accused of boasting of his intimacy with white women, which led to his being targeted one night after George Houston.

At approximately 7:45 p.m., Wadkins was assaulted in his home by three white men wearing white handkerchiefs as masks and holding guns. As the men approached him, he was able to race out the open rear door and into Col. Knight's back yard. At that point, three shots were fired, "one passing through his double-chin," and a second going "through his right leg just above the knee." The three original attackers, followed by four more, pursued Wadkins as he ran into Knight's front yard, entered Knight's house, and ascended stairs to the second floor, interacting with Knight's frightened wife and children.

Knight himself, who had been "reclining on the front veranda," and now believing that a mob was preparing to enter his house, grabbed a rifle and held it on the crowd as he tried to sort out the confusion. At that point, the attackers fled, and Knight phoned the police. Wadkins, covered with blood, was helped back to his own apartment where a Dr. Lawrence provided medical care, and a policeman was left to guard him overnight.[346]

The following day, the *Morning Tribune* reported that Wadkins had been warned by several white friends that he had narrowly missed receiving the same treatment as Houston and therefore should leave town immediately. At first, he resisted, but ultimately decided to leave his property in the care of an agent. He then fled via bicycle, arranging with a friend to meet him at Six Mile Creek, from which he could be driven to a railway station.[347]

In the same *Morning Tribune* issue of Sunday, August 2, 1903, still another article spoke of an African American man escaping a murderous white mob. In this additional case, which took place the morning before, police had arrested a man named Henry Jackson in the Scrub for allegedly "inciting the negroes in the vicinity to some show of violence, using incendiary language against the whites." He then had spent the day in a cell, absolutely stricken with fear over the possibility of mob violence.

At 10:30 that night, Chief Jones decided to walk the prisoner to the county jail by himself, "holding him by the arm" as they "walked on the dark side of Florida avenue, near the government building." Suddenly, a dozen men leaped out of the shadows and demanded that they halt. Supposedly, Chief Jones turned to defend Jackson, but his prisoner "broke loose from the chief's grasp and flew down the street like a thoroughbred racer." Although the mob chased him for a few blocks, "Jackson was too swift for his pursuers, and when he turned into the darkness back of the hotel, the mob gave up the chase."[348]

Seeing the police repeatedly attempt to move such men at night, with only one officer as guard, instead of in bright sunlight with a whole contingent of policemen for protection, it must be assumed that members of the all-white police force were collaborating with the castrating and murdering mobs. Further evidence comes from the facts that, whenever police attempted these moves at night, the mobs were always waiting, and no matter how heinous the crimes committed, none of their members were ever arrested, much less prosecuted. This was terror, pure and simple, imposed on a subjugated Black community by tyrannical whites, and one additional blurb in the same issue of the *Tribune* showed how well it worked: "Jim Anderson and H. Tillman, two negro hackmen who feared a dose of the Houston treatment, left the city last night for reasons of their own. A notorious white woman was also induced to leave last night."[349] Translation: After the initial attacks, others were threatened, and many of them fled for their lives. But not all.

The *Morning Tribune* of August 4, 1903 revealed that the latest citizen to be threatened by anonymous letter-writers was "no less a personage than Robert Mugge, member of the Board of Public Works and saloon owner extraordinary." In fact, ever since the attack on George Houston, Robert had received letters warning that, if he did not refrain from "certain conduct," which likely involved his close association with African Americans, he, too, could expect a mob attack. But according to the *Tribune*, "The letters caused a broad smile of half-amusement and half-defiance to fit over the Teutonic features of the Hon. Robert," and he sat down to dictate the following message, which he asked the *Tribune* to publish: "Editor *Tribune:* I have this day received certain anonymous threatening letters. I desire to put the writers thereof on notice that they are known to me and others. They are business competitors and take this cowardly method of annoying me. But, should they attempt to carry out their threats, they will meet a warm reception, as I have prepared for such an opportunity as they deserve. R. Mugge."[350]

That article was followed in the *Morning Tribune* of August 5, 1903 by a second article with the headline, "Mugge Now Carries A Gun." The article declared, simply and directly, that Robert had, the day before, secured a permit from the County Commissioners to carry a pistol and, therefore, should now be assumed to be "heavily armed and dangerous to meddlers." Mention also was made of a rumor that he had employed a bodyguard, fully protecting himself "against an anticipated attack from a mob."[351]

Considering that an uncomfortably large number of white citizens of greater Tampa had now declared at least short-term war on the Black population of the city, and that white police officers and deputy sheriffs appeared to be in league with them, Robert Mugge's active defiance of both groups was uncommonly brave. Then again, maintaining a strong public profile and making it known that he would respond in kind to attempted violence was likely a smarter move than cowering in fear. Many in the region would never approve of his primary occupation, much less of his hiring, supporting, and consorting with his African American neighbors. But remaining fearless, outspoken, and oblivious to the terror campaign signaled that any assault offered at least as much risk for the attackers as for him. And knowing that most of his family members were safely overseas likely made him that much more confident.

Still, it had to be tough seeing some of his natural political allies, including *Tampa Tribune* editor Wallace F. Stovall, buckle under to such forces. The following are brief excerpts from Mr. Stovall's August 8, 1903 editorial in which, under the title, "The Tampa Plan Is The Best," he seemed to approve of one form of mob law (one that white Tampa had recently been employing) as a means of suppressing another: "Since the emasculation of the negro villain, Houston, in this city by a number of indignant citizens a few nights ago ... the *Tribune* is of the opinion that the remedy adopted by Tampa is far better than lynching. It has had a salutary effect on all hoodlums. It has put the negroes to thinking and some of the whites have been very uneasy about the safety of their anatomy. Taking everything into consideration, the *Tribune* believes that Tampa has solved the mob law problem and the race question at the same time ...

"Mob law in this country is alarmingly on the increase, North as well as South," he continued. "It must be suppressed." And how did he propose to do that? "The *Tribune* recommends the Tampa treatment in preference to lynching every time." In other words, to Mr. Stovall's mind, castration was a lesser evil than lynching. Yet, he failed to acknowledge that castration, even more than lynching, was exclusively the product of mob law.[352]

Despite the chaos then afflicting the region in which Robert Mugge lived and worked, he attempted to turn his attention back to needs of the city, and Wallace Stovall followed suit. For instance, the *Morning Tribune* of August 11, 1903 published Robert's long and complex letter to the editor in which he declared the urgency of paving roads in Tampa and explained how the work could be afforded by the city. The article was titled, "Mugge On Bonding— Member of Board Of Public Works Shows That Funds Asked For By That Body Are Absolutely Necessary, And Gives Logical Reasons For The Asking."[353]

Of course, having just taken on the forces of lawlessness in Tampa, including those ironically working in law enforcement, Robert should have expected some sort of retribution. And perhaps he did expect it, only not in the form it eventually was delivered. Said payback was described in giddy detail in the August 13, 1903 issue of the *Morning Tribune* under the headline, "On A Moonlight Drive." The piece proclaimed that Robert had been "arrested Sunday night by Patrolman Lane, while driving on Rock Road in company with the notorious mulatto woman Panchita." As they were taken into custody, Robert reportedly "raised quite a kick," but paid a $10 bond for Panchita, and another for himself, as they were charged with violating Ordinance 175. In the process, Panchita informed police that her legal name was Mary Brown, and statements were made that police had been instructed several months before "to arrest all white men seen in public in the company of negro women or vice versa."[354]

So, was Robert out cavorting with a woman while most of his family was in Germany for the summer? Perhaps. Is it also possible that, because of the climate in the city at the time, he was simply giving a ride to a friend he thought could be in jeopardy while heading home late at night? That too is possible. But either way, the timing suggests retribution for his refusal to condone, or participate in, racist assaults on the African Americans around whom he lived and worked. It also suggests that the police had been watching him and waiting for an opportunity to find him in violation of the law—any law. That they should call upon Ordinance No. 175, the city's most repressive law of all—sexist, racist, and down-home authoritarian—made the irony that much richer, as did his and his companion's being arrested by Patrolman Lane, one of the two officers who had spied upon, and then arrested, George Houston, paving the way for his ultimate castration.

It should also be conveyed that Panchita's only infraction was being of mixed race (or "mulatto," as white people liked to say) and then having the gall to be on a city street after 9:00 p.m. with an influential white man. Regarding the aims of Ordinance 175, was she a woman of "ill repute," even by standards of the time? According to previous mentions in the *Morning Tribune*—two or three at most—she had friends who sometimes got rowdy, but she was also said to be a woman of means. Still, in Tampa, Florida, the most serious crime of 1903 was the mixing of races, and of that, she and Robert were clearly, perhaps shamelessly, at fault. For them, that meant a fine in court and public embarrassment; but for a Black man in Tampa, the same offense would have meant castration, death, or both in quick succession.

Chapter Thirteen
Rights and Wrongs

Days later, on August 15, 1903, the *Morning Tribune* announced the city's latest crackdown on saloon operators. Not surprisingly, the piece announced that Tampa Mayor James McKay was receiving increased pressure to keep saloon owners from opening on Sundays. Consequently, Chief of Police Jones informed George P. Raney, Jr., as attorney for the Liquor Dealers' Association of Tampa, that the Police Department would now have to "arrest the proprietors occasionally." In turn, Raney informed Liquor Dealers' Association President Robert Mugge, and Robert passed along Raney's letter to his membership, complete with his own skillfully worded addendum: "I trust you will carefully read the above and govern yourselves accordingly."[355]

Yet, regardless of new legal pressures, Robert never stopped stirring the political pot. For example, in the *Morning Tribune* of August 18, 1903, he addressed the matter of the city's privately owned Water Works Company, which was contracted to provide for all the city's water needs, but which was infamous for its poor performance. In the article, he recounted the ridiculous deal the city had been given

ten years before, and declared why Tampa should henceforth choose
a different course. It was a stance that would take on great irony in
the years to come.[356] Meanwhile, in the *Morning Tribune* of August
20, 1903, editor Wallace F. Stovall published a front-page editorial
which, without naming the newly notorious Robert Mugge, quoted
from his previous letters on bonding, paving, and the Water Works,
and did so under the headlines, "Why We Need Bonding—Prominent
Tax-Payer Talks On Important Subject—Waterworks Will Come
Later—Paving, Not Water, Is Now Needed."[357]

For Robert Mugge and Wallace Stovall, the rush to reassert
civic engagement may have been an effort to suspend recent terror
and bullying and replace them with a renewed sense of normalcy.
However, for county officials, just like city ones, a return to the
status quo simply meant resuming their assault on saloon owners,
including the usual emphasis on Robert, in particular. The *Morning
Tribune* of September 2, 1903 set the stage with an article titled "War
On Saloons." The subject was a meeting the day before of the County
Commissioners in which State Attorney H. S. Phillips questioned
the continuing granting of permits for alcohol sales in the area just
beyond Twenty-Second Street, which was known as "Hell's Half-
Acre." One of the two saloons at that location which Mr. Phillips
singled out for "vileness" was, of course, one of Robert's. In addition, attorneys Donald C. McMullen and G. E. Mabry sought to stop
the renewing of all licenses for saloon owners Robert Mugge, W. T.
Boyd, and others, "in the interests of the moral upbuilding of the
city." After a period of discussion, "the matter was laid over until
Thursday."[358]

Two days later, in an article titled "Sabbath Sellers," the *Morning
Tribune* chronicled the resulting battle over licenses for the Seminole
Saloon, owned by Robert Mugge, and the Red Light Saloon, supplied
by the Florida Brewing Co. Most invective was aimed at the Red
Light, which citizens from the district called one of the "wickedest
places on earth," emphasizing public drunkenness and "vile prostitutes assembling to drink and carouse in the dance hall to the rear."
For his part, the Rev. Dave Blount referred to both saloons as "dens
of iniquity," and although quite deaf, claimed to have heard "the

putrid curses uttered by drunken degenerates." He also claimed "he had seen both places open on Sunday, though R. Mugge proved that the door through which he alleged to have seen men at the bar did not exist."

During this fight, "the character of Mr. Mugge was assailed," his opponents pointing out that he had previously been arrested for selling alcohol on Sunday, plus mentioning his dalliance with Panchita. Yet, later in the afternoon, Donald C. McMullen agreed to quit his larger fight against the saloon men, so long as the two Twenty-Second Street saloons were closed and Robert agreed to "quit doing business on Sunday." In response, Robert rightly complained that it was unfair to single him out for special treatment, but told the Board of Commissioners he would "willingly submit to their decision in the case, if they would see to its enforcement throughout the entire county." He also declared the unfairness of allowing blind tigers (unlicensed liquor sellers) to continue functioning nonstop in the city, while licensed saloons were forced to shut down one day per week. At that point, Commissioner Branch drew up a compromise resolution stating that any saloon owner granted a license that day, but later found to be opening on Sunday, would have his license revoked. In addition, the applications for the Red Light and Seminole Saloons were both withdrawn, at least for the moment.

In a short statement at the end of the *Tribune* piece, Robert informed saloon keepers of the city that they would have to abide by this agreement.[359] Then, in an editorial in the September 5, 1903 issue of the *Morning Tribune*, editor Wallace F. Stovall echoed Robert's point to the County Commissioners about the unfairness of the current system: "Unless the Commissioners proceed, by the use of all the authority at their disposal, to put the illegal whisky-sellers under the same ban as the licensed liquor dealers, compelling them either to pay their licenses or to quit business every day and Sunday too, they will be giving the licensed liquor men the worst end of a very unfair deal.[360]

Robert could not have made this case better himself, and followed up with an expression of gratitude to editor Stovall in the form of a letter published the following day. But he also described some of his frustrating attempts to get city and county officials to address the problem:

> Many, many times have I suggested to the parties in authority that if we as liquor dealers received the proper protection against illicit liquor selling the necessity for selling liquor on Sunday by us, to make ends meet, would no longer exist. I invariably receive this reply: "You inform on the guilty parties and furnish the proper evidence and I will do my duty."
>
> Commissioner Ware accosted me in a fierce manner, when I spoke to the Board of County Commissioners of the blind tigers not being molested, and said, "We are dealing with you now," but I failed to see that the board took any action as to the blind tigers afterwards. Solicitor Simonton said as to my complaint of liquor men being punished continually for Sunday liquor selling and the tigers not being molested, "You fellows are easier caught up with ..."[361]

Chapter Fourteen
Storm Warnings

The *St. Petersburg Times* of September 12, 1903 lauded the recent Sunday selling ban by the Board of County Commissioners. Overall, the article was predictable in its praise for the action of the Board, but the revelation of the piece came relatively late: "Last Sunday only one establishment in the county, the 'Buckingham Theatre,' at Fort Brooke, is known to have sold liquor, and the proprietor, Lewis Chappell [sic], is now under $500 bond awaiting trial on the serious charge of selling whiskey without a license."[362] The *Morning Tribune* of the same date provided additional information, or at least assertions: "The *Tribune* learns that the license for the Buckingham theatre saloon which was pulled for violating both the law and the agreement among the saloon-keepers by selling last Sunday was taken out by R. Mugge, Chappell [sic] being only a hired bartender." The article went on to claim that a police officer had, between 2:00 and 3:00 a.m., discovered one of Robert's wagons carrying a load of liquors from his Crystal Saloon, at Harrison and Franklin Streets, to the Buckingham, presumably indicating "a pre-arranged plan to sneak a march on the other liquor-dealers by selling at this resort on Sunday."[363]

The next move belonged to Robert Mugge, as he paid for space to provide rebuttal in the *Morning Tribune* of September 16, 1903. In short, he denied all allegations directed at him personally, and he asked that Mayor McKay "investigate the charge of Police Officer Morgan," and for any teamster of his found to have delivered alcohol to the Buckingham on September 6 to be "severely punished."

Attached to Robert 's letter were two notarized affidavits. In the first, signed by him, he swore that none of the Chappelle Brothers (the correct spelling of their name) were ever hired bartenders for him, that "all parties doing business under his license were duly notified" on September 5, 1903 not to sell liquor on Sunday, and that, on September 6, 1903, no one had delivered alcohol on his behalf to the Chappelles or to anyone else. In the second signed and notarized affidavit, Lewis Chappelle swore that he was the manager of the Buckingham; that he was no "hired bartender"; that no liquor, beer, or wine had been delivered to him on the date in question; and that he had been instructed by Robert Mugge, both in the *Tribune* and via telephone, that he was "to close strictly on Sundays." Finally, printed below these affidavits, probably by the paper itself, was the following supporting information: "W. J. Rutherford stated to the *Tribune* yesterday that it was probably his wagon which Morgan saw, and that he was en route to the Brewery to secure a supply of beer for a day's outing at Rocky Point."[364]

The only way to understand any of this is to take a step back and get to know Lewis Chappelle's more famous brother, Pat. Like Lewis and their other brother James, Patrick H. Chappelle grew up in Jacksonville, Florida. Early on, however, Pat became a traveling musician, immersing himself in show business of the time, including Black minstrel shows. Eventually, he returned to Jacksonville where, in the 1880s, he opened a 500-seat theater and saloon which he called Excelsior Hall. From the start, he staged his own shows in the theater, which came to include African American singers, dancers, and comedians, as well as a brass band and a small orchestra. As his Jacksonville shows became increasingly popular, he also began taking shows on the road, featuring such major acts as blues artists W. C. Handy and Ma Rainey. Over time, he became so influential that he was dubbed the "Pioneer of Negro Vaudeville," the "Black P. T. Barnum," and the "Magnate of Afro American Stage."[365]

However, in 1899, the steady growth of his business took a turn. After a dispute with the landlord for his Jacksonville theater, who also happened to be the mayor, Pat Chapelle moved his headquarters to Tampa. There, he and a partner named Robert S. Donaldson, a fellow African American entrepreneur, opened two new theaters, which, like Jacksonville's Excelsior Hall, were combination theaters and barrooms. The first to open was the Buckingham Theatre Saloon,[366] and the second was the Mascotte Theatre Saloon.[367] As he had done in Jacksonville, Pat Chappelle produced large-scale shows for both establishments, as well as staging national tours, eventually under the name of his famous Rabbit's Foot Company.[368] Moreover, prior to the first show of the day at his theaters, he would organize a parade similar to those most associated with New Orleans: "Watch out for the Buckingham parade at 2 o'clock. Men dress in yellow coats, ladies riding in carriages, led by Master Arthur Howe, on horseback, with the Buckingham brass band."[369]

Another setback happened a year or so later when Chappelle and Donaldson fell out over finances. As a result, Donaldson took control of the Mascotte, leaving Pat Chappelle to run the Buckingham, assisted by his brothers, Lewis and James. Therefore, by the end of 1901, the "Chappelle Brothers" were listed in newspaper ads as "Sole Owners" of the Buckingham Theatre, while Pat Chappelle was now listed as "Sole Owner" of another venue called the Bijou Theatre.[370] In truth, both the Buckingham at 416-18 Fifth Avenue, and the Bijou at 302-04 Central Avenue, were being leased from Robert Mugge. But Robert was always happy for managers of his bars to become their public faces, thereby undercutting the perception he controlled the local saloon business. All that mattered to him was that his managers acquired all drinking stock from him, paid him promptly each week, and adhered to laws governing gambling, Sunday sales, and so forth, since their legal problems would quickly become his as well.

In any case, for the first few years, all went extremely well for the Chappelle brothers in Tampa. Despite Jim Crow segregation, their theaters drew large, multiracial, and multiethnic crowds—the "special boxes for white patrons"[371] probably helping—and the shows Pat Chappelle staged were hits both at home and on the road. Just as one indicator, *Morning Tribune* editor Wallace F. Stovall sold them lots of ad space and routinely praised their productions, as he did on February 6, 1903 in a review titled "Genuine Minstrel Show On At The Buckingham":

> Genuine negro minstrelsy and vaudeville was depicted in its true light, with all the frills and furbelows of anti-slavery days injected in the show put up by Chapelle Bros. at the Buckingham Theater last night. Taken as a whole, the exhibition is good, and when considered from the standpoint that it is an unadulterated negro production, devoid of black paint and burnt cork, so conspicuous in the impersonations by white artists, the situations are all the more interesting. While the attraction merits a fair patronage from among the American and Cuban negroes, it commands only a limited amount of patronage and respect from the white population, yet if the same was produced in the Tampa Bay Casino, all Tampa would flock to that famous resort to witness it and make its very walls tremble from center to circumference with laughter and applause.[372]

Unfortunately, the Chappelle presence in Tampa would not last out that particular year, and not due to facts that seven men had been arrested for gambling at the Buckingham on August 9, 1902;[373] that twenty-seven more were arrested for gambling there on February 14, 1903;[374] that Pat Chappelle had to sue the Georgia Minstrels for stealing his contracted "coon" cornetist, Elmer Dodd, the first week of March 1903;[375] or even that Pat Chappelle, himself, had to plead guilty to Sunday selling on March 19, 1903.[376] More on why momentarily.

While all the back and forth over Sunday licenses was taking place, other forces were having their say as well. On September 13, 1903, the *Morning Tribune* announced what everyone already knew: "Hurricane, With Driving Rain, Dealt Destruction To City Property."

Reportedly, the day before, Tampa was hit by a hurricane that cut off telegraph service, electric power, and electric lighting; shut down street cars; did an estimated $50,000 in damage to city buildings; and did "incalculable" harm to orange groves. In the city, effects of the storm were "mostly evident along Franklin Street, where business houses were unroofed, stocks ruined and general destruction caused by both wind and water." Robert's affected businesses included his Eureka Saloon (302 Franklin) which, having lost its roof early on, was "entirely drenched" inside and therefore "practically ruined"; his Shamrock Saloon (308 Franklin) which "was also flooded and much damage done to furnishings and stock"; and his wholesale house (304 Franklin) which received water "several inches deep."[377]

Further reports in the *Tampa Times* (as reprinted twenty years later) brought Robert more bad news: "Eighteen acres of sugar cane on the Robert Mugge plantation east of the city was leveled in Saturday's storm." And even worse, "R. Mugge's schooner Eva I. Shenton, valued at $8,000, was wrecked off the Louisiana coast in the hurricane."[378] But not until three days later, in the *Morning Tribune* of September 16, 1903, would the full story be told.

Due to the storm, Robert's 150-ton schooner, Eva I. Shenton, had been wrecked among the Chandeleur Islands, "near the mouth of the Mississippi River." Although the crew had been saved, the vessel was destroyed. Captain LaPenotiere, the same one involved with abduction of La Resistencia leaders, secured the aid of another schooner and "sent the sails and rigging to New Orleans where they were sold." In addition, a Mugge employee named W. R. Grambling sailed to New Orleans to help salvage as much of the wrecked ship as possible.[379]

Losing acres of sugarcane, the roof of a building, and assorted merchandise was bad enough. But losing a second schooner, plus cargo, meant the end of Robert's steamship line. And yet, there were setbacks still to come, both for him and for others.

The *Morning Tribune* of Saturday, September 19, 1903, under the headline, "That Buckingham Affair," described another wrinkle in the Lewis Chappelle case. Although Robert likely had purchased a city license for the Buckingham Theatre Saloon, he somehow had failed to secure the other permits needed. As a result, the *Tribune* was "ably informed that, within the last few days, Mugge sent in his check for $750 to cover the State and county license for the past year."[380]

Four days later, as reported in the *Morning Tribune*, the case finally went to trial with Lewis Chappelle, manager of the Buckingham, admitting to doing business "on the first Sunday of the present dry regime," and doing so without a license. He had been caught "serving thirsty customers in a room over his saloon, the drinks being conveyed from the saloon by means of an elevator [likely a mechanical conveyance along the lines of an old-fashioned dumbwaiter]."

The complicating factor was the lack of licenses, the securing of which had been Robert's responsibility. Probably for that reason, Solicitor Simonton asked Judge Graham to find Chappelle guilty only of selling on Sunday, and not for the other offense, "pending good behavior." Yet, strangely, the judge chose to do the reverse, and meted out a sentence of four months on the chain gang, plus an additional two months if Chappelle failed to pay a $500 fine plus court costs.[381]

Clearly, Robert was furious with Lewis Chappelle for disobeying him, especially after he, himself, had solemnly promised that none of his saloons would violate Sunday selling laws. Therefore, Robert claimed he would not assist with Chappelle's defense. Whether he did or not is difficult to know, though Lewis was represented by John P. Wall (unrelated to the judge of that name), a top attorney Robert often used himself.

Beyond that, the final sentencing was morally problematic, in that, again, the judge insisted on finding Chappelle guilty of operating without government licenses, the obtaining of which had been Robert's obligation, rather than for serving alcohol on a Sunday, which had been Chappelle's overriding crime, and which, in such circumstances, was likely thought to justify the severity of his sentence. Otherwise, Chappelle's race, the recent harsh treatment of African Americans, and the white community's disdain for Black saloons, may, together, have ensured the severity of his sentence.

Nevertheless, after the trial, the Chappelle brothers moved their operations back to Jacksonville, and the Buckingham Theatre Saloon never again opened under their control. However, for the rest of his life, Pat Chappelle would include Tampa as a stop on his highly successful tours, and whether due to the influence of the impresario or the saloon magnate, Lewis Chappelle never had to serve his sentence, in that he was pardoned by Florida's governor.[382] And just to show that affection for Pat Chappelle's work never diminished in the city he briefly called home, here are excerpts from a Wallace F. Stovall/*Morning Tribune* review of January 7, 1908:

> Last evening, an immense crowd of people attended the performance of "A Rabbit's Foot," given under canvas [a large tent] by the colored organization which started out from Tampa five seasons ago under the management of Pat Chappelle. Since that time Pat Chappelle has made one of the most signal successes achieved by any negro in business throughout the south ... Tampa feels proud that she has given to the world of business, particularly in a line as difficult as is the show business, a colored man who can hold his own with the best of the white showmen.[383]

The day Lewis Chappelle's trial ended, Robert left town as well, though not for long. The same *Morning Tribune* issue of September 24, 1903 which reported the trial results also reported Robert's plans: "Robert Mugge has gone to New York, to meet his family, who have been touring in Europe. He will return home with them."[384] Then, three weeks later, the *Morning Tribune* of October 14, 1903 shared the following brief announcement: "Brandon, Oct. 13.--Walter Hobbs, one of the efficient commissioners, was here Monday for the purpose of unloading and conveying R. Mugge's large cane mill to Bloomingdale," confirming not only that Robert was, indeed, now growing sugarcane on his 319 acres near Bloomingdale, Florida, as he was on his 560 acres at Six Mile Creek, but that some of his crop had weathered the recent storm.[385] [386] With pleasant news such as this, both Robert Mugge and the citizens of Tampa could have been fooled into thinking the turbulence of recent months had been put to rest. Sadly, that was not to be the case, and the Chappelle brothers were probably right to have left when they did.

The main headline of the *Morning Tribune* of December 5, 1903 was stark: "Jackson's Dead Body Now Swings From An Oak Limb." According to the *Tribune*, Lewis Jackson was a 25-year-old Black man who had been accused of perpetrating some unidentified horror against a young girl. For a time, he was held in the county jail while attorneys hired to prosecute him searched Florida statute books for a law that would match the "peculiarly heinous crime which he had committed." And yet, reportedly, they could find neither a precedent nor a statute that would fit. So, the sheriff "had no recourse but to release his prisoner, as there was no charge against him." And rather than do that by the light of day and provide him with police protection to assure his safe passage, the sheriff followed typical Tampa protocol, which was to push him out the door at 8:00 at night, suggesting that he "leave the country at once, for fear that some harm might befall him."

Naturally, a mob was waiting, which first castrated him, then argued whether to "take the negro to the colored hospital, as was done with Houston, where he could receive surgical attention," or simply to lynch him. Apparently, few in the crowd had read editor Stovall's proposal that, going forward, castration be considered Tampa's official alternative to lynching, because they did not see this as an either/or proposition. Otherwise, law enforcement had once again played its part in this recurring legal travesty, thrusting its prisoner into the night, as if a ceremonial fox released to waiting hunters and hounds.[387]

Lewis Jackson's fate having been sealed by a confederation of the county sheriff's office and a freelance mob, just four days later, local peacekeepers focused on Robert Mugge once again. The *Morning Tribune* featured the following headline, in which it managed to ridicule him both for being German and for being a saloon owner: "Mugge Drunk? Ach! 'Tis Hard Story to Believe—But Officers Say He Took Too Much of His Own Medicine."

According to the *Tribune*, Robert had been arrested the night before by Patrolman Parnell, who accused him of being "drunk and disorderly and resisting an officer" while riding a streetcar. He also was accused of "vomiting and using profane language in the presence of ladies," and then of giving officers "considerable trouble" as they arrested him and took him to the station where he was held until "a bond of $50 was produced for his appearance" in court. "Several witnesses testified that they had seen Mugge after his release from jail and that he did not appear to be drunk."[388]

Note that last statement about Robert not appearing drunk. To reiterate, Robert suffered from asthma and bronchitis throughout his life. The incident in question took place in December, decades before flu shots, cold remedies, and asthma inhalers, and excessive mucus, all by itself, can make a person nauseous as well as disoriented. In addition, during his adult years, Robert would suffer from rheumatism, eventually from kidney disease, and according to his son August, from an untreated hernia, two symptoms of which are nausea and vomiting. Moreover, for someone who routinely worked eighteen and more hours per day, and who owned dozens of horses, buggies, and wagons, it stands to reason that he only would have ridden a streetcar at night if he were ill but still trying to carry on business. Finally, it would seem extremely possible for a shaky streetcar to induce vomiting in someone who was already nauseous.

Throughout this period, the police were indisputably watching Robert Mugge, and targeting him and his businesses in any way they could. Could he have been drunk on this occasion? A century later, it is impossible to know. But in the vast public record of his adult life, as well as the personal record created by his son August, there is not a single reference to his being intoxicated. Instead, this has the feel of harassment, which would no doubt have thrown him into a rage, whether on the streetcar or in the courtroom, as both his dignity and his sense of personal responsibility were being questioned. That would seem the only explanation for the following story as well, as a person greatly respected throughout the region was once again accused of being a public nuisance.

The streetcar encounter culminated in a courtroom scene described in the *Morning Tribune* of December 10, 1903: "'Liars' said Robt. Mugge, member of the Board of Public Works and saloon magnate, in Municipal Court yesterday morning. The appellation was evidently intended for police officers and others who testified against him on the charges of being drunk, using profane language and resisting an officer, which were [proffered] against him as a result of the alleged disturbance raised by the well-known citizen on a street car Monday night." In response, Judge Gordon instructed Robert that public officials and saloon magnates can expect no preferential treatment, then fined him $25 and costs.[389]

And with that came the close of 1903. Few who had lived it—certainly not Robert Mugge, and certainly no member of the African American community—would wish to live it again.

Chapter Fifteen

Fair and Foul

1904 opened with the death of one of Robert Mugge's valued employees. As reported in the *Morning Tribune* of January 16, 1904, D. D. Jones, an African American engineer for the Mugge ice factory, got into a dispute with a neighbor named Matthew Hurst, a painter. Upset over attention Hurst allegedly had paid to his wife, Jones, a former firefighter, provoked a fight, but wound up the loser, leaving behind his wife and their baby.[390]

Six days on, another of Robert's employees got into trouble, though not for actions of his own. While socializing in the Scrub, Eugene Gill, the Black manager of Robert's Central Saloon, was robbed of $115. Gill alerted the police, and they arrested one Mary Cole, who still had $110 of his money on her person.[391] Of course, the best news for Gill was that, thanks to Robert repeatedly appealing his case, some fifteen months after initially being tried and convicted for use of a handheld slot machine, he had yet to serve a single day.

The next story of interest focused on Robert himself. It was published in the *Morning Tribune* of January 26, 1904 and concerned what he called his "bad habit of being charitable." Many times, it seems, "the heart of the saloon magnate" had been touched by hard-luck stories, leading him to provide aid, and ultimately to find the object of his care to be unworthy.

Only a few days before, a young man had told Robert such a touching tale of misfortune that he had once again been moved to act. Robert gave the man a job in his bottling works, provided him with clothes, took him to a boarding house, and paid his board for the next week. Yet, after working just two hours in the bottling works, the young man returned to the boarding house, ate his evening meal, and told the landlady that, if she would give him back the board money, he would pay her fifty cents for his supper. He then took off with Robert's money. But the worst part of all, Robert laughed, was that the man was "a Dutchman" (meaning German).[392]

The last of these stories involved another of Robert's employees, once again with an unhappy ending. The *Weekly Tribune* of February 4, 1904 reprinted an article from Tuesday's daily under the headline, "Bartender Was Killed." The bartender in question was Jeff Refo, manager of the African American annex of Robert Mugge's Crystal Saloon at Franklin and Harrison Streets. Contrary to the orders of his employer—and the instructions of Charles Massey, manager of the white section of the saloon—Jeff Refo supposedly had opened for business on a Sunday. That attracted Deputy Sheriff Robert W. Beagles, who later claimed to have ordered Refo to close the saloon and accompany him to the county jail but had met resistance. The only fact known for sure is that the unarmed Refo ended up with a bullet in his groin and another in his hand.

Arriving on the scene and finding Deputy Sheriff Beagles intoxicated and with a whiskey bottle in his pocket, Patrolman Parnell arrested Beagles and took him to the station. There, Beagles claimed that Refo had been drunk himself and, when approached by Beagles, had cursed him and attacked him viciously. As for Refo, the fatally injured saloon manager was taken to his home, where he was treated first by a white doctor, then by a Black one, and finally died of his wounds.[393]

So, was Jeff Refo actually "very drunk," as Special Deputy Beagles later claimed, even though Refo was working at the time, or was Beagles the only one who was truly intoxicated? Also, would Refo have been unwise enough to "curse," and then attack "viciously," a white officer of the law, or did Beagles make that up as well to excuse his own drunken homicide? Rather than moving on to the next story, it may prove worthwhile to examine how this incident affected everyone involved, including any immediate impact for Special Deputy Sheriff Beagles himself, and for his career as a law enforcement officer.

The *Morning Tribune* of February 9, 1904 provides a record of the deputy sheriff's full legal repercussions from the saloon annex assault:

> R. W. Beagles, who shot and killed Jeff Refo, a negro bartender, Sunday January 31, was given his liberty yesterday as the result of a preliminary hearing of the case before County Judge Robles ...
>
> J. E. Moore and Charles Massey were the witnesses to the fatal affray. Both testified that Refo was the aggressor and that Beagles was, in the first place, trying to enforce the law, and, secondly, acting in self-defense, in the protection of his own life against the assault made upon him by the bartender, who was very drunk.
>
> Judge Robles said that there was no case against the defendant under the testimony submitted, and discharged Beagles. While the case can be brought before the Grand Jury at its next session, it is not probable that it will be, as the witnesses produced yesterday were the only ones available in the case, and both agreed that Beagles was in the right.[394]

Without question, it is difficult to analyze a court case which was tried more than a century ago, and to do so simply by reviewing meager press coverage of the time. However, it also is difficult to reconcile an intoxicated white sheriff's deputy being able to shoot and kill an unarmed African American bartender in the latter's workplace and then be found innocent on the word of two white witnesses almost certainly not present for the altercation. One of those witnesses, J. E. Moore, was a prominent white businessman, so it makes no sense that he would have been drinking in the Black annex. As to the white manager, Charles Massey, if, as claimed, the white section of the Crystal Saloon was closed in keeping with the ban against Sunday sales, then he, too, should not have been present, much less passing time in the Black annex. Finally, if, as charged, Jeff Refo had opened his section, rather than, say, being there on Sunday just to clean up or do accounts, there would have been African American customers present, yet none were produced in court. Instead, the only witnesses called were two white men who presumably would not have seen a thing. For the court to solicit their word alone suggests a straight-out whitewash.

But reason and morality aside, that was the City of Tampa's response to the deadly shooting of Jeff Refo. And how did this response, coupled with the murder itself, affect Refo's loved ones? According to the *Morning Tribune* of the following day, "Mary Refo, widow of Jeff Refo, the colored bartender who was shot and killed January 31 by R. W. Beagles, died yesterday at 6 A.M. She had grieved deeply over her husband's death and this hastened her own demise [presumably from suicide]. The funeral occurs today at 10 A.M. from Beulah Baptist Church."[395]

Taking this one step further, was R. W. Beagles at least suspended for using deadly force when far less would have sufficed, or was he even reprimanded for drinking on the job? If so, neither was reported. Instead, according to the *Morning Tribune* of February 23, 1904, Beagles attended the annual Military Ball of the Tampa Light Infantry at the new Armory (ironically, the upstairs section of a large new building owned and constructed by Robert Mugge) where he was appointed a noncommissioned officer by Captain M. Henry Cohen, who also served as the deputy sheriff's attorney at the recent hearing.[396]

Over the next nine years, as Beagles switched back and forth between the city Police Department and the county Sheriff's Office (not unlike the way problem police officers today are dismissed by one department, only to be hired by another), his escapades were periodically mentioned in the local press. What follows are three notable examples.

For one, in the *Morning Tribune* of February 23, 1908, Beagles was described as "pulling out a big Smith & Wesson hammerless revolver in the lobby of the Tampa Bay hotel late yesterday afternoon and pointing it carelessly around the rotunda where over a hundred guests were assembled." Patrolman Beagles had been specially appointed by the city to attend a party given by German Ambassador Speck von Sternberg. But by the time the party took place, he was thoroughly intoxicated and had to be forcibly disarmed by Assistant Manager Bredel of the hotel, to protect its guests.[397] Three days later, Mayor Frecker dismissed him from the force.[398]

Four years after that, Mr. Beagles was a deputy sheriff once again, and the *Morning Tribune* of February 4, 1912 reported his latest public display. The night before, he had driven "joyously" down Lafayette Street while it was filled with Saturday night shoppers. In each hand was a pistol, and as his car passed the Dairy Kitchen, "he pulled the trigger twice." One of the bullets bounced and then hit the waistband of L. D. Geiger, who was standing on the curb near Val Antuono's, but fortunately did no damage.[399]

Finally, the *Morning Tribune* of January 6, 1913 revealed that "R. W. Beagles, who has been connected with the sheriff's office as a deputy was arrested Saturday night by Patrolman Cane, charged with being drunk and disorderly and drawing a gun on another." The trouble was said to have taken place at the Cosmopolitan Saloon in Ybor City where Beagles "pulled his pistol and threatened to make things lively." At that point, he was arrested, taken to police headquarters, and asked for a $50 bond.[400]

To review, this was a highly regarded officer of, alternately, the Tampa Police Department and the Hillsborough County Sheriff's Office. Yet, for nearly a decade after he killed Jeff Refo, an African American manager of the annex to Robert Mugge's Crystal Saloon, Beagles repeatedly exhibited drunken and reckless behavior in public, both on and off the job. He was fired for some of this behavior, then inexplicably rehired by one agency or the other. And never did anyone think to punish him for these actions, or even to revisit his killing of an unarmed Black man in 1904. In other words, R. W. Beagles had a career which, on the surface, was devoted to law and order, but which, as Twain and Warner had written of the Gilded Age overall, was thoroughly rotten at its core.[401]

On the more positive side, Robert's farms at Six Mile Creek and Bloomingdale were proving productive. In a large ad placed in the

Morning Tribune of January 19, 1904, he advertised two thousand dollars worth of seed cane for growing new plants, five thousand one-gallon cans of syrup, five thousand stone jugs of syrup, one thousand bushels of sweet potatoes, and poultry. The ad was prominently placed by "R. Mugge, proprietor of the largest and best stocked liquor house in the South, 305-11 Franklin Street, Tampa, Fla.," from which he conducted much of his business.[402]

Two months later, even better news was reported in the *Morning Tribune* of March 18, 1904, involving the wedding of Robert Mugge's eldest child: "Mr. Herman Regener, of the *Herald*, and Miss Louise Mugge, daughter of Mr. and Mrs. Robert Mugge, were united in marriage last evening at 7 o'clock, at the residence of the bride's parents, Rev. F. W. Siebelitz, pastor of the German Lutheran church officiating. The ceremony was performed according to the German custom ... Mr. Regener and his bride are the recipients of many congratulations."[403]

But the news turned bleak again the following month, as a devastating fire hit West Tampa. The *Morning Tribune* of Tuesday, April 5, 1904 described the carnage under a series of screaming headlines, but the key estimates of loss included twenty-five acres burned, 130 buildings destroyed, four factories leveled, $250,000 in damage versus $100,000 in insurance, 100,000 people left homeless, and 600 out of work. "The fire started at 1:15 in a bowling alley operated by Robert Mugge, on Pine Street near Howard Avenue. It grew and spread like a whirlwind. By the time the local volunteer firemen, with their horse wagons, arrived, the flames were shooting heavenward in great sheets." Chief A. J. Harris called out Fire Companies One and Five, but they reportedly had trouble getting their heavy equipment to the scene via West Tampa's sandy streets.[404]

On this occasion, Robert lost several buildings, but it barely seemed to faze him. The following day's *Tribune* recorded his typical resilience: "Robert Mugge, who lost $10,000 worth of buildings and stock in the West Tampa fire, had the lumber on the ground early yesterday morning for rebuilding his houses better than before."[405] Then, only a day after that, the paper said he would have a temporary structure in place by Saturday, whereupon he would resume his saloon business, while also erecting a new brick building.[406]

On April 25, 1904, Robert's longtime friend and supporter, Adolphus Busch, having seen alarmist newspaper coverage of the Tampa fire during a visit to San Francisco, wrote to express his concern, also advising Robert to "insure at least 60%" of his buildings in order to reduce future losses: "Therefore, take my advice, Mugge, and profit by the experience you have had in this fire; cover yourself somewhat for the sake of yourself and your family."[407]

Perhaps unknown to Adolphus, Robert's problem was not that he wasn't carrying insurance, but that he also owned the insurance company, and therefore had to cover his own losses, as well as those of others. Six months later, the *Morning Tribune* of October 4, 1904 would carry Robert's notice to policyholders of his National Aid Association, an industrial life insurance company he had started sometime before, that they should ignore misrepresentations from agents of other firms regarding his company's financial condition, because protections would remain the same in the future as in the past.[408] And yet, a year after that, probably having suffered continuing fire-related losses, Robert sold his firm to the Industrial Life and Health Insurance Co., which, strangely, celebrated by giving away ashtrays as souvenirs.[409]

At any rate, in the same letter, Busch went on to express delight that two of Robert's sons (he did not specify Robert's daughter, Frances, as well) were now studying in "the Old Country," mentioned that he would be visiting there in late June, and declared that, "If I can do anything for the boys, or if you have any commission you would like to entrust to me, rest assured it will be attended to with pleasure." Finally, he encouraged Robert to pay off "accumulated interest" due on Robert's longtime loans from Anheuser-Busch, before it grew "to such dimensions that it will be disagreeable for both of us," and provided closing reassurance of his ongoing affection: "With kind personal regards, I am your friend."[410]

Of course, there were more challenges still to come. That same month, as explained in the *Morning Tribune* of April 20, 1904, "a very important case" was argued before Judge Wall concerning the opposing rights of the Seaboard Air Line Railway on one side, and Water Street property owners on the other. The railway was attempting to condemn the section of Water Street in front of Robert's La Brisa Saloon, and Robert took the position that property could not simply be seized on behalf of a corporation.[411] Sadly, the court sided with the railroad, and gave the defendants twenty-four hours to explain, again, why the property should not be taken. In reality, the only remaining question was one of damages.[412]

Certainly, whatever face Robert showed the public, after a year of nearly unrelenting clashes, losses, conspiracies, and public embarrassment, he had to feel assaulted from all sides. And yet, if he did, giving in to such feelings—letting them cloud his judgement—may have led to even bigger problems, largely of his own making.

Periodically, newspaper editors of the time adopted causes, and urged their readership—especially local businesses—to support them. In Wallace F. Stovall's case, perhaps the biggest to which he offered support was the South Florida Fair of 1904. As the fair's finance committee solicited subscriptions for what Stovall termed "this great movement," he would offer praise for those who made significant contributions and chide those who made none. For instance, he pointed out that the Florida Brewing Company had contributed $500, saloon owner B. M. Balbontin had made a personal donation of $250, and smaller liquor dealers had given according to their ability.

By contrast, Robert Mugge had offered nothing, even though, as Editor Stovall asserted in the *Morning Tribune* of October 20, 1904, he owned "a greater number of saloons in Tampa and suburbs than are owned by any of the saloon trust individuals of cities with ten times more inhabitants than Tampa, in view of which, in the natural course of events, he will reap thousands of dollars from the selling of his liquid sources of inspiration to the thousands who will attend the fair during the two weeks it will be in operation." As the piece continued, it became increasingly clear that, for whatever reason, Stovall saw Robert's refusal as a personal affront, and therefore, he was prepared to cast aspersions of his own: "A man who will make hundreds or thousands of dollars out of a movement of this character, and still refuses to make any appropriations whatsoever, would make a decidedly interesting exhibit for a certain branch of the live-stock department of the fair."[413]

Placing such a dispute in context, it must be noted that Robert Mugge gave to charities all the time. He contributed to the Children's Home for Orphans every month. He also raised money for, and contributed money to, many who had suffered misfortune. For instance, in December of 1901, in a move the *Tampa Times* called "characteristically generous," Robert gave the *Times* 100 bottles of high-quality Sauterne wine, and asked the paper to advertise it at a discounted $1.00 per bottle and then donate the proceeds to the Children's Home on Christmas Day.[414] He also loaned money and resources to those trying to get started in business—like the time in the 1880s when, according to August Mugge, Robert loaned $10,000 to two poor, newly arrived cigar makers named Cuesta and Rey, and a year later, when the loan was repaid, would not even accept the $800 in interest offered.[415]

In other words, Robert Mugge was a compassionate and civic-minded person. So, why would he not placate Wallace Stovall by contributing to the South Florida Fair? Was he feeling vulnerable after recent losses from fires, the sinking of two schooners, the loss of one-seventh of his saloon income due to Sunday closings, and even the cost of sending three teenagers to school in Germany? Conversely, had he been appalled by Stovall's support for abduction, lynching, and castration, or embarrassed by the snide coverage given to his Panchita and streetcar arrests? Or, finally, was he sick of editors feeling they could compel handouts, whether for ad buys to keep their ragtag publications going, or for obsessions like the South Florida Fair? In short, in a free country, why should others decide when, or with whom, Robert should share his wealth?

Any of those might have been valid excuses for opting out. And yet, doing so meant alienating, even antagonizing, a trusted ally; one who had given public attention to Robert's proposals, as well as his grievances, and only rarely asked for anything in return. On this occasion, Robert could have helped, and he certainly should have helped. For five hundred or a thousand dollars, he would have appeared the hero instead of the chump. Yet, for whatever reason, he could not bring himself to do it. And so, he made himself a new and costly enemy.

For the *Morning Tribune* of October 29, 1904, W. F. Stovall wrote a long editorial in which he called Robert Mugge "a hog in human attire" and said that "his monumental penuriousness and unmitigated selfishness stamp him without question as an imported production of swine—whose gelatinized ideas permit him to wallow in his own putridness and flourish like a tadpole in slime." After many more insults, he added that, "Like the red woman of Babylon, who stood in the marketplace and advertised her shame and degradation, this Robert Mugge stands alone in this city as the only business man of any magnitude who has thus far unequivocally refused to contribute a penny toward helping one of the greatest enterprises that the city has ever undertaken."

It was a hurricane of purple prose, and it had not yet even struck the mainland. Editor Stovall then went on to defend himself from remarks Robert allegedly had made to the *Tampa Times*, surely the dominant cause of his growing so unhinged:

> Just listen at this barefooted contortionist of the truth:
>
> "I have never sold myself and money has never made me do anything I did not consider right. Can the *Tribune* make and substantiate the same claim? Mr. Stovall himself has said to me: 'If you and the other (saloon men) would pay each of us (*Times*, *Herald* and *Tribune*) $1,000 per year, we would all say nice things about you.' My reply was: 'I consider that local papers should be published in the interest of the community, and if you think it would help the city of Tampa to run me down, do so if you wish, every day, and on Sunday twice.'"
>
> The above is one of the blackest and most contemptible lies ever uttered.
>
> Here is what was really said to Robert Mugge and a witness to the conversation will substantiate the assertion:
>
> "The newspapers treat you all right, but you never reciprocate and if I conducted a business of the nature of yours, I would at least spend a thousand dollars a year with every paper in the city, then you could at least expect something kind from them."

Mugge knows this to be the truth and he knows that he willfully lied when he wrote the opposite.[416]

Frankly, such passionate insults were as common in newspapers of that day as were requests for money, and Stovall's account of their meeting was not so different than that of his former friend. Still, Robert's contrariness on this occasion was bound to do him more harm than good, and the results were easy to see in the paper's reporting for months to come. For example, less than a week later, Stovall asked readers not to miss voting for "ratification of the $300,000 public improvement bond issue," yet managed to refer to Robert Mugge as "swinish," even though Robert had done as much as anyone to create this opportunity.[417] And the next week, when *Tribune* staff arranged to have the presidential election returns projected onto canvas hung from the building opposite theirs via "electric stereopticon" (an early slide projector utilizing two lenses), with the returns themselves coming in all evening via Western Union,[418] he also could not resist hiring a political cartoonist to draw caricatures of Robert and others and inserting them into the coverage.

While the biggest US cities had been covering elections via stereopticon and Western Union feeds since 1892, the 1904 contest between President Theodore Roosevelt and Judge Alton B. Parker was the first to be presented that way in Tampa, and the *Tribune* deserved credit for making it happen. The election took place on November 8, 1904, and the *Morning Tribune* of the following day recounted not only the winners and losers but also the *Tribune's* own minute-by-minute coverage.

From 8:00 p.m. until midnight, a great many people had packed Franklin Street between Polk and Cass to watch the election returns as they "flashed from Averill's electric stereopticon on a large canvas suspended from the Boyd building, across the street from the *Tribune* office." Because the Republican landslide was evident early, the largely Democratic crowd remained quiet. However, "many negroes were in the crowd and most of the cheering for Roosevelt came from them." Otherwise, according to the *Tribune*, "the big audience was entertained as well as instructed. Mr. Barnes, a talented sketch artist

... furnished much amusement for the crowd by his catchy cartoons of Mugge and others."[419]

For months, Wallace Stovall's grudge against Robert would be reflected in his papers, and Robert appears to have reciprocated by placing few ads in the *Tribune*. Certainly, the decision not to help support the fair was Robert's to make, just as Stovall had the First Amendment right to brand him every sort of "pigheaded." But the short-term feud enhanced the reputation of neither.

Of course, whatever Robert's thinking on this occasion, it is easy to imagine his becoming a target for every worthy cause of the time, and easy also to picture him growing weary of repeated requests. In his memoirs, August Mugge told a story that may or may not relate to his father's tiff over the South Florida Fair, but at least illustrated the wit with which Robert sometimes deflected such requests.

> There was a drive on in Tampa for some charity. When the callers came to see my father, he told them to go and make the rounds, and when they have completed it, to return to him and he would double the highest amount pledged. The committee called on John Trice, President of the Citizens Bank and Trust Company, and told him to put down $500 (which he never intended to pay) that they would pull Mr. Mugge's leg for $1,000. When they came back to my father, he said, "Well, I shall keep my promise and give you a check for $1,000; however, with this reservation, I am going to write on this check: To be paid when Mr. Trice pays the $500." His check was returned a few days later in the mail.[420]

Illustrations

Robert Mugge, probably in Germany before emigrating to the United States in 1870 at age seventeen. (Courtesy, August B. Mugge.)

Augusta Römerman Kiefer, Robert's first cousin, who preceded him in emigrating to the United States. (Courtesy, Kiefer-Hartung family, via Lorna Cooper Snow.)

Ludwig (later Louis) Mügge, Robert's father. (Courtesy, August B. Mugge.)

Luise (later Louise) Mügge, Robert's mother. (Courtesy, August B. Mugge.)

Alice Janthe McCullough Mugge, Robert's first wife. (Courtesy, David Byron McCullough.)

Caroline Rautenstrauch, before leaving Germany to become Robert's second wife. (Courtesy, Martha Washington Mugge, via Patricia Mugge Andrews).

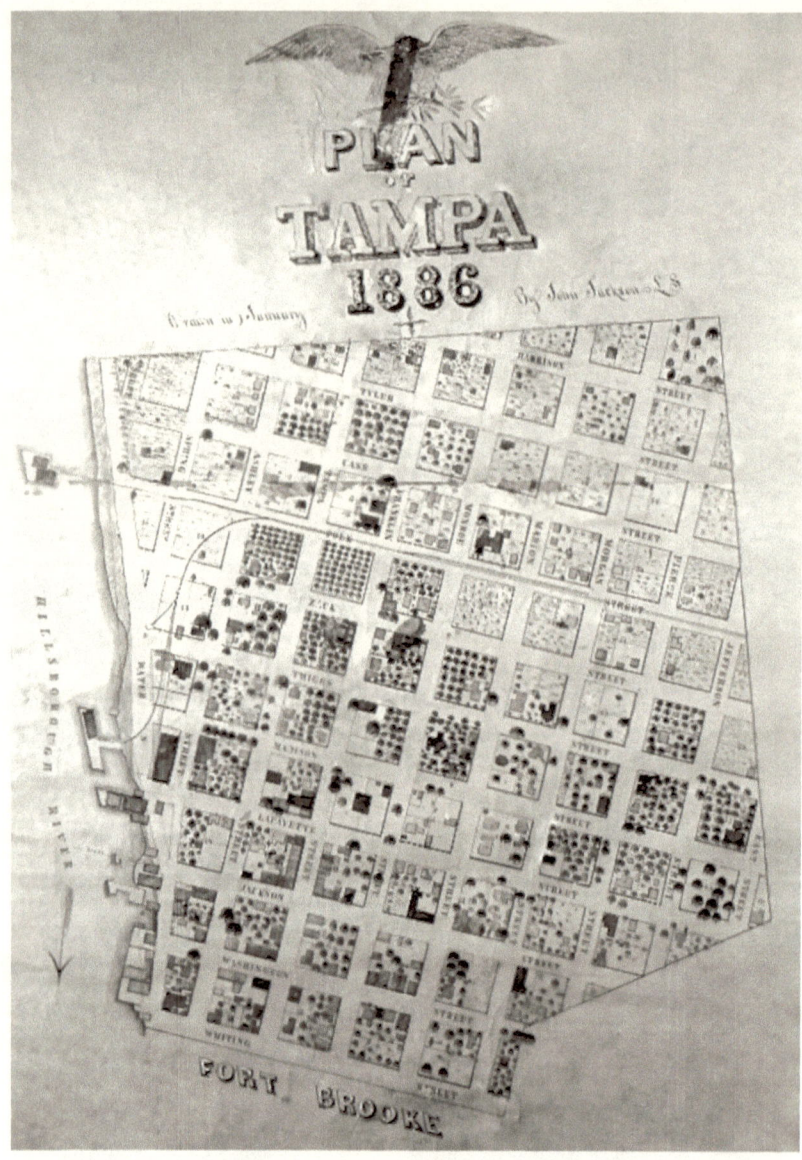

An 1886 map of Tampa, Florida created by John Jackson and photographed by local commercial photographers, the Burgert Brothers. Robert Mugge's original lot was three blocks from the bottom and four blocks from the left; the lower right quarter of that block, centered on the corner of Marion and Jackson Streets. (Courtesy, Tampa-Hillsborough County Public Library System.)

A 1922 Burgert Brothers photo of the Mugge family home built by Robert in the 1880s. (Courtesy, Tampa-Hillsborough County Public Library System.)

A second 1922 Burgert Brothers photo of the Mugge family home including Caroline's large garden (replacing the original ice plant) and with the storage and rental building at the back. (Courtesy, Tampa-Hillsborough County Public Library System.)

A photo of Dr. Frederick N. Weightnovel, physician and escaped Russian Nihilist, from his 1880s business card.

The reverse side of Dr. Weightnovel's 1880s business card, mentioning the "Mugge house."

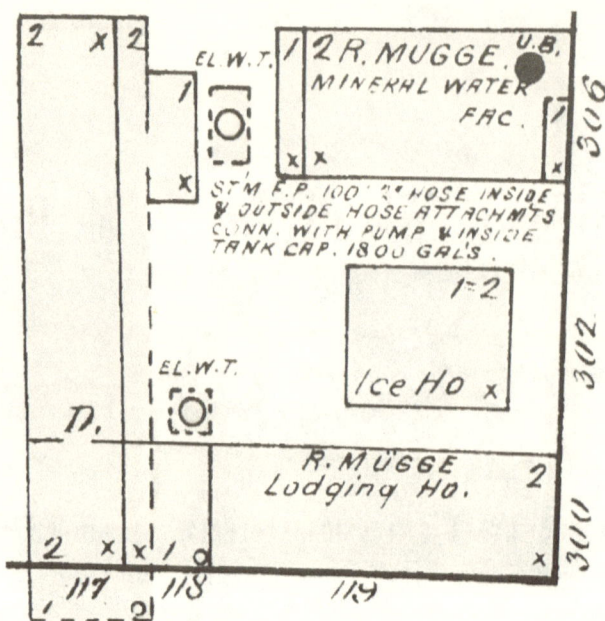

MARION

JACKSON

An 1892 Sanborn fire insurance map for Tampa shows the Mugge family home and lodging house at the corner of Jackson and Marion Streets, Robert Mugge's original ice plant to the right of the house, Robert's bottling works to the right of the ice plant, and a long, two-story building at the rear of the property. (Courtesy, University of Florida Digital Collections, George A. Smathers Libraries, ufdc.ufl.edu.)

An Anheuser-Busch Brewing Association ad from 1890, the year Robert began representing it in South Florida. (Courtesy, Anheuser-Busch Archives.)

An 1893 illustration of the Tampa Bay Hotel and grounds. (Courtesy, Tampa-Hillsborough County Public Library System.)

Anheuser-Busch president and co-founder Adolphus Busch and wife Lilly Busch in the 1870s. (Courtesy, Missouri Historical Society.)

A large whiskey bottle produced by Robert Mugge's wholesale liquor company. (Courtesy, Tampa Bay History Center.)

A soda water bottle produced by Robert Mugge's bottling works. (Courtesy, Tampa Bay History Center.)

An 1890s Burgert Brothers photo of the northwest corner of Fifteenth Street and Seventh Avenue in Ybor City, then known as Robert Mugge Corner, due to the prominence of Robert's Golden Eagle Saloon and other of his businesses. The saloon is on the right side of the image and includes a sign advertising Anheuser-Busch beer. (Courtesy, University of Florida Digital Collections, George A. Smathers Libraries, ufdc.ufl.edu.)

The Morning Tribune of February 26, 1887 published this ad for May Cameron's
London Gaiety Company, a female vaudeville troupe performing at Robert Mugge's
Saratoga Saloon

An 1899 Burgert Brothers photo of forty-six-year-old Robert Mugge, rediscovered by Internet historian Dan Perez in the Tony Pizzo Collection at the University of Florida Libraries. When Mr. Perez found the photo, it had been mislabeled "Robert Hugge." There is no record of a person with that name living in Tampa during that era. It also is logical that a formal photo of Robert Mugge would have been shot in 1899 because, in the winter of 1900, in recognition of the new century, the Tampa Tribune *published its glossy "Midwinter Edition 1900" featuring formal photos and descriptions of many top Tampa businessmen. Since Robert Mugge was one of the most successful in the region, it is odd for him not to have been included. Perhaps this photo was misplaced or mislabeled right from the start, or perhaps Robert had a minor dispute with the paper that led to his being excluded from the special edition. Apparently, the photo was then not correctly identified for more than a century. (Courtesy, University of Florida Digital Collections, George A. Smathers Libraries, ufdc.ufl.edu.)*

An 1899 Burgert Brothers photo of the west side of the 300 block of Franklin Street
in downtown Tampa. The corner building with the balcony, 302 Franklin Street, was
the longtime home of Robert Mugge's Eureka Saloon, and the building to its right, 304
Franklin Street, held his wholesale liquor business until he moved it to the opposite side
of the street. (Courtesy, Tampa-Hillsborough County Public Library System.)

An 1898 Burgert Brothers photo of a portion of the United States Army encampment in Tampa during the Spanish-American War. (Courtesy, Tampa-Hillsborough County Public Library System.)

A gift to Robert and Caroline Mugge from their friends, Adolphus and Lilly Busch, probably celebrating the Christmas Eve 1899 birth of Nellie Busch Mugge, named after the Busch's second daughter. Donated to the Tampa Bay History Center by Nellie's daughter, Gretchen Petri Harrington. (Courtesy, Tampa Bay History Center.)

In 1900, the Burgert Brothers shot this typical interior of a Tampa saloon at the corner of Eighteenth Street and Twelfth Avenue, which may or may not have been owned by Robert Mugge. (Courtesy, University of Florida Digital Collections, George A. Smathers Libraries, ufdc.ufl.edu.)

Distiller and Rectifier
Wholesale Dealer

IMPORTED ᴬᴺᴰ DOMESTIC
WINES AND LIQUORS.

—Dealer in—
ANHEUSER-BUSCH

St. Louis Keg and Lager Beer,
Budweiser and Black and Tan.

ROBT. MUGGE,
TAMPA, FLORIDA.

MANUFACTURER OF
ICE

BOTTLER OF SODA
AND MINERAL WATER

Electric Lights.

Having greatly increased and improved the facilities at my electric lighting plant, I am now prepared to furnish first-class lighting service at reasonable rates.

ROBERT MUGGE.

Telephone 202.

The Morning Tribune *of July 9, 1901 carried this ad for several of Robert Mugge's core businesses of the time.*

Wallace F. Stovall, the founder and longtime editor of the Tampa Tribune *newspapers. (Courtesy, Tampa-Hillsborough County Public Library System.)*

A studio photograph of 16-year-old Louise Mugge, eldest child of Robert and Caroline Mugge, apparently shot in 1900. (Courtesy, Margaret Regener Hurner.)

A political cartoon in the pro-temperance St. Petersburg Times *lampooning Robert Mugge who owned a local saloon but resided in Tampa.*

Caroline Mugge and her two youngest surviving children, Martha Washington Mugge and Nellie Busch Mugge, during a 1903 visit to Germany. (Courtesy, Margaret Regener Hurner.)

CHAPPELLE & DONALDSON,   PAT CHAPPELLE,
Proprietors.   Bus. Mgr.

BUCKINGHAM THEATRE-SALOON
416-418 Fifth Avenue.

MASCOTTE SALOON
CORNER PIERCE AND POLK STS.

Imported & Domestic
Wines, Liquors & Cigars.

—◆— Remember —◆—
We have the best Vaudeville Show
in Hillsborough County. We employ
none but professionals.

An ad (circa 1899) for two of the Tampa saloons operated by "pioneer of Negro vaudeville" Pat Chappelle, one of which (the Buckingham Theatre-Saloon) was owned by Robert Mugge. (Courtesy, Tampa Bay History Center.)

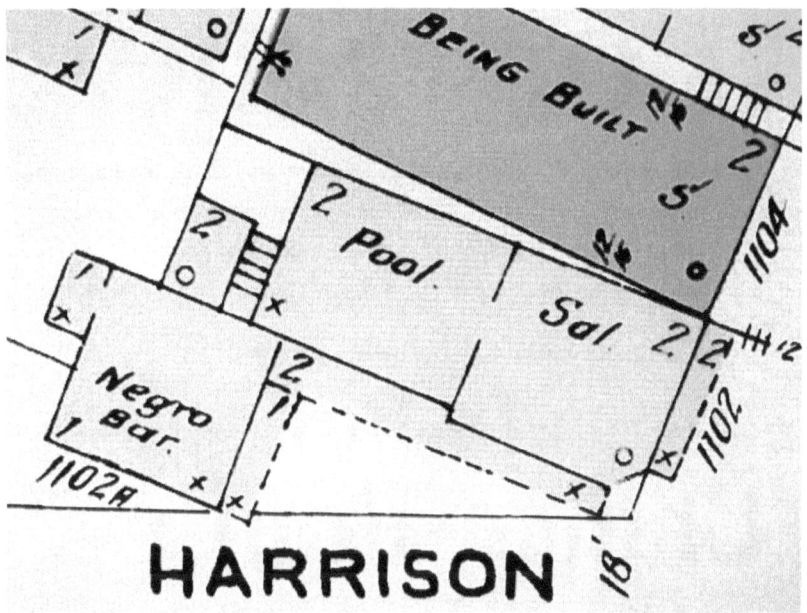

A 1903 Sanborn fire insurance map shows Robert Mugge's Crystal Saloon at Franklin and Harrison Streets. Due to Jim Crow segregation, the front room on Franklin was designated for white patrons, and the back room on Harrison was created for Black customers. (Courtesy, University of Florida Digital Collections, George A. Smathers Libraries, ufdc.ufl.edu.)

TUESDAY, JANUARY 19, 1904.

For Sale.

Two thousand dollars worth of Seed Cane, both green and ribbon, at either my Six Mile Creek or Bloomingdale Farms.

Five thousand one-gallon tin syrup cans, 12c per can.

Five thousand first class stone jugs from 1-2 to 5 gallon capacity, 12c per gallon.

One thousand bushels choice sweet potatoes.

To Buy

Choice Poultry.

R. MUGGE,

Proprietor of the largest and best stocked liquor house in the South, 305-311 Franklin street, Tampa, Fla.

All orders filled the day they are received.

The Morning Tribune of January 19, 1904 carried an ad in which Robert Mugge offered to sell thousands of dollars' worth of products grown or raised on his two large farms.

Adolphus Busch, second from right, standing with associates at one end of his railway car. (Courtesy, Anheuser-Busch Archives.)

A June 12, 1904 postcard from August Mugge in Darmstadt, Germany to two of his younger sisters at home in Tampa. (Courtesy, August B. Mugge.)

A 1905 photo of brother and sister August and Frances Mugge while they were attending school in Darmstadt, Germany, here probably posing on the floor of a factory in Giessen, Germany where their older brother Eugene had been assigned to work as part of his own schooling. The cost of sending three teenaged children to school in a foreign country must have been considerable. (Courtesy, August B. Mugge.)

HOW THE RETURNS WILL BE READ.

An image from the Atlanta Constitution of November 4, 1894 illustrating stereopticon coverage of presidential election returns, as was first used in Tampa during the 1904 presidential election.

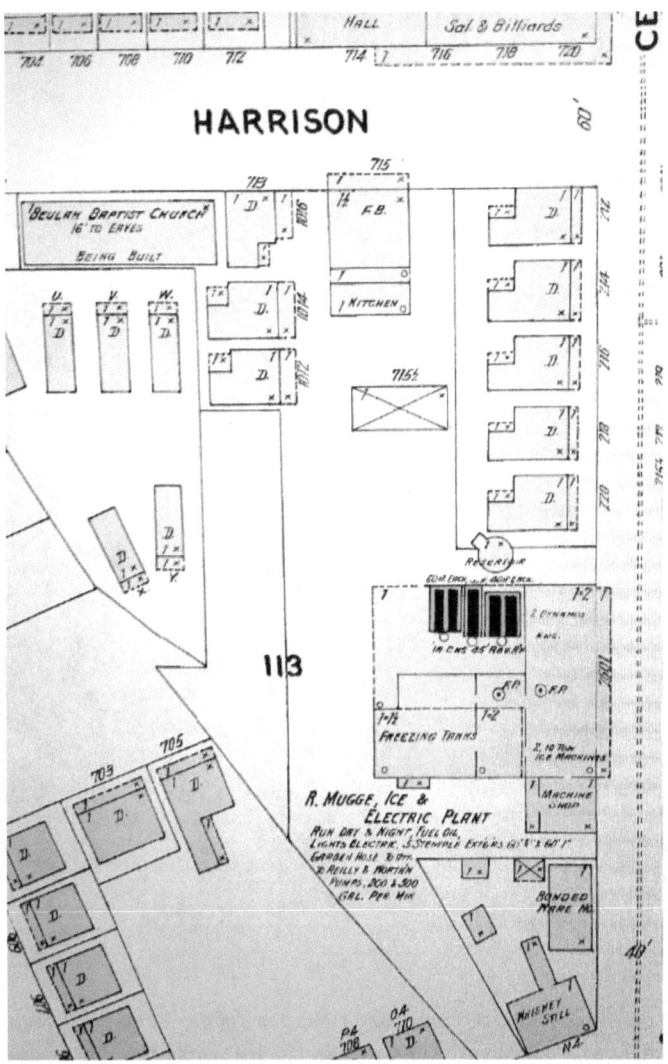

A 1903 Sanborn fire insurance map shows Robert Mugge's growing presence along Central Avenue between Harrison and Cass Streets in the Scrub. At the upper right was Robert's Central Saloon. Moving south along the western side of Central Avenue were some of Robert's rental properties, his ice factory and electric plant, his machine shop, and his distillery. At the upper left, on the south side of Harrison, was Beulah Baptist Church, an African American house of worship to which Robert donated property, and for which he reportedly paid off a mortgage. (Courtesy, University of Florida Digital Collections, George A. Smathers Libraries, ufdc.ufl.edu.)

In 1899, the Burgert Brothers undertook a group photo of the Tampa Police Department. (Courtesy, Tampa-Hillsborough County Public Library System.)

A 1906 photo of Caroline Mugge, now approximately forty-five, and her eldest son Eugene, approximately twenty, chatting beside a horse and buggy in Tampa. (Mugge family photo.)

A 1910 photo of temperance firebrand Carrie Nation shot by German photojournalist Philipp Kester.

A 1910 photo of Martha and Nellie visiting their older brother August in Germany. (Courtesy, Martha Washington Mugge, via Patricia Mugge Andrews.)

A 1911 Burgert Brothers photo looking north up Franklin Street from the intersection of Franklin and Zack Streets. Note that, as of 1911, horses and buggies, automobiles, and streetcars all shared the downtown streets of Tampa. The city, like the country, was in a continuing state of transition. (Courtesy, Tampa-Hillsborough County Public Library System.)

Early in 1912, Robert ordered construction of a beach house for his family on Anna Maria Key. According to the Morning Tribune, *he named it Sorgenfrei, which loosely translates as "free of care." (Mugge family photo.)*

From 1910 until 1913, August Mugge was a member of a university dueling fraternity in Stuttgart, Germany. In this photo, circa 1912, he is seated at the lower left. (Courtesy, August B. Mugge.)

Increase in Population
(United States Census Reports)

Year	Population	Increase
1880	720	
1890	5,532	668 P.
1900	15,839	186 P.
1910	37,782	138 P.
1912*	48,321	543 P.

*Directory Census

TAMPA, FLORIDA
1912

MAKES MORE HAND-MADE CLEAR HAVANA CIGARS THAN ISLE OF CUBA
AVERAGING A MILLION A DAY

"The City With the Pay Roll"

Land Locked Harbor—24 feet of water
Municipal Owned and Controlled Docks
Nearest Adequate Port in America to Panama Canal

Copyrighted, 1912
Board of Trade
Tampa, Fla.

In 1912, the Tampa Board of Trade distributed this map of the city. (Courtesy, Tampa-Hillsborough County Public Library System.)

Tampa, Fla., Aug. 28, 1912.

To Whom it May Concern:

According to my opinion, when it comes to crime, vice and corruption New York City is but a sleepy Sunday school village as compared to the lawlessness existing in Tampa, and the sheriff's office and the police department are responsible for ninety per cent of it.

Respectfully,

R. MUGGE.

After years of harassment from the Tampa Police Department and Hillsborough County Sheriff's Office, Robert Mugge took out an ad critical of both in the Morning Tribune *of August 29, 1912.*

A 1913 Burgert Brothers photo shows Robert's ten-story warehouse under construction on Jackson Street. To the building's right, at the corner of Jackson and Franklin Streets, is his former Eureka Saloon. (Courtesy, Tampa Bay History Center.)

The Mortal Triumvirate On the Morning After

Stovy (awakening): What a horrid dream! Methought the people had swatted me favorite che-ild, Commission Form, And that The Times' extra was cried upon the streets!

Mugge: No dream; 'tis the stern truth. So badly wert thou stricken that I gave thee of my tea— It was doped a-plenty and you slept.

St. Don: Yea, and more and worse 'tis rubbed in.

With Comish went Nish and Ref and little Recall too—all are gone! The Common People swatted each and all; 'twas a mighty swat. I know this lad Common People—his brother, Public Opinion, Likewise hath a mighty arm. I met him two years agone—to my sorrow. And yet, I had but obeyed the beckonings of my Pinellas friends.

All: 'Tis over and the best of friends must part. (Exeunt.)

The Tampa Times of April 9, 1913 published a political cartoon attacking charter-change proponents Robert Mugge, Donald C. McMullen, and Wallace F. Stovall.

A 1942 photo of the African American Central Hotel, built by Robert Mugge and designed by his twenty-three-year-old son August. It opened in the spring of 1914 and sat across Harrison Street from Robert's Central Saloon. (Courtesy, University of South Florida, Tampa Library Special Collections.)

As prohibitionist forces won victories across the country, Robert ran this Anheuser-Busch ad in the Morning Tribune of June 10, 1914. It equated beer consumption with personal liberty.

A colorized postcard image of the Bay View Hotel, apparently from 1915, the year the hotel opened. (Courtesy, Patricia Mugge Andrews.)

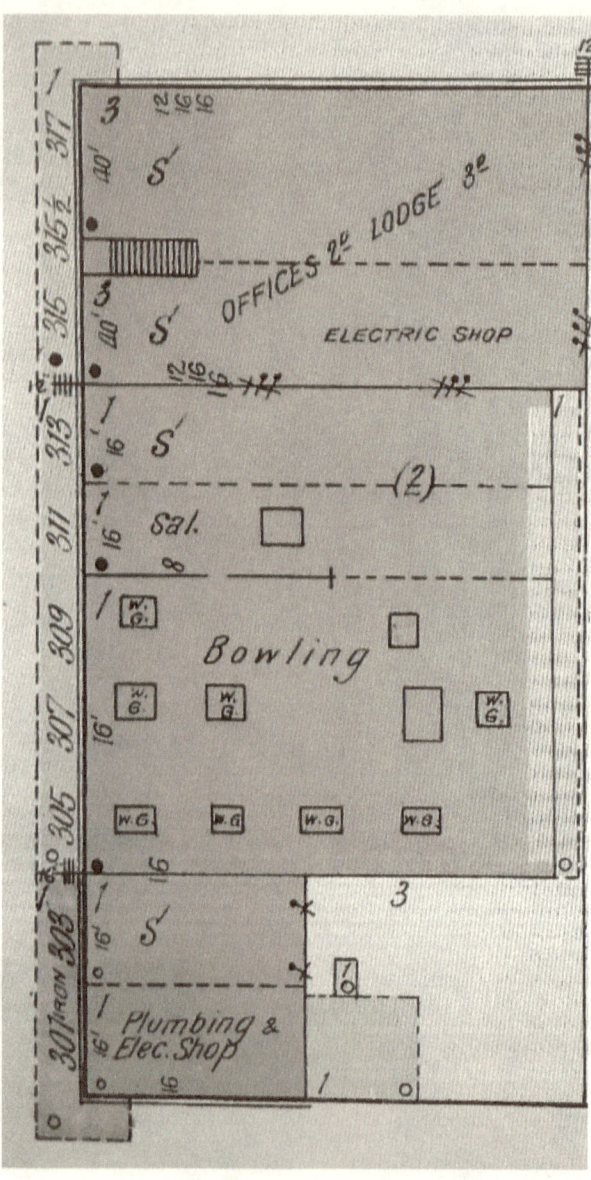

This 1915 Sanborn fire insurance map includes five buildings on the east side of the 300 block of Franklin Street in downtown Tampa, three of which (305-07-09) had previously housed Robert's wholesale liquor business, but now contained his elaborate new bowling alley and pool hall complex, and one of which (311) housed his St. Louis Cafe. (Courtesy, University of Florida Digital Collections, George A. Smathers Libraries, ufdc.ufl.edu.)

PARTIAL VIEW OF TAMPA, FLA., THE CITY BEAUTIFUL.

Church of the Sacred Heart.   Bay View Hotel.   Tampa's $350,000 City Hall.
Tampa's Newest and Best.

This postcard, probably released in 1916, features a colorized image of the Church of the Sacred Heart, a Catholic church built in 1905, as well as the Bay View Hotel and City Hall, each of which opened in 1915. (Courtesy, University of Florida Digital Collections, George A. Smathers Libraries, ufdc.ufl.edu.)

A less-than-flattering candid photo of Robert Mugge, wearing work clothes, probably taken by one of his children in 1915 when he was approximately sixty-two and likely suffering from oncoming kidney disease. (Mugge family photo.)

A candid photo of Robert Mugge reading a newspaper at his dining room table, likely shot by one of his children in 1915. (Mugge family photo.)

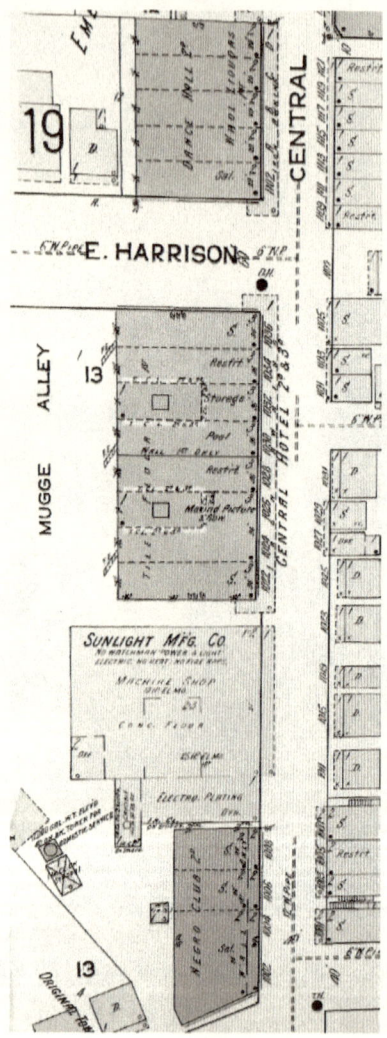

Throughout Robert Mugge's career, the center of his business empire was the west side of Central Avenue, stretching from Harrison Street to Cass Street. From top to bottom, this 1915 Sanborn fire insurance map shows his Central Saloon and newly relocated wholesale liquor business; his Central Hotel, complete with seventy-two guest rooms and eight first-floor businesses, one of which was a movie theater called the Grand Central Theatre; his Sunlight Manufacturing Company and attached Hillsborough Machine Shop; and, replacing his distillery, a new brick building leased to an African American fraternal organization. (Courtesy, University of Florida Digital Collections, George A. Smathers Libraries, ufdc.ufl.edu.)

The Mugge family plot at Tampa's Woodlawn Cemetery, purchased when Robert Mugge died in December of 1915. (Shot by the author in November of 2018.)

A photo of August Mugge in his World War I army uniform, probably shot in 1919. (Courtesy, August B. Mugge.)

This photo (circa 1917) shows Mugge family friend William Petrich, Eugene Mugge's first wife Mimi, Eugene and Mimi's daughter Marie, and Robert Mugge's widow Caroline at the Mugge beach house, its name now changed from Sorgenfrei to The Gulf View. (Courtesy, Margaret Regener Hurner.)

After Robert's death, his son August commissioned a local artist to create this painting of his father, based upon a section of a 1915 photo. (Courtesy, Dr. Robert H. and Mrs. A. Elizabeth Mugge.)

On May 15, 1922, the Burgert Brothers shot this photo at the intersection of Franklin and Jackson Streets. At the center was the completed Bay View Hotel, then still owned by the Mugge family. To the right was the block of buildings on Franklin Street which had once included Robert's Eureka Saloon and his wholesale liquor business. (Courtesy, Tampa-Hillsborough County Public Library System.)

On June 26, 1927, Caroline Mugge, now known affectionately as Grossmama, celebrated her sixty-sixth birthday at the Lake Magdalene home of Herman and Louise Regener. For the occasion, the Burgert Brothers photographed her surrounded by twenty American grandchildren, with more to come. (Courtesy, Margaret Regener Hurner.)

In 1936, Robert Mugge's eldest son, Eugene, constructed a new distillery, declaring it kin to Robert's from 1890, and reviving such favorites as Old Mugge corn whiskey. It was a short-lived effort, but a sweet reminder of glories past. (Courtesy, Anthony P. "Tony" Pizzo Collection, University of South Florida, Tampa Library Special Collections.)

Chapter Sixteen

Never on Sunday

The 1905 publication of the Tampa Board of Trade included a prominent profile of businessman Robert Mugge. Apparently based on an extensive interview with Robert himself, it offered a rare, detailed inventory of his primary business interests and holdings at that time, and confirmation of his prior moves within America. What follows is a series of brief excerpts:

This old established business was founded in 1876 on a very small scale with practically no capital, and now it is the most extensive house of the kind in Florida. The premises occupied are Mr. Mugge's own property and cover an area of 105x100 feet. Here a very large stock of goods is carried embracing all kinds of imported and domestic wines and liquors, cordials, Bass' ale and Guinness' stout, etc. In whiskies ... Mr. Mugge also makes a specialty of his own brand which by the familiar name of "Old Mugge" is very popular ... Mr. Mugge is also the owner of a distillery on Central avenue where he has also an ice factory. The capacity of the distillery is fifty gallons a day, that of the ice factory twenty tons daily. The business of the house extends throughout South Florida generally, both to the trade, and to individuals in packages ... Mr. Mugge represents here the far famed Anheuser-Busch Brewing Association. This company's lager and Budweiser may be ranked as the finest beers in the world ... Mr. Mugge sells of this product an average of $2,000 weekly. Mr. R. Mugge is a native of Hanover, Germany. He came to the United States in 1870 and lived for a time in Kentucky and Indiana. He has been a resident of this city for twenty-eight years ... Mr. Mugge is an extensive real estate owner here. He is also the owner of some twenty liquor houses in Tampa. In connection with all his interests we believe that he is the second largest payer of taxes in the city ... There can be no doubt that altogether this enterprise forms one of the most important items of Tampa's interest and is entitled to be quoted as among the leading business establishments.[421]

On January 24, 1905, as reported by the *Morning Tribune* of the following day, the Mugge family experienced an event offering great joy, as Robert and Caroline's eldest daughter, Louise, gave birth to their first grandchild, Hermina Regener: "Born, to Mr. and Mrs. Herman Regener, last night at 7:30, a fine girl. Papa Regener and Grandpa Mugge are equally overjoyed."[422]

Still, after a couple of months of familial bliss, Robert stepped right back into the thick of public controversy, as he enlisted the help of Adolphus Busch in pressuring Tampa's City Council not to dispose of the now-city-controlled Tampa Bay Hotel to outside corporate interests. The *Morning Tribune* of March 26, 1905 covered the situation in detail, including its typical questioning of Robert Mugge's motives under the headlines, "Injunction To Stop Hotel Sale Secured By Millionaire Brewer—Busch, From His St. Louis Brewery, 'Buts In' [sic] To Tampa's Affairs—But Who Hides In The Busch?"[423] However, a more concise, more accurate, and less inflammatory description of events was offered the following day by the *Ocala Evening Star.*

The *Star* pointed out that the late Henry B. Plant had spent approximately $3 million in constructing the Tampa Bay Hotel and grounds, and that the city was in the process of acquiring both from his estate for $125,000, "in order to prevent the demolition of the big hotel and the cutting up of the beautiful botanical gardens into building lots." Yet, now, the City Council of Tampa was also considering selling the property to E. John Kauffman and Associates of New York City for only $140,000. Because Mr. Kauffman represented a syndicate which wished to convert the property into a winter racetrack, and because the property was worth far more than was being offered, "Adolphus Busch, the millionaire St. Louis brewer, acting as a tax payer of this city, yesterday ... secured a temporary writ of injunction in the circuit court to prohibit the city council of Tampa from selling ..." As the *Star* went on to make clear, had not Mr. Busch intervened, the sale would have been consummated that day.[424]

Although questions regarding the hotel's future would not be resolved until later in the year, the *Morning Tribune* of March 28, 1905 gave a dramatic, and somewhat distorted, account of what happened next under the headlines, "Brewer Busch Loses His Injunction Suit—Judge Wall, After Hearing Argument, Dissolves Injunction—Mugge Appears In Case—The Man Behind The Busch Comes Forth And Signs The Bond." Aside from reporting that the injunction had failed the day before, what seemed to interest the *Tribune* most was that Robert Mugge had been behind the entire effort, even to the point of signing a $5,000 bond which would now permit the city to sue him for costs related to their failure to sell the property as expected.[425] But more on that shortly.

A day later, the *Morning Tribune* reported Robert Mugge's latest request to City Council for fairness in the enforcement of laws governing alcohol sales. Only this time, instead of supporting Robert's solid arguments, Wallace F. Stovall, clearly still furious over Robert's failure to help underwrite staging of the South Florida Fair, ridiculed him in a story headlined, "Poor, Persecuted Mugge!"

Robert's frequent lawyer, J. J. Lunsford, spoke to the Council in support of Robert's petition to have something done about drug stores and houses of prostitution in Tampa selling liquor without a license. In response, President Webb maintained that a petition from someone of Robert's character was not to be taken seriously, and that Robert was no doubt frustrated knowing that local brothels were not buying their liquor from him. Robert's petition charged that Tampa's Police Department was aware of these facts yet refused to enforce the law in such cases. In the hearing, Lunsford declared that they were ready to substantiate the accusation. But Webb said he would prefer someone other than Robert Mugge bring charges against the police or any other city officials.[426]

Still, in many respects, the future of the Tampa Bay Hotel continued to be the biggest story of the moment. With that in mind, the *Morning Tribune* of March 30, 1905 revealed that Frank Q. Brown, head of the Ocean and Gulf Realty Co., had arrived in Tampa. Brown's company controlled the hotel and surrounding property, and he was there in the hope of finalizing an agreement with the city. Negotiations had moved slowly since the killing of the injunction filed by Adolphus Busch and Robert Mugge, but at least their actions had prevented a sale that would have meant destruction of the hotel.[427]

What neither the *Morning Tribune* nor anyone else seemed to understand at the time was that Mugge and Busch were quietly helping the City of Tampa to save its most precious assets, which were Henry B. Plant's luxurious hotel and adjoining properties. In his memoirs, Robert's son, August B. Mugge, relayed the full story, beginning with the fact that, most likely, the hotel "was never a paying proposition." So, after Henry Plant died in 1899, his estate looked for ways to dispose of it.

For his part, Robert believed the city should take it over. And when he learned that Northern speculators were preparing to buy it, he rushed to the hotel one morning and convinced his friend Adolphus, who was there on a visit, to loan the city what was needed to purchase the hotel on its own. "Mr. Busch agreed, but wanted the hotel deeded to my father, who consulted with his attorney, J. J. Lunsford." Papers were then prepared and the deal consummated. Afterwards, the city floated a bond issue which gave them the money to reimburse Busch, and the property was deeded to the city. The building was then "operated for a number of years as a hotel," before being donated to the University of Tampa. "In deeds of this kind," August recalled, "my father, as so often, became the forgotten man."[428]

Meanwhile, the city police, whom Robert had criticized once again before the City Council, were on the watch for any infraction of his they could use to repay him. Regrettably, in his disdain for the police, he became careless and gave them what they wanted. The *Morning Tribune* of April 11, 1905 took delight in telling this sordid, if entertaining tale, under the quasi-scandalous headlines, "Mr. Mugge Out For A Lark, Run Down By Two Policemen."

The first thing to know about the piece is that it admits—even brags—right from the top that Robert Mugge was a target, and offers both explicit and implicit reasons why:

> Acting under instructions from Chief Jones, who had received complaints from respectable residents of Tampa Heights, Detective J. W. Ahn and Patrolman H. C. Thompson sallied forth late last night on the trail of Robert Mugge, the eminent moralist who has recently made such strong appeals in behalf of the observance of the law before the City Council and the County Commissioners. Mr. Mugge, it was reported to the Chief, had been enjoying midnight drives through the quiet streets of that delectable section, in company with a "lady of his acquaintance," who enjoys some reputation in police circles under the name of Miss Ollie Cummings.

The chief gleefully told his men that, "if they caught Mr. Mugge in such company," both persons should be arrested, making use of the ever-oppressive Ordinance 175.

Later that night, at the intersection of Palm and Nebraska Avenues, the two officers did, indeed, spot their intended prey—the offending saloon magnate and his female companion—as well as an unexpected third person, Henry Smith, who was a whiskey drummer at Robert's distillery. But Robert saw them as well, at which point their carriages' leisurely strides turned into buggy-on-buggy pursuit, ending, as planned, at Central Avenue and Cass Street. There, upon

Robert's instructions, Cummings raced into his ice factory, while Robert and the whiskey drummer greeted the police.

At the station, cases were docketed against both men for being in the company of a woman of questionable character after 9:00 p.m., and Robert provided $100 in bail money for the two of them. Then, Detective Ahn said he would return to the ice factory for Cummings, at which point Robert posted $50 for her as well.

With the first act completed, the *Tribune* provided a helpful summary: "This is Mugge's second arrest recently under the same ordinance, his company on the first occasion being also a female, but of a somewhat shadier hue than his companion of last night."[429] The closing racist statement aside, Robert's disdain for authority, perhaps coupled with what, today, we would term a midlife crisis, or even simply a reaction to too many years of nonstop, round-the-clock work, had now given his enemies a cudgel with which to beat him. Police, politicians, and newspapers would have a field day responding to these events, using them, in effect, to question his moral authority to question theirs.

Was Robert having an affair with this woman, and possibly even providing her a place to live, as some neighbors (one of them a patrolman) would go on to claim? Or was she simply someone met at one of his saloons, or dance halls, or other businesses whose occasional company he enjoyed? In the end, it did not, and does not matter, except to him and his family, and except for the ways in which it weakened him for a time, at least in the public eye.

Regardless, the show did continue. The *Morning Tribune* of April 12 featured the following article under the headline, "Neighbors Object to Mugge's Woman." Again, notice that Robert's primary accuser is a member of the Police Department purporting to live in the same neighborhood as Cummings, and that events are being intentionally sensationalized by both the police and the press, with each of them feeling previously victimized by the saloon magnate.

The hearing began with Henry Smith, the whiskey drummer, explaining he had been out for a leisurely drive with Mugge when the latter suggested stopping to pick up Cummings. He testified he was unaware of her reputed bad character, and Judge Whitaker gave him a suspended sentence.

"Attorney J. J. Lunsford appeared for Mugge and Miss Cummings, and a warm colloquy ensued between him and Patrolman H. C. Thompson who, with Detective Ahn, had made the arrests." The patrolman claimed that he and other residents of their neighborhood, along the ironically named Liberty Street, believed that Robert was openly keeping Cummings in said neighborhood, and "he did not propose to stand for anything of the sort under the very noses of his family." The argument between Attorney Lunsford and Patrolman Thompson became so heated that Judge Whitaker had to call for order.[430]

The melodramatic coverage continued in the *Morning Tribune* of April 13, 1905. Reportedly, Judge Whitaker granted a continuance to permit Lunsford to "get Miss Bowers, matron of the Door of Hope, to testify to Ollie's reformation." In addition, the court sent a subpoena to Cummings, instructing her that her rights would be preserved, but she would either testify the following day or go to jail. Finally, it was brought out in the two-hour session that, when the officers demanded to search Robert's ice factory, he warned that he and Cummings's lawyer had advised her to get a pistol, and that he had advised her to use it.

At the end of this brief second act, the *Tribune* provided another helpful summary: "The indignation of the people of the neighborhood where it is alleged Mugge maintains the young woman is very great, and talk has been heard of drastic actions if the open scandal continues."[431] One thing was certain: Whenever someone proposed taking law into his own hands, W. F. Stovall would always lend support.

The *Morning Tribune* of the following day, April 14, 1905, documented what was, contrary to assertions, likely the final chapter of this riveting saga. Naturally, the journalistic dispatch began with a series of Wallace Stovall insults:

> Hon. Robert Mugge, saloonkeeper, injunctionist, member of the Board of Public Works, and censor-general of Tampa, was

fined $25 and costs by Municipal Judge Whitaker yesterday, for violating ordinance 175, prohibiting citizens of Tampa from being in the company of prostitutes on the streets. Should Mr. Mugge feel indisposed to pay this huge amount, which is the maximum penalty for keeping certain kinds of bad company, he will have the option of serving his beloved city for 30 days on the streets to which as a member of the Board of Public Works he gives much attention.

Otherwise, the only new development was that the matron of the Door of Hope, although served with a subpoena, failed to act as a character witness for Ollie Cummings. Perhaps someone in law enforcement had warned her not to appear, or perhaps a donor who resided in Tampa Heights had done so. But Cummings herself showed up, and "testified that she had walked in the path of rectitude since her residence with that organization." She also admitted having spent time with Robert Mugge the previous Monday, and "Constable Louis Callenberg testified to seeing them drinking together at the Metropolitan theatre." And with that, the entire drama simply faded away, aside from J. J. Lunsford giving notice of a motion for a new trial, which almost surely never happened.[432] Of course, there still was the matter of Detective J. W. Ahn.

Twelve days after Detective Jim Ahn helped to arrest Robert Mugge, Henry Smith, and Ollie Cummings for taking an evening ride that offended the high moral character of the Tampa Police Department, the *Morning Tribune* of April 22, 1905 reported that two employees of the Criterion Theater in Ybor City had sworn out warrants against Detective Ahn for assaulting them without provocation at their place of work.[433] Then, two weeks after that, the *Morning Tribune* of May 6, 1905 revealed that J. W. Ahn was actually an alias for one J. Wesley Ashburn, a longtime professional gambler who had come to Tampa to run a gambling house; who, after helping apprehend a gang of "safe-blowers" with whom he was intimately acquainted, was invited to join the Police Department as a detective; who allegedly had served time in Missouri for homicide; who was currently married to at least two women, one living in Virginia and the other living in Tampa; and who was preparing to marry a seventeen-year-old girl in Jacksonville as well. Upon the discovery of this information, Detective Ahn was quietly asked to resign from the force, and he promptly left the city in order to avoid further scrutiny or prosecution.[434]

However, the *Morning Tribune* of the following day announced discovery of still another not-yet-divorced wife in Virginia.[435] And thirteen months later, the *Morning Tribune* of June 16, 1906 reported that Ashburn, previously known as Detective J. W. Ahn, had arrived in Lexington, Kentucky "with a handsome young bride and found a warrant for bigamy awaiting him. He was locked up and will probably be prosecuted to the extent of the law."[436]

For one further example of the moral imperatives governing Tampa's law enforcement and journalistic coverage during the era in question, nothing better exists than a piece in the *Morning Tribune* of May 14, 1905, appearing a month after the Mugge-Cummings story. According to the *Tribune*, John Paul, an African American dishwasher at the California Restaurant on Polk Street, as well as Paula Frieble, a young German woman formerly employed there, had been arrested the day before on a charge of "disorderly conduct." The specific crime alleged was that Ms. Frieble sat in Paul's lap in the kitchen of the Chinese restaurant.

Paul, not able to provide a $50 bond, had been locked up overnight, while Chief Jones had released Frieble on her own recognizance, instructing her to be in Police Court the following morning to answer the charges against her. "The negro declares that the girl, on passing back into the kitchen where he was sitting by the door, stumbled and fell in his lap, getting up again at once." One of the proprietors backed up his statement and identified Maude Moore, a white waitress at the restaurant, as the source of the false accusation. It seems Moore was angry about having been fined $25 for attacking Paula Frieble with a razor, and now she was seeking revenge.

The *Tribune* writer, almost certainly Wallace F. Stovall, seemed intrigued by Frieble, describing her as "a very pretty German girl with blue eyes and black hair," about 20, who had come there from New York, and who spoke with "a decided German brogue." When

Stovall asked her about the incident, seemingly evoking the world-weariness of future German film star Marlene Dietrich, she simply shrugged her shoulders and said, "she did not care what they did with her."

Stovall declared this likely an accident. Still, returning to form, he wrote, "In case it should be shown to be similar to the disgusting affairs that threw the city into an uproar a couple of years ago, the authorities should push the matter to the limit. Until this is shown, however, the public should keep cool, and let the law take its course."[437]

As to Robert's recent adversity, the trial itself had ended, but not the reverberations. Back on March 10, 1905, the *Kissimmee Valley Gazette* had reported Robert's purchase of Kissimmee's Eagle Saloon from R. T. Butler, the Chairman of Osceola County's Board of Commissioners. In fact, at the time, Robert had ingratiated himself by claiming he "would not take a dollar away from Kissimmee," but instead would "spend two dollars for every one—of his profits—in buying and improving property and otherwise contributing to the upbuilding of the town."[438] Yet, after publicity resulting from the Ollie Cummings affair, the *Gazettes* of May 5 and May 12, 1905 reported the Woman's Christian Temperance Union leading strong community protests against him, as well as against the three top male citizens of Hillsborough County whose affidavits swearing to Robert's good character had won him a license for his new saloon.[439 440]

Then, as the *Morning Tribune* updated an older story in its issue of May 17, 1905, it also took another swing at Robert:

> Upon application of the defendant, endorsed by the Chief of Police, the Council remitted the remainder of the sentence against Eugene Gill, convicted several years ago for operating a gambling device. Gill was barkeeper for St. Robert Mugge, the sweet aroma of whose character ascends like incense into the heavens, compelling the admiration of three representative citizens of Hillsborough County and the laudation of the public at large. While the law required that Gill should

be the one to suffer, the Councilmen expressed the opinion last night that his Saintship was the one who was morally deserving of arrest.[441]

Without question, the owner of a concern promoting illegal activity should be at least as subject to prosecution as an employee overseeing such activity. However, it was never established in court whether Eugene Gill, manager of the Central Saloon, had utilized the toy slot machine on his own as a means of driving up profits, or whether his employer had assigned him to do so. Regardless, Gill did not spend "several years" incarcerated for this crime, as the article implied. Instead, after he was convicted on December 3, 1902,[442] his employer had subsidized a lengthy appeal of his case, and it was public knowledge he had not yet been imprisoned by January 22, 1904, when the *Morning Tribune* reported his having been robbed during social activities in the Scrub.[443] Therefore, he likely served a year or less before having his sentence commuted. Moreover, it was absurd to criminalize use of a toy game of chance which, instead of money, awarded the winner a small discount on products sold.

In any case, just one week later, Stovall could stop beating up on his former friend, because nature, an exploding gas lamp, and the poorly functioning Water Works Company took over for him, and with much more devastating effect. The *Morning Tribune* of May 24, 1905 described perhaps the worst fire yet to strike Robert Mugge directly.

According to the report, Tuesday morning, a man named White, the chief clerk of J. W. Jones's Bee Hive store, struck a match to light a gasoline lamp so he could see while sweeping. In an instant, a gas tank exploded, sending flames racing throughout the store, then on into the rest of the two-story Armory Building at Franklin and Cass Streets in Tampa. The building, constructed by Robert Mugge with backing from the Anheuser-Busch Brewing Association, was the only brick building at that intersection. It also contained Robert's Armory Saloon and the Tampa Light Infantry Armory, in which, in addition to staging its events, the infantry stored fifty-five army rifles plus ammunition. "Within an hour after the fire started, both the east and south walls, on Franklin and Cass streets respectively, had fallen in with a crash, and 5,000 rounds of cartridges in the Armory were discharged by the heat and kept up a fusillade for more than a quarter of an hour."

The saloon, itself, was a wreck, uninsured, and with a loss of approximately $20,000. "Formerly the handsomest bar in Tampa," wrote the *Tribune* reporter, "it is now black and desolate enough to point the moral of a temperance tale." But overall, the losses of this building and others on Franklin Street—especially the adjacent building holding Gordon's pawn brokerage—were thought to be approximately $40,000.[444]

Robert Mugge had lived this scenario before, and just as in the past, he did not waste an instant preparing to rebuild. The following day's *Morning Tribune* reflected as much: "Robert Mugge has announced that the Armory Building, burned in Tuesday's fire, will be replaced with a one-story brick building [since he would no longer include space for the armory]. The work of cleaning away the debris was begun yesterday."[445]

Yet, since Robert had long criticized the Tampa Water Works Company for its poor performance as a public utility, the news revealed nearly four weeks later should have come as no surprise. According to the *Morning Tribune* of June 23, 1905, Robert planned to sue the utility for $25,000, claiming, in the process, it had provided insufficient water pressure to firefighters attempting to save his Franklin Street Armory Building.[446] And with that announcement, Robert launched what was to be one of his greatest obsessions for years to come, even as he also set about resolving, at last, two of his key interests of years past, which were the saving of the Tampa Bay Hotel and the paving of city roads.

Those efforts, too, were recorded in the January 23, 1905 issue of the *Tribune*, though without mention of the key roles played by Robert Mugge and Adolphus Busch in the former of the two. At least the excitement of the moment was conveyed through some decidedly emotional headlines: "City Now Owns Tampa Bay Hotel— Property Upon Which Henry Plant Expended Over Three Million Dollars Bought By City of Tampa Yesterday For $125,000—Cash Was Paid D. H. Thomas, Representing The Owners, By City Officials And Deed Was Delivered To President Fuller, Of Board Of Public

Works—Money For The Improvement Bonds Also Now Available—
How It Was All Done." And the article itself was equally informative,
aside from that one crucial omission, probably due to editor Stovall's
continuing animosity toward Robert Mugge.

All at once, the day before, the city had come into "full and
complete possession and ownership of the Tampa Bay Hotel and
its magnificent grounds," while also securing "the proceeds of the
public improvement bond issue, which will give the city 20 miles of
fortified brick paving and complete the Waring sewerage system."
With respect to the hotel acquisition, the *Tribune* dubbed it "one of
the most unique experiments in municipal socialism ever made,"
and noted that the Board of Public Works would soon be receiving
proposals for the leasing of the hotel, considering "what is to be done
with it, now that we have got it."[447]

Neither Robert nor Adolphus needed credit for any of this; they
only cared about saving the hotel. And now that they had, Robert could
focus on a range of issues currently being considered by the Board of
Public Works. For instance, as was reported in the *Morning Tribune* of July
15, 1905, with the city now owning the Tampa Bay Hotel and grounds,
the Board voted to lease "the race-track and fair grounds portion of the
Tampa Bay Hotel property to the State Fair Association for five years, at
a nominal fee." Robert argued that the city should be paid at least $5,000
per annum for use of the fairgrounds, but he was outvoted.[448]

Still, the biggest news came on September 20, 1905. It was then
that the *Morning Tribune* revealed the decision of the Board of Public
Works to lease the Tampa Bay Hotel to David Lauber of St. Louis, in
partnership with the *Tribune's* own Wallace F. Stovall, for a period of
five years. The rental would be $25,000, due in payments of $2,000
the first year, $3,000 the second year, $5,000 the third year, $7,000
the fourth year, and $8,000 the fifth year, with the hotel scheduled
to reopen that coming November 1. At the Board's public meeting
the day before, Robert Mugge had moved that the bid of Lauber and
Stovall be accepted, S. J. Drawdy seconded the motion, and all four
members voted aye. At that point, "Col. Knight was instructed to
prepare a formal lease and, on motion of Mr. Mugge, the bond was
fixed at $10,000.[449]

In short, with the most stunning irony, *Tribune* Editor W. F. Stovall, the same man who had spent months ridiculing and even libeling Robert Mugge, was now being awarded a five-year lease for the Tampa Bay Hotel, and within the Board of Public Works, it likely was Robert who had made it happen. That is, in one fell swoop, Robert had saved a priceless part of Tampa heritage, while also mending fences with a former friend and ally. So, perhaps a less-than-perfect year could yet be saved.

But whatever gains were made in the foreground, there was, behind the scenes, still the rising drumbeat of the temperance movement. As just one reminder, the *Morning Tribune* of October 1, 1905 recorded a talk by Don C. McMullen—local attorney, prohibitionist, and staunch critic of Robert Mugge—delivered at the aptly named Christian Endeavor convention. His subject was the temperate life.

McMullen led off with the notion that, "Common sense and experience enjoin us to be temperate in all things, thought, word and deed," then posited that, of all forms of intemperance, the one most "hideous" in all respects was "the use of intoxicating liquors as a beverage." After that, he suggested that Robert Mugge and the Florida Brewing Company appeared to own, between them, nearly all the saloons in Tampa, and that he believed they pulled as much as a million dollars a year from the pockets of the people of Hillsborough County. His basic message was that, because of the saloon industry's wealth, local politicians and even religious leaders were afraid to criticize them. But he closed with the following proposal: "The question ought to be submitted to the people of Florida, and no man who claims to adhere to and believe in the principles of majority rule can advance any reason why the people of this State should not be allowed to say whether they want the saloon or not."[450]

In other words, the battle lines had long been drawn, with personal liberty on one side, and the will of the majority on the other. For the temperance movement, there was one ultimate ambition, which was termination of alcohol use; if not in the whole country at once, then state by state, and beginning with the saloons.

Chapter Seventeen

Opposing Forces

The playful relationship between Robert Mugge and Wallace F. Stovall had clearly returned because, in the January 12, 1906 issue of the *Morning Tribune*, W. F. Stovall wrote, "Mr. Mugge seems to be sleeping. No injunctions in a month."[451] Robert responded in the following issue: "Editor *Tribune:* Mugge never sleeps and is ever ready to look after the interests of Tampa and her people."[452]

In the next issue, Mr. Stovall agreed with the contention that Robert never slept, affirming, "We have seen him out rather early in the morning."[453] The exchange is interesting for at least three reasons: first, it offered proof that the largely one-sided feud between them truly was over; second, it illustrated that both men slept very little, since one was out in time to see the other already working; and third, it showed that both of them exploited the *Morning Tribune* much the way people would utilize Internet-based social media more than a century later. In that latter case, each one used the newspaper to establish his identity in the community, to express himself on issues of the day, to promote a political or business-related agenda, and, as here, simply to be playful. The overriding point is that each of them had a life in print that existed independent of his actual life, and it is that shadow image of each which, fortunately, has survived, making it possible to tell their story.

Nonetheless, just as Robert Mugge rarely slept, so, too, did temperance forces, patiently pushing their own agenda for decades, just as, say, anti-abortion and pro-gun forces would do in late twentieth and early twenty-first century America. The *Morning Tribune* of January 14, 1906 related the next shell lobbed in Robert's direction under the headline, "Wet And Dry Election Seems To Have Gone Against Saloons." In fact, the voters of Kissimmee, the county seat of Osceola County, had reportedly voted to go "dry" by a majority of just sixty-eight votes, and returns coming in from other of the county's precincts indicated a defeat for sellers and buyers of alcohol. "Heretofore, Kissimmee has boasted of three saloons, R. Mugge, of Tampa, being among the liquor dealers interested in the town."[454]

This appears to have been an extremely small plurality by which one half of the public was able to impose its moral view on the other half. Yet, democracy had, and still has, few safeguards against democratically imposed tyranny, even by the slightest of margins. Of course, political philosophy aside, Robert was now stuck with a nonfunctioning Eagle Saloon which he had only just purchased there the previous spring.

Regardless of setbacks, Robert Mugge kept building. The *Morning Tribune* of February 13, 1906 indicated that crews were now completing work on a three-story hotel in West Tampa. It would open as the Madrid Hotel and Restaurant. Later, under the management of Robert's son Eugene, it would be renamed the Grand Occident Hotel and Restaurant, and years later, it would be known as simply the "Mugge Hotel." But at this point, the *Tribune* referred to it as a "lodging house," despite its having sixty rooms for guests: "Many improvements are being added to the surroundings of the R. Mugge lodging house, corner Howard and Walnut Streets. This is the largest building of its kind in the city."[455]

Yet, nothing pleased Robert more than conceiving complicated solutions for intractable problems, instituting those solutions, and then explaining them to everyone involved. For instance, donning his Board of Public Works hat again, Robert used the *Morning Tribune* of April 10, 1906 to spell out new procedures for the paving of roads. "Editor *Tribune*: Daily I am asked the question: How much will I have to pay as my share for paving?" He then clarified the complex formula by which homeowners and business owners would be expected to help pay for the paving and curbing in front of their properties. As Robert explained, for each section of pavement, the city would pay a third of the cost, and the property owner on either side of the road would also pay a third. Meanwhile, the Board of Public Works would issue "paving certificates" which the city would use to pay the contractors, and property owners would pay off the value of their respective certificates in one, two, or three years, with eight percent interest accruing.[456] More than likely, Robert's explanation was repeated more than once.

At any rate, while the goals of good paving included relative permanence, that was not the case with elected officials, and a new municipal election was set to take place in June of 1906. For that reason, throughout the month of May, the *Morning Tribune* was filled with political endorsements of assorted candidates. For instance, the issue of May 6, 1906 featured a letter to the editor from Robert Mugge, the declared purpose of which was to endorse mayoral candidate Frank C. Bower, a favorite of Tampa business interests. In asserting that average Tampans should entrust their government to someone from the corporate community, he shared more information about his own attitudes as an employer than he did about Bower's qualifications for the city's highest office. What follows, then, are comments he made about himself:

> Editor *Tribune:* The poor man is entitled to his full rights, and, according to my view, and which I have practiced, he should receive much more consideration than the rich, because they can help themselves. Yet the poor man does much more good for himself to stand by the man who is in position to help him ...

I employ a large number of men, pay them good wages, and am their friend all the way though. I am acting for them in all their troubles as lawyer, doctor and preacher ...

The liquor business does not cover all I do. I had buildings erected in 1905 at a cost of $35,000. A contract is let now for a $3,000 building. I keep two painters at work the year round on repair work. My average wages for builders and mechanics are no less than $200 a week. During the next five years I expect to spend no less than $100,000 for new buildings ... R. Mugge[457]

Although Robert likely did not intend it, his words came across as boastful and patrician, if only because what he regarded as simple truths mostly reflected his own position of power. Still, at a time when few in the white power structure were watching out for the needs of minorities and the poor, and unlawful vigilantes were seen as a legitimate extension of law enforcement, a white employer willing to hire, support, and protect largely unwelcome workers would have been seen, at least by those workers, as a positive force in a highly destructive environment. By contrast, others in the community—especially those who had fought a war to preserve slavery—would have viewed his remarks quite differently.

Another possibility is that, with a Board of Public Works election coming up as well, Robert saw these comments as an indirect way of promoting himself, without having to mount an active campaign. Admittedly, in the four years since his previous run, his reputation had suffered. And yet, many were still willing to sing his praises, and that included the *Morning Tribune* itself. Setting things into motion this time were two separate commentaries in the May 10, 1906 issues of the *Daily* and *Weekly Tribune*. One was a letter to the editor, and the other was an editorial: (1) "We hereby announce R. Mugge for member of the Board of Public Works for the First Ward at the coming election. We do this, not for the benefit of the individual, but for the benefit of the public, [signed] Many Voters."[458] (2) "Robert Mugge has made Tampa a most excellent member of the Board of Public Works. He is absolutely honest, capable and progressive and those who vote in the First Ward will have to go a long way and look for some time before they can locate a man who will more assiduously look after the interests of the people."[459]

Unfortunately, the bad publicity surrounding Robert's interactions with police had apparently taken a toll upon public perceptions. According to the *Morning Tribune* of June 6, 1906, in the First Ward, his run for the Board of Public Works seat was defeated by Elmore Webb in a vote of 321 to 298.[460] True, it was only a plurality of twenty-three votes, but that was all it took. Of course, predictably, the loss of an election did not cause him to lose even a step, as he had too many battles yet to fight. And in case anyone doubted that Robert Mugge and Wallace F. Stovall were largely fighting on the same side again, in the *Morning Tribune* of June 12, 1906, Mr. Stovall praised the record of Robert and his fellow commissioners:

> The showing made by the retiring Board of Public Works, which turned over the affairs of the department to the newly elected Board yesterday, is one which any right-thinking man must commend ...
>
> The old Board found not a cent to its credit when it entered upon its duties. It found, however, considerable paving and other work which had been left to it by the former Board, which it was necessary for it to carry out, securing the necessary funds in any manner possible.
>
> It was the retiring Board that carried through the negotiations which resulted in the floating of the city's public improvement bonds and which began the work of completing the city sewage system and adding eighteen miles of vitrified brick to the city's public improvements ...
>
> President Fuller stated that the old Board left to the credit of the new Board the sum of $38,000 in cash, together with the certificates for the paving already done, which bear interest. The Board has also recently purchased a new cremating plant, which will shortly be erected and will prove a valuable aid in disposing of the city's garbage. Many other improvements have been installed and perfected under the

able administration of Messrs. Fuller, Drawdy, Balbontin, and Mugge ...

Well done, thou good and faithful servants.[461]

Yet again, despite old struggles recently resolved, another batch was newly under way. As just one example, the day after election results became public, the *Weekly Tribune* of June 7, 1906 featured the following report under the headlines, "Before Supreme Court— Attorney Goes to Tallahassee to Argue Important Suit." This was Robert's suit against the Tampa Water Works Company, in which he charged his Armory Building at Franklin and Cass Streets had been destroyed due to that company's failure to provide fire companies with sufficient water pressure. By this point, Judge Wall of the Circuit Court had ruled against Robert's claim, asserting that he did not have standing to file such a suit. However, Attorney J. J. Lunsford expected better results on appeal to the State Supreme Court, in that the US Supreme Court had recently rendered a decision upholding "the right of a private citizen to recover damages under such circumstances."[462]

Next, in the *Morning Tribune* of July 11, 1906 was an ad for a new addition to Robert's business portfolio: "New Machine Shop. Started at R. Mugge's Ice Factory, Corner Central Ave. and Cass St. All kinds of machine work. Steam, gasoline, piping and mill work. All work promptly executed. Hillsborough Machine Shop. Tampa, Fla. Phone 202."[463]

Regrettably, a return to business as usual also meant returning to the constant threat of serious fires, including one in Ybor City reported in the *Morning Tribune* of July 13, 1906: "The costliest fire for a long time occurred on Seventh Avenue in the vicinity of Twenty-Second Street, early yesterday morning. Several alarms were turned in, but owing to the system being out of order, were not received by No. 2, the nearest fire station, and the firemen were unaware of the conflagration until warned by a citizen."

By the time the Fire Department arrived, the entire north side of Seventh Avenue, between Twenty-First and Twenty-Second Street, was engulfed in flames. Firefighters managed to keep them from spreading to the north and west, but the fire "leaped across Twenty-Second Street, catching the Seminole Saloon, and the building of Dr. Maximo Diaz, in which was situated the drug store of R. E. Hendrix. Both buildings were destroyed." Although some estimates placed the total loss at $40,000, Robert Mugge said he believed it would reach $50,000. The value of his Seminole Saloon Building had been $4,000, and the saloon itself $3,000, with neither having been insured.[464]

Ironically, the same day, the *Pensacola Journal* of Pensacola, Florida reported that Robert had won his fire-related lawsuit before the Florida Supreme Court. The *Associated Press* story read as follows: "Tallahassee, Fla., July 12.—The Florida supreme court decided that, a water works company is liable for damage for failure to supply sufficient water pressure to extinguish a fire in the case of Robert Mugge, a Tampa brewer, who sued for $25,000 damages because of the loss of a building through alleged lack of water pressure. This reverses the decision of the lower court and remands the case for further proceedings."[465]

The *Morning Tribune* of Saturday, July 14, 1906 expanded on the previous story, laying out the actual decision. The heart of it was that the Water Works, as a public utility, enjoyed "extensive franchises and privileges." But in return for those rights, it had taken on an absolute "public duty" to provide sufficient water for the fighting of fires. Therefore, if adequate water was not supplied in such circumstances, and negligence led to the destruction of property, then the Water Works Company was liable to the property owner for the damage suffered.[466]

Meanwhile, a new front had opened over what comprised the "closing" of saloons on Sundays. The city released its initial volley on Sunday, July 15, 1906, and Robert and his employee fired back via the *Morning Tribune* of Wednesday, July 18, 1906. The paper included a letter to the editor from J. H. Hubbard, manager of Robert's St. Louis Cafe at 311 Franklin Street, in which Hubbard described his July 15 arrest for allegedly having the saloon open that previous Sunday morning.

Hubbard wrote that, at 8:00 a.m., he had passed through Robert's wholesale house and then entered the saloon through a side door, solely for the "purpose of turning off stale water, rinsing out cuspidors, etc., which would become very obnoxious and unsanitary by Monday morning, after having been closely shup up from 12 o'clock Saturday night until 5 o'clock Monday morning." He also pointed out that he was paid for six days a week and therefore enjoyed having Sunday to himself, but that Robert asked him to stop by briefly in order "to keep my place in a neat and sanitary condition."

That day, during the short time Hubbard was present, Officer Tompkins stopped by and "exacted a $50 cash bond" due to the saloon being "open." As the officer was leaving, Hubbard asked if he could finish cleaning up before exiting himself. The officer said yes, but that he needed to be out before the next officer showed up. Predictably, twenty minutes later, as Hubbard prepared to go, Officer Woolweaver stopped by, arrested him a second time, and took him to the station where he was given a lecture by Chief Walker.[467]

To the relief of both Robert and his employee, such publicity led to a quick resolution in court the following day. The *Morning Tribune* of July 20, 1906 portrayed Judge M. Henry Cohen getting right to work and, in every sense, taking no prisoners. In the words of the reporter, Mayor William H. Frecker's first legal showdown with saloon operators had "resulted in a victory for the saloonists."

The city had intended to make this a test case regarding Sunday openings, and then have the verdict applied to others arraigned. But Judge Cohen acquitted Hubbard and "ruled that that part of the ordinance restraining a man from going in his place of business on Sunday was absurd." In the opinion of Judge Cohen, it was necessary for saloons to be cleaned on the Sabbath, and he therefore dismissed all other cases against saloonkeepers, while still warning them not to permit customers into their premises.[468]

Six days later, the July 26, 1906 issue of the *Morning Tribune* noted someone else's arrival, and with no warning whatsoever: "Eugene Mugge, eldest son of Robert Mugge, after six years absence, pursuing mechanical and civil engineering studies in the German universities, is at home to spend six weeks with his parents."[469] In point of fact, however, as was later explained in the memoirs of his brother August, he was back in the country to stay: "After Eugene left Giessen, he went to Chemnitz to perform his studies, but for some reason unknown to me to this day, he fell out with Professor Stammler [the man hired by Robert Mugge to look after his children while they were studying abroad], and took off for Tampa. This infuriated my father, who would have nothing to do with him and ordered him back to Germany." But Eugene refused to go, and instead "found employment elsewhere."[470]

The *Morning Tribune* of September 5, 1906 brought Robert even more bad news. Although he had previously owned a controversial saloon called the Seminole at Twenty-Second Street and Seventh Avenue in Precinct 28, that saloon had been destroyed by the big Ybor City fire of a few months before. Now, he had rebuilt the Seminole and asked the County Commissioners for a new license. But due to previous complaints about the old Seminole, as well as about other saloons in that district, his petition was refused. At that point, four or five other petitions for saloons in the same precinct were withdrawn. However, Robert did not withdraw his, the general assumption being that he would not give up the fight.[471]

Robert's refusal to accept the Commissioners' decision was confirmed in the *Morning Tribune* of October 12, 1906, which reported work proceeding on his Seminole Saloon building: "The new Mugge building, Seventh avenue and Twenty-second street, is mounting rapidly upward. It will be the only two-story brick building in that vicinity ... The Twenty-second street vicinity is a rapidly growing business center."[472]

Six decades before computers inspired the term "multitasking," Robert already worked on multiple fronts. Despite his spending every day running a range of businesses, nearly any edition of the *Morning Tribune* could describe another effort of which he was a part, and which might not be fully explained until later. As one example, the issue of October 19, 1906 noted that the Florida Supreme Court had denied a petition for rehearing his recent victory there, which meant his case would now return to the Circuit Court to determine "whether or not the water-pressure furnished by the company, on the occasion in question, was sufficient."[473] In a second example, the issue of October 27, 1906 shared a rumor that Robert Mugge was "negotiating the purchase of the McKay waterfront property from Capt. James McKay" for a possible payment of $35,000.[474] And in a third example, the issue of November 3, 1906 declared that Robert, his attorney J. J. Lunsford, and his son-in-law Herman Regener, along with William A. Riddle and William H. Thayer, had together created a new corporation called the US Light Manufacturing Company, with business to be conducted as follows: "The manufacture and sale of lighting, heating or power equipment and appliances for the generation, distribution and general utility of light, heat and power through the use of gasoline, alcohol, gas, electricity, or other fuel or energy, now known to commerce or which may hereafter be discovered ... "[475]

And yet, a story about heat could just as easily be followed by one about ice, as in the November 6, 1906 headline proclaiming that, "Another Big Ice Plant Proposed, More Ice and More Invested Capital Promised By This Large Enterprise." The upshot of this story was that, despite the Florida Brewing Company already having an ice plant with 100 tons capacity, the Tropical Ice Company also having one with 100 tons capacity, and Robert still having the oldest ice factory in Tampa, currently with twenty tons capacity, a Mr. J. W. Chandler from Baltimore, Maryland planned to open a new one with 125 tons capacity. Clearly, even in subtropical Tampa, ice could soon be a glut on the market.[476]

Although August was in Germany at the time, his father relayed what happened next. According to August's memoirs, after the new ice plant opened in 1907, a representative came to his father and offered him a daily supply of ice at a cost lower than it cost him to make it himself. The lone proviso was that he accept a minimum daily amount. Robert agreed, selling whatever he did not need himself to "two Italian venders who checked with him every Sunday night." August continued, "This proved to be a money making proposition, and for fear that the contract would not be renewed after one year, my father kept the transmissions running daily under the proper supervision, so as to keep the machines intact for any eventuality. He could afford to do this, since the contract was so lucrative."

After a year, the representative returned, asserting that the contract could only be renewed at a higher price. Without answering, Robert picked up his phone and told his supervisor, "Sam, steam her up, we are in business again." Never imagining that Robert had kept his operation in working order, the company backed down, renewing his contract on the same terms, and doing so for years to some. "Ice was also sold to drug stores, and I understand that my sister Martha collected from them for ice delivered."[477]

Meanwhile, Robert Mugge's rumored purchase of Captain James McKay's waterfront property was finalized, because the *Morning Tribune* of November 10, 1906 announced that ship owners from New York and Chicago had leased the McKay docks "from Robert Mugge, who recently purchased the property from Capt. James McKay." The plan was for a line of passenger and freight steamships to run between Tampa and New Orleans.[478] In other words, Robert could now be back in the shipping business, but without the risk of losing his own schooners.

As all his other enterprises rose and fell, turned a profit or were cast aside, Robert Mugge's saloons and other alcohol-related businesses remained the heart of his operations, and he fought fiercely for their survival and success. Sometimes that meant fighting various battles at once. For instance, the *Morning Tribune* of November 8, 1906 described his latest renewal of an ongoing conflict, which was then one of several under way.

In this case, Robert was asking County Commissioners for the right to operate his rebuilt Seminole Saloon in Precinct 28, where no saloon currently existed, and the dispute had dominated the Board's entire meeting of the day before. Advocating for Robert, Attorney J. J. Lunsford cited court decisions by Judge Wall, while Davis and Hampton expressed the opposition of "two churches and a number of the Christian people of Gary and Antioch." More specifically, Col. Davis cited a Legislative statute of 1903 which declared alcohol was not then sold in precinct 28, and that saloons were forbidden "within four miles of a church or schoolhouse." Furthermore, he pointed out that the area enjoyed no police protection other than from county constables. But the Board ultimately adjourned, delaying a decision until the following day.[479]

That was succeeded by an update in the *Morning Tribune* of November 10, 1906, revealing that the County Commissioners had rejected Robert Mugge's petition. Of course, Robert's attorneys, Lunsford and Dickenson, responded by declaring they would mandamus the Board, and H. S. Hampton, speaking for the other side, threatened to "fight the case even to the Supreme Court if necessary."[480]

This case and like ones were making J. J. Lunsford and his partner extremely busy attorneys. For instance, just three days later, the *Morning Tribune* of November 13, 1906 pointed out that Lunsford was also scheduled to appear before the Supreme Court in Tallahassee in a case meant to test "the validity or invalidity of the City of Tampa raising the city liquor license from $250 to $500," and Lunsford's partner, E. R. Dickenson, had secured an alternative writ of mandamus from Judge Wall, directing the County Commissioners to permit Robert Mugge to open his new Seminole Saloon at Twenty-Second Street and Seventh Avenue. "The case was made returnable to November 26, when it will be argued before Judge Wall."[481]

In the meantime, as the battle against higher license fees was being fought before the Supreme Court of Florida, the City continued to demand the increased fees which the saloon owners were currently refusing to pay. The *Morning Tribune* of December 1, 1906 reported that, inasmuch as City Attorney E. R. Gunby was "in the country enjoying a hunt," the cases of "saloonists" who had not paid their license fees would instead be heard on Wednesday. "There will be at least 30 defendants on that day, although the bulk of these will be represented by Robert Mugge, the Florida Brewing Co. and A. H. Rawlins."[482]

At this point, a delayed court appearance merely meant that Robert Mugge could continue with his building efforts, as described in one last article of 1906, this one appearing in the *Morning Tribune* on December 30: "The Mugge Block, corner Frances Avenue and Main Street, which partially burned last week, is to be remodeled and used as a one-story building."[483] For a moment, neither fires, nor legal judgements, nor any other opposing forces would hold him back for long.

Chapter Eighteen

Idea Man

1907 began with an announcement in the *Morning Tribune* of January 4 that the corporation started months before by Robert Mugge and others would, for now, focus on a single product: "W. A. Riddle has gone to Chicago to purchase machinery for a plant to be established in Tampa within the next few months for the manufacture of gas lamps." The article also noted that the business would be "incorporated and capitalized at $25,000," that Robert Mugge and J. J. Lunsford would be prominent among the stockholders, and that the plant would "be placed on some of Mr. Mugge's property in the downtown section."[484]

In his memoirs, Robert's son, August B. Mugge, provided more details: "In 1906, he became interested in the Sunlight Manufacturing Company. This company produced individually operated gas installations for small towns where there were no gas accommodations. He became a stockholder and created a two-story brick structure at the corner of Cass and Central Avenue, in which the machine shop was housed."[485]

Happily, the *Morning Tribune* issue of March 9, 1907 revealed positive news on the home front as well. According to a notice sent to the *Tribune* by a New York advertising agency, "Merchant Eugene George Mugge ... the son of manufacturer Robert Mugge and his wife [the former] Caroline Rautenstrauch," was to be wed to "Miss Wilhelmina Franziska Matilde Margarethe Petri ... of Giessen,

Hessen."[486] In his memoirs, Eugene's younger brother August would later explain that, although their father had been feuding with Eugene, Robert had finally relented and given the elder son permission to marry "Mimi" Petri, his German girlfriend. The wedding took place in the Catholic Church in the German city of Giessen, with August and his sister Frances in attendance. After what August described as a "wonderful reception," Eugene and Mimi visited with his two siblings in Darmstadt, then Eugene took Mimi back to New York.[487]

Eventually, the newly married couple arrived in Tampa, where they would settle, at least for a time. By contrast, Robert, having lost his position on the Board of Public Works, was anything but settled, wondering how to share his latest ideas for civic improvement. Fortunately, he still had the Tampa press as his soapbox.

In the March 10, 1907 edition of the *Morning Tribune*, editor Wallace F. Stovall kicked off a series of Robert's "thoughtful suggestions."[488] The first, offered as a letter to the editor, proposed the hiring of a topnotch landscape gardener who would plant all manner of fruit trees, as well as pecan trees, on city-owned land west of West Tenth Avenue. According to Robert, after perhaps a decade, income from the fruit and nuts produced would pay all expenses for looking after the city's parks, plus provide a profit of perhaps $15,000. In endorsing this plan, Wallace Stovall, now very much in Robert's corner again, wrote, "Matters concerning Tampa are of great interest to him, and he has shown much intelligence in his advice and criticism."[489]

Four weeks later, in the *Morning Tribune* of April 7, 1907, editor Stovall reiterated key points of Robert's recent letter proposing formation of a "Million Dollar Steamship Co." Robert contended that "vessels plying from Tampa to the various harbors would redound to the benefit of the cities thus connected, the intermediate territory, and the people concerned in the company." He further asserted that railroads would happily cooperate since now, "instead of bringing to the city full cars and returning with empty ones, the merchandise brought in by the vessels would find its way into the cars and would have this mode of departure from Tampa." To bring about this million-dollar steamship line, Robert proposed that the people of Tampa contribute $400,000, the people of New Orleans contribute another $400,000, and the people of South Florida towns contribute the final $200,000.[490]

Two months after that, the *Morning Tribune* of June 5, 1907 shared Robert's concern about a lack of cleanliness in cities throughout the South. In this case, Robert proposed that "The city should be divided into cleaning districts," and in each one should be a team made up of an overseer and a squad of workers. The team would move along district streets, cleaning adjoining lots and alleys, repairing fences and sidewalks, and giving all a "clean and tidy appearance." According to Robert, all occupants would be notified beforehand when their lots were to be cleaned, with such occupants expected to pay, quite modestly, for the work being done.[491]

Then, in another month, the *Morning Tribune* of July 13, 1907 shared Robert's solution for handling basic health care needs of the city; an idea perhaps prompted by his own repeated loss of family members. As he pointed out, "Naturally only the rich can afford the services of the professional nurse, and all the rest, when sick, depend on the family members and kind-hearted neighbors. As a result, frequently several members of the same family get sick, one after another, being overtaxed." To improve this situation, Robert suggested local physicians start a night school to train a corps of professionals, including some to specialize in midwifery. By his estimate, if women wishing to enter the field could spare a few hours per evening, those women who currently worked for $3.00 to $7.00 per week could soon "find steady employment from $10.00 to $25.00 and board."[492]

Certainly, local power centers were more receptive to some of Robert's ideas, and to some of his businesses, than they were to others. For instance, for a time, as indicated in the *Morning Tribune* of April 10, 1907, the Board of Trade, the Chamber of Commerce, and the Wholesale Grocer's Association all endorsed Robert's proposal for a million-dollar steamship company, and began pressuring city and county officials to explore the possibilities.[493] In fact, as noted in the *Tribune* three days later, this initial excitement led Robert and others to begin planning their next moves: "A pile driver is hard at work near the McKay docks building a new dock for R. Mugge. Bulk heading is going on on the Lykes property and a big dock will be built by the Hendry & Knight Co."[494]

Robert's spirits also must have been lifted by an article in the *Morning Tribune* of May 19, 1907 under the headline, "Mugge Wins Liquor License Fight With Commissioners." Once again, Robert and his attorneys, Lunsford and Dickenson, had prevailed through sheer determination, first by gathering a petition from a majority of voters in Precinct 28, and then by convincing Judge Wall to order the granting of a new permit. So ordered, the Board of County Commissioners approved the opening of Robert's new Seminole Saloon at Seventh Avenue and Twenty-Second Street, and with one or two ironic twists still to follow.[495]

Just three days after a petition from a majority of citizens had helped Robert win a liquor license in Precinct 28, the *Morning Tribune* of May 22, 1907 announced that such petitions would no longer be needed when requesting saloon licenses. In 1899, Robert had successfully pushed for a law which eliminated that need, but Judge Wall had declared the law unconstitutional, in that it supposedly granted County Commissioners the "same powers as a tribunal of justice." So, Robert had asked attorney J. J. Lunsford to sue on behalf of his clerk, John S. Hubbard (apparently the same Mugge employee called J. H. Hubbard in a previous story), regarding attempts to get a new license for Robert's Seminole Saloon. And after arguments from Mr. Lunsford, the State Supreme Court agreed to eliminate the petition requirement still again.

The act of 1899 required only that applicants advertise their intent to request a liquor license for a particular district; show that the district has, at some point, included such a business; and prove that the applicant is of "good character" and over the age of twenty-one. Of course, at the time of the original application from Robert, the most serious objection had been "that the site of the saloon for which permit was asked was located just outside city limits, thus being out of the jurisdiction of the police, but near enough to attract patronage from the city." However, the territory of Fort Brooke had since been added to the City of Tampa, thereby overcoming that argument as well. So, in this instance, Robert won from all directions.[496]

And yet, even with these victories, Robert Mugge did not let up on his separate campaign to have so-called blind tigers—unlicensed sellers of alcohol products—properly penalized by law. The *Morning Tribune* of June 2, 1907 noted a rare win in that area as well under the headline, "Selling 'Bitters' Alleged Violation of Revenue Law": "Charged with the sale of intoxicating liquors without license, E. Berger, as manager of the Tampa Drug Co., was before County Judge Robles for a preliminary hearing yesterday ... The case, it appears, arose from the alleged sale of malt whisky, a proprietary preparation, and certain 'bitters,' between the Tampa Drug Company and Robert Mugge. Judge Robles held Berger for trial in bond of $500."[497]

In addition, the *Morning Tribune* of August 10, 1907 showed that, as in previous years, Robert was going ahead with his usual application for multiple county liquor licenses: "Whereas, Robert Mugge has filed with the Board of County Commissioners for Hillsborough county, Florida, an application for permit to sell liquors, wines and beer in election districts, 1, 6, 14, 19, 20, 22, 25, 26, 27, 28, 29, 30, 31, 32, 33, of said county and state; any citizen of such election district may show cause, if any there be, at the meeting of the Board to be held on Tuesday, the 3rd day of September, 1907, next, why such permit should not be granted."[498] Of course, these filings did not indicate whether Robert owned more than one saloon in certain districts, or mention any that he owned outside of Hillsborough County.

At the same time Robert's beer, wine, and liquor businesses were expanding, other of his businesses were coming online as well. According to the *Morning Tribune* of June 20, 1907, at Central Avenue and Cass Street, "the site of his old distillery," Robert was almost finished constructing the large brick building that would house his new Sunlight Manufacturing Company.[499] In fact, six days later, *Tribune* editor Wallace F. Stovall appeared to be positively effusive regarding Robert's new company. First, he praised the construction of its modern new factory building, equipped with "the most up-to-date and serviceable machinery that this country produces," thereby permitting it "to do general machine shop business, both construction and repairing work." Second, he waxed eloquent about the company's prospects, and how those could affect the city as a whole: "At present the company is only manufacturing various extremely powerful gasoline lamps on which they have a number of patents, but they expect to branch out into the production of various metal goods, and every article that will be sent by this company to points all over the country will bear the stamp 'Tampa' on it, thus aiding to advertise this city throughout the country as a general manufacturing center and not merely the home of cigars, as is now the impression."[500]

Of course, every year included setbacks as well. For example, the *Morning Tribune* of November 1, 1907 noted that another of his businesses had been under attack. Early the previous morning, a fire had started at the corner of Arch Street and West Ninth Avenue, leading to $5,000 in damages. Included among the buildings destroyed was a two-story wooden structure owned by Robert Mugge with a saloon downstairs and a lodging house upstairs.[501]

But overall, the year ended on an upswing, with water balancing fire once again. The *Morning Tribune* of November 21, 1907 carried the following ad indicating increased business for Robert's waterfront property: "Steamship Morgan Plying Between Tampa, Mobile and New Orleans. Office, Warehouse and Wharf, Mugge's Dock."[502] This was bolstered by an ad in the *Morning Tribune* of December 6, 1907 showing that Robert continued to hire more full-time employees: "Wanted—Three girls to work in bottling shop, good pay, light work, steady the year round. Apply to R. Mugge, 305 Franklin street."[503] No doubt, some in the community were unhappy to see him hiring both female and minority workers. But Alice would have been pleased as, presumably, Caroline and their daughters were.

Chapter Nineteen
Arrested
Development

F ollowing on the panic of late 1907 which, itself, is thought to have been a response to the catastrophic San Francisco Earthquake, 1908 kicked off with a recession causing financial distress throughout the country.[504] Never one to sit idly by during times of emergency, Robert came up with a multileveled strategy for how Tampa could get through the current situation. With many working people believing he asked too much of them in order to get businesses functioning again, his proposal in the *Morning Tribune* of January 26, 1908 led to a lively debate, only a portion of which is documented here. Kicking things off, Robert acknowledged that everywhere he looked, people were using such terms as "Hard Times!" and "No Money," and asking "How long will this last?" He then asserted that Tampa's situation was somewhat different than that of the rest of the country, though still serious, and that if people of the city would follow certain plans of action, prosperity could be "re-established in sixty days."

Next, he identified what he saw as the biggest problem, which was that, during the past year, "an enormous lot of suburban property was laid out in lots and sold through skilled advertising at from a hundred to a thousand times the actual value on weekly or monthly installments." In short, unscrupulous trade practices had become widespread, leaving "deluded purchasers" scrambling to make their payments (not unlike the subprime mortgage crisis of exactly one hundred years later). One answer, he felt, was for "all lines of trade" to stop extending "over one week's credit" until the situation could be reversed. In addition, he recommended that laborers take "a uniform cut in wages of twenty-five per cent and re-establish a nine-hour day for one year." If businessmen would then make similar concessions, he believed Tampa would have its "biggest building boom" ever. He went on to contend that, unless such changes took place, the economy would remain at a standstill, and ended with a bromide that likely rang true for some: "Fifteen to twenty dollars a week beats loafing any day in the week."[505]

Two responses to this letter were printed in the *Morning Tribune* of February 4, 1908 and are excerpted here. The first was from A. J. Garrett: "Mr. Mugge wants the laboring man to reduce his wages in order that the speculator may realize a good income on his investments ... The generous (?) hearted Mr. Mugge does not mention that rent and the necessities of life be reduced so as to be in reach of the laboring man, but seems to think that a nine-hour day, and 25 per cent cut in the building mechanics' wages would be a panacea for all ills caused by the recent money stringency."[506]

The second was from J. I. Jenkins: "If he, R. Mugge, wants something done by reducing wages, first let Mr. Mugge reduce the prices on liquor and beer or reduce the rent on his property to his renters or donate a liberal sum to some of the charitable institutions first, then let him organize labor, come together and decide what is necessary to be done on their part."[507]

The last response, from R. F. Turman of Riverview, Florida, arrived more than a month later, as financial conditions continued to worsen, and was published in the *Morning Tribune* of March 6, 1908: "Only a few months ago we were reveling in prosperity the likes of which the country never saw. Railroads were unable to handle the traffic for lack of rolling stock and men to man their trains. Today idle cars and locomotives are numbered by the thousands. While a corresponding number of men are out of work and clamoring for the very means of existence. It would seem that Mr. Mugge is better read up on the subject than his critics. I think the sooner laboring men come to realize the true conditions the better it will be for all concerned."

Mr. Turman also noted that the situation for organized labor had worsened just since the publishing of Robert's letter. Apparently, three recent US Supreme Court decisions had left workers "at the mercy of employers," even to the point where, if job actions were taken against contractors engaging in interstate commerce, those companies could sue both unions and individual workers for three times their resulting losses. He then closed with the following admonition: "So now don't you think you would better be good and hurry up and accept Mr. Mugge's proposition, for he really wrote better than he knew, and that is a whole lot."[508]

Tough economic times meant fewer jobs for everyone, and therefore, the situation was likely even worse for women and minorities. However, one position was never in short supply, and that one, in terms of gender, was known for being "equal opportunity." The position was political rabble-rouser, and during the early part of the century, no one served that role more effectively than hatchet-wielding Carrie Nation (sometimes symbolically spelled "Carry A Nation"), widely known for bashing in the doors of decadent saloons. In early 1908, she came to Florida, making several well-publicized stops. The *St. Petersburg Times* of January 29, 1908 announced her arrival under the primary headline, "Carry Nation Still The Life Of The Town."

The previous Saturday night, Ms. Nation reportedly spent more than an hour confronting an audience filled with "men only," during which she ironically offered a "scathing denunciation of men, their manners, morals and methods." The presentation had earned her forty-two dollars towards the "establishment of a sexual purity farm at Cherokee, Okla.," raising the question of whether she was largely addressing men, not only because she saw them as the cause of the problems, but because they were better situated than women to help underwrite her operations.

The *Times* writer described her as "a matronly woman, small of stature with shrewd grey eyes which could twinkle, flash or blaze as the discussion warranted, dressed quietly in black with a white silk scarf knotted around the throat," and bearing no resemblance to her cartoon image as "irate female, bonnet askew and hatchet in hand." Yet, in their conversation at her hotel, she blasted what she considered to be the worst habits of men, one being tobacco, which she called "a terrible curse, worse than liquor." Of course, she saved her greatest ire for saloons, which she termed "breathing holes of hell," insisting that "St. Petersburg is too lovely a city to allow these plague spots to defile her streets and lure her young men to ruin."[509]

Four days later, the *Morning Tribune* greeted her arrival in Tampa with mention that her "Sex and Purity" lecture for men would be given at the Tampa Bay Casino at 3:00 that afternoon. Reportedly, Ms. Nation already had stopped by the *Tribune* office and extended a special invitation to saloon operators and their employees to attend her presentation. She went on to say, "I am going around to see all my friends, the saloonists, to talk with them and persuade them to give up the business. I have already been encouraged by receiving two 'communications' from one saloon, and I am going to call on that saloon at once, as the gentleman must be interested in my cause to write."

Considering Robert Mugge's delight in debating the merits of saloon culture, as he often had with prohibitionist preachers, it seems likely, though not certain, he would have been the "saloonist" inviting her for a chat.[510] And considering his ongoing concern with American liberty, it seems equally likely he would have advised her that, threatening to take away men's rights to drink beer or whiskey with friends was not the smartest way to convince the same men to extend women the vote, much less invite more of them into the workplace. Of course, by this point, the causes of suffrage and temperance had become closely intertwined, so there would have been little point.

Probably of less interest to Robert, except in terms of potential customers for his saloons, would have been the arrival of Confederate War Veterans later that same month. According to the *Morning Tribune* of February 19, 1908, their group was given "The Key to Tampa," including "free admission" to the South Florida Fair.[511] However, just ten days later, with scenes evoking the 1864 burning of Atlanta by Union troops under Major General William T. Sherman,[512] the *Sunday Tribune* described "The Most Disastrous Fire in Tampa's History," which utterly ravaged Ybor City.

Although the paper offered breathless descriptions of an urban inferno, it best captured the depth of the horror in a single sidebar: "Jose Gonzalez owned one of the prettiest coal-black horses in the city, and one of his first cares was for the animal. But the stable was afire, and when he reached the scene the beautiful animal was tearing madly down the street, a mass of flames and screaming with the pain of his cremation."[513]

As always, the *Morning Tribune* did not publish on Monday. But that allowed its staff to assemble all the gruesome statistics for their "Fire Extra" on Tuesday, March 3, 1908. As they reported, the fire had raged for four and a half hours, beginning at a boarding house owned by Antonio Diaz, and ending at Robert Mugge's saloon at "Twentieth Street and Fourteenth Avenue." In all, it had burned through fifty-five acres, constituting eighteen-and-a-half city blocks, with 308 buildings destroyed, among them five cigar factories, fifteen restaurants, six saloons, fifteen boarding houses, twenty stores, and 240 private homes. The estimated cost of all damage was $1 million, with only half of that amount covered by insurance. While on the more personal side, 2,500 were now homeless, and 1,000 were out of work.

Incredibly, the same issue which Robert Mugge had taken all the way to the Florida Supreme Court, and which would soon be argued a second time in Circuit Court, was moving to the forefront still again. In an interview, Mayor Frecker said he would sue the Water Works Company, believing as he did "that the lack of water supply for the fire caused a more serious loss than would have resulted had the pressure been all that it should have been." However, Superintendent C. R. McFarland, who had responsibility for such matters, claimed "that everything possible was done to make the pressure in Ybor City as strong as possible, but that it was a physical impossibility to put on top pressure on all of the hydrants that were being used."[514]

The latest water pressure debate played out in two more issues of the *Morning Tribune*. First, the issue of March 7, 1908 revealed that the City Council had adopted one resolution to stop paying the Tampa Water Works Company for hydrant rental, and another to consider revoking its franchise.[515] Second, the issue of March 12, 1908 quoted a six-page report submitted by Fire Chief Tucker Savage in which he declared that, "had water pressure been what the contract with the city calls for ... the fire could have been contained to the building in which it originated."[516]

Although not reported by the *Morning Tribune*, on March 13, 1908, Eugene's wife Mimi gave birth to their first child, whom they named Margarete Wilhelmine Eugenia Mugge.[517] However, on April 5, 1908, the Tribune carried less happy news concerning Herman Rautenstrauch, the visiting German nephew of Robert and Caroline, and the younger son of Caroline's brother George. Reportedly, Herman had been riding a bicycle north on Franklin Street when he fell while trying to avoid an automobile. At the time, he was on his way to the First National Bank, intending to make a deposit for his uncle, when he and the car crossed paths, and he fell beneath it. "Neither of the wheels of the auto struck the boy, but the gearing underneath the car caught in his clothing and dragged him several feet."

Mrs. Fielding, who was driving, stopped as quickly as possible, and several men pulled Herman out from under the car. He was then taken to the home of his aunt and uncle, with minor injuries of the head and left elbow treated by Dr. Oppenheimer. At the time of the accident, the contents of his uncle's bag had been scattered over a wide area. But that, too, was gathered up, with only six dollars missing from the original total. "At a late hour last night, the young man was resting quietly."[518]

Already weakened by the current recession, Hillsborough County liquor dealers now faced a looming collision of their own. Local prohibitionist attorney Donald C. McMullen was running for state senator on a platform of pushing for a "local option vote" for Hillsborough County, which could ban alcohol sales entirely in Tampa and the surrounding region. In addition, a key issue in the current gubernatorial race was whether Florida should embrace prohibition at the state level. Fortunately, many of Tampa's business and political leaders came out strongly against such possibilities at either the state or county level, warning that many industries attracted to the region would flee if their workers' personal lives were thus restricted. Wallace F. Stovall supported these beliefs in a series of editorials, including one in the *Morning Tribune* of April 28, 1908, which not only warned of how the local economy could be further decimated, but even spoke of the effects on the saloon industry itself. As he pointed out, each saloon employed an average of five persons, and multiplied times eighty saloons in the city alone, that meant "four hundred human beings, many of them with families dependent upon them, would be left without the means of earning a livelihood were their present occupation taken away from them."[519]

Prospects were bleak enough for a time that Robert and the other saloon owners he represented publicly sided with local government on the issue of banning Sunday sales of alcohol. The *Morning Tribune* of May 28, 1908 disclosed as much by quoting from their recently signed resolution: "Be it resolved by the undersigned that we will do everything in our power to see that not only our places of business are closed, but that the other saloons of the city are closed, and that we shall lend our assistance to the proper authorities, whenever necessary, for the detection of those who violate the law."[520] The resolution was signed by Robert Mugge and eighteen other sellers, then reaffirmed by Robert four weeks later in the *Morning Tribune* of June 24, 1908. On that occasion, he added that, "Sixty-five per cent of the Tampa saloonkeepers are virtually bankrupt, in consequence of the outrageous high license and unfair competition, inasmuch as perhaps fifty or more concerns dispense liquors, wines and beer on Sunday without ever paying any license except U. S. revenue of $25.00 a year, yet for all that the saloonkeepers are a unit on the Sunday closing proposition so far as they are concerned."[521]

Perhaps because Robert and his peers in the saloon business continued to feel put upon by authorities, he sometimes also came to the aid of others he felt were being unfairly targeted. Such a case was evident in a *Morning Tribune* story of July 4, 1908, in which ten men, some of them older, and most or all of them of Latin American descent, were arrested for shooting craps. The paper reported that, "Bonds were furnished for each of the ten by Robert Mugge."[522] Of course, Latinos were not the only ones whose rights were under attack, whether on Independence Day or any other."

The war on Tampa's minorities took another turn in 1908, going from mob-driven threats and nighttime attacks to the shameless, highly visible suppression of Constitutionally guaranteed voting rights. Despite an 1885 Florida Constitution that offered the legislative option of a poll tax and other provisions to keep Black men from voting (as well as mandating segregated schools and prohibiting interracial marriage),[523] by the early years of the new century, African Americans in Tampa were increasingly well organized, were running successful businesses, and were trading their votes for promises to help their community. In the process, their support was becoming decisive in some city elections, leaving many white power brokers alarmed. How the latter responded was explained in the *Morning Tribune* of July 24, 1908, under the straightforward headlines, "Party Formed To Have White Voices—Purpose Is To Eliminate Negroes From Politics."

The night before, the first public mass meeting had been called of the White Municipal Party, the city's newest and most exclusive organization, with 100 of its 350 official members attending. Following up on their slogan, "A White Political Tampa," they drew up a resolution expressing the need to "remove the negro from balance of power in the city elections" and provide for "a white primary election" to be held "at least thirty days before a municipal election. The rising vote taken on these resolutions brought all those present, save three, to their feet. The three did not vote." (Note: Perhaps the three not voting were Tampa citizens with a conscience, or perhaps they were visitors from other Florida cities, simply getting tips on how to disenfranchise their own minority populations.)

To help attendees understand the steps they would need to take to stay within the law while "barring the negro as a factor from the city elections," attorney J. J. Lunsford read the section of the city statutes which permitted any party "to hold a city primary just as county and state primaries are held." It also was explained by party leaders that members of all other parties—Republicans, Democrats, Socialists, etc.—were eligible for membership in this new party, "provided only they are white."[524]

Wishing to better enlighten the *Morning Tribune* of the new party's intentions, Mitchell F. McKay, clerk of the Criminal Court and brother of Donald B. McKay, *Tampa Times* editor and future long-time mayor of the city, sent a follow-up letter to the editor which was printed on August 4, 1908. In it, McKay argued that, in the recent mayoral election between William H. Frecker and Francis Lyman Wing, "both sides made a strong play for the negro vote and it is hard to tell which side received the larger part of it." Yet McKay suggested that it was demeaning for white politicians to have to make deals with people of color to secure their votes: "We do not mix with the negro in his social affairs between elections, and to do so for merce-nary purposes is disgusting and degrading." Therefore, the White Municipal Party would hold white-only primaries to determine all future winners of elections without the participation of African American voters.[525] In other words, members of various political parties would choose among the candidates standing for office in the so-called white primary, would determine the most popular, and then, in the later municipal election, would vote together for the previously selected winners, ensuring that any votes belatedly cast by Black citizens would be rendered meaningless.

No evidence exists that Robert Mugge had anything to do with this party or ever supported its candidates. However, as previously mentioned, Robert's longtime attorney, J. J. Lunsford, did play a role, and although it may be coincidental, once their collaboration on the Water Works suit was finished, Robert did not employ him again. As to *Tribune* editor Wallace F. Stovall, in print, he remained noncom-mittal about the party and its hateful agenda, simply reporting on its activities, the same as he did for other political organizations.

Robert, of course, continued to enjoy exhaustive coverage by local press. But there were times when even he wished for less atten-tion. For example, the *Morning Tribune* of August 13, 1908 reported that Robert and other liquor wholesalers of the area had been before city officials, once again requesting reductions in the steep license fees they paid. "Seven members of the city council [one of whom was Herman Regener, son-in-law of Robert Mugge] assembled at the office of Mayor Wing yesterday afternoon, pursuant to a call for a special session, to listen to a petition from the liquor dealers of the city relative to the lowering of the whiskey license." In the process, Robert also requested a clearing of press from the room, making what must have been a tongue-in-cheek reference to their influence on the citizenry: "Before anything was done Robert Mugge, who recently filed a petition with the board of county commissioners for permission to operate saloons in twenty or more places in Tampa, said that he did not think it wise to allow newspaper men to attend the meeting. He explained that as one-fifth of the population of Tampa only are of sufficient intelligence to read the newspapers, and as this one-fifth is always a disturbing element, he saw no reason why the proceedings should be given to the public as it would only cause trouble."[526]

In the *Morning Tribune* of August 15, 1908, editor Wallace F. Stovall responded with humor of his own to Robert's comments about newspaper readers under the headline, "A Disturbing Element." In his piece, Stovall divulged that, on the same day Robert had made the remark, someone from Robert's household had phoned the *Tribune* to complain of inconsistent delivery. He went on to write, "Mr. Mugge certainly does not consider himself a 'disturbing element,' but rather, judging from his frequent contributions to the local press, as one of the pillars of our commercial strength and most valiant defenders against the forces of evil which from time to time assail us. There are degrees of disturbance, and Mr. Mugge's idea of a 'disturbing element' is probably that awakening of public sentiment which is at times prone to curb his peculiar private interests."[527]

Naturally, most news concerning Robert Mugge still focused on his saloon business, and the next few *Morning Tribune* stories were no exception. One on October 13, 1908 announced that Eugene Mugge, Robert's elder son, was also entering the saloon business. Since Eugene had previously managed Robert's three-story hotel on Howard Avenue in West Tampa, both the hotel and the saloon were likely Robert's way of establishing his son in business. According to the piece, "Eugene Mugge, a well known young business man and son of R. Mugge, now owns the Central saloon at Seventh avenue and Fourteenth Street, so long conducted by Villamil. The deal was consummated several days ago and Mr. Mugge yesterday took full possession."[528]

Then, a month later, Robert wrote a letter to the editor in which he shared Wallace Stovall's concern with the increasing number of saloons in the city. Of course, in Robert's case, the bigger concern was decreasing revenue for current owners and managers due to increased competition, but each man found his own way to the same compelling goal. According to Robert, "Efforts have been made by liquor dealers repeatedly to have a law enacted prohibiting more saloons than one to every thousand people, and that when one remains closed over twenty-four hours to declare it vacant. They were unsuccessful, because the city needs the $50,000 revenue paid as license."

But Robert went even further, accusing city officials of being predatory and corrupt: "It is somewhat strange ... that the Council is so timid in abolishing negro clubs, owned and conducted by professional gambler-politicians. The ordinance Mr. Turner intro-duced at last meeting in reference to clubs was entirely my work; he had nothing to do with it further than introducing it. In these clubs even minors are served with strong drink and are permitted to gamble. They are kept open all night and Sundays and are beyond the control of the police ... and but for the fact that the owners are politicians, they would not be tolerated one minute." He concluded by beseeching members of Council to "muster courage for once and drive these dives out of business."[529]

In the same issue, editor Wallace F. Stovall added the following comments to Robert's own: "St. Petersburg is deeply agitated over the proposed opening of its third saloon. Tampa has been having a bit of a row over the opening of its eighty-first ... Robert Mugge, in a signed communication on this page, endorses the stand taken by the *Tribune* yesterday with reference to the indiscriminate placing of saloons. Mr. Mugge is a wise man in his day and generation and he sees just where this sort of thing is leading."[530]

Chapter Twenty
Crusaders at the Gates

B y the start of 1909, the American economy was stabilizing again, and Robert felt good about his own prospects as well. However, in more personal terms, the year could not have begun worse. On January 4, Eugene Mugge and his wife Mimi lost their ten-month-old daughter, Margarete Wilhelmine Eugenia Mugge. According to the *Morning Tribune* of the following day, the child "died yesterday morning at the family home, Sixth avenue between Marion and Morgan streets."[531] [532] Not surprisingly, this brought the couple crippling distress, and probably was the reason Eugene, or more likely his father, sold the business they had purchased only four months before. The *Morning Tribune* of January 14 made the following announcement under the headline, "Saloon Changes Hands": "Charles Gerken has purchased the Seventh avenue cafe, Seventh avenue and Fourteenth street, and has taken charge of it. This was conducted formerly by Eugene Mugge."[533]

Newspapers of earlier eras, such as those under study here, focused largely on the activities of men in the public sphere, with little consideration of women who were functioning primarily at home. The world of women and children was not thought worthy of public discussion, except in terms of social events, scandals, or personal tragedies, as in the loss of Robert's first wife, four of his children, and now one of his grandchildren. However, thanks to Robert's stature in the community, even modest family gatherings were sometimes recorded, providing the briefest of glimpses beyond his multifaceted workplace. Such was the case with the *Morning Tribune* of Thursday, June 17, 1909:

> Mrs. Robert Mugge [Caroline] was agreeably surprised on the occasion of her birthday, and also Mrs. Bertha Berger [Robert's sister], whose birthday is Friday. Mrs. Mugge and children and grand-children had just left the house intending to attend the matinee at the Iris, when they were suddenly and pleasantly surrounded by a number of friends, who made themselves at home and a comfortable and pleasant afternoon was spent. Refreshments and cake were served and many good wishes were expressed. Mrs. Mugge was presented with a beautiful drawn-work scarf.[534]

As no one knew better than Robert, his wholesale and retail liquor businesses had given his family that comfortable life. But now, everywhere he looked, businesses like his were under attack. For instance, Memphis, Tennessee had just become "the largest city in the world where prohibition prevails," and the saloon industry there was in nearly full denial. According to the *Morning Tribune* of July 5, 1909, for now, most saloons were still open, and even the bar in the venerable Peabody Hotel was still selling beer, whiskey, and mixed drinks, causing police to "seize a bottle of whiskey and one of beer to be used as evidence." Signs at other uptown bars claimed only soft drinks or "near-beer" were being sold, but customers known to bartenders "were not allowed to go away thirsty."[535]

Then, only six days later, the *Morning Tribune* reported (via *Associated Press*) that prohibition had struck an entire Southern state. At midnight the day before, more than a thousand Texas saloons had ceased operating due to a new state law regulating the sale of liquor. The law limited the number of saloons in each county to one for every 500 people and barred the issue of new licenses except for those run "in conjunction with a hotel." Certainly, with even the legacy of Western watering holes endangered, the days of public drinking appeared to be numbered. In Texas and elsewhere, every saloon now felt like a modern-day Alamo.[536]

Still, despite city, county, and state dominoes falling to temperance forces, Robert found the time to write a book, which he self-published in 1909. It was titled *Practical Humanity: A Suggestion for the Destruction of Poverty the Curbing of Cupidity and the Lessening of Crime* and was much like one of his complex letters-to-the-editor yet extended to book length. In fact, *Practical Humanity* was nothing less than an attempt to combine American history and values, national and international politics, an unfortunate prejudice or two picked up in Robert's adopted country, his own experiences battling prohibition forces, and some fascinating utopian prescriptions for how American society could be completely restructured through a merging of capitalist and socialist ideas. One section was especially enlightening in terms of his business philosophy, and of the increasing pressures under which his alcohol-related companies had to function. That section was titled "The Liquor Question," and it opened as follows:

> Right here it becomes necessary to say something on the question of allowing or not allowing beer, wine and liquors within the colonies [his nostalgic name for the new American society he envisioned], for there is no doubt whatever, should the government think proper to establish them, a cry will be raised by the fanatics to keep them out ...
>
> It will not be possible in this little work to go into everything that is said for and against prohibition, so I will deal with the subject in a broad and general way, presenting some self-evident facts that any intelligent man or woman can observe with but very slight effort on his part. As far back as we can go in history, taking also the history of the Bible,

we find that intoxicating liquors in some shape or form were used by all civilized nations and by most peoples and tribes who were not civilized.

Certain religions came in from time to time, some of which, like the Mohammedan [Muslim] forbade their use, and others like the Christian, not only allowing the use of wines and strong drink but in some cases advising it. Looking at the world then, as we see it today, I ask the questions, "What nations are ahead?" "What are the most civilized?" "What have made the most rapid advances in the arts and sciences?" "What are the most moral and free from vices?" "Are they the nations who have used intoxicants from as far back as we can learn, or are they the Turks whose religion will not allow their use?" According to the rule of the prohibitionist, the total abstaining nations ought to be far in the lead, but is it so? On the contrary, is it not true, that where liquors and wines were forbidden, dangerous drugs took their place ... Better a hundred fold the licensed sale of beer and liquors, than a nation of dope-fiends ...[537]

For all of Robert's time, effort, and expense in writing and publishing a book that few of his contemporaries would read, the project afforded him another means of expressing himself, and perhaps a distraction from periodic challenges to his integrity. So, all in all, it was a good investment, not unlike the way he stood by his son Eugene, even when the two of them were at odds.

On July 7, 1909, the *Morning Tribune* posted some welcome news for the Mugge family, helping a bit to dispel the pain with which the year had started: "Born, to Mr. and Mrs. Eugene G. Mugge, of 1501 Morgan street, a 12-pound girl baby. The young father is a happy man, and mother and child are doing well."[538]

To everyone's relief, new baby Marie was healthy. Yet her parents, Eugene and Mimi, continued to grieve their recent loss. Robert found ways to support them both, as was revealed in the *Morning Tribune* of September 2, 1909:

Eugene Mugge, one of the best known young men of the city, left Tuesday morning for Chicago, where he will hereafter make his headquarters. Mr. Mugge has secured the position of traveling representative throughout the north and west for one of the largest cigar manufacturing firms in this city, in which his father, R. Mugge, has secured an interest. Mr. Mugge is a clever and capable gentleman and cannot fail to make good. Mrs. Mugge will not join him at present, but will shortly leave to spend a year in her old home in Germany.[539]

Presumably, Robert invested in this new firm largely to give Eugene another chance to succeed, while also enabling Mimi to visit with her much-missed family. Still, for Robert, that meant a further dispersing of his own family once again, and a sad reminder he had not seen his daughter Frances in the six years since she left for Darmstadt. In his memoirs, Robert's son August, away just as long, reported that, in 1909, his father "expressed the wish" that Frances return home. Hulda Kreher, a young friend of the family, happened to be visiting Germany that summer. So, the family contacted her, and she agreed to accompany Frances back to Tampa.

The plan was for August and Frances to meet Ms. Kreher in Hamburg after a visit to the home of Eugene Ohme, a relative of the Ohme family in Tampa. But while there, "Frances slipped on the polished living room floor and sprained her foot." At a nearby hospital, they were told to apply cold compresses, which they did. Then, the next morning, August and Frances met Ms. Kreher at the local train station, and all three took a train to Cuxhaven, where Frances and her friend "boarded a steamer of the Hamburg-American line." The ship made it safely to New York, with the *Morning Tribune* of November 2, 1909 announcing the young women's arrival in Tampa the day before, together with another of Frances's friends, Hattie B. Moffatt, whose presence on the trip August apparently had forgotten. As for August himself, he returned to Darmstadt, of course, now completely on his own.[540] [541]

The year ended with *Morning Tribune* articles of December 20 and 29 setting the stage for a big finale of Robert Mugge's longtime legal action against the Tampa Water Works Company. The first reminded readers how the case had progressed to this point:

> After an intermittent delay of fight and rest for four years the trial for Robert Mugge and the one for [pawn broker] Jacob Gordon are likely to come to trial during the present term of the circuit court. Messrs. Mugge and Gordon are suing the Tampa Waterworks Company for damages for failure to furnish enough water to extinguish the fire at the Armory building, Franklin and Cass streets, May 23, 1905, and which fire spread to the building occupied by Mr. Gordon.

The piece also advised that the Mugge case had been to the State Supreme Court, which ruled that a water works company could be held liable for damages when not providing proper fire protection. Then, for the first of many times, it noted that the verdict here would set precedent for the suits filed after the more recent, and more costly, Ybor City fire.[542]

Nine days later, the *Tribune* repeated the basic facts, named the *eleven* competing attorneys, and monitored jury selection, which was the only task completed before a holiday recess. Finally, after the break for New Year's, the city, state, and Robert Mugge most of all, prepared for the battle of a lifetime.[543]

Chapter Twenty-One
Burden of Proof

A decade into the new century, Tampa was now trying to prove it had advanced far enough out of the primordial sand, pioneer brutality, and Confederate insurrection to be considered part of the civilized world. In many respects, the entire country was trying to prove the same. Among the waiting challenges were the following:

(1) Could the Constitutionally guaranteed rights of the individual be preserved under an expanding state that, increasingly, wanted to control all aspects of American life, often at the behest of politically connected corporations and interest groups?

(2) Could the rights of workers be preserved in a time of concentrated and monopolistic wealth and power?

(3) Could the rights of minorities and women be preserved and extended under a constitution written by, and for, Caucasian men of European descent?

(4) Could government and law enforcement become sufficiently free of corruption to ensure relative safety, security, and fairness for all citizens?

As of the start of 1910, the jury was very much out. But at least a court case was beginning which could answer some of these questions, though perhaps not the biggest one of all, which was: What did citizens mean when they asked for a "moral city?"

The case of Robert Mugge vs. the Tampa Water Works Company was covered in the *Morning Tribunes* of January 2, 4, 5, 6, 7, 8, 9, 11, 12, 14, and 15, 1910. Naturally, the proceedings began with witnesses testifying as to the poor pressure provided by city water hydrants, and how that led to streams of water so weak that firefighter hoses could not reach the second floor of the burning Armory Building. Also established were facts that the fire was started by an exploding gas lamp, and that the building contained a large cache of weapons and ammunition, property of the Tampa Light Infantry, which erupted midway through the fire. One amusing story involved the owner of the Central Pharmacy, located opposite the Armory Building, who refused to leave his building until he had finished his breakfast, "whether my store burned or not."[544]

The second day of the trial was taken up with contractor B. H. Davidson and owner Robert Mugge discussing construction of the Armory Building and its dollar value before and after the fire. Also of interest was the city engineer's declaration that "the water main at the corner of Franklin and Cass is three feet under ground," clearly making the water travel three additional feet upwards before reaching a burning building.[545]

By the third day of the trial, boredom experienced by the *Tribune* writer was palpable, after he complained of having "water on the brain." Still, energetic debate followed the plaintiff's contention that, "under the contract, the water works company was in duty bound to maintain a certain static pressure." Attorney S. M. Sparkman replied, "If there was a fire and all spigots in the city should be turned on, it would be impossible for the city to maintain the pressure." Therefore, he continued, the company's one obligation was to maintain a "certain pressure at the time of the fire." In response, Attorney M. B. Macfarlane offered a sarcastic twist of his own: "Then one squirt is all that is necessary to relieve the company from any liability."[546]

On the fourth day, the plaintiff closed out its testimony with five additional witnesses, after which attorneys for the Water Works Company asked that the jury render a verdict of "no cause for action," claiming that Mugge's side had failed to prove liability.[547] That request was answered on Day Five, as Judge John P. Wall denied the motion of the previous day, stating his opinion that evidence showed the Fire Department had offered efficient service, so it would be up to the jury "to determine whether or not the water works company had supplied a sufficient quantity of water." After that, witnesses for the water works company testified that, at the site of the fire, "forty pounds of pressure had been available to the firefighters, and that the pumping station was working at "fifty revolutions per minute," both of which purportedly proved the company was meeting its responsibilities.[548]

Coverage of Day Six began with the statement, "Hammer and tongs is the manner in which the defense went at it in the Mugge $25,000 damage suit against the Tampa Waterworks company yesterday." The highlight of an otherwise "tedious and uninteresting day" revolved around testimony by Fire Chief A. J. Harris that, when arriving at the scene of the fire, he had first entered Robert Mugge's Armory Saloon. After that statement was made, Attorney M. B. Macfarlane pointed out that, in recent depositions made in the law office of Glen and Himes, as well as in the office of Judge John P. Wall, Chief Harris had said he first entered the Beehive store. When faced with the discrepancy, Chief Harris replied that he simply could not remember.[549]

On the seventh day of the trial, the water works company continued "piling up evidence" that the water supply had been "ample" during the Armory fire. That was followed by Tampa Water Works Superintendent C. R. McFarland claiming he had "tested the water gauge at the pumping station three months after the fire and found it not adjusted right." After readjusting it, he estimated the company supplied sixty-six pounds of pressure when the fire broke out, and sixty-three pounds at the finish, with a five-foot drop in the water at the tower.[550] Then, on Day Eight, Mr. McFarland went on to testify that, on the day of the fire, the "normal supply of 5,000,000 gallons" of water had been available, with an average water pressure of "sixty-four pounds."[551]

The highlight of Day Nine was the testimony of J. D. Walker from West Tampa, who said he had asked Chief Harris "why he had not put out the fire in the Armory building before it had reached the Gordon building." According to Walker, Chief Harris had replied, "he could not get water enough."[552] However, with that issue still unresolved, the final hour of Day Nine began a "six-and-a-half-hour" summation by Attorney Peter O. Knight, whose oratory on behalf of the Water Works Company went five and a half hours more on Day Ten, interrupted only by a two-hour break for lunch. Thus, by the estimation of the *Tribune* reporter, who calculated that Knight, a fast talker, had spoken an average of 108 words per minute for, arguably, 375 minutes, "he spoke about 67,500 words in his masterly presentation of the case to the jury." And it was that "logical and painstaking resume of evidence" which extended the trial by one extra day.[553]

On the eleventh and final day of the trial, Judge Wall addressed the jury, telling them, on the one hand, that they "should not consider for one moment whether the plaintiff in this case is engaged in the liquor business," or on the other hand, "take into consideration that the defendant is a corporation," because the liquor business was a "legitimate" one, and corporations had "the same rights as individuals." He told them further that, if they believed the defendant had "failed to furnish water as called for by its contract with the city," and that that had led to the destruction of the plaintiff's property, they should find for the plaintiff. But if, to the contrary, they believed that the company had complied with its contract, or that failing to do so was not a factor in the destruction of the plaintiff's property, they should find for the defendant.

Once the judge's instructions were complete, the jury retired to consider the evidence. Only two hours later, the jury returned, offering a verdict for the plaintiff "for $11,500 and interest at the rate of 8 per cent from the time of the commencement of the suit, which brings the total amount of the verdict close to $16,000," with court costs expected to drive the amount still higher.[554]

After Robert Mugge's big victory in court—still not the final word, since the Water Works Company would now appeal this latest decision to the State Supreme Court—he had the pleasure of welcoming his son Eugene back to Tampa, though under curious circumstances. According to the *Morning Tribune* issues of January 26 and May 18, 1910, Eugene had returned from three months in Chicago, where he had been "connected with a jewelry firm" called Loftis Brothers. Reportedly, Eugene would now travel all over Florida on behalf of that firm, while making Tampa his headquarters.[555] [556]

Since Eugene had moved to Chicago only four months before, accepting a tobacco company position arranged by his father, such a rapid reappearance must have baffled his family, especially considering his many previous career changes. But whatever Eugene's reasons, the prodigal son had indeed returned, and according to the US Census of 1910, he was once again living with his father and mother, presumably along with his wife Mimi and daughter Marie.

As for Robert, by now, the varied parts of his life had grown increasingly routine. Naturally, on the personal side, he continued to support his family. For instance, the *Morning Tribune* of May 5, 1910 announced that Caroline and her younger children would shortly leave on a six-month trip to Germany, during which they would visit with relatives and friends, including Robert and Caroline's son August, who had now been away for seven years.[557] As August mentioned in his memoirs, the trip also permitted his mother and sisters to accompany Eugene's wife Mimi and daughter Marie as they made their way to an extended visit with Mimi's family in the German city of Giessen.[558]

Meanwhile, on the business side, government harassment was even worse than routine. As a case in point, the *Morning Tribune* of Sunday, May 22, 1910 reported that, on Friday afternoon, US Department of Revenue officers had seized four bottles of seventy-proof whiskey which were on sale at Robert's Panama Restaurant/Saloon (1324-26 Franklin Street), the issue being that the seventy-proof bottles bore a government stamp declaring them to be 100 proof. Officers had also seized three barrels of whiskey, alleging that, as the bottles were emptied, Robert's employees had refilled them from the barrels, selling them again without stamp or brand, and thereby violating federal law.[559]

Finally, ever present was Robert's industrial cycle of life, wherein older projects were pushed aside, and newer ones took their place. As the latest example, an ad in the *Morning Tribune* of May 26, 1910 requested bids for tearing down the Mugge ice plant building on Central Avenue, so as to make room for his Sunlight Manufacturing Company.[560] Yet, for someone who had started more businesses—and in the process, overseen more construction—than probably anyone in the state, and had done so based on his own ideas and his own labor, merely reconditioning a building would offer little challenge, and little inspiration. No, for Robert Mugge to feel alive again, what was needed was a whole new direction.

The first sign that Robert wanted a break from all that routine— wanted to top off his illustrious career with something truly astounding (a white whale of ambition, if you will)—came in the *Morning Tribune* of July 14, 1910: "Automobiles To Be Built Here— Tampa's Biggest Building To Be Their Home." Seemingly out of nowhere, Robert reportedly would erect "the greatest building ever constructed" in Tampa, and in so doing, would become "Florida's pioneer automobile manufacturer."

The plan was to build a "brick block eighty feet wide and 250 feet deep, with concrete floors, and as nearly fireproof as possible." It would stretch from Central Avenue to Tampa Street, "covering Tyler Street entirely," and would include space formerly occupied by his ice factory. At each end would be a large opening permitting cars and other vehicles to enter and exit. As to expense, construction of the building would cost $50,000, but then he would spend another $100,000 to $150,000 to fill it with machinery sufficient to build and repair automobiles. This would be supplemented by $40,000 in tools he already owned in conjunction with his Sunlight Manufacturing Company, and that business, too, would be housed in a portion of the building.

Asked to comment, Robert declared that automobiles were "in the land to stay," and since they were, they should be manufactured in Tampa. That way, money spent to purchase them would stay in the city as well. And with that goal in mind, he had ordered one million bricks from the Tampa Brick Co.[561]

Undeniably, as was always the case with Robert Mugge, his proposal was audacious, transcendent, and brilliantly detailed. And no doubt, it took the city by storm. And yet, just as storms eventually pass, so, too, did Robert's big idea. After that one walloping article, in which he shared his exciting plans, there was never another mention.

Had it all been a monstrous hallucination? A joke at the public's expense? A passing fancy of the most imposing sort? Most likely, it had merely been a trial balloon: a proposition meant to flush out finance. But maybe investors never stepped forward. Or maybe his own excitement flagged as he thought how such a massive project would dominate his life, while also bringing a level of risk beyond any he had yet known. Maybe, by the light of day, he simply set it aside, just as he had prior projects that were equally well designed, but beyond his means to carry out at the time.

The obvious truth was that, deep down, Robert Mugge was an idea man. Just as, decades later, Alfred Hitchcock would find more enjoyment in planning out classic suspense films than in directing them,[562] Robert, too, was an artist at heart—one who adored dreaming big dreams, and working out fixes for the most staggering problems, but who did not have the time or the means to carry forth all he could envision. So, no doubt reluctantly, he let the factory go. Yet, this would not be his last big idea, nor the last fully realized effort that could yet come to define him. Yes, even more than being the saloon magnate of Tampa. And on the practical side, there was the question of what to do with all those bricks he had ordered.

Then, as today, the world never stopped changing, and to the extent possible, Robert remained at the cutting edge. That was true of big things, like automobile factories, but also of smaller ones that most people took for granted. For instance, the *Morning Tribune* of August 11, 1910 carried Robert's ad regarding innovation in the area of beer packaging and distribution. The subject was crown caps, which were invented by William Painter in 1892, and which later became known simply as bottle caps.[563]

The ad expressed Anheuser-Busch's longstanding belief that "beer sealed with corks was superior to that sealed with crown caps," but also conceded that five years of testing had proven both kinds of top were equally effective. The implicit message? Ready or not, change was on the way![564] And that was true in Tampa as well, where, very soon, an entire city would blow its top.

Chapter Twenty-Two

The Public Good

As one of the city's two major newspapers, Tampa's *Morning Tribune* could not avoid covering the lively, multi-union parade commencing her latest cigar makers' strike. And truthfully, *Tribune* coverage of August 12, 1910 seemed measured and respectful. Yet, just below the surface was an obvious wariness regarding the ethnic nature of both the event and the job action to come. A cigar makers' strike in Tampa? What could go wrong, especially when it started so upbeat?

The parade was made up of 2,500 allied craftsmen, tradesmen, and workmen showing support for cigar makers in their disputes with the Cigar Manufacturers Association. It had moved through the streets of Ybor City with strong encouragement from the Spanish, Cuban, and Italian families of striking cigar workers, until stopping for the delivery of passionate speeches in multiple languages. Jose de la Campa, president of the Joint Advisory Board, presided, introducing assorted speakers, and speaking himself about the difficulty of gaining union recognition and about the poor treatment he said had been inflicted upon the workers. He then went on to assure anyone listening that theirs was a peaceful movement, and that recognition would usher in a new era of mutual respect and tranquility.[565]

The goal of a peaceful strike lasted only a month. Tensions were already starting to build because of the length of time with no progress. But then, as reported by the *Morning Tribune* of September 15, 1910, someone allegedly in a crowd of striking Cuban and Italian workers shot a bookkeeper named J. F. Easterling in the back as he was entering the idle Bustillo Bros. & Diaz cigar factory. The shooting, whether carried out by a provocateur favoring the strikers or one planted by the manufacturers, turned a tinderbox into a full-blown explosion, and the press, including *Tribune* editor Wallace F. Stovall, returned to its usual role of fanning the flames, with the formerly implicit concerns about ethnic violence now dominating its coverage. According to Stovall, the shooting of Mr. Easterling meant that a "lawless element, now attempting to intimidate a peaceful citizenry" would "spare no effort to attain their desired end.[566]

After such provocation, a traditional Southern mob was quick to respond, with typically little pushback from law enforcement. Moreover, the attackers were given all the publicity they could have wished, as in the *Morning Tribune* of September 21, 1910. The story was that two Italians, Angelo Albano and Castenge Ficarrotta, had simply been picked up for questioning about the shooting. But when a deputy sheriff, aided by an off-duty fire captain, attempted to transport them at night to the county jail, a mob forcibly grabbed them, drove them a short distance, then lynched them just three and a half miles from the county courthouse.[567]

The aftermath was predictable, with the ritual bloodletting providing too many citizens with a sense of relief, followed by a general calm. The one complication was the nationality of the victims, which led to a brief international incident. Otherwise, the *Morning Tribune* of the following day provided an update: "The coroner's jury, which had been empaneled the night before, met yesterday morning, at 9 o'clock ... at the place where the lynching occurred. The bodies were still hanging just as they had been left. A number of photographers also put in an appearance, taking views which found a ready sale at various downtown stands during the day ... The place was thronged with hundreds of people, eager to see the work that had been accomplished by the mob, which had been graphically told them through the columns of the *Tribune.*"

Approached by a reporter, Sheriff Jackson expressed surprise that the two men had been lynched. Hearing they had been taken from his officers, he had assumed the goal would be to deport them, as had happened during previous Tampa cigar strikes. The reporter then asked if he had any clues as to members of the mob. But he responded, "I do not think it advisable to discuss that." In closing, the reporter asked if the sheriff hoped to bring them to justice, and he answered, "Most assuredly."[568]

Then, according to the *Morning Tribune* of October 4, 1910, into the midst of all this came Robert Mugge's wife Caroline and two youngest daughters—Martha thirteen and Nellie ten—newly returned from their five-month stay in Europe. While away for the summer, they had toured through Germany, Switzerland, Italy, Belgium, and France, much of that time accompanied by Caroline's son August, who was now studying engineering and architecture in Stuttgart, Germany. The highlights of the trip had been attending the Oberammergau Passion Play in Bavaria and traveling through "the picturesque Alps."[569]

For her part, thirteen-year-old Martha kept a journal of the trip, a highlight of which was getting reacquainted with her older brother August, who met up with them in the town of Braunlage in the Harz Mountains: "Indeed, we had forgotten him. The last time I saw him I was six, but at home we had always heard that we had another brother who was studying in Germany." August hired an automobile for the visit and, on July 1, Martha's birthday, drove his mother and two sisters to the town of Lauterberg where Robert and his sister Bertha had been born and lived until leaving the country. A few months before, August had visited there on his own, taken a photo of the house where Robert was born, and sent it to his family. Now, according to Martha, "We were longing to see it for ourselves ... A man by the name of Junge, the owner of the house, showed us the rooms, and the back yard, where Papa used to play. We had a funny feeling to think that Papa, who has made America his home, spent his boyhood here."[570]

During the family's absence, all of Tampa had been touched by the strike, the shooting and eventual death of the cigar company bookkeeper,[571] and the lynching of two seemingly random Italians. One effect had been a severe downturn in business for the saloons, probably a result of thousands of cigar workers going without pay for two months and concerned potential visitors staying away. The *Morning Tribune* of October 5, 1910 revealed that, of the sixty or so saloons operating in the city, twenty would not seek new annual licenses. Those closing were largely in Ybor City and West Tampa, where the loss of business from cigar workers had been ruinous. According to Robert Mugge, "The strike is putting us out of business in the Latin sections of the city. The business is going to the bad and I don't see any good reason why we should expend our money in paying high license, with no chance of getting it back."[572]

Staying true to form, the City of Tampa responded to recent lawlessness by punishing strike leaders, who were charged with being accessories to the murder of J. F. Easterling, as well as for alleged intimidation to "prevent workmen from returning to work." What was perhaps most surprising was that, according to the *Morning Tribune* of October 19, 1910, these leaders were arrested[573] on the same day that the city carried out the official hanging of a Black man named Derry Taft, who had admitted to the gruesome murder of his wife,[574] but also the same day that a major storm hit Tampa, "destroying telegraphic and telephone communication with the outside world," putting two trains out of operation, and apparently doing "disastrous" damage to the orange crop.[575]

As the city worked to clean up the mess left by its recent storm, the state worked to clean up its own mess regarding Robert's long-running suit against the Tampa Water Works Company. With the case now being appealed again to the Florida Supreme Court, hired attorneys made a desperate, last-minute attempt to reverse the recent Circuit Court decision in favor of Robert Mugge and against their client. However, having thus far been defeated on the merits, they were now endorsing a different approach. This was clear in the statement of lead attorney Peter O. Knight which appeared in the *Morning Tribune* of November 18, 1910: "The case of the Tampa Waterworks Company, plaintiff in error, appealing from the decision of the Circuit Court in the suit of R. Mugge, which was argued in Tallahassee and which occupied the whole of Tuesday before the Supreme Court, is one of the most important ever coming before that tribunal, as a number of other suits are pending the decision in this case."[576] In other words, Attorney Knight, viewed as a key spokesman for Tampa's business and political establishment,[577] was signaling that, if Robert's lawsuit against the Tampa Water Works Company were allowed to succeed, it would assure similar success for the million-dollars' worth of other suits filed after the Ybor City fire.

His point, of course, was that, in 1910, a million-dollar judgement would almost certainly bankrupt the utility and exact financial pain on the entire city. But even if that were true, did the Tampa Water Works bring the situation upon itself? Very much so. And had Robert repeatedly urged City Council to cancel its costly contract with this ineffective company and oversee Tampa's water needs itself? Absolutely. But a growing convergence of corporate and governmental interests had made course correction impossible. So, with both investors and taxpayers on the spot, and with no way to separate Robert's case from all the cases still to come, the only hope was for a panel of politically connected jurists to void the commonsense judgement of Robert's fellow citizens. Yes, in twenty-first century terms, the Tampa Water Works was deemed "too big to fail."[578]

Meanwhile, as Robert and counsel awaited the inevitable, the *Morning Tribune* of November 24, 1910 recorded an equally predictable verdict for leaders of the Tampa cigar workers union. First, however, the paper noted that the courtroom the night before had held "one of the biggest crowds in its history." According to the reporter, "When the verdict was read there was not a sound heard." It was "almost death-like."

Officers had anticipated demonstrations, whether positive or negative, from the large contingent of strikers and their supporters. But there was nothing. Was this an honest response, whether conscious or unconscious, to a major miscarriage of justice, and the realization that, in such an environment, nothing could or would be done about it? Possibly. But it also could have been a sign that everyone, on all sides, was simply exhausted and wanted this ugly chapter behind them.

For the record, the three strike leaders on trial that night—"Brit" Russell, J. F. Bartlum, and Jose de la Campa—were all found guilty and expected to be sentenced to "the dull task of boxing turpentine timber or working the roads in convict garb." Yet, de la Campa, most of all, accepted his fate with equanimity, smiling as "friends expressed their disappointment," and projecting the same desire for peace that had characterized his speeches on the day of the big labor parade in support of the strike. For whatever reason, Tampa still seemed incapable of having peaceful and respectful job actions without spinning off into uncontrolled violence, recrimination, and legal malfeasance.[579]

At any rate, with that trial consigned to history, short of its eventual pro forma sentencing, the only remaining suspense in Florida legal circles was whether Robert Mugge, whose case against the Tampa Water Works had prevailed in the State Supreme Court once before, would do so again, with that body this time upholding the recent Circuit Court decision in Robert's favor. If it did, the ultimate victory would be his. But if not, his case, in progress since 1905, would be returned to Circuit Court for still another hearing.

As it happened, just before the Christmas holidays of 1910, the Supreme Court of Florida presented a massive and widely expected gift to the Tampa Water Works Company. The *Morning Tribune* of December 21, 1910 announced the decision,[580] and the paper of the following day shared the entire (rather muddled) text, a small part of which follows:

> In view of the fact that the defendant Water Works Company had no sort of connection with originating the fire that consumed the plaintiff's property, and are liable only on the theory of failure to comply with their contract duty to supply water for fire protection at an agreed pressure of forty pounds to the square inch in its water mains and that the

plaintiff's property would have been saved from destruction but for such failure, and in view of the further fact—that of necessity of arriving at the solution of the question of the defendant's liability in the performance of another agency—to-wit: the city fire department, in its efforts to subdue the fire—have to be considered, we are of the opinion that the burden of proof is at all times on the plaintiff in such and that he is required to show by a preponderance of the evidence, first, that the Water Works Company failed to supply water in the quantity called for by its contract with the city, and, second, that but for such failure the plaintiff's property could have been saved from destruction. Does the plaintiff's proofs [sic] come up to this requirement? We do not think it does ...

The judgement of the court below is reversed.[581]

Indeed, it was. And even though the reversal in the Supreme Court left one more hearing of the case in the Circuit Court, few would expect a different outcome. In such cases, when the higher court has spoken, the lower courts tend to listen.

Finally, as the year drew to a close, one remaining body presented its findings, and that was the grand jury investigating bloodshed during the 1910 cigar workers strike. Its utter lack of success, likely due to zero support from law enforcement, was reported in the *Morning Tribune* of December 23, 1910. With a seeming sense of regret, the foreman offered the grand jury's report:

In regard to the lynching of the two Italians, Angelo Albano and C. Ficarrotta, we have failed to find any evidence connecting any parties with the lynching of said Italians.

In the assassination of Mr. J. F. Easterling, we have summoned many witnesses but have failed to find any evidence that would warrant our finding a true bill against any persons connected with the assassination.

> We trust the officers will continue to do their utmost to find out and secure evidence to convict the perpetrators of the assassination [but not the lynching?].[582]

Regretful or not, the City of Tampa and County of Hillsborough could not keep safe a bookkeeper who worked for one of the cigar manufacturers and who had lately received multiple written death threats, and neither could they keep safe two Italian men who were in police custody and had been charged with nothing. Then, when all three were murdered by persons unknown, law enforcement could not find a single clue regarding identities of the killers. Their one accomplishment in the months-long affair was to arrest three strike leaders and, without evidence, convict them of conspiracy charges because they appeared not to be aware of who, among the thousands of strikers and their supporters, might have been making threats or engaging in either lethal or nonlethal violence against individuals seen to be working against them. In Tampa, throughout 1910, accountability was in short supply.

Chapter Twenty-Three
Onward and Upward

S till searching for a massive new project that could come to define him, not until the spring of 1911 did Robert claim to have found it. However, even his plans announced in the *Morning Tribune* of Tuesday, May 16, 1911 were preliminary at best.

Reportedly, Robert had contracted with B. H. Davidson to construct a five-story building on Jackson Street between Franklin and Tampa. The structure was expected to be seventy feet wide and 105 feet deep and would be built on a vacant lot with the Greeson Theatre to one side and Robert's Eureka Saloon on the other. Once erected, it would house a wholesale grocery firm projected to be one of the largest such businesses in the state. According to the *Tribune*, "The location is well suited for the purpose, being both near the water front and accessible to the tracks of Seaboard and Atlantic Coast Line Railways."[583]

Robert's plans were among those praised in another piece of civic boosterism published in the *Morning Tribune* of May 27, 1911. The article provided a brief history of the greatest past periods of construction in the city but declared the current period to be the greatest of all. As a key sample of such activity, the paper cited Robert's forthcoming building on Jackson Street, now slated to feature six stories instead of five, with his grocery business on the bottom floor and other businesses above. The latest news was that, over the coming days, he expected to assemble much of the material he would need in the construction of his building.[584] However, in the subsequent issue of June 22, 1911, Robert added that he would commence work just as soon as promised railroad tracks were laid adjacent to his site.[585]

On the personal front, the *Morning Tribune* of June 17, 1911 gave the first indication that Eugene Mugge's Tampa jewelry franchise had not worked out, inasmuch as he was now employed by his father once again. According to the *Tribune*, at approximately 10:00 a.m. the day before, Eugene had "suffered a severe fall" while aboard one of his father's trucks. It was speculated that the truck was overloaded with kegs of beer, because "one of the axles broke and he was thrown to the brick pavement." Although not breaking any bones, Eugene was "severely bruised and shaken up," and was later treated at home by Dr. J. B. Wallace.[586]

As for Robert, his empire continued to expand, with his latest acquisitions revealed in the *Morning Tribune* of July 30, 1911. The piece declared that he had just purchased three lots at the northwest corner of Zack Street and Nebraska Avenue for $15,000, which the paper termed "a splendid one for business purposes." That was because his new lots were directly across from Tampa's fancy new Union Station, which was then under construction and expected to open the following year.[587] In fact, on these lots, Robert would build his well-received Kentucky Mail Order House, and if not for his other latest news, this transaction alone would have been the talk of the town.

Instead, all eyes were on the "Notice to Contractors" in the *Morning Tribune* of August 6, 1911, which not only announced that the Parker Engineering and Construction Company was seeking "sealed proposals" from those wishing to erect Robert's big new building, but described the structure as a "ten-story reinforced concrete warehouse."[588] In other words, the planned height of the building had gone from five stories, to six, and now to a grand total of ten. And yet, there was nothing like another saloon battle to return Tampa to its baser instincts.

A month later, as documented by the *Morning Tribune* of September 6, 1911, Robert Mugge was back applying for county saloon licenses, and once again receiving neighborhood pushback, this time based entirely on racial animus, which the parties in question did nothing to conceal: "A delegation of citizens from West Hyde Park and vicinity appeared before the Board of County Commissioners at its session yesterday afternoon, strongly protesting against the establishment of a proposed saloon on Grand Central avenue, near the Shaw storage warehouse, or in any other portion of Precinct No. 26." This was prompted by notices by both Robert Mugge and the Florida Brewing Company that they planned to open saloons in this precinct where none currently existed. However, the main cause of their ire was their assumption that Robert planned to open one in a two-story building on Grand Central Avenue, which already featured an African American restaurant on the first floor and an African American dance hall on the second floor.

The delegation, led by E. Lamar Sparkman and W. B. Gray, contended that, while African Americans of that section known as Dobyville were "for the most part respectable," in some smaller cottages lived "some characters tougher than many found in the 'Scrub,' and would be made worse by alcohol." W. B. Gray went on to allege that, if a saloon were opened in the planned location, "It will be unsafe for any white woman to pass the place, especially at night."

County Attorney John P. Wall was then asked if the county could refuse to grant Robert a permit. But Mr. Wall replied that, if Robert had complied with all applicable laws and they tried to refuse a permit, he could "mandamuse" [sic] the County Commissioners and force them to grant it. He explained that, under the law enacted in 1899, "if any petition signed by two-thirds of the voters of the precinct" had been submitted since October 1, 1897, and a permit had been granted, then other applications for permits must be honored as well. A search of the records showed that, in 1889, the

Tampa Bay Hotel Company had been granted a permit, and that was considered a binding precedent. Therefore, even if the dates cited in the reporting did not entirely add up, Robert prevailed once again,[589] though he would not prevail in all matters.

Chapter Twenty-Four
A Mighty Fortress

As 1912 began, much of Robert Mugge's attention was on family. For one thing, he had a summer home built on Anna Maria Island, which, until 1922, when a wooden bridge was completed, could only be reached by boat. The island was discovered by Caloosan and Timucan Native American tribes, then, in 1539, by Spanish explorers including Hernando de Soto. However, of more immediate relevance, early in the twentieth century, it was settled by Madison Post, a one-time mayor of Tampa, who named it after his wife Anna and sister-in-law Maria.[590] According to the memoirs of August B. Mugge, "The entire family took turns in visiting the island every summer for years," but his father never saw the house.[591] It was simply something he wanted to do for his family.

As for August, 1912 would bring the climax of a situation which had been building for some time. As previously mentioned, in 1910, he had moved to a university in the German city of Stuttgart to study engineering and architecture. And like many other of the largely male students, he eventually joined one of the exclusive fraternities on campus. This permitted him to live in a beautiful house on a hill overlooking the city, and to engage in such communal activities as singing, dancing, and drinking beer. Robert, August's father, had not wanted him to join what was then known as the "corps," preferring that he focus on his studies. But because August knew virtually no one in Stuttgart, he joined in search of companionship.

As August recalled in his memoirs, these fraternities also were known for swordplay: "The custom of dueling originated in the Middle Ages and was revived in the War of Liberation against Napoleon in the early part of the 19th century." Even in the early twentieth century, members of the corps learned to duel in order "to teach themselves courage." Although dueling was illegal, in most cities, students could walk about with bandages on their faces and not arouse suspicion. But in Stuttgart, the police were expected to take stronger action than elsewhere. So, when conducting duels, the corps met at night on the outskirts of the city, and usually had no problem. But perhaps once every ten years, the police were tipped off, and anyone caught was sentenced to three months in the fortress Hohenasperg near Stuttgart. Incredibly, that happened to August.

In November of 1911, August had to appear before the German Tribunal. He was found guilty of dueling, sentenced to the usual three months in the fortress of Hohenasperg, and told he could serve his sentence any time within six months from the date of his trial. Another student named Saenger received a similar judgement, so they decided to serve their sentences together, beginning on February 1, 1912, "since it was very close to the end of the winter term and would take in the Easter holiday." According to August, "The Fortress Hohenasperg was built in the 18th century and served at one time as a castle and later as a penal institution ... It is located on a mountain, and from its walls can be seen a beautiful view of the surrounding country."

"A jailor by the name of Carst" assigned them to a "cell in the basement of a building," along with a servant, Heinrich Netting, who "was once sentenced to death for murder, but now was serving a life sentence." Every day, Netting brought them their meals and drinks from a nearby inn. Otherwise, members of the four corps visited frequently, bringing bottles of beer from the inn, and by 6:00 in the morning, all were so intoxicated that "they would beg the jailor, if they could spend the night in another cell." Additional visitors came as well, and packages were sent to them "containing cakes, wine, champagne, and eatables of all kinds in such an abundance, that the jailor had to assign to us an adjoining room for storage purposes." For August and his friend, it was more of a vacation than a punishment.

Best of all, Saenger's mother sent bed linen for them both, enabling a sound sleep on perhaps every night but one. Netting, their servant, had a collection of canaries and brought them two birds in a cage along with a container of worms. One night, after feeding the canaries, Saenger forgot to close the container. When they awoke, worms were covering their beds.

After an appeal, their sentences were reduced from three months to ten weeks, which meant they would be dismissed on April 15. When that day arrived, "the jailor presented us with a bill for 1300 bottles of beer, in addition to wine and our meals. When the corps had visited us, all of the beer was charged to us. In American money, my share of the beer was about $30.00, and I was well pleased." Thanks to paying no room rent back in Stuttgart, they wound up saving money.[592]

Ironically, at the same time August was in Germany celebrating his family's ethnic heritage, many in the American South were doing the same regarding race. Inspired by the bright, electric lights installed throughout New York's Theater District,[593] one Southern city after another was establishing its own "Great White Way," ostensibly a downtown shopping district fully illuminated by electric light. As reported in the *Tampa Times* of January 30, 1912, Birmingham, Alabama was the latest city to embody the new trend: "With the initial lighting of its 'Great White Way' system Saturday Birmingham was added to the long chain of southern cities who have adopted this method of illumination of their principal streets."

That Saturday, the system was inaugurated with "much formality and splendor." At noon, the membership of the Hustlers and Boosters marched through the streets. And that night, a gala event included public speaking, a torchlight procession, and a performance of "Dixie" by Nappi's twenty-piece white ensemble. But the greatest source of pride for the people of Birmingham was that their "Alabama Made Great White Way" featured decorative posts designed and manufactured within their own state.

The article ended with a reference to the Tampa Electric Company's intention to undertake a similar project closer to home. Perhaps paying tribute to another civilization built on slavery, the company had selected Egyptian style ornamental posts for eventual installation along all of Franklin Street and, for the time being, had set up a sampling in front of the courthouse between Lafayette and Madison Streets.[594] Of course, in its own way, Tampa, like Birmingham, was already as much of a "Great White Way" as its Black minority could handle. But in Tampa, as in Birmingham, white folks would never even know, since African Americans were not allowed to vote. And considering how ebullient Tampans were over such development in other cities, they would likely not be waiting long for a brightly lit white downtown of their own.

Robert Mugge, too, was obsessed with new technologies, but developed them on the Black side of town known as the Scrub, with both white and Black employees. The *Tampa Times* of February 19, 1912 carried a large ad for his Sunlight Manufacturing Company based at Cass Street and Central Avenue, which was still producing and distributing the Sunlight Lighting System, described as "the standard of gasoline lights and suitable for lighting homes, stores, mills, factories, construction work and street lighting." And even though Robert no longer planned to mass-produce motor vehicles on this block, the company's elaborate machine shop was now repairing and rebuilding automobiles, including rebuilding transmissions and creating virtually all automotive parts. In addition, its brass foundry was furnishing light and heavy brass castings, and its electro plating services dealt in silver, nickel, gold, and aluminum, with "special attention given to nickling auto parts and surgical instruments," as well as the "resilvering" of mirrors and the refinishing of brass beds.[595]

Yet, beginning in 1912, Robert's primary focus was construction. As just one example, the *Tampa Times* of March 2 announced that, on the three lots he had acquired at Zack Street and Nebraska

Avenue, he would build a two-story brick building. Again, once completed, it would house one of his best-known saloons, which was his Kentucky Mail Order House.[596] Of course, what continued to capture the city's imagination was his forthcoming ten-story building on Jackson Street between Franklin and Tampa. The *Times* of May 11 noted it would have "two acres of floors" and be the "city's second skyscraper." Reportedly, Robert was now planning to use the bottom two floors for his wholesale liquor business, and to rent out the other eight for light manufacturing and storage purposes.

A reinforced concrete construction was planned, and all floors would have a steel structure. Approximately 2,500 cubic yards of concrete would be used (the most for any building in Tampa to date), and 175 tons of steel. The walls and interior portions would be made of terra cotta, and the outside would utilize pressed brick. Yet, perhaps most impressive at the time, the building would be completely fireproof, including a fireproof elevator enclosure, and metal windows with wire glass would be featured on the buildings three exposed sides.

Work had begun the past Monday, and already half of the foundation was in place, with general contractor Jack L. McGucken and civil engineer C. H. Hyer predicting the rest would be ready by the following Sunday. From there, they expected to finish an additional floor every two weeks, and to complete the entire building within six months.[597]

Of course, despite the massive new projects Robert was undertaking, smaller matters required his attention as well. A reminder of that fact appeared in the *Morning Tribune* of July 10, 1912, imparting how he had been counting change in his wholesale liquor establishment on Franklin Street when two of his friends entered. Agreeing to take a break, he left his money in a bag on his desk while escorting the two friends to his saloon next door. Returning to his office after a drink or two, he found the bag of coins and checks missing from his desk and informed the Police Department.[598] More often than not, however, the police were not the solution; they were the problem.

Chapter Twenty-Five

Law and Disorder

I t went without saying that Robert had had enough. In the top righthand corner of page two of the August 29, 1912 *Morning Tribune*, he placed a large, unmissable ad with a simple message:

> Tampa, Fla. Aug. 28, 1912
> To Whom It May Concern:
> According to my opinion, when it comes to crime, vice, and corruption New York City is but a sleepy Sunday school village as compared to the lawlessness existing in Tampa, and the sheriff's office and the police department are responsible for ninety per cent of it.
> Respectfully,
> R. Mugge[599]

If anything would have caused the entire city to go deathly silent for a time, then suddenly break into whistles, shouts, and other exclamations of surprise, like opening the door of a sealed room and stepping directly into a noisy street (as Buster Keaton later suggested in his 1924 silent film classic *Sherlock Jr.*), it would have been that ad. Perhaps this was something others believed as well. But Robert had said it out loud, for everyone to hear. Worse yet, he had written it on page two of the Thursday morning paper, and now everyone in the city, whether agreeing or not, would wait to see what would happen next.

In a sense, it did not matter if the statement were true. What mattered was, he had said it; he had reached his limit, and he had called them out in the most public of ways, like a gunfighter waiting in the street for his well-armed nemesis. Because living with such a reality means living a lie, and a dangerous one at that. It means giving up on constitutional guarantees that make our daily lives possible. If the lawmen are lawless—if they solicit bribes from lawbreakers, if they collaborate with vigilantes, if they suppress a portion of the populace, if they shoot unarmed men with impunity—then justice has no meaning. And Robert was not just addressing Deputy Sheriff Beagles, who had gunned down one of his Black saloon managers eight years before, or the former Detective Ahn, who had arrested Robert and others for a joyride in 1905, only to be exposed himself as a professional gambler, a bigamist, and a convicted killer.

Everyone in Tampa knew that, for quite some time, law enforcement had conspired with racist and union-busting mobs; they knew it whether they said it aloud or not. All proof needed was there in the local press. But was it corrupt in other ways as well? Over the past decade, the *Tribune* had carried periodic articles about patrolmen, detectives, or deputy sheriffs being arrested for assault and battery,[600] [601] soliciting bribes from brothels and gambling houses,[602] [603] [604] engaging in relationships with women of ill fame,[605] and committing murder while drunk.[606] So, yes, for many years, corruption had run deep in both the Hillsborough County Sheriff's Office and the Tampa Police Department.

Returning to the present, however, in the *Tampa Times* of September 3, 1912, a saloon owner named A. H. Rawlins launched an attack on the city's most successful liquor wholesalers, claiming that Robert Mugge, the Florida Brewing Company, Ed Dominguez, and more were "backers of the saloons which are operating in the face of the law." In particular, he asserted that, "There are four bars on Central avenue, run by negroes, but the licenses are in the name of the wholesale houses,"[607] as if this were especially damning. Certainly, at least a couple of those saloons (those at Central and Harrison and Central and Scott) were owned by Robert Mugge, and unashamedly so.

The leading point of Rawlins's tirade seemed to be that the long-accepted practice of allowing liquor wholesalers to own saloons but engage others to run them meant that many licensed saloons were being operated by individuals—even African Americans—who would not have been able to secure licenses on their own, due to whatever arbitrary "character" issues might have been raised, were the government licensing bodies to know the identities of all operators from the beginning. However, since this practice had never been ruled illegal, Rawlins did not say how he, simply a fellow saloon owner, could have the practice changed, and he also seemed to be acting on an additional motive not immediately revealed by the article. Perhaps he felt that, with several wholesalers owning ten or twenty saloons each, the city contained more saloons than represented healthy competition for his own, or perhaps he was making these charges on behalf of some other group.

Whether or not Rawlins, himself, was acting as a surrogate for the police, the following day—less than a week after the appearance of Robert Mugge's ad casting aspersions against the County Sheriff's Office and City Police Department—both of those groups did shoot back. Their joint move was recorded in the same issue of the *Tampa Times* as the attack by Rawlins:

> Following the publication by Robert Mugge in a morning paper several days ago reflecting upon the sheriff's office and the police force, a petition was presented to the board of county commissioners this afternoon asking that Mugge's liquor license be taken from him on the ground that he is not a law-abiding citizen nor is he a person of good moral character. The list of signatures on the petition is composed

of members of either the sheriff's office or of the city police force.[608]

Notably, the list included R. W. Beagles who, for years, had literally gotten away with murder, reckless firearms use, public drunkenness, and disorderly conduct while a Tampa patrolman or Hillsborough County deputy sheriff.

In the September 4, 1912 issue of the *Tampa Times*, A. H. Rawlins continued his calls for a "higher standard in the liquor business" and said he would "push law against wholesalers who 'farm out' their permits from the county commissioners to sell wines, beers and liquors that were advertised in August." Six of those applications were from individuals or corporations requesting annual licenses for between twelve and fifteen saloons—Robert among them, of course—and six were from individuals requesting licenses for two saloons each. Below the list, the *Tribune* writer pointed out one curiosity, which was that, even though Rawlins had been railing against anyone purchasing a license for a saloon he did not plan to operate personally, "Rawlins himself asks for two permits in one of the queer things shown."[609]

In the *Morning Tribune* of September 5, 1912 (just as in the *Tampa Times* of September 4, 1912) were printed the results of the tumultuous County Commissioners meeting of the day before, including this key fact: "Robert Mugge, wholesale liquor dealer who recently criticized the police and sheriff's administrations, was yesterday granted by the Board of County Commissioners fifteen applications to sell liquor in various parts of the city." Despite complaints from George Bell, who spoke for the protesting officers, the commissioners voted to grant all licenses requested. Then, at the conclusion of the session, Commissioner Phil Collins declared that, if the Board refused the applications of Robert Mugge, while granting all others, it "would be guilty of partiality." He went on to state that, "no citizens other than the officers, who felt some irritation because of Mr. Mugge's recent advertisement charging that the city was full of crime because of lax enforcement of the law, had made complaints about Mr. Mugge's character or the places he conducts, and that, on the other hand his applications had the endorsement of John Trice [President of the Citizens Bank], Eugene Holtsinger [Fourth Ward Commissioner of Public Works] and R. M. Prince [President of the Florida Local Underwriters' Association]." He also pointed out that, in 1896, the board had attempted to refuse Robert's liquor permits, and "he compelled the board to grant them by taking legal action. Should the board refuse the permits he undoubtedly would again sue the board, win his point and the County would have to pay the cost of the litigation."[610] [611]

With that win solidly under his belt, Robert Mugge then dispensed with A. H. Rawlins via the *Tampa Times* of September 6, 1912. In his lengthy interview, Robert began by giving the best explanation ever of his business model, while also decrying the failure of the city and county to clamp down on the illegal competition facing licensed saloons. He charged that three out of four places selling alcohol in Tampa were blind tigers, by which he meant "drug stores, restaurants, bawdy houses, and hidden dispensaries" selling liquor without purchasing state, county, and city licenses. Since acquiring such licenses cost a single establishment $1,750 per year, the law-abiding businesses were at a financial disadvantage, made that much worse when city and county officials would not enforce the laws.

Shifting to his rebuttal, Robert said, "Rawlins' talk about enforcing the law, and stopping the wholesale houses from securing permits for the places they rent is absurd. Do you know what the last thing a mule does before dying? He kicks. That's what Rawlins is doing—kicking, because he's nearly broke ... He says he is trying to raise the standard of the whisky business here. Ask him whether he started into business himself on a high standard?"

Robert then claimed that permitting the Florida Brewing Company, a few other wholesale houses, and himself to take out licenses for legitimate saloons was the only thing keeping the latter afloat. "If we did not pay the license, the saloonkeeper could not, and it would more than halve the number of licensed saloons and correspondingly increase the number of blind tigers." He went on to ask what it mattered whether one name or another was on the permit, so long as a license was purchased and the business operated. "If I take out the license for a place, then rent the place, location, license and all, to a man, and stock him up in business, I am the loser if he goes broke." Moreover, if his agent should violate the law in any way—selling whiskey on Sunday, for instance—Robert would be held accountable, unless, of course, he could prove he had instructed the man to observe the law.[612]

Still, there were bound to be repercussions for Robert Mugge after taking on local law enforcement and winning. One came less than two weeks later, as noted in the *Tampa Times* of September 21, 1912. On a warrant sworn out by Chief Bailey, Robert was arrested for "violating the sanitary ordinances." The charge made in court was that Robert had permitted "all kinds of refuse to be placed in a single container and had neglected the alley out back of his Franklin Street saloon. Robert pleaded not guilty, but paid the $10 fine imposed, even as Chief Bailey was threatening to arrest more saloon owners for the same dubious offense.[613]

Then, a month after that, a confrontation took place that could have been foreseen early in the year when newspapers were gushing about the "Great White Ways" established in other Southern cities. According to an editorial in the *Tampa Times* of October 24, 1912, Robert Mugge was having none of it: "With all but 104 feet signed up out of 4,600 feet, the Great White Way for Franklin street, inaugurated by The *Times*, will be put in as soon as it is possible to get the material here. Forty of the eighty posts can be had in four weeks and the balance in another three weeks, and Mr. Woodsome said yesterday he believed the street would be lit by Christmas week." Robert, though, as the only Franklin Street merchant who had not signed up to participate, was being blasted for his "notorious lack of public spirit." According to the *Times*, Robert had consistently refused to bring his 104 feet of frontage between Jackson and Lafayette Streets into the "Great White Way." And as a punishment befitting his crime, "Mr. Mugge will be left out unless the great Busch interests who are back of him see they ought to be in."[614]

Ever since the White Municipal Party was organized in 1908, and Donald B. McKay became its successful 1910 candidate for mayor of Tampa (while remaining editor of the *Times*), Robert may have looked forward to a quiet, symbolic way to demonstrate his disapproval. Perhaps this was also a chance to pay back the Tampa Electric Company, which had done everything in its power (in every sense) to cripple his own rival Tampa Electrical Illuminating Co. which, at one point, had lit much of Ybor City and the Scrub. And finally, perhaps he did not appreciate the *Tampa Times* expecting him to help underwrite this pet project of theirs any more than he had liked the *Morning Tribune* expecting him to be the biggest underwriter for the South Florida Fair.

In any case, there was only one Great White Way and, again, that was the Theater District of New York City, which was first lit by bright electric lights in 1880, and given its new nickname mostly due to a headline in the New York *Evening Telegram* in 1902.[615] By contrast, these were merely cities of the former Confederacy symbolically suggesting that their growing downtowns were the exclusive domains of white people, while African Americans were largely restricted to neighborhoods of their own, as separate and unequal in life as the Tampa City Council of several years back had insisted they be in death. No, whatever Robert's motivations, and it may have been all of the above, he could be said to have rendered a public service by disrupting a gaudy and oppressive symbol of united whiteness, even if presented as municipal progress.

Chapter Twenty-Six
View from the Top

I n 1913, not all news centered around saloons and ten-story buildings. As a case in point, the *Morning Tribune* of January 19, 1913 carried the latest predictions from inventor Thomas A. Edison under the headline, "Edison Says 'Talkies' Will Replace 'Movies.'" In presenting his newest invention, "a talking motion picture machine called the knietophone," Mr. Edison proclaimed the coming end of the legitimate stage, asserting that talking pictures would permit the smallest villages around the world to experience "$2.00 shows for one-twentieth that amount." He also predicted that barnstormers (theater companies touring small towns) would cease to exist, because no one would be "willing to pay for second-class acting when the foremost actors are performing for the 'talkies' and can be seen and heard for a dime."[616]

As exciting as Edison's predictions of wrenching social and cultural change likely to result from his latest technological advancement, including the end of both traveling theatrical companies and silent cinema, he perhaps was getting ahead of himself. Certainly, silent films would not even reach their zenith until the 1920s features of Chaplin, Keaton, Lubitsch, Lang, von Stroheim, Gance, Eisenstein, and others, and the so-called "talking pictures," which he already had named, would not begin taking over movie production and distribution for another fourteen years.[617]

In the same way, while Robert knew that his new ten-story building was one of the great achievements of his life, he had not yet settled on the reasons for its existence. But raison d'être aside, he quickly discovered how much fun it was to start 1913 literally on top. The exhilaration of reaching his summit could not have been more obvious than in the *Morning Tribune* of February 10, 1913, under the headline, "New Mugge Building Reaches Tenth Story." The paper revealed that, as soon as the top floor was completed, contractors McGucken & Hyer "hoisted the stars and stripes, which now float proudly from the building, which is seven feet higher than the new Citizens' Bank and Trust Company building."

Watching the hoisting of the flag, and inspecting the roof of his new building, Robert "enjoyed a hearty laugh." Asked for the source of his pleasure, Robert pointed to the flag and exclaimed, "I am tickled to death; I am seven feet nearer heaven than 'old John Trice' [president of the Citizens' Bank]."[618]

A couple of weeks later, however, "obstructionist" Robert Mugge returned, and in retrospect, it is easy to understand why. The Atlantic Coast Line railway company, in conjunction with his old nemesis, the Tampa Electric Company, wanted to infringe upon his property rights. And as tends to happen as communities grow and utilities become corporate, everyone was expected to bend to their will. Robert, however, decided on a different approach. The March 4, 1913 issue of the *Tampa Times*—again, the paper owned and edited by the mayor—carried much of the story.

It seems that, together, this regional railroad and local electric company were partnering with the City of Tampa in constructing an intracity rail line from Union Station out to Ybor City, and the line was set to run alongside Robert's new saloon, the Kentucky Mail Order House, which stood directly across Nebraska Avenue from the station. As the urban trinity of railroad, electric company, and city government saw it, even if Robert had been within his rights in building his saloon flush with the edge of his property, his having done so could now mean a danger of intoxicated patrons walking out his doors and into the paths of their trains. Therefore, the group wanted to erect crossing gates at that point, but could not do so without placing a post on Robert's property. Robert resisted the idea, filing an injunction with the novel claim that Nebraska Avenue had never been dedicated as an official street of the city, which Mayor McKay asked the city attorney to investigate.[619]

The *Morning Tribune* of the same day added the further information that, on February 27, railroad employees had begun digging a hole on Robert's property, in which they intended to place a post, from which one of the new gates would be hung. Robert had forbidden them to proceed further, but they ignored him and completed their work. At that point, he filed his injunction, alleging that the post on his property interfered with the value of his brick saloon building. Of course, Robert's concern was less with the work being done than with the fact they had done it without first seeking his permission. And if anyone doubted it, he was quoted as follows in the *Weekly Tribune* of May 29, 1913: "I am reasonable when people come to me, but when they don't come to me, I'm like a bull."[620] [621]

As Richard White wrote in his 2011 book, *Railroaded: The Transcontinentals and the Making of Modern America*, the Gilded Age construction of the transcontinental railroads shaped the American economy and, in many respects, the American personality, by combining corporate initiative, federal subsidies, immigrant labor, and brilliant engineering in an effort to connect all corners of North America. However, even if previous historians had seen these efforts bringing positive, transformative change to the United States and its neighbors, White's research revealed the railroads to have been "overbuilt, prone to bankruptcy and receivership, wretchedly managed, politically corrupt, environmentally harmful, and financially wasteful."[622] In other words, White doubled down on Mark Twain and Charles Dudley Warner's contention (laid out in their 1873 novel, *The Gilded Age: A Tale of Today*) that the glittering gold surface of nineteenth century progress could not conceal the corruption below,[623] and he also implied that anyone seeking to interfere with such massive undertakings could expect to be *railroaded*, by which he meant subject to a harsh governmental and corporate response: "Although historians have tried to diminish the corruption of the Gilded Age, it is hard to study the era without being aware of how corrupt the normal procedures of business and governance became in the late nineteenth century ... Corporations used the federal government to punish rival corporations while gaining advantages for themselves."[624]

That being the case, when Robert Mugge challenged a consortium in his own city, even thirteen years into the twentieth century, he knew to expect similar treatment. As his statements of the time suggest, not only was he incensed by the loss of democratic norms meant to ensure fair dealings between individual taxpayers, landowners, and entrepreneurs on the one side, and autocratic bullies on the other, but also by the basic lack of respect shown to private citizens. In other words, if the press wished, it could paint him as an enemy of progress and the public good. However, for Robert, as for many others, this was a matter of liberty, and of basic human values.

In truth, this "gate post" standoff was hardly the Watergate of its time. Instead, as early as March 18, 1913, few were even paying attention because, on that day, the afternoon *Tampa Times*—followed a day later by the *Morning Tribune*—announced Robert Mugge's revelation. As the *Tribune* of March 19 calmly reported, "R. Mugge, who is having erected a ten-story building on Jackson street, between Franklin and Tampa streets, which was originally intended for storage and warehouse purposes, has changed his mind, and the structure will be arranged for a hotel. It is Mr. Mugge's intention to give Tampa another hostelry, to be ready for the next tourist season." The new plan was to create hotel offices and a restaurant on the first floor, perhaps a garden on the roof, and a total of 126 hotel rooms split among the other nine floors, each room being fifteen-by-fifteen feet and with its own bathroom. Robert projected that the building itself would be completed in another thirty days, but that the hotel would not be ready until the fall.[625] [626]

The new vision was quite exciting. Yet, as often happened with Robert Mugge, execution would lag. Furthermore, as also often happened, right as one project reached for the sun, another began to fade. The sad news could be read in the *Morning Tribune* of April 3, 1913. Reportedly, papers had been filed to place Robert's Sunlight Manufacturing corporation in voluntary bankruptcy, naming Robert himself as the principal creditor. The company was still manufacturing and selling gasoline lamps, and still had its offices at 1002 Central Avenue, with Robert listed as president and W. T. Jamison as general manager. But its assets were calculated to be $35,000, versus liabilities of $40,000, which was the reason for the bankruptcy.[627] In his memoirs, August B. Mugge, Robert's son, wrote that, following the bankruptcy, Robert took over as the company's sole owner.[628] Of course, at this point, as Robert had long pointed out, government, too, could use some sunlight.

In April of 1913, Tampa voters considered adopting a new City Charter. *Tampa Tribune* editor Wallace F. Stovall supported the change as a way of reducing corruption in city government, and Mayor Donald B. McKay, also editor of the *Tampa Times*, opposed it. Debate between the two sides grew heated, and so it was inevitable that Robert Mugge would weigh in, providing, in the process, another treatise on his own political thinking. His letter to the editor was published in the *Morning Tribune* of April 6, 1913:

> Editor *Tribune*: Horace Greeley [politically active founding editor of the *New York Tribune* during the mid-nineteenth century] said, "Not every Democrat is a horse thief, but every horse thief is a Democrat." One can just as easily say, Not every opponent of commission form of government for Tampa belongs to the lawless element, but every professional law breaker and those who help to divide the spoils from lawlessness, is opposed to change in the form of government the people of Tampa now enjoy. These facts alone should be sufficient for any honest thinking man to guide his vote on Tuesday next.
>
> The foundation for all civilized nations to enjoy life, liberty and property is law and its execution, and when that is denied, mob law and anarchy rule. Numerous crimes are

committed in Tampa daily with full knowledge and consent of men who have sworn that they will execute all laws as found on the books of the city ...

Once upon a time a highway robber and murderer was about to be executed, when he saw his mother, he asked permission from the sheriff to kiss her goodbye, and this was granted. Instead of kissing his mother, he bit off her nose. When asked his reason for committing his last crime, he made the following statement: "When I was a little boy, playing with neighbor children at their homes, I stole small things and carried them to that woman, she would pick me up and kiss me, and in consequence I landed where I am now at ..."

Our present form of government is as autocratic as it can possibly be. If the Mayor and a majority of the Council agree that the city shall be ruled by the lawless element, there is absolutely no legal power to stop them and the people have to submit to anything that element selects to do for them and that is the existing condition right now.

Another silly argument against the charter is made by otherwise sensible men, stating that their intention had been to vote for the new charter, but since it became known that certain prohibitionists, socialists, etc., were also in favor of commission form, their minds changed. I presume that in the revolutionary war when a colonist offered his services, he was first examined as to his religion and political faith and only when his answers were satisfactory to the examiner was he enrolled. I also presume that when the flood sufferers are offered food and clothing, they first inquire if the donor is a prohibitionist or socialist and if either, food and clothing are refused. The voting is done for a principle not for men ...

The five commissioners to be elected by all the people will be nothing more or less than servants who are hired to do certain things. Failing to do their full duty, any or all can be ousted inside of ninety days, and not every four years. It will be simply impossible For Them To Wink At Crime And Hold Their Jobs.

The people of Tampa, by a large majority, favor lawful government, which permits them healthful recreation and pleasure, and also gives them fair returns for the money wrung from them in the shape of taxes and licenses. R. Mugge

Editor Stovall added the following practical information just below Robert's philosophical musings: "The commission charter abolishes the cumbersome system of two boards, conflicting in duties and responsibilities, and centers duty and responsibility in five men. Vote for it Tuesday."[629]

Not surprisingly, this led to the publishing, in the next day's issue of the rival *Tampa Times*, an editorial comment intended solely to insult Robert Mugge without addressing any of the issues he had raised: "Robert Mugge setting himself up as an authority on morals is a spectacle to make Old Nick [an English name for Satan] himself turn green with envy. If there is one man who is more than all others in Tampa notorious for his low standard of morals, that man is Mugge. And probably no man who ever lived in Tampa has exerted a worse influence than this same man."[630]

Although, on occasion, Robert did thumb his nose at conventions he considered foolish or oppressive, his critics in government and the press (with one man representing the top echelon of both) liked to imply that his legal sale of alcohol, his support for racial and ethnic minorities, and his fight against rampant corruption proved a lack of personal morality when, in fact, only a community largely devoid of healthy human values could consider Robert the problem.

Regardless, Mayor/Editor Donald B. McKay need not have stooped to such a level to protect his own political station, because his ethnic allies in Ybor City were offering him full support, and African Americans were still being denied a vote. The *Morning Tribune* of April 9, 1913, in a heartfelt response clearly penned by editor Wallace F. Stovall himself, reported the election results under the headline, "Ybor City Defeats The Commission Charter." According to Mr. Stovall, the charter change had won handily everywhere in Tampa except in the two Ybor City wards, where the largely Cuban, Spanish, and Italian population sent it to overwhelming defeat, apparently wanting to support the current administration, which they believed best represented their own interests. Mr. Stovall's belief was that the outsized vote from those two wards was unfairly influenced, not only by the city "machine," but also by the county sheriff, his deputies, and his "henchmen," all of whom benefitted from the current unnatural order: "The result is deeply regrettable from the standpoint of good government. It is sufficient to cause the blush of shame to the respectable citizen when he reflects that a movement of civic betterment may thus be defeated and destroyed. It was a bad day for Tampa ..."[631]

Once again, the *Tampa Times* responded, not with passionate and articulate debate, but with simple invective, this time in the form of an insulting political cartoon. The illustration, which appeared just a few hours later under the headline, "The Mortal Triumvirate On the Morning After," offered three smiling men in bed together, fully dressed but mostly under the covers. The three—Tampa businessman Robert Mugge, prohibitionist attorney Don C. McMullen, and *Tribune* editor Wallace F. Stovall—were identified by labels on their respective pairs of shoes at the foot of the bed. All were known to be prominent and vocal supporters of the charter change, and in view of that initiative's defeat, they were ridiculed in the text below the cartoon.[632]

Naturally, these being dueling newspapers, editor Stovall responded somewhat in kind in the *Morning Tribune* of April 11, 1913, writing some comic verse under the headline, "An Appeal to Reason—(From the Administration)." The poem is quite long, and its many period references would have to be heavily footnoted to be understood and appreciated by contemporary readers. However, knowledge of a few facts will make at least the middle section understandable: (1) Donald B. McKay, a founder of Tampa's White Municipal Party and the longtime owner and editor of the *Tampa Times* newspaper, served as Tampa's mayor from 1910 through 1920; (2) Charles "Cousin Chollie" McKay Wall, a well-known cousin of the mayor, ran Tampa's lucrative numbers racket out of Ybor City; (3) J. E. "Jolly Jim" Etzler was another founder of the White Municipal Party, the owner of a liquor business, and the mayor's key ally on City Council; (4) bolita was an illegal game of chance played in the saloons, gaming houses, and brothels of Ybor City; and (5) the term "Dutch" was a pejorative for Germans, as in the residents of "Deutschland." So here, then, is that middle section of Wallace Stovall's poetic response:

> We like Jim lots better than Mugge,
> For Mugge's name's awfully Dutch;
> And another thing much against Mugge,
> He tells the folks too blasted much.
> If he'd keep his mouth shut about grafters,
> And swear there's no gambling in town,
> And say he just loves to pay taxes
> Because they forever go down;
> Then we'd think lots better of Mugge,
> And the Dutch in his name we'd forgive;
> He could keep his back doors open on Sundays,
> And in peace we together could live.
> We'd treat him just like "Cousin Chollie,"
> "Jolly Jim" and the rest of the boys;
> Here's your chance, Mugge, now for redemption:
> Just stop making quite so much noise ...
>   —Bolita.[633]

Robert was so delighted by Wallace Stovall's poem that he whipped up one of his own, and the *Morning Tribune* published it the following day under the headline, "A Reply To Bolita." The references made are the same, with the addition of an implied, tongue-in-cheek German accent, resembling what was used in the popular cartoon strip of the time, "The Katzenjammer Kids." The latter section read as follows:

> And Mugge say for me to write
> And tell you he declined,

To brag upon dot government,
Unless he lose his mind.
He also say for me to write,
And say dot he's some sinner
But by the crowd dot you are mit,
He's hardly a beginner.
He say he's gettin' careful,
About who goes mit him.
And so he say good-bye to you,
And your frien', "Jolly Jim."
            —Anheiser.[634]

The final stanza of Robert's poem was likely a self-satirizing reference to the public furor that developed when he was arrested for nighttime joyrides with women of supposed ill fame—Panchita in 1903 and Ollie Cummings in 1905—but now extended to the notion of his not wanting to associate with Mayor Donald B. McKay and his allies (politicians of ill repute).

Chapter Twenty-Seven
Arrivals/
Departures

No matter what was happening with his businesses or his family, Robert Mugge never stopped thinking about what would be good for the future of Tampa. As just one example, with all the recent talk of improving the estuary, and therefore the harbor, which was prompted by recent visits to the city by engineer Henry C. Long of Boston, Robert decided to make a preemptive recommendation of his own in the *Morning Tribune* of April 17, 1913. It began with the following words to a *Tribune* reporter: "The citizens of Tampa should pay for the dredging of the Hillsborough river and not wait for the government. I have taken up the matter with the property owners and will, myself, contribute $10,000 toward the project." Robert went on to say he would employ an engineer to create a map of the Hillsborough River, designating property owners on either side, and attempt to convince all to contribute to the effort.

By Robert's estimation, the river should be made "twenty-four feet [deep] as far as the Lafayette street bridge, twenty feet deep from that point to Michigan avenue, and sixteen feet deep from Michigan avenue to Sulphur Springs." By contrast, the plan currently being discussed by the government called for only a twenty-foot deepening below the bridge and twelve feet to Michigan Avenue. Robert calculated that the cost of his own proposal would be approximately $400,000 and believed that, if he and other property owners along the river should pay that cost, their investment would be returned to them at least ten times over. "The deepening of the river will mean the life of West Tampa in particular," he said. "Both West Tampa and Tampa have the dry rot at the moment."[635]

The *Morning Tribune* of April 23, 1913 announced that, at their meeting that afternoon, the Board of Governors of the Board of Trade would discuss Robert Mugge's idea for deepening the Hillsborough River as far as Sulphur Springs. Quoth the *Tribune*, "Since the article was published much favorable comment has been heard regarding the plan, which promises quicker and better results than would be secured from the government."[636] But the *Morning Tribune* of the following day reported the Board of Governors had not acted on the plan, due in part to pessimism from the mayor regarding the federal government agreeing to pay for the deepening. Of course, Robert's plan was that property owners along the river would pay, and that hit a roadblock when some of the property owners present resisted the idea.[637]

Next, in the *Morning Tribune* of May 9, 1913, Robert proposed still another means of paying for the dredging. His latest suggestion was for the cities of Tampa and West Tampa, together, to borrow $500,000, and for Hillsborough County to borrow another $500,000, thereby providing $1 million to accomplish this important work. Then, between them, the three could raise riverfront tax assessments by $2 million, providing the income needed to repay the loans. And why, asked the reporter, should the region expend so much effort, or take on significant financial risk? To which, Robert responded with his vision for the city's future: "Some people in Tampa do not seem to realize the tremendous possibilities of the Hillsborough River. If properly dredged it would accommodate 300 ships. Along its banks would be scores of factories of all kinds. The opening of the Panama Canal will mean more commerce between Tampa, Central America and South America. Among other things, we can import coffee from Brazil and sell it throughout the United States."[638]

The *Morning Tribune* of May 10, 1913 added the following: "Mr. Mugge believes that Tampa should become a manufacturing center for other things besides cigars and that the 'Made in Tampa' brand should mean a standard of excellence. 'Perhaps the deepening of the river will not be carried out during my life time,' commented Mr. Mugge, 'but after I am dead and gone, the people will remember what I have said, and they will remark: Mugge was right, after all.'"[639] In the process, Robert not only acknowledged his mortality for the first time, but also the goal of the larger good—that is, working for the betterment of others, including generations yet to come.

The following day, *Tribune* editor Wallace F. Stovall weighed in as well:

> There is nothing ephemeral or eccentric about Robert Mugge's proposition to deepen the Hillsborough River all the way to Sulphur Springs. It is a natural improvement which, in the logical course of our progress, must come sooner or later and will, in time, be absolutely demanded by our commercial needs. Mr. Mugge insists that work to this end be begun now, in order that we may all the earlier realize the great benefits which will come from such improvement.[640]

The same edition of the *Morning Tribune* also announced that Robert's idealism was once again carrying over to the "Tampa Bay Park." Editor Stovall, who had his own longtime concern with the welfare of the hotel and its grounds, condemned the current city administration for "allowing the Tampa Bay Hotel gardens and park to go to pieces." By contrast, he noted that Robert Mugge, upon hearing the city was refusing to furnish gardener Waldie with fertilizer for the park, offered to furnish it from his own stables, assuming only the city would convey it.[641]

Robert's next appeal for civic improvement, as advanced in a letter to the *Morning Tribune* of May 22, 1913, supported the Tribune proposal for funding road building throughout the county. In the process, he considered how the region had developed since he first arrived there. "I have made Tampa my home since 1876, and have resided here permanently ever since, have been a taxpayer since 1878, and am today one of the largest individual taxpayers of Hillsborough county, Tampa, West Tampa, Plant City, and Port Tampa City." He then spoke of how, when the county had proposed bonding of $400,000 for the purpose of building roads, he had used all his influence to support the effort. And now that the county proposed bonding again, this time to raise $1 million for the same purpose, he was once again in favor:

> All counties are preparing to build good roads and Hillsborough, to retain her prestige must be in the lead. The convenience of the farmer and settler must be considered. With brick paved roads merchandise may be transported in auto trucks and delivered at the customer's door, thereby saving in freight, hauling to and from depot and time in transit. Good roads will add to the pleasure of tourists, many of whom will be thereby induced to purchase winter homes, put them in charge of our people and thereby open another avenue of revenue.

As to the sum of one million dollars, Robert called it (probably with an unseen twinkle in his eye), "not much, when you say it quickly." Then, with his usual attention to detail, he went on to propose exactly how the roads should be built, how the money should be raised, and who should administer the funds and oversee the work.[642]

Following that, the *Morning Tribune* of July 6, 1913 announced another of Robert's gifts to the city. Plans were being made to "cut a short street through the City Hall block from Lafayette street to Jackson, when the city is ready to begin laying the foundation for the new City Hall." Ensuring the new street would be of sufficient width, A. J. Knight, owner of the building occupied by the Keller Clothing Company, and Robert Mugge, owner of the adjoining property, informed the mayor that they each planned to present the city with ten feet from the rear of their respective buildings.[643]

Meanwhile, as detailed in the *Tampa Times* of April 19, 1913, conversion of Robert's ten-story building into a luxury hotel was facing a cluster of fresh problems. First, because the building was designed to be a warehouse, its walls were close to property lines, with metal window frames holding opaque glass, none of which was suited for light or ventilation. The latest plans called for fourteen rooms per floor, which meant one room per window already installed. But the windows comprised 1,575 panes of glass from the second floor to the tenth, making 3,150 that would have to be changed in order that occupants could see out.

Second, the city had recently passed new building laws, and building inspector Paul Gasser was helping Robert to understand the changes needed to meet new requirements. In short, he would have to "reconstruct much of the building," including adding "light and air shafts, vents from every toilet, shafts from the kitchen ... and a flue for said kitchen or water heating apparatus." Inasmuch as the building was built "right up to the property line," such flues and chimneys would have to be built up through the building, as would the vents from the toilets. Assuming all these matters were corrected, plus others raised by the building inspector, permission would be given for making the building a hotel. Of course, at this point, even with Gasser's support and enthusiasm, Robert had no assurance that his vision would yet be realized.[644]

Happily, though, confirmation followed in the *Tampa Times* of May 31, 1913, as reflected in the article's headline: "Mugge To Have 126-Room Hotel." After working closely with building inspector Gasser, Robert was finally given the permit needed to proceed. The approved plans provided for "a lobby, dining room, kitchen, boiler room, store room and buffet on the first floor, and for fourteen bedrooms on each of the nine upper stories."

According to an excited Paul Gasser, the hotel would have 126 bedrooms, each with its own private bath. All rooms would be "outside rooms," opening onto a large central hall which, on each floor, would run from north to south. Also included would be the latest models of fast elevators and steam heating throughout. Because other, shorter buildings were extremely close on either side, the placement of fire escapes was perhaps the biggest challenge, but the solution was to place them on the front of the building, tastefully integrated into its design. Besides, as inspector Gasser loved to point out, the building's construction had made it "the most fireproof hotel in the city." And considering the extent to which Robert's businesses had been beset by fires over the years—especially his arson-ravaged saloons—he was easily as pleased as inspector Gasser by these advances, which is why even the building's marble stairway and elevator shafts would be encased in fireproof material.

The article ended with the prediction that work would be rushed so the hotel could be opened by the fall, just in time for the "transient winter trade." All of which was great news, except for the fact that, understandably, Robert was once again getting ahead of himself.[645]

By contrast, the next news was disappointing. The *Morning Tribune* of June 7, 1913 announced the government's decision on funding the proposed improvement of the Hillsborough River. In brief, it was an unfavorable report, which nevertheless could still be appealed to the Board of Engineers for Rivers and Harbors. "It is stated that the engineers who have examined the river thus far do not believe the amount of commerce justifies the expense."[646] Of course, anticipating this news, Robert Mugge had proposed other sources of funding, including having property owners along the river contribute, and that possibility had not yet been ruled out.

Only a week later, the *Morning Tribune* revealed a second disappointment, which was the failure of Robert's attempt to exercise his own rights in opposition to those of the city. More specifically, he could not stop the railroad, in alliance with the electric company, from building a structure on his property. Judge F. M. Robles ruled that the Atlantic Coast Line Railway Company could proceed with erecting gates "at the intersection of Polk street and Nebraska avenue," which included infringing on Robert's saloon property at that corner.[647] But on the positive side, the new streetcars between Union Station and Ybor City would now begin operation, and the city would no longer have concerns about a potentially dangerous crossing, even if one of its own making. Moreover, although Robert had lost his right to say who could plant a post on his property, he still had won, in that all the traffic moving in and out of Union Station would ensure the future success of his Kentucky Mail Order House, now perfectly positioned across the street.

Also of note, despite completion of a construction project Robert had opposed, he, himself, was engaged in a major new project of his own, over and above what was being done with his ten-story building. As mentioned in the *Tampa Times* of September 24, 1913, he had resolved to replace all his wood buildings with brick ones, thereby making them both more attractive and less vulnerable to fire. "As a starter he will tear down the old wooden building at Central avenue and Harrison street occupied by the [African American] Central saloon and replace it with an attractive building of modern design and build." According to the *Times*, the old building had been in use for more than twenty years and was "a landmark" in that section of the city but was badly in need of repair.[648]

However, even as Robert moved forward on all fronts, he suddenly was faced with the biggest loss of his life, outside of family. The *Morning Tribune* of October 19, 1913 reported news he likely knew already, which was that his longtime friend, supporter, and ally in all things political and financial, Adolphus Busch, had died in Germany, right as his home city of St. Louis was celebrating the hundredth anniversary of German independence. The report of Mr. Busch's death included a review of his remarkable career.

According to one of his associates, Mr. Busch had died with a personal wealth of some sixty million dollars (at this writing, nearly two billion), a number which would have been much higher, were it not for his lifelong philanthropy. Born into an old German family in Kastel, a district of Mainz in the Grand Duchy of Hesse, on July 10, 1837, he was well-educated, but being the twenty-first of twenty-two children, he assumed he would need to make his own fortune. He therefore emigrated to America in 1857 at the edge of eighteen, settled in St. Louis, worked a couple of early jobs, served in the Union Army for six months, inherited a bit of money when his father died, created a brewing supply company, became partners with Eberhard Anheuser who had acquired the Bavarian Brewery, married Anheuser's daughter Lilly, and upon the death of his father-in-law in 1880, took full control of the brewery, which was renamed the Anheuser-Busch Brewing Association. Under Busch's leadership, the company instituted many innovations, including refrigeration, pasteurization, and investment in related businesses, from bottling factories to ice-manufacturing plants. Other major investments ranged from a bank to a railroad, and he built a hotel in Dallas, Texas that was then the tallest building in the state.[649]

In other words, Adolphus Busch had been a German immigrant in America who succeeded in much the way Robert Mugge had, though on a far grander scale. Therefore, it made perfect sense that the two of them had become friends and allies, and it also made sense that, after Busch's death, Robert's relationship with Anheuser-Busch would continue, yet never again be the same. Now it would simply be a business relationship, and not a deep and enduring personal one as well.

The extent to which Robert had been shaken by this loss was revealed in what he did next. Just as he responded to the death of his first grandchild by calling home his daughter, Frances Bertha Mugge, after six years away, he now brought home his son August, more than a decade after sending the two of them to study in Germany. But why, exactly?

Had the death of Adolphus caused Robert to face his own mortality? Had it made him realize he should train a successor, to the extent that was even possible? Was his strength beginning to fail, right as his workload was most ambitious? Was he even facing the fact that, out of love, he had sent three of his children to top schools in Germany and, because of that, had not seen his son August since he was a boy of thirteen; whereas, now August was a man of twenty-three? Perhaps for all these reasons, Robert called August home a year and a half before he would have earned his Doctor of Engineering degree, which had long been the goal to which father and son were both committed. But whatever Robert's reasons for recalling him, August responded immediately.

According to the passenger list of the *Kronprinzessin* (Crown Princess), August Mugge sailed from Bremen, Germany to New York City, arriving there on November 26, 1913.[650] The *Morning Tribune* of

December 2, 1913 announced his arrival in essentially royal fashion, which made sense since, during the time August had been away, his father had become a king of Florida commerce, which made his son a kind of prince:

> August Mugge, son of Robert Mugge, for ten years having been in Germany has returned home to remain permanently, arriving unexpectedly and surprising his family. Mr. Mugge has been studying engineering and architecture during his absence and returns to the city prepared to begin business for himself. He has devoted a great deal of his study to harbor engineering and has visited the principal ports of Europe and the British Isles for this purpose. Mr. Mugge is astounded at the improvements made in the city in the last decade and he states that as these changes were made in ten years the advancement during the next decade will be greater than the fondest expectations of Tampa's most enthusiastic boosters.[651]

Such packaged praise was fine for the public. But privately, in his memoirs, August had far more to say about this abrupt transition. For some time, he had been hearing "disquieting news" about his father's health, which had caused him to worry. If there were any chance his father might die, he felt it important he head home where he could assist his family, just as Robert had when his own father passed. Then, in the fall of 1913, he received a cable that read, "Father low, come home at once," and it had been signed by Robert himself. August therefore packed his possessions, took a train from Stuttgart to Hamburg, booked passage on a steamer of the Hamburg-American line, and proceeded to Bremen. There, he stayed with a student friend named Walter Putenson, whose father loaned him 900 marks to purchase a ticket on what he later remembered being the S. S. Prinzessin Caeceloa of the North German Lloyd line.

After a "stormy crossing," August arrived in New York City and immediately left for Tampa by train. He reached there early in the morning on the Friday after Thanksgiving, stopping at Union Station, which had been built during his absence. Leaving the station, he was somewhat at a loss. But he walked down Twiggs Street and, passing the old Convent of the Holy Names, finally got his bearings and found his way to the family home at the corner of Marion and Jackson Streets.

Robert had not mentioned to anyone that August was returning home, so his arrival was a complete surprise. At five feet and eleven inches, he was not nearly so tall as his father, and certainly not as tall as his six-foot, three-inch brother Eugene. Yet, the charming European gentleman who entered the house at 302 Marion was a far cry from the awkward adolescent who had left there a decade before. Many years later, August still reveled in the fond and excited greetings he received from his mother, Caroline; from his sisters Frances, Lanie (Melanie), Martha, and Nellie; and perhaps most passionately from Annie, the African American woman who had helped to raise him, and who had not seen him since he left for Germany.

After having breakfast with the family, August walked the two blocks to his father's office in the wholesale establishment on Franklin Street, just above Jackson. Naturally, the greeting was warm, because they, too, had not seen each other in a decade. Bewildered that his father looked well, he learned that Robert had "recovered," but still wanted him to remain at home. Naturally, August had hoped he would be able to return to Germany and complete his studies, but Robert told him that, from then on, "he would be my professor."

Robert also informed August that he could begin work on Monday, but that now he should go greet other members of the family, which he did. Over the course of the day, he visited his Tante (Aunt) Bertha in the upstairs portion of the house; his older sister Louise and her three daughters—Hermina, Fonnie, and Anna—at their home near Michigan Avenue; his brother Eugene, along with wife Mimi and young daughter Marie; and Fritz Petri, the brother of Eugene's wife Mimi, who had come from Germany the year before, probably accompanying Mimi and Marie. Fritz, too, was now working for Robert, and would later marry Nellie, Robert's youngest daughter.

Caroline set up August in a corner bedroom on the second floor of their home, and Robert informed him that he would be given free board, clothes when necessary, and $15 per week for himself. Robert also gave him money to pay back Walter Putenson's father in Hamburg for the loan of 900 marks to make the trip home. Of course, returning to Tampa was one thing, but finding his place there was quite another.

"On Sunday morning, according to German fashion, I donned my cutaway, striped pants and with derby, kid gloves and cane went into my father's office." There, he met B. H. Davidson, his father's contractor, who was paid on a weekly basis to do whatever construction work Robert currently needed. At that time, Davidson was converting the Central Saloon building at Central Avenue and Harrison Street from a wood-frame building into a two-story brick one. August described him as "a self-made man with very little schooling, but vast experience."

After greeting them both in his fashionable German clothes, August proceeded to stroll down Franklin Street. Unbeknownst to him, after he had left, Robert said to the equally amused B. H. Davidson, "Well, he will soon have that thing off." In fact, August recalled that everyone on the street had stared at him, so he quickly returned home and never wore the suit again.

On Monday morning, an office was established for August on the fifth floor of Robert's ten-story building, now standing on Jackson Street, midway between Franklin and Tampa. A corner of that floor was enclosed, an old desk brought in, and equipment installed for the processing of blueprints. Otherwise, having brought his own "drawing paraphernalia" from Germany, August required only paper and a few additional items before getting straight to work.

What Robert asked him to do was design the African American hotel which he was planning to build at the intersection of Central Avenue and Harrison Street, directly across from his Central Saloon, which Davidson already was rebuilding, and next to his Sunlight Manufacturing Company. Robert's only specifications were that the new three-story building be eighty by 160 feet, have eight stores on the first floor, and have a combined seventy-two hotel rooms on the second and third floors. He left all other details to August who, in turn, immediately started consulting with B. H. Davidson, the man assigned to erect this building as well.

Right from the start, Mr. Davidson was a huge help, including teaching August to work in yards, feet, and inches, instead of the metric system he had used in Germany. Another of August's German customs which amused Mr. Davidson was wearing a smock to protect his clothes. But it was a good collaboration, with each of them working separately during the day, then coming together in the evening so that August could get Davidson's input on his latest drawings.

Since Robert was still very much engaged in the liquor business, August soon assisted with that as well, taking over the Monday morning collections from Robert's many saloons. As he did so, traveling around Tampa and Ybor City, he was amazed by the changes made over the past ten years, yet reassured by certain familiar landmarks, among them the blacksmith shop next to the family home, the livery stable that adjoined it, the old Court House, and the bandstand on the Court House Square (actually rebuilt a few months before August's return), which still featured concerts on Saturday night. Life in Tampa was remarkably different from what he had known in Europe, but he quickly adapted.[652]

As for Robert, after all these years, it must have been comforting for him to have his son back in the family home and already serving key roles in his businesses. And yet, their reunion was not the only positive note on which the year would end. The *Morning Tribune* of December 29, 1913 offered another welcome announcement, which was that, "A new steamship line will start operations between Tampa, Punta Gorda, Boca Grande and Havana on the first of the year and it is expected the line will prove to be a great asset to Tampa throughout the coming year. This line will use the Mugge docks for terminals which will be a convenient place for shippers."[653] After a year in which Robert had scored notable successes, taken risks, shared his visions with an often uncomprehending public, and suffered at least one devastating loss, he had, for now, once again established a balance between unscheduled departures and reassuring arrivals.

Chapter Twenty-Eight

Somebody Bet on the Bay

Augustus Mugge, having only just returned to Tampa in late 1913, was not listed in the 1914 *Tampa City Directory*, even though he was now acting as an architect for his father, as well as doing weekly collections from his father's saloons. For his part, older brother Eugene, back in the fold as well, was now listed as manager of the Sunlight Manufacturing Company, and he and his wife Mimi and daughter Marie were apparently living in the family home. Therefore, for the first time since 1901, when Eugene had left for Germany, followed by Frances and August in 1903, Robert Mugge's entire family—his wife and seven surviving children—were living nearby, along with his sister Bertha, his son-in-law Herman, his daughter-in-law Mimi, and his four surviving grandchildren. So, for Robert and his wife Caroline, this must have been the sweetest of times, even if Robert, true to form, never stopped working.

For instance, his latest project, described in the *Morning Tribune* of December 30, 1913 as a "Hotel For Negroes," and in the *Tribune* of January 4, 1914 as "$40,000 apartments," was an unexpected challenge for someone already building a ten-story hotel. Regardless, he saw a need, and so decided to fill it. According to the first article, Robert, "owner of a lot at the corner of Harrison Street and Central Avenue, is having five small cottages moved from it preparatory to erecting a brick building which will be used as a negro hotel."[654] And according to the later piece: "Plans are out for a $40,000 hotel for negroes which R. Mugge will put up at Harrison Street and Central Avenue, in the Scrub. The first floor will be occupied by eight stores, and the stories above will be devoted to apartments. The building will stand on a lot 163x80 feet. Drawings made by August Mugge, son of Mr. Mugge, have been put into the hands of building inspector Paul Gasser for approval. It is likely the permit will be granted during the week and the work begun."[655]

Please note that, at the time, the word "hotel" could designate a resting place for travelers, or a building offering long-term rentals. Most likely, this hotel was to function as both. Yet, either way, why would Robert take on another large-scale effort at such a hectic time? Was he building a Black hotel out of guilt that, under Jim Crow segregation, his white whale of a building could only accommodate white guests? Was he doing it as a practical consideration since, as the article of December 30 added, "A well known negro citizen constructed a similar building in the 'Scrub' last year and now has one of the best paying businesses in that part of the city?"[656] Or was there a symmetry for him in having created a Black subdivision when he first arrived in Tampa, and now, late in his career, erecting an African American hotel in the same locale?

Whatever his reasons, it was a meaningful gesture to his friends, workers, and neighbors of color, if only because, under segregation, African Americans had limited housing options, and when they traveled, Black hotels were few and far between. Most often, African American salesmen, musicians, theater groups, and even relocating soldiers had to stay with friends or the members of local Black churches. So, Tampa apparently having two such hotels as early as 1914 made it an oasis, at least in terms of shelter.[657]

Meanwhile, day after day, week after week, month after month, work also advanced on Robert's other hotel. Periodically, new information was revealed to the press, including the hiring of Ernest G.

Stanford, formerly of the Tampa Bay Hotel, to oversee the furnishing of the building and, later, to serve as manager. According to the *Morning Tribune* of January 29, 1914, other recently disclosed information was that each bedroom would be fitted with a bath or shower, the building would be steam-heated, the kitchen would be "in charge of a competent German chef from New York," and further features would include "several beautifully appointed reception rooms, a large lobby and writing room."[658]

Progress on the so-called "negro hotel" was soon announced as well, including in the *Morning Tribune* of March 24, 1914: "Architect August Mugge and Contractor Davidson are rushing work on the Mugge Building, Central Avenue and Harrison Street, which is to be a hotel for negroes." Reportedly, the hotel would be completed and ready for occupancy by May 1. The three-story brick building had "white trimmings, which give it an ornate appearance." The only other new information was that the building stood ten feet back from the street, "thus widening Central Avenue at that point," and it was said to be the most impressive building "yet erected in that portion of the city."[659]

In his memoirs, under the title "Central Hotel," August shared his memories of being a twenty-three-year-old architect with his first major building already nearing completion. Of course, for him, the most satisfying part of the experience was seeing his sometimes difficult father "well satisfied with the plans." In passing, he also noted that concrete from his father's old swimming pool "was crushed and used in the foundation of the hotel." In addition, he confirmed that the Sunlight Manufacturing Company, now managed by his brother Eugene, had taken the place of Robert's former ice factory and electric plant. But as to the hotel, his foremost recollections were that, "It was quite a building ... and it was completed in the late spring of 1914 and occupied by tenants.[660]

Affirmation of these facts appeared in the *Morning Tribune* of May 13, 1914: "The banquet that will be held as part of the program of the meeting here of the Negro Medical, Dental and Pharmaceutical Association, will be held in the banquet hall in the new Mugge building at Central Avenue and Harrison Street, instead of in a restaurant, as inadvertently stated in yesterday's paper."[661] Since the two main Tampa papers did not cover much about the African American community, this impressively routine notice about something other than violence, illegal behavior, arrests, or repression in the Scrub was a definite step forward, perhaps linked more to interest in the hotel than in the event itself. However, it also indicated that, almost immediately after its opening at 1030 Central Avenue, the hotel was able to attract, both as guests and as diners, a large, Black professional organization.

Returning to Robert's ever-evolving ten-story building, more news about that appeared in the *Morning Tribune* of April 9, 1914: "Workmen are busy transforming the structure into a luxurious hotel." Currently, plumbers and electricians were installing fixtures, which was expected to take approximately sixty days, while "the job of putting in partitions" would take perhaps two weeks. Meanwhile, a great many "unique ideas" had been "planned in detail by R. Mugge" and were then being instituted, including a central hall, twenty feet wide and 100 feet long, on each of the top nine floors. The floors, themselves, were being decorated with "rich carpets and handsome furniture, ornate illuminations and wide windows overlooking the city," which should make them "fine places to talk, smoke and enjoy an occasional drink." The guest rooms would be arranged as suites, with each pair of bedrooms connecting, and each of those having its own bathroom. Robert explained that, because men tend to like showers, and women tend to like baths, one bathroom in the suite would contain a tub, and the other would contain a shower. But perhaps most intriguing was the paper's note that, "Aiming at constant renovation, Mr. Mugge has a plan to overhaul the hotel completely once a year, without ceasing business for a day. As there will be nine floors it will be possible to put one floor at a time out of service."[662]

Throughout his career, Robert had balanced creativity and practicality in everything he did. That was true in his construction of new buildings, and it was equally true in his courtroom appearances related to his wholesale and retail liquor business. While known for hiring talented attorneys, overseeing their arguments, and working on his business accounts while monitoring the progress of each hearing, Robert's legal cunning and dry wit, even when he himself said nothing at all, could make such hearings extremely entertaining affairs.[663] Take, for example, the Federal trial described in the *Morning Tribune* of May 26, 1914.

As noted previously, during a US Bureau of Internal Revenue arrest in May of 1910, Robert had been charged with selling alcoholic beverages from containers of liquor, the contents of which was different from what government labels had attested it to be. With the trial finally under way, gauger Miller, who had tested thirteen casks in Robert's establishment, testified that he had found the whiskey weaker than branded by the government. More specifically, he claimed that whiskey in the "packages" (the government's word for casks) was three to seven percent less potent than was labeled. "By a mathematical calculation he reached the conclusion that the packages were short two and three gallons each."

Next, in cross-examination, attorney M. B. Macfarlane asked the witness if the packages tested contained corn whiskey, but Mr. Miller could not remember. So, Col. Macfarlane then asked a hypothetical question: Assuming that some of the casks had held corn whiskey, would the contents still be corn whiskey, even if the proof had been reduced by the addition of water? "The line of questioning was adopted to show the jury that the addition of water would not necessarily change the kind and character of the spirits." Mr. Miller admitted that corn whiskey with water added would still be corn whiskey, but stated that the question itself implied tampering, and that "sod corn whiskey when it is drowned by hydrant water is a poor beverage when compared with the bare footed product of the mountain stills."

Still taking this notion that corn whiskey weakened by water does not cease to be corn whiskey, Col. Macfarlane then asked "if the whiskey might not take the water by absorption through the barrel staves." An expert imported from upstate then confirmed that corn whiskey could absorb moisture from "the exhilarating atmosphere of South Florida, and that this accounts for the convivial effect of the 'white mule' which it was suggested, rivaled champagne, fittingly described as 'the imprisoned laughter of the peasant girls of France.'"[664]

All of this was followed later that afternoon by a terse statement in the *Tampa Times:* "Judge Rhydon M. Call this morning instructed the jury to render a verdict of not guilty in the case of Robert Mugge charged with adulterating liquors. The case against Mugge was deemed insufficient to convict, after the United States had completed its testimony, and no defense was required of Mugge or his attorneys, Macfarlane & Chancey."[665] Victory in such a case is always sweet, but that much more so when ingeniously earned, with the "burden of proof" placed squarely where it belongs.

Moving from one manner of spirit to another, the *Morning Tribune* of Tuesday, July 21, 1914 included the following announcement: "Rev. L. C. Wambsganss, wife and daughter Louella leave this morning for Anna Maria Beach where they will spend the remainder of the week as the guests of Mrs. R. Mugge and family at their cottage 'Sorgenfrei.'"[666] As mentioned, Robert would never even see the beach house he had ordered built on Anna Maria Island, but it made him happy knowing that his family enjoyed it, and that they would do so for years to come. His German name for the dwelling translated as "free from care."

Between 1909 and 1916, Rev. Wambsganss served as the pastor of Zion Evangelical Lutheran Church at the corner of Tyler and Marion Streets in Tampa. At the time, it occupied a humble wood-framed building with little ornamentation. In 1922, August Mugge would become president of the congregation, and after the death of his first wife Dorothea in 1924, would commit himself to building a handsome brick church and parsonage at the corner of Warren and Highland Avenues. But until that time, all Tampa Lutherans worshipped in the small wooden building. And since most were German immigrants, all but two special services per month were conducted in German.

Caroline and her children were active members of the church, but Robert did not attend. According to August's memoirs, although his father had been baptized and was confirmed a Lutheran while growing up in Germany, as an adult, he never belonged to any church. However, he routinely quoted Bible passages, and August believed he was "a Christian in his own way."

August also remembered a Sunday morning in the summer of 1914 when a Rev. H. Niedernhoefer had stopped by his father's office, representing himself as affiliated with the American Lutheran Church and wanting to speak with Robert about his desire to start a church in Tampa. Believing his father would not be interested, August told him he was wasting his time. But Rev. Niedernhoeffer elected to wait, and when Robert arrived, he invited the preacher to sit and chat. August then excused himself, but when he returned later that evening, the two were still talking, presumably on matters of religion. And due to that one visit, although Rev. Wambsganss would continue to be the family's pastor, officiating for such occasions as weddings and baptisms, on one future occasion, it was Rev. H. Niedernhoeffer, based in Ocala, Florida, who would receive the call.[667]

As Tampa grew, many houses of worship were founded, including two early synagogues, one established in 1894 and the other in 1902, when a split took place between Orthodox and Reform members. Although Jews had been successfully woven into the white community since the mid nineteenth century—serving as mayors, judges, doctors, and merchants[668]—Christians were dominant, of course, as were their churches, divided not only by denomination but also by race. Segregation was as prevalent in matters of the spirit as of the flesh, and how Black churches were treated by Tampa's white power structure was on full display in the City Council meeting of August 11, 1914. The Morning Tribune of the following day recorded that session, which also included a darkly humorous debate about euthanizing cats. The piece was headlined, "From Sublime to Ridiculous," which was at least half right: "Entertainment of a various character was offered by the council last night and an entertainment, which, if it could have been well advertised, would surely have filled the council chamber to overflowing ... There were moments of genuine solemnity and others of almost riotous laughter."

The Council session opened with a petition from Tampa's Afro-American League which was backed by Black and white church congregations throughout the city. The group was requesting that houses of prostitution "be removed from close proximity to certain colored churches." It was later followed by discussion of a proposed ordinance to license all cats in the city and to have the police department kill those which continued to be unlicensed and untagged. Both propositions led councilmen to highly unusual bouts of "oratorical display," and the first to a kind of sermonizing that appeared pious but was clearly unsympathetic.

Once again, the opening complaint was that, having "houses of ill-fame" so near to churches helped to undo the good the churches were trying to accomplish. However, the councilmen were quick to respond that the Black churches bore responsibility for this situation, in that most of the brothels had occupied their present locations much longer than the churches that had moved in around them. Councilman James Etzler went even further, stating that, "He, for one, would not vote to change the present state of affairs if it meant that the women who reside in those houses at present are to be scattered all over the city thereby, because he did not propose to do injury to other sections in order to relieve the situation among the people of the colored section which they had brought upon themselves." But that was followed by Councilman Anderson who launched into a quasi-sermon about "the incident of the Magdalene woman whom the Christ protected from the mob when they would have stoned her to death," extending the message to a defense of "the women who are obliged from the force of circumstances to be inhabitants of such places," and warning everyone present "to beware how they cast the first stone against them." Ironically, this was likely the first time "women of ill fame," the primary target of Ordinance 175, had been defended in Council. Yet, it demonstrated that even prostitutes were accorded a higher status there than were respected members of the Black community.

The petition from the Afro-American League was finally referred to the police committee where it would no doubt die of neglect, and Council then took up the proposed ordinance regarding the licensing and killing of cats. This discussion quickly descended into a competition among councilmen to see who could tell the worst jokes on the subject, coupled with serious concerns from Chief Woodward about his men using the ordinance as excuse for target practice in the streets. The petition also turned out to have been introduced by M. R. Mills, the president of the Tampa Audubon Society, who was more than ready to sacrifice the city's cats in exchange for protecting local birds. Ultimately, though, this proposal, too, went nowhere, councilmen perhaps having learned from recent history, they were better off doing nothing than being ridiculed for wrongheaded actions.[669] Yet, more serious lessons could be drawn as well.

Tampa's white citizens could vote the Council in or out, whereas Black citizens had been stripped of that right. Therefore, all understood that, for Council members, the top priority was ensuring that problems facing Black neighborhoods did not migrate to white ones. Equally clear was the sway of interest groups, as in the Audubon Society being allowed to urge the killing of cats in order that the city's birds be protected. With animals as with humans, access to power determined health and safety.

That same month, the health and safety of Eugene Mugge's wife Mimi and daughter Marie became an issue as well. According to the *Morning Tribune* of August 2, 1914, the two had left on May 15 for another extended visit with Mimi's family in their German hometown of Giessen.[670] This was significant because, on July 28, in response to the assassination of Archduke Franz Ferdinand and his wife Sophie, Austria-Hungary had shelled Belgrade, Serbia, which officially began World War I. Then, on August 1, in support of Austria-Hungary, Germany entered the war as well, intent on defeating France and Russia.[671] As nations from around the world—not yet including the US—piled on for one side or the other, a second article in the *Morning Tribune* of August 29 revealed that Eugene had received a letter from Mimi dated August 2, which was "about the time the mobilization of German troops was under way." The *Tribune* declared its hope that both Mimi and her young daughter Marie were not enduring "extraordinary hardships" while residing in the "warring country."[672]

Meanwhile, the ongoing wars between saloon owners and government officials continued apace, with City Council passing another law aimed exclusively at saloons. According to the *Morning Tribune* of July 20, 1914, the upshot was that, as of October 1, the city would allow only one saloon for every one thousand residents.[673] Of course, since Robert had lobbied for such a law, hoping to head off increased competition, he could hardly complain now. However, by early the following year, he would surely wish he had.

But returning to Robert's much-anticipated ten-story hotel, articles about its progress were appearing with increasing frequency. One in the *Tampa Times* of September 15, 1914 mostly repeated old news, yet did mention that the construction was not merely fire-proof, but also "noise-proof," that Robert was said to be spending $60,000 on the interior changes alone, and that the name of the hotel would be the Bay View, because of the "excellent view to be had of the bay from its windows."[674]

Two days later, the *Morning Tribune* added a few additional facts, as well as enhancing some already disclosed in the *Times*. For instance, the first floor would now be comprised of a lobby, a dining room, a pantry, a kitchen, an office, and a buffet. In addition, two large passenger elevators would be encased in fireproof boxes and would move through fireproof shafts; a four-foot-wide marble stairway would lead from the ground floor lobby to the top of the building; and the view from uppermost floors made ships in the river and trains on the land below look like miniatures.[675]

After August Mugge and contractor B. H. Davidson finished work on the Central Hotel, Robert put them to work on completion of the Bay View. According to August, his father initially placed B. H. Davidson in charge. But soon thereafter, Mr. Davidson went on a binge, infuriating Robert, who dismissed him and placed August in charge instead. Suddenly under August's purview were carpenters, bricklayers, painters, and plumbers, all of them working "incessantly," which was quite a challenge. Accordingly, the payroll was approximately $2,500 per week, and August did not know how his father could stand the pressure. "Architecturally, I did the best I could with the painting of all rooms, in decorating the lobby, having front doors installed according to my design, also the entrance, over-head paneling under the marquee, and the columns were boxed in and appropriately painted. I made a perspective drawing of the hotel which was used on the stationery."[676]

One piece of information not included in the newspapers of the time, but later mentioned in August's memoirs, was that his father preferred "not to depend on utilities but to own the installations outright." For that reason, he "installed his own telephones and switchboards" in the Bay View, "instead of yielding to the telephone company," which would have charged him a monthly fee.[677] Beyond that, however, there were few details not reported by local press.

For example, the *Morning Tribune* of October 18, 1914 published an article that focused both on new metal windows ordered for the hotel and on how fireproof the building had become. First, it announced the arrival of a large shipment of double-hung metal windows which would be installed on three sides of the Bay View, the front side not requiring them because of being "reasonably free from fire." Second, it relayed building inspector Paul Gasser's contention that the hotel was now so fireproof that, "If I were on the tenth floor, and somebody were to yell 'Fire!' I wouldn't even turn over in bed." That was because, with the interior walls and floors being fireproof, and the elevators being encased in fireproof shafts, any fire would be confined to a single area.[678]

Finally, the *Morning Tribune* of November 7, 1914 conveyed Manager Ernest Stanford's promise that remaining details were being rushed so that the hotel would be ready for occupancy "as soon after December 15 as possible." For instance, large groups of workmen were now adding "interior designs over plaster on the ceilings and walls, with a different pattern and shade for each room." In addition, furniture had been purchased, "all of modern and elegant design," and was ready for installation.

Stanford also announced that he had personally overseen purchase of equipment for the dining room and kitchen, including "every known labor saving device and every invention for improving service," as well as silverware specially designed and intended to last fifty years. As to "dining room arrangements," those would be under the personal supervision of B. H. Bostain, who would leave his present establishment under the charge of his brother, J. M. Bostain, so that he could give his full attention to the "banqueting feature, as the second floor lobby can be used for this purpose and will seat 400 persons." Moreover, "afternoon teas for the ladies" would be "served in private reception rooms."

Although manager Stanford did announce that, regrettably, it would not be possible to include a roof garden as originally planned, other fascinating features had been added. For one, the only wood used in the entire hotel was for doors and window frames, and if they should catch fire, they could easily be doused by fire hoses available on every floor and connected to a large water main. For another, cleaning would be accomplished by "vacuum machinery," with the dust and dirt transported through the walls and into containers in the basement.[679]

Everything was now proceeding perfectly. So, what could prevent Robert Mugge's full enjoyment of this moment? Nothing less than a saloon-related drama in which his son and employee, Eugene, was at least a supporting player. No, what was written in the *Morning Tribune* of November 29, 1914 would not have brought Robert joy.

The complicated story began as Rev. W. E. Thompson was preparing to give a temperance address from an automobile on a street in Plant City. At that point, Robert's son Eugene introduced himself, and they had a pleasant conversation. But once the address began, Eugene interrupted, asking the source of statistics Rev. Thompson had recited. The preacher replied, then continued. But a short time later, Eugene interrupted again, demanding to know where the preacher had secured his information. Rev. Thompson answered that he was quoting from testimony given before a United States Senate committee, to which Eugene responded, "the committee is a set of thieves."

Eugene then went on to say that, as a rule, preachers tended to be "the biggest class of criminals," causing Rev. Thompson to counter that, although it was possible some "unrighteousness" could be found among members of his own profession, their "career of vice did not extend over so broad a field as did the liquor traffic." This led to a period of confusion, including pushing and shoving between those favoring Eugene's point of view and those favoring the minister's.

Among those mistreated during the melee was an older man named E. W. Wiggins who was pushed to the ground by a former saloon proprietor, Jack Garner. Mr. Garner was then arrested by Marshal Ed Vestel, taken to the station, booked, and released on bond.

Although told to go home, Mr. Garner returned to the meeting "with the announced intention of making an apology." But when he arrived, he was confronted by Charles Wiggins, the son of the man he had knocked down. A fight ensued, and Garner stabbed Wiggins three times, "the third thrust proving effective."

For a time that night, while Wiggins was under the care of Dr. J. C. Knight, it was thought that an artery might have been severed, and that he could die. This led to further tension between the two groups, and some even spoke of taking the law into their own hands (usually code for lynching). Finally, though, Dr. Knight announced that the condition of Charles Wiggins was good, and that he should survive, "unless unexpected complications set in."[680]

The follow-up to this event was reported in the *Morning Tribune* of December 1, 1914: "Eugene Mugge, of Tampa, and W. J. Sanderson and Jack Garner, of this city, were fined in Police Court here this morning for disturbing the peace during the progress of the meeting held here Saturday night by the 'drys' after which serious trouble was narrowly averted following the cutting of Charles Wiggins by Garner, a former saloonkeeper ... Mugge pleaded not guilty, claiming he had a right to interrupt a speaker, but the judge decided that the Tampa liquor man had gone too far with his questioning ... The fair-minded people of this community heartily deplore the affair which they fear will cast a reflection upon the city."[681]

From there, the year could only get better. And so, on December 13, 1914, the *Morning Tribune* announced the following: "Mugge Building Finished."[682] Strictly speaking, that was not yet the case. But the finish line was approaching, and "The Bay" was sprinting ahead.

Chapter Twenty-Nine

Accommodations

The Tampa *City Directory of 1915* no longer mentioned Eugene Mugge at all, and Robert was now listed as manager of the Sunlight Manufacturing Company, a position he had recently entrusted to Eugene. Therefore, it seems safe to assume that father and son had fought hard over recent events, prompting Eugene to move to New York City where he could pursue other prospects, his wife and daughter presumably still being stuck in Germany.

In Tampa, meanwhile, Robert's own ambitions continued to grow. As if he did not face a big enough challenge opening two large hotels, simultaneously, he decided to open a new bowling alley and pool hall complex as well. This effort, like the others, looked to the future, while also bearing resonance from his past. The *Tampa Times* of January 9, 1915 made that clear: "R. Mugge has moved his wholesale liquor stock to his Central avenue building [meaning his two-story Central Saloon Building at Central Avenue and Harrison Street, opposite his new Central Hotel] and has torn out the inside of the place so long used by him on Franklin street preparatory to putting in a bowling alley and pool room. He will have eight bowling alleys and seven pool and billiard tables and will run the place on a high plane. Mr. Mugge had a grocery store on this same location thirty-five years ago when he first came to the city and has occupied it ever since."[683]

Translation? The buildings which once housed Bartholomew C. Leonardy's general store, then contained Robert Mugge and William Mahn's grocery store, and later were converted for use as Robert's wholesale house, would now feature the largest number of high-quality bowling lanes and pool tables ever seen in the City of Tampa. In other words, despite his plan to open a luxurious new hotel which the law required be exclusively white, supplemented by an entertainment complex a half-block away, he would conduct his remaining businesses out of his newly renovated Black saloon and his handsome Black hotel in the heart of the Scrub.

A week before the much-heralded Bay View Hotel opening, the *Tampa Times* of Monday, January 11, 1915 announced an event of at least equal importance, which was the wedding of Frances Bertha Mugge to Frederick Otto Reiner, a bookkeeper for the Tampa-Cuba Cigar Company, and soon to be a key executive for Mugge family businesses. The quiet ceremony had taken place on Saturday afternoon at the German Evangelical Lutheran Church, with Rev. Louis Wambsganss presiding. According to the *Times*, "The impressive German double ring ceremony was used and the witnesses to the wedding were a few relatives only. The bride was attired in a becoming coat suit of midnight blue, with accessories to match. Her attendant was little Miss Frances Regener, a niece and namesake. This little girl acted as ring bearer and her dress was a dainty white lingerie, with blue sash and ribbons. The best man was Mr. William Petrich."

After the ceremony, Mr. and Mrs. Reiner led their guests to the Mugge family home where an informal reception was held, and at 3:30 p.m., the couple left for a honeymoon on the "west coast" (presumably the west coast of Florida). Upon their return to the city, they would move into a "beautiful new bungalow" at 3110 Tampa Street. "The young couple enjoys the friendship of a large circle, all of whom join in wishing them every happiness in life."[684]

An interesting addendum to the wedding (though actually a prelude) is the fact that, just five months before, in the *Morning Tribune* of August 6, 1914, four young German American men had told a reporter that, if asked, they would return to Germany and fight for the fatherland in World War I. The four were Otto Reiner, Frances Mugge's new husband; William Petrich, manager of Tampa's German American Club, and Otto's best man; Fritz Petri, the recently arrived brother of Eugene's wife Mimi, and a clerk for Robert Mugge; and A. Haule, who was the current manager of the Tampa Bay Hotel.[685] Of course, it must be said that all of these men likely had been born in Germany, and the United States itself would not enter the war for another two and a half years. But the conflicting emotions of first-generation German Americans could not have been better illustrated.

For Robert, the wedding of Frances Bertha Mugge—a daughter whose intellect so impressed him that he sent her to school in Germany, at a time when few women were being properly educated—would have been absolute bliss, but likely also a welcome diversion just a week before his scheduled hotel opening. In fact, if he was trying to push the opening from his mind, perhaps he did not even care—not at first, anyway—how much reporters were now focusing on the hotel's manager, sometimes to the detriment of its long suffering and sacrificing owner. The change was clearly on display in the *Morning Tribune* of January 12, 1915, including this gushing description: "A strong personnel of experienced hotel men will conduct the house. It will be managed by E. G. Stanford, who has had wide experience in the business. Formerly he was steward at the Tampa Bay Hotel, was later supervisor and, in the summer of 1912, he successfully managed it for H. L. Coe. His reputation as an able and affable host is already well established in South Florida."

The article went on to give Mr. Stanford personal credit for overseeing the "brilliant artistic effects" to be found throughout the hotel. These included "handsome lighting fixtures" hanging in the tiled lobby; two rapid elevators, one of which could travel 300 feet a minute and the other 175 feet a minute; "luxurious furniture" of mahogany on the eighth floor and fumed oak everywhere else; bedrooms with "harmonious color schemes" comprised of tinted walls, carpeted floors and furniture, plus grip racks, metal waste paper baskets, thermos carafes, ladies' writing desks, and wardrobes; as well as bathrooms containing crystal shelves and towel racks, and all needed accessories. Most of the bedrooms contained twin beds, and some of the rooms were connecting. But otherwise, the styles of furniture and other aspects varied according to the needs of traveling men, of ladies, and of families, for whom suites had been prepared.

Given special attention were the reception halls on every floor, which featured upholstered chairs, stylish tables and lamps, and shades which harmonized with the rest of the furniture. These halls were further said to be "bathed in soft floods of light from many overhead lamps," to have carpeted floors on which were placed lovely little rugs, and to have card tables available for "sociable games."

The story ended with two interesting side notes. One was that Stanford had taken out a three-year lease on the Knight Building on the opposite side of Jackson Street as a place to show off sample rooms for the hotel; and the other was a mention that guests would have access to Mugge's new bowling alleys and pool hall, just around the corner on Franklin Street.[686] Then, while patronizing these recreational facilities on the east side of Franklin, they would likely be tempted to have a meal and a few drinks in his St. Louis Cafe next door to them. In other words, this was the sort of vertical integration for which Robert had long been known, but with new variables in the types of businesses involved. Regardless, though, the ultimate point was that years of work were soon to culminate in the grand opening of a grand hotel, and anticipation was growing throughout the city.

The day after the Monday night opening, both Tampa newspapers were exuberant in their praise, perhaps at least in part because an opening night dinner had been held in their honor. The *Morning Tribune* led the charge: "Mayor McKay [also still the editor of the rival *Tampa Times*] headed a delegation of newspaper workers who accepted the hospitality of Manager E. G. Stanford last night at the opening of the new Bayview Hotel, the latest and, perhaps, most modern hotel in the South." The article went on to effuse that, "The lobby and upper stories also show that the hand of a genius has been at work fitting the building for a hotel," then reported that the dinner for the press had been "one of the most delightful ever served in Tampa."

The menu "served by Manager Stanford to his guests" included the following: "Martini Cocktail, Blue Points on Half Shell, Terafin Alvarez Sherry, Consome Bay View, Celery, Radishes, Olives, Broiled Spanish Mackeral, Maitre d'Hotel, Pommes Natural, Haute Sauterne, Filet Mignon a la Stanford, Rice a la Conde with Peaches, G. H. Mumm's 'Extra Dry,' Roast Stuffed Philadelphia Squab au Cresson, Green Peas, Mashed Potatoes, Salad Terfoglia, Neapolitan Ice Cream, Assorted Cake, Camembert Cheese, Demi Tasse, Benedictine, Chartreuse, Creme de Menthe, Cigars, Cigarettes."[687]

The *Tampa Times* of the same day was at least as complimentary: "Ranking with the finest hotels of the country in point of provision for the entertainment of its guests, the Bay View hotel was formally opened last evening, the beautiful dining room being crowded from the opening hour of 6:30 o'clock until late in the evening. It was with pardonable pride that Manager Stanford led his guests through the building, pointing out arrangements provided for the special comfort of the hotel's guests. On all sides were heard words of praise for the excellence of the building and its appointments, for R. Mugge, the owner of his enterprise, and for the management to whom the task of selecting fittings and furniture fell."

The *Times* reporter went on to describe how the "exquisite finishings furnished an excellent background for the roses and carnations that decorated the lobbies and the dining room in profusion." He then called attention to the woodwork and lighting of the dining room, and stood in awe of how "the table occupied by the newspapermen stretched for the entire room, and next to the windows." Finally, he reported how Mayor McKay, as the evening's first speaker, "took occasion in his remarks to speak of the good work Robert Mugge had accomplished in this city and his progressiveness" (traits not so much admired when the mayor's newspaper was viciously attacking him for his support of the proposed charter change), then "highly praised the Bay View hotel and its manager Ernest G. Stanford for the manner in which the work of fitting up the hotel had taken place."[688]

What was strange, of course, was that the man responsible for all of this—the man who had the original vision, who stuck with the project for years, and who risked his financial well-being, and possibly his health, in the process—had decided not to be present for his own moment of glory. In effect, he had thrown a giant dinner party, and then taken himself off the guest list. The one person who could speak to that phenomenon was Robert's son August, and he did so fifty years later for his memoirs: "At the Grand Opening, the dining room was filled to capacity, and in the center, Mr. Stanford had reserved a table for his guests, amongst these Mayor D. B. McKay. He had naturally asked my father, who declined and told him that I would represent him. I had on my tuxedo, and it was quite an elaborate affair with speech making, etc. On behalf of my father, I thanked them all. Looking towards the window, I saw my father standing on the sidewalk looking in, and he supposedly made a remark to somebody, 'Now, all of this belongs to me, and I have to stand on the outside.'"[689]

Robert Mugge's exile was self-imposed, of course, and perhaps indicated some deeper sense of alienation from the Tampa, Florida of 1915. At the very least, it implied strong second thoughts about the project, about what it was costing him, and about the man he had placed at its helm. The latter was safe to assume, since all he had repressed would soon come crashing to the surface. But even knowing the melodrama soon to unfold, it seems proper to savor this moment just a bit longer, allowing *Tribune* editor Wallace F. Stovall the final word. His editorial appeared in the January 20, 1915 issue of his morning paper:

> The formal opening of Tampa's new hotel, The Bayview [sic], is worthy of special chronicle in the development of the city. By what must strike the observer as a wonder work of architecture, this massive building, erected originally for warehouse purposes, the tallest structure in the city, has been converted, in a few months time, into a modern, up-to-date and well-appointed hotel, with metropolitan equipment, said to be the best furnished hotel in the South ...
>
> It is proper in greeting Tampa's newest establishment and one so creditable as this, to speak of the man whose

indomitable energy and progressive spirit have provided the
city with such an attraction ... Building a ten-story building
and then deciding it could not be used for the purpose
intended, Mr. Mugge adopted the idea of making it a hotel
and, despite the scoffing of the skeptical, proceeded to carry
out that idea ... It has been done and it stands a monument
to the energy and persistence of its builder and owner. And
those who have at times decried Mr. Mugge should now do
him the simple justice of acknowledging that he has given
Tampa something of which it may be proud.[690]

Editor Wallace Stovall's observation that Robert's latest accomplishments came "despite the scoffing of the skeptical" echoed similar comments made thirty-eight years before by the editor of the *Sunland Tribune* (unrelated to Stovall's later *Tribune* newspapers), shortly after Robert and Alice Janthe arrived in Tampa: "As an industrious and enterprising citizen we can not speak too highly of Mr. R. Mugge ... Many of the older citizens were disposed to laugh at Mr. Mugge when he commenced improving his place, but he has certainly set them an example of enterprise, and we cannot but wish that many more such as he would settle in our town."[691] For Robert, it was always a blessing, yet also a curse, to see things others could not; to try things others would not; and to believe things others felt he should not. Such was, and is, the plight of the immigrant—and also the supremely gifted individual—to be ever out-of-sync with the time and place he or she has come to inhabit. Indeed, as Stovall went on to say, it was time to acknowledge "that he has given Tampa something of which it may be proud." Regrettably, the city was still not ready to do so.

On the same day Wallace Stovall delivered his earnest appreciation, the *Tampa Times* reported how the City Council showed him none. Only hours after opening his hotel, Robert went before them asking simply that they change the ordinance limiting the number of saloons in the city. That way, he would be able to buy a liquor license for his hotel, without which it surely would not succeed. Council's response was, "If Mr. Mugge wishes to gain a license for the bar in his new hotel he could do so by closing up one of his many other bars in the city and have the license transferred."[692] And yet, as Robert tried to explain, in building, reworking, and furnishing his hotel, he had gone so deeply into debt that he could not afford to close even one of his saloons. As a result, the evening ended in a standoff, with his request postponed until the next regular meeting.

Apparently, the strain of this situation, and perhaps some resentment from all the credit his new hotel manager was taking for its successful completion, led to a confrontation between owner and manager. The result of that confrontation was explained in the *Morning Tribune* of January 31, 1915. "A change was made in the management of the Bay View last night when August B. Mugge, son of Robert Mugge, owner of the hotel, assumed charge, relieving Ernest G. Stanford, who opened the house two weeks ago." Quickly moving to a positive slant, the *Tribune* opined that the new manager, August Mugge, was both "widely traveled" and "highly cultured," having attended leading German universities. The reporter also touted August's knowledge of both American and European hotels, his charming personality, and his promise to operate on the same high level as had Mr. Stanford.[693]

The following day, the *Tampa Times* got a statement from Robert Mugge: "'I don't like to engage in a newspaper controversy about a business matter that the public is not interested in, and will only say as does the government when they remove a head of a department that I let Mr. Stanford go for the good of the service." He went on to say that he did not wish to harm Mr. Stanford in any way and was sorry that the matter had become public.[694]

Many years later, in his memoirs, August elaborated. He remembered being summoned by his father and informed that he would take over as manager of the hotel. At first, August had protested that he knew nothing of running a hotel, but Robert told him that he would learn on the job, which he did. August remembered retaining the rest of the office help, and recalled further that, "things went along very smoothly until after the South Florida Fair and the winter season. Daily receipts were turned over, and on Saturdays the payrolls were met, and at the end of the month the utility bills were paid." The one initial challenge was that his predecessor had failed to pay the bills for the opening night banquet he had hosted, leaving August to manage that as well.[695]

From then on, the hotel functioned well, and Robert worked to stabilize his finances which, like him, were under stress due to all the projects he had taken on simultaneously. Ironically, right at that point, August Busch, son of the late Adophus and Lilly Busch and new president of the Anheuser-Busch Brewing Association, decided to send his representatives into the field for a major audit of the company's far-flung agents. Their arrival in Tampa was announced in the *Morning Tribune* of February 6, 1915: "E. S. Clauss, of St. Louis, vice president of the Anheuser-Busch Brewing Company, was a recent arrival at the Bay View accompanied by Mrs. Clauss ... While in the city they were shown around by August Mugge who demonstrated that Tampa is a wide-awake city."[696]

Once again, fifty years later, August provided more details. According to his recollection, Mr. Clauss "was on a rampage, traveling from one agency to another throughout the State of Florida and throwing them into bankruptcy." As part of that trip, Clauss came to Tampa, intending to evaluate Robert's performance as an Anheuser-Busch distributor and his increasingly large debt to the company. But unaware of the potential seriousness of the visit, August invited the Clausses for an afternoon drive around the city and then to dinner at the Bay View, during which he presented Mrs. Clauss with flowers and informed them that he had spent ten years being educated in Germany. The following day, E. S. Clauss met with Robert, told him about August's wonderful hospitality, and of how pleased he was to learn that Robert's son had studied in Germany. After a few days, the Clausses left for St. Louis, but it was not until years later that August learned he likely had saved the day for his father, simply by being gracious to a business associate and his wife.[697]

On February 11, 1915, the *Morning Tribune* gave notice of the opening of Robert Mugge's new bowling alleys at the Mugge Building on Franklin Street and featuring six teams competing for a local championship. The paper also announced that the alleys would be under the supervision of Jack Daley, newly arrived from Boston,

Massachusetts, and purportedly both an expert bowler and an experienced manager of bowling alleys.[698] Then, two days later, the *Tribune* followed up with news of the strong reception given to Robert's new alleys, which were said to be the best yet offered in Tampa.[699]

Still, one key problem remained. Robert knew his Bay View Hotel could not succeed without a liquor license, and so far, City Council was refusing to honor his request. The *Tampa Times* of February 24, 1915 reported his latest ritual effort, this time with a slightly different spin. Since Council repeatedly informed him that the only way he could secure a permit for his hotel was by transferring one from another establishment, he offered up a license "issued to him for a saloon on the northeast corner of Garcia avenue and Arch street." Unfortunately, the councilmen knew he had not operated a saloon at that location for more than two years, when it was destroyed in a fire. So, this attempt failed as well.[700]

Basically, Robert and City Council were playing a proverbial game of chicken. He wanted that governing body to give him a new license for beer, wine, and liquor sales at his hotel, while they wanted him to transfer a license from one of his existing saloons, which meant his giving up the profits he made from that location, violating his agreement with its manager, throwing multiple bartenders and porters out of work, and probably getting no future use from a piece of property he owned and had furnished for this purpose. Without a license to go with it, and with City Council saying no new permits would be issued, he could not even sell such a saloon to someone else and would be forced to take a major loss.

As noted in the *Tampa Times* of February 27, 1915, the matter of Robert operating the Bay View bar without a license finally resulted in his arrest, as well as a bit of confusion. When he had appeared in Police Court that morning, Judge Bailey was serving as acting judge, because Judge M. Henry Cohen was confined to his home due to illness. Otherwise, Robert was represented by attorney E. R. Dickenson, who asked for a continuance until the following Thursday. The continuance was granted.[701]

With his liquor license situation spiraling out of control, Robert decided it was time to beg. He therefore made his case in a formal petition to City Council, and that petition was printed in the *Tampa Times* of March 3, 1915. His argument continued to be that he could not afford to give up the income from any of his saloons simply to secure a license for his new hotel. But he also proclaimed that he had both built and furnished this hotel for the benefit of the city as it attempted to lure tourists and travelers to South Florida, that he had gone into debt to do so, and that it was unfair to penalize him by making him give up one profitable business to make another one flourish. He then concluded with a final plea, showing more desperation than humility: "I wish to state that I have spent thirty-nine years of hard labor to help build up Tampa, with very little enjoyment for myself. I have paid out several hundred thousand dollars for wages, many times without getting any profits or benefits myself, and I believe I am entitled to some consideration. Respectfully, Robert Mugge." Sadly, the only response from Council was a noncommittal referral of his letter to the Police Committee.[702]

Such maneuvering dragged on for another three weeks.[703] [704] [705] Then, just when it seemed Robert's standoff with Council would never end, he finally won the day with some skillful sleight of hand. As reported in the *Tampa Times* of March 24, 1915, what Robert did was purchase the West Coast Mail Order House, a saloon at Polk and Jefferson Streets which had been owned and formerly operated by Peter Joh, then have its liquor license transferred to the Bay View Hotel.[706] This satisfied the City Council requirement that no new licenses be issued, convinced Judge Cohen that the hotel would not violate city liquor laws, and restored to Robert Mugge the fundamental right to conduct his business.[707]

With all the legal and financial pressure on alcohol-related enterprise, another sign that Robert was trying to diversify came indirectly in a *Morning Tribune* piece of April 16, 1915. Reportedly, a man named Manuel Cabrera had been charged with stealing four electric fans and a drum "from a motion picture theater on Central Avenue, the property of R. Mugge." In fact, when Robert built his new African American hotel with room for eight shops on the first floor, one of those spaces was earmarked for a new "picture show," as a later article called it, and which the Tampa *City Directory* listed as the

Grand Central Theatre. Most likely, the electric fans were installed to cool audiences during warmer weather, and the drum suggests that musicians were accompanying silent features, that the space was being used for vaudeville performances, or both.[708] Beyond that, little more is known of this intriguing enterprise, which seemed a logical next step after Robert's many years of presenting vaudeville.

Nevertheless, with the issuing of a "new" liquor license, Robert's dream project was complete at last. And in case he doubted that the Bay View already was integral to Tampa's identity, the *Morning Tribune* of April 23, 1915 announced that the Board of Trade's new photo envelopes featured a panorama view from the top of his hotel. The envelopes also described Tampa as being "one of the fastest growing cities in America," with the "nearest available port to the Panama Canal, center of the citrus industry, largest phosphate shipping port in the world," and "eleventh revenue producing port of the United States which ships naval stores and lumber to all foreign ports."[709] Yes, the City of Tampa was on the move, and its glittering, irrepressible center was saloon magnate Robert Mugge and his glorious new hotel.

Chapter Thirty

John Barleycorn Must Die

In his memoirs, August Mugge recalled the spring of 1915. As the Bay View's first winter tourist season ended, the number of guests began to decline, and with them the hotel's income. "One day I received a letter from my father in which he informed me that I would have to curtail expenses, and he advised me to discharge Mr. Abbott, the head clerk." August went to his father's office and told him that he would not fire Mr. Abbott, but Mr. Blanchard instead. Robert responded that, had August followed his original instructions, he himself would have been discharged. In other words, it was merely a test of his abilities. As August summed up the situation, "You had to be on your guard."

At this point, August was paid fifty dollars per week to manage the hotel, but most of that went for "entertaining guests." As he noted, a great many so-called traveling men were now coming to the hotel, among them white entertainer Bert Leigh and his troupe who stayed with them for three months while performing at the Greeson Theatre next door.

By May, profits had fallen to the point where Robert ordered August to close the hotel for the summer. However, believing momentum and customer loyalty would be lost by shutting down at all, August refused. Instead, he suggested that he operate the hotel on his own, open a bank account, and at the end of each month, write Robert a check for whatever was left after bills had been paid. And with that understanding, the hotel stayed in operation.[710]

Winter may now have ended, but the air was newly chilled for everyone in the beer, wine, and liquor business. In an editorial in the *Morning Tribune* of April 30, 1915, Wallace F. Stovall gave his best imitation of Paul Revere in announcing the latest, and clearly most serious, assault yet on Robert's core business: "The Davis saloon regulation bill, which has now passed both Houses of the Legislature, is not a measure in the interest of temperance. If our prohibition friends think it is, they are sadly mistaken." What the bill promised to do was prevent saloons from selling alcohol by the drink, insisting that it only be sold by sealed package, meaning bottles, which then would have to be drunk elsewhere. As foreseen by Mr. Stovall, this meant the end of draught beer, the end of social drinking, and the encouragement of drunkenness, since only larger amounts of alcohol would be sold. It also meant that regular drinkers of draught beer in a social setting would become private whiskey drinkers and, because forced to purchase entire bottles rather than mere shots, they would now imbibe far more. Certainly, the *Tribune* editor was correct in writing that, "Such a measure can prove no more than a farce ... It is not based on common sense or reason. In addition to making drunkards, it will make law-breakers and criminals [by encouraging social drinkers to turn to illegal establishments]." Yet, to the detriment of the saloon industry, he was wrong in predicting that, "It will not be supported by public sentiment and, therefore, will become a dead letter."[711]

How had it come to this? In his book, *Last Call: The Rise and Fall of Prohibition*, author Daniel Okrent explained the larger context as follows: "The party of change will always be more motivated than the party of the status quo." He reinforced that with a quote from American humorist George Ade in his 1931 elegy, *The Old Time Saloon*: "'The Non-Drinkers had been organizing for fifty years and the Drinkers had no organization whatsoever. They had been too busy drinking.'"

Okrent went on to describe the "archetypal American" of that time as the latest of several generations of family members to live in a midsized town, to attend the local Protestant church, and to have difficulty identifying with the so-called "wet" activists, who tended to be urban and ethnic, including wealthy German brewers like Adolphus Busch, who had been decorated by the Kaiser. In other words, the so-called "drys" did not like foreigners, and the same "progressives" who supported labor unions, who fought against big-city political machines, and who rallied against saloon culture, also believed in restricting immigration as a means not only of protecting labor but also of combatting saloons. Moreover, when German Americans and Irish Americans opposed the use of a moral or religious pretext for the weakening of personal liberties, progressives saw this not as patriotism, but as resistance to their own morality-based crusades. And of course, as Okrent points out, resistance to foreigners and their ethnic traditions took root most easily in the region of the country built upon slavery: "Xenophobia was yet more intense in the South, even though—or perhaps because—in some Southern states the population was as much as 99 percent native stock. When foreigners showed up on their turf, many Southerners recoiled ... The Klan, which supported woman suffrage in behalf of Prohibition, in turn supported Prohibition as a weapon against the immigrants. This was obviously very fertile soil for the Anti-Saloon League."[712]

It also offers the perfect lead-in to 1915 Florida, where the righteous rumbling of morality-based social engineering had become a roar. However, in attempting to find partial success in momentary compromise, the temperance forces and their political allies had arrived at something truly twisted: a law that would kill saloon culture—and the regulation and taxation that had evolved with it—yet replace it with a system sure to increase public drinking, intoxication, and lawlessness in the process. This would not be prohibition; but if successful, it *would* be a final, fatal hatchet swing to all saloon doors, and no one in Florida would be more affected than Robert Mugge.

By late summer and early fall, Robert and other liquor dealers were growing increasingly nervous. Of course, saloon owners and their patrons were not the only ones panicking, in that, if the new law resulted in the number of saloon closings predicted by local dealers, then state, city, and county coffers would be affected as well. For instance, the *Morning Tribune* of September 14, 1915 reported that "the Davis Package law is a wrench thrown into the machinery of the city government." As illustration of this point, at its session the day before, Tampa's Finance Committee predicted that enforcement of the law would "curtail the city's license taxes approximately $25,000," requiring a similar amount to be cut from budgets if the city were to live within its means.[713]

As for the liquor dealers, they determined among themselves how to proceed. Those in Tampa resolved to let Jacksonville dealers take the lead, as was made clear in the *Morning Tribune* of September 16, 1915. Their friends to the north planned to prove in court that the Legislature had exceeded its powers, in that the State Constitution allowed only one form of prohibition, which was that created through local option elections. Meanwhile, ostensibly, no liquor licenses would be renewed in Tampa until the State Supreme Court had made its ruling.[714]

Yet, among the signs of impending doom was an article in the *Tampa Times* of September 21, 1915: "Fire insurance companies are instructing their agents in Florida to cancel policies in retail saloons and stock and write no more insurance on such hazards." The reason given was that, wherever prohibition laws had thus far been enacted, "disastrous fires [had taken place] among saloons, resulting in losses to the companies with insurance on building and stock."[715]

Then, as announced in the *Morning Tribune* of September 30, 1915, "closing time" arrived at last: "Midnight tonight practically sees the end of the open saloon in Tampa. The Davis Package Law goes into effect on the stroke of twelve, and thousands of dollars' worth of property in this city will be almost a total loss to the liquor men." According to the paper, while some dealers planned to ignore the law, thereby risking a thousand-dollar fine and twelve months of imprisonment, others planned to get out of the business entirely, and still others sought to skirt Davis Law regulations by incorporating existing saloons as fraternal organizations.

For example, just the day before, the *Tribune* revealed an application for a so-called Crystal Club, the name of which was suspiciously like that of Robert's well-known Crystal Saloon. In the club's articles of incorporation, it was described as "an organization for fraternal, social and intellectual advancement of its members," attempting to sell itself as exactly what it was not. Yet, at the same time, City Council was creating tough new criteria for what constituted private clubs, while also passing new club-related license fees as high as $750. In other words, all means by which dealers and drinkers were preparing to skirt the dictates of the law, including these, were being noted, and just as quickly as such efforts were mounted, counter measures were devised.

Even owners getting out of the business entirely faced a heavy financial blow, because the finest in "bars, brass railings, ice chests and coils, bric-a-brac and art a la nude" purchased in headier times were now impossible to unload. As one example, the *Tampa Times* later told the story of Paul Hornlein, the owner of a saloon building in St. Petersburg, whose saloon fixtures had cost him $3,000. However, now that he was leaving the business, he had been forced to sell them for ten dollars, with the buyer agreeing to remove them himself. In short, other than awaiting the Supreme Court ruling and, in the interim, failing to renew city, state, and county licenses, the saloon men really had no good options.[716] [717] [718] [719]

The final effect of this law was described in the newspapers of Friday, October 1, 1915, as the curtain came down on Tampa's saloon era. In the *Morning Tribune*, the headlines alone told the tale: "John Barleycorn Back In Second Line Of Defense—Davis Bill Effective At Midnight Spells Death Knell Of Many Saloons." Yet, in his extensive coverage, editor Wallace Stovall sometimes waxed poetic, while

other times sharing basic and even brutal facts: "Florida took its
first step towards total prohibition at midnight last night when the
Davis Package Law became effective. For the first time since this
State countenanced the open saloons these places will not open their
doors this morning until 7 o'clock. And they will close at 6 this
evening. For it is the law."

Taking for granted that scenes in Tampa were no different than
ones elsewhere in the state, he reported that, "Business in most of
the Tampa saloons was better than usual all evening. The regular
attendants at the saloons were augmented by those who occasionally enjoyed the diversion of 'foot on rail and elbow on bar' ... In
some," he went on, "grotesque conviviality was indulged in and
many discordant voices joined in singing 'Auld Lang Syne.'" But
henceforth, Tampans would have to drink at their homes, in private
offices, or on the street, no longer able to "linger over the brass and
mahogany and depend on it for support."

According to his interviews with saloon owners, of the seventy-
seven saloons previously operating in Tampa, West Tampa, and Port
Tampa, only twenty-five were expected to reopen the following
morning. And of the sixteen or so "adjacent to Franklin Street and
this side of Harrison," only five, at most, would open again, at least
until the Supreme Court ruled on the law's constitutionality. As for
the court fight itself, liquor dealers of the state were challenging the
first, fourth, and seventh sections of the law which regulated hours
of operation, restricted the sale of alcohol to sealed packages, made
it unlawful for liquor to be consumed on the premises where it was
purchased, and forbade the hiring of women to work in so-called
mail order houses.

Of course, during past disputes, saloon magnate Robert
Mugge had dependably been the first into the fray: advocating
for fellow liquor dealers, petitioning City Council or the County
Commissioners, raising his voice in public forums, heaping scorn
upon law enforcement, writing letters to the editors, filing injunctions, provoking test cases, and even proposing compromise rather
that accepting defeat. But this time around—and for several months
past—Robert had refrained from public debate; his ever-present voice

had gone silent, leaving questions only he himself could answer. Had he grown weary of the battle—day in, day out, and year after year—fighting for his rights as a citizen? Was his health failing? Did he feel he had invested so much in his new hotels, bowling alleys, brick buildings, and more that he must, for the first time, avoid speaking out, lest he be assaulted by vengeful authorities? Or did he see this crisis was different: that it was a kind of checkmate; that the law, though awkwardly written, debated, and passed, had nevertheless left little room for the ingenious, unexpected, last-minute, and game-changing gesture, which had always been his specialty? Whatever the answer to that multipart question, on this, the darkest night of Robert's career, the *Tribune* reporter did manage to seek him out, provoking at least a modicum of optimism, even as his lack of action spoke volumes.

"One prominent saloonist [most likely Robert Mugge, but clearly not on the record] stated last night that attorneys in charge of the fight had promised a decision from the Supreme Court by October 15. 'Those of us who are closing, are doing so only temporarily,' he said." Robert also informed the reporter *on* the record that, of the ten city saloons he had opened in Tampa the day before, only three would remain open. One of these was downtown (likely the St. Louis Cafe), one was near Union Station (obviously the Kentucky Mail Order House), and the other was in Ybor City (probably the Seminole Saloon).[720]

For his part, as described in the *Morning Tribune* of October 3, 1915, Sheriff W. C. Spencer, too, was seeking guidance as to which behaviors would be acceptable. To that end, he decided to swear out warrants against four liquor dealers, then use their cases to test the new law. Perhaps the most daunting section was the one "prohibiting the consumption of liquor in the premises of the vendor." Most saloon owners still doing business had partitioned off rooms to the back or side of their establishments and arranged separate entrances from a street or alley, but was this enough to meet new requirements? "There are about thirty saloons operating now, and the Sheriff desires to secure a ruling on the legality of the devices which they employ to avoid violating the law."[721]

Drinkers, themselves, also had to adapt. Seeing the humor in this, the *Morning Tribune* of Monday, October 4, 1915 catalogued assorted solutions for the law's many challenges. For one, the hip pockets of men's suits, which once had been adapted for "weapons of self-defense," now would be shaped for pint versus quart bottles. In the same way, four-ounce vials were seen as a perfect fit for vest pockets, causing drug stores "to neglect their stamp trade" to keep up supply. In addition, restrictions on where drinking could take place had increased demand for office refrigerators and ice boxes, thermos bottles, storm curtains for automobiles, and access to back rooms and livery stables.[722]

Ten days later, *Tribune* editor Wallace F. Stovall decided to explore, even more fully, the humorous part of what was a deadly serious loss of rights for many of his readers. Implicit was how much the liberty of the average citizen had been curtailed since the days when Tampa was little more than a settlement:

> "This here ain't like it used to be when I was a boy," remarked a human specimen of the vintage of '65 [1865] yesterday in one of the new fangled emporiums which have sprouted up in the city during the fortnight the Davis Law has been in effect.
>
> "Why, when I was a young man, you could get beer and whiskey at the grocery store. It was sold over the counter just like flour and sugar. It was as free of regulation as syrup. And it wasn't made out of chemicals, either."
>
> The old man leaned on his cane and spat tobacco juice into a cuspidor. "In them days," he continued, "a feller when he wanted to take a drink, walked up like a two legged human and took it, and didn't have to go through any side doors, get lost in stinkin' alleys and hit any three knocks against the hard pine, alias mahogany, to git what he was after. Since this din-busted Davis law come along a feller don't know whether he's a human being or some sort of dumb brute that ain't worth considerashun [sic]."[723]

In his memoirs, August Mugge recalled how his father had responded, and he gave an update on their relationship as well. Just in terms of the Bay View Hotel, Robert had closed the bar, removed its fixtures, and made a small dining room out of it. The main dining room was operating at a loss, but August managed to rent it out. Drinks were now disbursed to guests at the back of the small dining room, and it was there that Robert maintained a modest workspace for himself. At the end of every month, August gave Robert a check for approximately $600. Robert knew August was keeping nothing for himself, so he offered to pay him $50 per week, as he had previously. Robert said to consider this rent for his own use of the small dining room.[724]

The final hammer came down just over a month after the Davis Package Law had gone into effect. The *Morning Tribune* of November 5, 1915 delivered the crushing blow: "History was made in the Supreme Court of Florida today when the court suspended its rules and announced a decision upholding the constitutionality of the so-called Davis package law." Three justices had voted in support of the law, and two justices had dissented. "The decision of the court was not unexpected here, but there was some surprise expressed that there should have been a division of opinion."[725]

Although no one who mattered was listening, Wallace F. Stovall attempted one last, well-reasoned broadside against the law in the *Morning Tribune* of November 20, 1915, laying out (under the headline, "The Folly of the Law") all the negative effects already taking place throughout his city and others across the state.[726] Then, when that had no effect, he tried again in the December 2, 1915 issue, delivering something quick and to the point: "The Davis law has merely cut down the number of saloons. It is doubtful if it has decreased the quantity sold by so much as a quart. Besides, in those places which dodge the law, the sale is carried on without regard to hours. It is sold at all hours of the night and all day Sunday. The drinker sits at a table instead of standing at a bar. It is behind closed doors without police supervision or public scrutiny. The Davis law is the biggest farce ever put on the statute books. Prohibition and temperance people would do well to appeal to the next Legislature to repeal it and restore the old system."[727] Or to quote twenty-first century *The New York Times* columnist Bret Stephens, himself quoting eighteenth century Irish stateman and philosopher Edmund Burke: "At the core of Burke's view of the [French Revolution] is a profound understanding of how easily things can be shattered in the name of moral betterment, national purification and radical political transformation ... [Burke was] a man who saw, more clearly than most, how 'very plausible schemes, with very pleasing commencements, have often shameful and lamentable conclusions.'"[728]

Yet, the damage was now done, to the city in general and to Robert Mugge in particular. As August wrote in his memoirs, "He must have been going through hell." Most evenings that November, August found his father racking up balls for customers in his new bowling alleys on Franklin Street. He appeared depressed but would not complain. The Davis Package Law had forced him to close nearly all his saloons, and the business that had brought him wealth, fame, and influence—that had fed his family, endeared him to Adolphus Busch, and made him the target of both police and prohibitionists—was beginning to unravel. Still, some of that old spark remained because, as he removed the bar fixtures from his building at Franklin and Cass Streets—once the site of his Missing Link Saloon, then his Armory Saloon, and finally his White House Saloon—he arranged to replace them with bowling alleys and pinball machines. And no matter how bleak things became, he would never reduce the weekly allowances for Caroline and their daughters.[729]

In the end, it was always about family. The inevitable dilemma of the immigrant, and perhaps the final challenge for Robert Mugge, was to be caught between an old love and a new one, between ancestors and descendants, and between a country of origin and a country of rebirth. By nature, any American immigrant was the sum of two parts, and nothing was more painful than having to choose between the two.

As the perfect example, World War I had been under way since the summer of 1914, and even though America would not join in until April of 1917, Tampa contained many expatriated Germans who cared deeply how Germany would fare. Because of that, Robert, through no fault of his own, suddenly found himself in a controversy with his fellow German Americans. The *Morning Tribune* of December 10, 1915 explained the cause of their concern: "The plant of the Sunlight Manufacturing Company, at Cass and Central, is to be used in the manufacture of equipment with which war munitions are to be produced, the plant having been leased to the Gulf Iron Works. This concern is said to have large contracts ahead covering fourteen months for the output of this equipment and is adding to the productive capacity by taking over plants here."

When word got out that Robert's factory had been leased for production of Allied war munitions, his friends from the German American Club began burning up phone lines to the Bay View Hotel, demanding an explanation from Robert's son, August. What August told them was that his father had leased his plant to B. L. Hamner of the Tampa Board of Trade, and that they had agreed no war munitions would be manufactured. Yet, through an oversight, the written contract included no provision preventing subleasing for that purpose. Therefore, Robert now realized his mistake, and he promised to make it right, just as soon as Mr. Hamner returned from out of town.[730]

Next, in what seemed like the city, or at least the local police, managing one final shot to the heart, Robert was arrested for an alleged Sunday liquor sale at the Bay View Hotel. And just as the *Morning Tribune* had done with Robert for decades, on Sunday, December 12, 1915, it shared all the details, this time under a familiar main headline: "Mugge Charged With Liquor Law Violation." In brief, "R. Mugge, proprietor of the Bay View Hotel, and Ray Wakely, steward at the hotel, were arrested on information filed by Solicitor W. H. Jackson, charging them with selling liquor without a license [that is, making it available to someone who was not a guest of the hotel]. An attempt will be made by the solicitor to have the cases tried in Criminal Court either this week or next."[731]

Conclusion

Tears of Angels

No one had a better right than August Mugge to tell this next story, in that he played a starring role. As Robert's heir apparent—or understudy, perhaps—it became his story as much as his father's. Like the rest of his memoirs, he would not write it for another fifty years. But when he did, the memories were as vivid as they were painful.

According to August, by December of 1915, the nights were bitter cold, yet Robert continued to wear his typical summer-weight clothes. Therefore, on one such evening, Caroline laid out a dark vest for him to wear as he returned to work. His response? "No, you can put that on me when I'm dead."

At approximately 4:00 a.m. on December 15, 1915, August, who had been sleeping at the Bay View Hotel, was awakened by a phone call. A policeman informed him that his father was lying on the sidewalk at Central Avenue and Harrison Street (site of his Central Saloon and Central Hotel on opposite corners), the apparent victim of a stroke. After a short drive to the scene, August found his father still breathing, still on the sidewalk, surrounded by concerned Black neighbors, and wearing the vest he had formerly refused. Wasting no more time, August phoned an ambulance and had his father taken to the Plant Park Infirmary near the Tampa Bay Hotel.

Once Robert was settled in, August returned to the Bay View, phoned his elder brother Eugene in New York, and urged him to hurry home. Then, at 7:00 a.m., he and Fritz Petri, Eugene's brother-in-law, headed to 302 Marion where they informed the family. Everyone dressed quickly, rushed to the hospital, and were present when, later that morning, Robert regained consciousness and asked to be taken home.

Despite his friendship with Frederick N. Weightnovel (or perhaps because of it), Robert had never trusted doctors, and largely avoided hospitals as well. But August had spent a decade in Germany, where schools instilled blind obedience to authority. So, when attending physicians Oppenheimer and Mitchell diagnosed a stroke (then called a stroke of apoplexy) and insisted that Robert remain, August readily complied. And to be fair, at first, that seemed a good decision. Robert rested comfortably throughout the afternoon, inspiring positive reports to the press. However, by evening, he suddenly took a turn for the worse, leading doctors to recommend "blood letting," and August once again agreed.

As a student of American history, Robert would have known that President George Washington died when his doctors treated his upper respiratory infection by draining half the blood from his body. Washington expired due to that aggressive bleeding, and Robert may have feared his own results would be the same. Granted, American and European medicine had little else to offer at the time, so this was an all-purpose strategy that appeared to help in some cases, hurt in others, and have little effect in the rest. Regardless, once the process was finished, and Robert was resting again, August urged the family to return home, assuring them he would spend the night in an adjoining room.

At approximately 2:00 a.m., August was awakened by a nurse who told him to come quickly. "Realizing that the end was coming, I stood grief-stricken by his bed side, took his hands into mine, and prayed the Lord's Prayer. Whether he was conscious of this, I do not know; he was sinking rapidly. And then it was all over, and I called

Joe Reed the undertaker." According to Robert's death certificate, he died of Bright's Disease of the Kidneys, which was a catchall for various maladies of the time, though mostly kidney-related.

Suddenly realizing the business implications of his father's passing, August returned to the Bay View, where he and Fritz sent telegrams to Anheuser-Busch and to E. B. Drake, a financier in Lexington, Kentucky who had loaned initial funding for Robert's ten-story building. Then, once again waiting for sunrise, August made a second trip to the family home where he broke the news to his mother and sisters. "All became hysterical, but I calmed them, and told them not to worry."

Later that morning, August met with John P. Wall, now the family attorney, and with the support of his mother and sisters, became administrator of Robert's estate. Unfortunately, his father had died intestate—without a will—which, over time, would cause problems. But for now, August simply needed to hold things together. For instance, at the Bay View Saturday night, he prepared the weekly bills, which, Monday morning, allowed Fritz to make the weekly collections. But in between came the massive Sunday funeral.[732]

Although the *Tampa Times* from that month is unavailable, coverage in the *Morning Tribune* was extensive. Excepting biographical information, which was largely inaccurate, the press provided a useful window on what ensued. For example, the first mention of Robert's passing came in the issue of Friday morning, December 17, 1915, only hours after he died: "Robert Mugge, pioneer citizen, energetic and far seeing business man, and prominent in financial circles of Tampa, died this morning shortly after 2 o'clock at the Plant Park Infirmary following an attack on Central Avenue yesterday morning when he fell fainting on the street." The paper noted that, despite his stroke, his condition the previous evening was so improved that his subsequent death would "come as a surprise to his many friends."[733]

The next notice was in the *Morning Tribune* of the following day under the headline, "Robert Mugge Dead." It recalled that Robert "had lived in Tampa for many years," and had "demonstrated a remarkable capacity for public service." It went on to observe that he was never "ostentatious in his acts," instead doing much "quiet charity for those most in need." It also declared he was "one of the most industrious men in the city, working from daylight often far into the night and never seemed to feel fatigue. He began with nothing and leaves a large estate, acquired through his genius for hard work. To those he leaves, *The Tribune* speaks a sincere condolence."[734]

The same issue included a much longer article as well, this one announcing that Robert's funeral service would take place at the family home, 302 Marion Street, at 9:30 a.m. Sunday morning, Rev. Niedernhoefer of Ocala, Florida presiding. The minister was expected to arrive Saturday morning to help with preparations, while Robert's older son, Eugene, was expected Sunday morning before the start of the service. Active pallbearers would include Herman Schenck, Henry Kruse, Ernest Berger, Peter Verri, D. B. McKay, Charles Ewing, Harry Howard, and George Stecher; and honorary pallbearers would include Guy M. Clarkson, Dr. L. A. Bixe, R. M. Prince, W. F. Stovall, W. C. Spencer, John P. Wall, Peter S. Joh, Salvador Ybor, G. Ferlita, M. Gonzalez, and Bert Frecker.[735]

In his memoirs, August described Robert's Saturday viewing and Sunday funeral, including the undertaker informing him that hundreds of people of assorted races and nationalities had paid their respects. The funeral, as previously announced, was held at the family home, with Rev. Niedernhoefer officiating. In his sermon, conducted entirely in German, the reverend recalled his visit with Robert only a year before, and eulogized him as someone "misunderstood" and, as August would often say, "a Christian in his own way."

Robert's eldest child, Louise Regener, had suggested they purchase a plot in the newer Woodlawn Cemetery, rather than in the older Oaklawn where Robert's previous family was buried. August complied,[736] also purchasing a flat, horizontal stone resembling a mat for sleeping. At one end was added a rounded, cushion-like head-stone on which, figuratively speaking, Robert could lay his head for eternity. On that rounded stone, a mason had carved simply, "Robert Mugge" and "1852-1915," as if all else went without saying. And that might have been the case, had not the listed year of Robert's birth been incorrect. As was mentioned at the start, he was born on January 5, 1853, a fact apparently buried with him, aside from unremembered baptism records at the Evangelical Lutheran Church of St. Andreas, (Bad) Lauterberg, Germany.[737]

Robert would later be joined by his wife, Caroline (Lena); his daughters, Louise and Melanie (Lanie); his sons, August and Eugene; Louise's husband, Herman Regener; and August's first two wives, Dorothea Schoel Mugge and Minna Worthman Mugge, each of whom died a few years into marriage, and only after birthing two children apiece. Ironically, the family's slowly fading wealth could be gauged by the declining size of subsequent headstones. Yet, under comforting branches of an ancient and stately oak, much of Robert's family did unite with him one final time, sharing with him the sort of peaceful resolution that eluded him in life.

For their part, Frances and her husband, Otto Reiner, would be buried in the Oaklawn plot, along with Alice Janthe McCullough Mugge and her sons, plus three others who died as young children: Thomas Paine Mugge, Alice Roosevelt Mugge, and Margarete Mugge, who was Eugene and Mimi's short-lived firstborn. Many years later, they would be joined by Dr. Ernest Reiner, son of Otto and Frances, and his wife Doris, while others found resting places elsewhere.

The *Morning Tribune* carried its own lengthy coverage of Robert's funeral on Monday, December 20, 1915 (by then, it published on Mondays) under the primary headline, "Mugge Funeral Is One Of Largest Ever Held." A few brief excerpts follow:

> Some of the most beautiful floral offerings ever seen at a Tampa funeral were in evidence on the big flower van, which was utilized to convey these tokens of esteem as the funeral carriage wended its way to the Woodlawn Cemetery, where the interment took place.
>
> Men who had associated with Mr. Mugge in his business and social life were present. They brought their wives and daughters, who were the friends of the wife and children of the deceased. There were also those who had been employed in the many different industries promoted by the pioneer citizen.

The retinue of employes from the Mugge places of business followed the funeral train yesterday morning to the cemetery, marching in orderly procession behind the numerous carriages drawn by the black stallions.

Eugene Mugge, eldest son, arrived from New York late last night and was not in attendance at the funeral. The widow and children of the deceased are prostrated with grief at the sudden and untimely death of the husband and father.

Amid coverage veering from the perfunctory to the sentimental, the most distressing portrayed a woman of color—probably Annie, the family's longtime domestic—from the vantage point of a master race:

One of the most touching of all the scenes was enacted at the undertaking parlors of J. L. Reed late Saturday afternoon, when an old negro "mammy," feeble with age, tottered in and pleaded with Mr. Reed for one last look at "her master"; and Mr. Reed granted her request. She was too old to attend the funeral, she said, and she wanted to see him for the last time. She made a pathetic sight with her basket on her arm, leaning heavily on her cane, and two tears were coursing down her wrinkled cheeks as she emerged from the inner room where the body lay groomed for burial.

And yet, beyond layer after layer of racist cliché, an angel was seen to grieve, unrecognized, by the side of a righteous man.[738]

This was followed on Tuesday, in the *Morning Tribune* of December 21, 1915, by the following "Card of Thanks": "For the many kindnesses shown to the family of Robert Mugge in the hour of its bereavement, it is desired to express our sincere appreciation and thanks. For the family, Mrs. Robert Mugge."[739] According to August's memoirs, at this point, he moved out of his room at the Bay View and into his father's former bedroom at the house, whereupon Caroline declared to her daughters still living at home, "Now, August is going to be our Papa."[740] And in many respects, as children and grandchildren suffered multiple hardships during Prohibition and the Depression,

Frances Mugge Reiner would become a second mother for the family, helping to raise assorted nieces and nephews along with her own three sons, and keeping everyone in touch through prodigious letter writing. That she and husband Otto would then be buried with many of the family's more tragic figures—Robert's first wife Alice, her two infant sons, Caroline's two lost children, and Eugene and Mimi's lost daughter—implied that they were as much the family's support system in death as they had been in life.

Not exactly fading from view himself, Robert Mugge's name would be mentioned twice more in the *Morning Tribune* of Christmas Eve, December 24, 1915. In the first case, Circuit Judge F. M. Robles signed an order making August Mugge administrator of Robert's estate, and thereby "authorized to continue the several lines of business formerly operated by him."[741] And in the second, just before adjourning for the term, Tampa's Criminal Court confirmed that "Proceedings against Robert Mugge, who was charged with selling liquor without a license at the Bay View Hotel, were stopped by his death."[742] In fact, judging from the evidence, if Tampa law enforcement could have hounded him into the next world as well, it certainly would have done so.

Robert likely came to mind again on New Year's Eve which, thanks to the Davis Package Law, was expected, by the *Tribune*, to be far different in 1915 than in all prior years. That is, with public drinking now largely forbidden, this holiday, like Christmas Eve before it, would surely be free of horn blowing, the firing of blank gun cartridges, and other forms of "hullabaloo and rowdyism." In summary, the Davis Package Law was "exacting a price of silence, and the noise makers of olden days are no longer in a noisy mood."[743] Or, as the *Miami Herald* noted on Christmas Day: "Prohibitionists, who jammed the Davis law through the last Legislature, do not seem at all pleased with the results of their handiwork. How could they be?"[744]

Robert would also come to mind the following April 3, 1916, when the *Tampa Times* announced that August—just twenty-five years old, attempting to run his father's remaining companies for the benefit of the family, and trying to get along with the city power brokers he barely knew—had reversed one of his father's most singular decisions. The overly exuberant headline, "August Mugge Signs Up For Installation Of Great White Way," nearly said it all. But indeed, August had authorized his father's old nemesis, the Tampa Electric Company, to install "white way lights" in front of the Bay View Alleys, which was Robert's bowling alley/pool hall/cafe complex on Franklin Street, just around the corner from his Bay View Hotel. According to the *Times*, which had initiated the project, the "white way system" had thus far illuminated downtown Tampa for more than three years, but now would extend nearly an unbroken mile from Jackson Street to Scott Street. "This evidence of Mr. Mugge's public spirit will be pleasing to all who have known of the circumstances,"[745] though perhaps not to everyone living or dead.

Robert would have been remembered still again on August 1, 1917 when his former assets were announced in the *Morning Tribune* in connection with the family's efforts to restructure them under a new corporation called the Robert Mugge Company. The following Monday, the estate would be sold "at the doors of the courthouse by order of Circuit Judge F. M. Robles," reportedly because the heirs could not divide his property equally under current conditions. "According to an inventory made of the estate, it is worth $1,419,011.27. As there are accounts payable to the amount of $15, 292.68 and bills payable secured by mortgages and otherwise to the amount of $374,856.70, the total assets over liabilities are placed at $1,028,861.89."[746] At the time, that was a considerable amount, which is why the term "millionaire" still had meaning.

Robert also would have come to mind when the *Morning Tribune* of June 16, 1918 reported that August Mugge, who had spent ten years of his young life attending school in Germany, was among those drafted for World War I military service, would be reporting to his draft board on June 24, would depart for training on June 27, and had selected his brother-in-law, Otto Reiner, to run the Robert Mugge Company in his absence.[747] Most likely, Robert would have been proud because, despite his own German roots, he had lived his remaining life in pursuit of American ideals. And like so many other immigrants, both before him and since, he had come for the chance to remake himself, yet managed, in the process, to remake the country as well. Until the day he died, he fought for the liberty which all had been promised—some from the start, and others over time. It should also be noted, however, that around the time the United States entered the war against Germany, probably due to growing anti-German sentiment, Tampa's German American Club was closed for good,[748] and the name of the Mugge beach house was changed from the German "Sorgenfrie" to the safely Anglo "The Gulf View."

It goes without saying that America in the late nineteenth and early twentieth centuries was severely flawed. And the worst of its flaws—intolerance and inequality—have yet to be entirely eradicated. But also still present is its potential for greatness, which is what drew the immigrants then, and what always will draw them. As a man of his time, Robert, too, was flawed, yet he never stopped believing in his own capacity for reinvention, or in that of his adopted country.

In the February 1, 1918 issue of the *Tampa Times*, editor Donald B. McKay, also Tampa's longtime mayor, presented the following editorial under the headline, "One German's Opinion Of Uncle Sam." America was then at war with Germany, which gave the piece special resonance:

> In these days when the patriotism of the German born … citizen is being questioned it is indeed pleasing to hear or read the utterances of one of such birth or origin who has a deep appreciation for the blessings that are accorded energetic immigrants from all countries who make their homes in this republic.
>
> Among these was the late Robert Mugge, one of the deepest thinkers who ever made Tampa his home. Several years prior to his death Mr. Mugge wrote a book on the subject, *Practical Humanity*, in the appendix of which he paid a characteristic tribute to Uncle Sam. He wrote in part:
>
> "It was in the fall of 1870 when I first met him (Uncle Sam) and felt then that it was impossible for any one to see him and get acquainted with him and keep from loving him.

While he had been brought into the world in 1776, he did not appear to me to be any older than a youth of about 19 summers—strong, robust and a picture of health. I found him also very kind hearted, honest to a fault and possessed of good will toward men. Being of great interest to me, I studied his history and learned that at birth he was much smaller than the average infant, but strong and healthy from the first. The men assisting at his birth have never been excelled in character or talent by any that the world ever produced, while his ancestors were the best of people. His birth, while most important for the world at large, was not accomplished without much labor and bloodshed. These men have ushered the infant into active life, framed a set of rules by which he should be reared and guided, while at the same time he was surrounded by wise, foreseeing councillors, who were always ready with the best advice. He was told to be honest and true-hearted; to be kind to everybody; to open his heart and doors to the poor, the weak, the infirm and all those who may have been driven from their home by religious intolerance or grasping tyrants. He was instructed to mind his own business; to give no cause for trouble, and to allow every one to go to heaven after his own fashion, and not to permit any church or creed to force itself upon his private affairs. He was advised to be frugal, to exclude luxury and to be industrious. All the above were embodied in the rules laid down and the advice given by his experienced councillors."[749]

Taken from *Practical Humanity*, an imperfect but heartfelt book, self-published in 1909 by Robert Mugge, a man who conducted business as an artist, a philosopher, and a patriot.[750]

On December 18, 1918, the US Senate proposed the Eighteenth Amendment to the Constitution, which was approved by the thirty-sixth state on January 16, 1919. The following October 28, over the veto of President Woodrow Wilson, Congress passed the Volstead Act, which also was known as the National Prohibition Act. Effective

January 17, 1920, the law plus prior amendment created a nation-wide ban on the manufacture, importation, sale, and possession of alcoholic beverages.[751]

The *Morning Tribune* of January 16, 1920 announced "inauguration of the nation's first saloonless year."[752] And it surely was, in that a once lawful business, now forbidden, would employ nonlegal means for meeting demand. That is, even as temperance officials were claiming victory, the true winners of Prohibition were Robert's longtime nemeses, the blind tigers, in that, just as he had warned, formerly licensed saloons would become speakeasies, and the men who ran them public enemies. At least, that would be the case until December 5, 1933, when global Depression brought the country to its senses, and the Twenty-First Amendment reversed the Eighteenth.[753]

Granted, this was not the first time American liberty had lost its way, and neither would it be the last. But for the former Wilhelm August Robert Mügge, it was the sad inversion of a moral tale.

A Sampling of Robert Mugge Saloons

Alhambra Cafe, southwest corner of Habana Avenue and Alvaro Street, West Tampa.

Armory Saloon, 902 Franklin Street (northwest corner of Franklin and Cass Streets), Tampa.

Bay View Hotel Bar, 208 Jackson Street (north side), Tampa.

Bijou Theatre, 302-04 Central Avenue (northwest corner of Central Avenue and Harrison Street), Tampa.

Buckingham Theatre Saloon, 1412-18 Fifth Avenue (north side), Fort Brooke.

Budweiser Theater, 1415-16 Fifth Avenue (north side), Fort Brooke.

Central Saloon, 302-04 Central Avenue, then 1102 Central Avenue (both northwest corner of Central Avenue and Harrison Street), Tampa.

Crystal Saloon, 1102 Franklin Street (northwest corner of Franklin and Harrison Streets, Tampa.

Delmonico Saloon/Cafe, 290 Main Street, then 702 Main Street (both southwest corner of Main Street and Francis Avenue), West Tampa.

Eagle Saloon, Kissimmee.

El Dorado Saloon, Port Tampa City.

Eureka Bar/Saloon, 302 Franklin Street (northwest corner of Franklin and Jackson Streets), Tampa.

Gaiety, northwest corner of Franklin and Tyler Streets, Tampa.

Golden Eagle Saloon, 1332-34 (later 1432-34) Seventh Avenue (both northwest corner of Fifteenth Street and Seventh Avenue), Tampa.

Greater New York Sample Rooms and Billiard Hall, 1102 Franklin Street (northwest corner of Franklin and Harrison Streets), Tampa.

Green Goose Saloon, Port Tampa City.

Kentucky Mail Order House, 702 Nebraska Avenue (northwest corner of Nebraska Avenue and Zack Street), Tampa.

La Brisa Saloon, 201-03 Water Street (northeast corner of Water and Washington Streets), Tampa.

Madrid Saloon, 48 Howard Avenue (southeast corner of Howard Avenue and Pine Street), West Tampa.

Missing Link Saloon, 902 Franklin Street (northwest corner of Franklin and Cass Streets), Tampa.

New Parlor Theatre, northeast corner of Central Avenue and Rock Road (Scott Street), Tampa.

New York Exchange Saloon/Cafe, 208 Lafayette Street (north side), Tampa.

Noah's Ark Saloon, Michigan Avenue near Florida Avenue, Tampa.

Panama Restaurant/Saloon, 1324-26 Franklin Street (southwest corner of Franklin and Constant Streets), Tampa.

Panchoro House, 1202 W. Ninth Avenue (northeast corner of 12th Street and Ninth Avenue, Tampa.

Parlor Wine Rooms/Saloon, northwest corner of Franklin and Lafayette Streets, Tampa.

Peninsular Saloon, St. Petersburg.

St. Louis Cafe, 311 Franklin Street (east side), Tampa.

Saratoga Saloon, 802 Franklin Street (northwest corner of Franklin and Polk Streets), Tampa.

Seminole Cafe/Saloon, 2102 (later 2202) Seventh Avenue (both northeast corner of Twenty-Second Street and Seventh Avenue), Tampa.

Seventh Avenue Cafe, 1401 Seventh Avenue (southeast corner of Seventh Avenue and Fourteenth Street), Tampa.

Shamrock Saloon, 308 Franklin Street (west side), Tampa.

Vulcan Mail Order House, 1002-06 Scott Street (northeast corner of Scott Street and Central Avenue), Tampa.

West Coast Mail Order House, 709-11 Jefferson Street (northeast corner of Polk and Jefferson Streets), Tampa.

White House Saloon, 902 Franklin Street (northwest corner of Franklin and Cass Streets), Tampa.

White Rose Saloon, 213-15 Lafayette Street (south side), Tampa.

Winner Saloon, St. Petersburg.

Other Mugge saloon addresses mentioned in period materials:

Twentieth Street and Fourteenth Avenue, Tampa.

Eighteenth Street and Thirteenth Avenue, Tampa.

Fifteenth Street and Ninth Avenue, Tampa.

2401 Seventeenth Street (southeast corner of Seventeenth Street and
      Thirteenth Avenue), Tampa.

Northwest corner of Nineteenth Street and Third Avenue, Tampa.

Northwest corner of Arch Street and West Ninth Avenue (later Arch
      Street and Garcia Avenue), West Tampa.

205-11 Green Street, West Tampa.

146 Howard Avenue, West Tampa.

187 Howard Avenue, West Tampa.

Bibliography

Archives:

Alexandrian Public Library, Mount Vernon, Indiana.

Anthony P. "Tony" Pizzo Collection, University of South Florida, Tampa Library Special Collections, Tampa, Florida.

Archives of August Bremer Mugge, Eau Gallie, Florida.

Archives of David Byron McCullough, Belcher, Louisiana.

Archives of Martha Washington Mugge, Jacksonville, Florida.

Archives of Patricia Mugge Andrews, Jacksonville, Florida.

Archives of Patricia Mugge Reams, Greenville, Florida.

Archives of Dr. Robert Herman and Alma Elizabeth Mugge, Silver Spring, Maryland.

Archives of Hartung and Kiefer families, Henderson, Kentucky.

Bureau of Vital Statistics, State of Florida, Jacksonville, Florida.

Burgert Brothers Collection of Tampa Photographs, University of South Florida, Tampa Library Digital Collections, Tampa, Florida.

Burgert Brothers Photographic Collection, Hillsborough County Public Library Cooperative, Tampa, Florida.

City of Terre Haute Board of Cemetery Records, Terre Haute, Indiana.

Collections, Anheuser-Busch Companies, Inc., St. Louis, Missouri.

Evangelical Lutheran Church of St. Andreas, Bad Lauterberg, Göttingen, Lower Saxony, Germany.

Florida History & Genealogy Library of the John F. Germany Public Library, Hillsborough County Public Library Cooperative, Tampa, Florida.

Florida Photographic Collections (Burgert Brothers Photos), University of Florida George A. Smathers Libraries, Gainesville, Florida.

Genealogy/Local History Archives of the Henderson County Public Library, Henderson, Kentucky.

Henderson County Circuit Court, Henderson, Kentucky.

Special Collections of the Vigo County Public Library, Terre Haute, Indiana.

Tampa Bay History Center, Tampa, Florida.

Books:

Browne-Hazen, Mrs. Pauline, *The Blue Book and History of Pioneers, Tampa, Fla., 1914*. Tampa: Tribune Publishing Company, 1914.

Grismer, Karl H., *Tampa: A History of the City of Tampa and the Tampa Bay Region of Florida*. Edited by D. B. McKay. St. Petersburg: The St. Petersburg Printing Company, Inc., 1950.

Ingalls, Professor Robert P., *Urban Vigilantes in the New South, Tampa, 1882-1936*. Gainesville: University Press of Florida, 1993.

Jacksonville, Florida City Directories. 1886-1887.

Johnson, Paul E., *Sam Patch, the famous jumper*. New York: Hill and Wang, 2003.

Mugge, August B., *My Memoirs*. Eau Gallie: Self-Published, 1967.

Mugge, Robert, *Practical Humanity: A Suggestion for the Destruction of Poverty the Curbing of Cupidity and the Lessening of Crime*. Tampa: Self-Published, 1909.

Mugge, Robert, *Watchmakers & Jewelers Hand Book*. Terre Haute: Self-Published, 1874.

New Orleans, Louisiana City Directory. 1886.

Okrent, Daniel, *Last Call: The Rise and Fall of Prohibition*. New York: Scribner, 2010.

Peeples, Harry A., *Twenty-Four Years in the Woods, On the Waters and in the Cities of Florida*. Tampa: Tribune Printing Co., 1906.

Rerick, Roland H., *Memoirs of Florida*. Edited by Philp Francis Fleming. Atlanta: Southern Historical Association, 1902.

Tampa, Florida City Directories. 1886-1918.

Tampa, Florida: Its Industries and Advantages. Tampa: Tampa Board of Trade, 1905.

Terre Haute, Indiana City Directories. 1860-1879.

Twain, Mark and Charles Dudley Warner, *The Gilded Age: A Tale of Today*. Hartford: American Publishing Company, 1873.

White, Richard, Railroaded: *The Transcontinentals and the Making of Modern America*. New York: W. W. Norton & Co., 2011.

Newspapers:

Atlanta Constitution, Atlanta, Georgia.

Baltimore Sun, Baltimore, Maryland.

Clearwater Sun, Clearwater, Florida.
Evening Gazette, Terre Haute, Indiana.
Florida Times-Union, Jacksonville, Florida.
Inter Ocean, Chicago, Illinois.
Jacksonville Metropolis, Jacksonville, Florida.
Kissimmee Valley Gazette, Kissimmee, Florida.
Lakeland Star, Lakeland, Florida.
Miami Herald, Miami, Florida.
Miami News, Miami, Florida.
The New York Times, New York, New York.
New York Tribune, New York, New York.
Ocala Evening Star, Ocala, Florida.
Pensacola Journal, Pensacola, Florida.
Pensacola News, Pensacola, Florida.
Sanford Chronicle, Sanford, Florida.
St. Petersburg Times, St. Petersburg, Florida.
Saturday Evening Mail, Terre Haute, Indiana.
Springfield Daily Republic, Springfield, Ohio.
Sunday News, Wilkes-Barre, Pennsylvania.
Sunland Tribune, Tampa, Florida.
Tampa Advance-News, Tampa, Florida.
Tampa Daily Journal, Tampa, Florida.
Tampa Herald, Tampa, Florida.
Tampa Journal, Florida.
Tampa Morning Tribune, Tampa, Florida.
Tampa Times, Tampa, Florida.
Tampa Tribune, Tampa, Florida.
Tampa Weekly, Tampa, Florida.
Tampa Weekly Journal, Tampa, Florida.
Tarpon Springs News, Tarpon Springs, Florida.
Terre Haute Daily Gazette, Terre Haute, Indiana.
Terre-Haute Evening Gazette, Terre Haute, Indiana.
Terre Haute Express, Terre Haute, Indiana.
Terre-Haute Saturday Evening Ledger, Terry Haute, Indiana.
Terre-Haute Saturday Evening Mail, Terry Haute, Indiana.
Terre-Haute Weekly Express, Terry Haute, Indiana.

Terre Haute Weekly Gazette, Terry Haute, Indiana.

Weekly True Democrat, Tallahassee, Florida.

Wilkes-Barre Times Leader, The Evening News, Wilkes-Barre, Pennsylvania.

Essays and Interviews:

Brown, Canter, Jr. and Larry Eugene Rivers (2018), "'The Negroes are There to Stay': The Development of Tampa's African-American Community, 1891-1916." *Sunland Tribune:* Vol. 29, Article 6.

Dunn, Hampton (1980), "Those Hell-Raisin' Tampa Newspapers," *Sunland Tribune:* Vol. 6. Article 6.

Gray, Major Wilbur W., (October 20, 1992). "Prussia and the Evolution of the Reserve Army: A Forgotten Lesson of History," *Strategic Studies Institute, U.S. Army War College.*

Hartung, Bertha and Moose Hartung Interview (February 1, 1991). Henderson County Public Library, Henderson, Kentucky.

Hurner, Margaret Regener (1989), "Robert Mugge—Pioneer Tampan," *Sunland Tribune:* Vol. 15, Article 8.

Mugge, Robert Edwin, 2018 Interview with Gretchen Petri Harrington.

Rivers, Larry Eugene and Canter Brown Jr. (2018), "'Rejoicing in their Freedom': The Development of Tampa's African-American Community in the Post-Civil War Generation," *Sunland Tribune:* Vol. 27, Article 3.

Rivers, Larry Eugene and Canter Brown Jr. (2007). "'The Art of Gathering a Crowd': Florida's Pat Chappelle and the Origins of Black-Owned Vaudeville." *The Journal of African American History,* Vol. 92, Article 2.

Stephens, Bret L., "Why Edmund Burke Still Matters," *The New York Times*, August 9, 2020, section SR, p. 6.

Stiles, T. J., "The Constitutional Amendment That Reinvented Freedom—The 14th Amendment, the one that empowered the Bill of Rights, turns 150 on Saturday." *The New York Times*, July 26, 2018, https://www.nytimes.com/2018/07/26/opinion/the-constitutional-amendment-that-reinvented-freedom.html.

Tucker, Abigail, "The Financial Panic of 1907: Running from History—Robert F. Bruner discusses the panic of 1907 and the financial crisis of 2008," October 9, 2008, *Smithsonian.com.*

Film Produced by Author:
Mugge, Robert Edwin, 2003 film *Last of the Mississippi Jukes* (MVD Visual).

Websites:
annamariaislandchamber.org.
ancestry.com.
bbictampa.org/history.
beerandbrewing.com.
britannica.com.
brookings.edu.
centenarynews.com (First World War 1914-1918).
chroniclingamerica.loc.gov.
genealoger.com.
germanculture.com.
greatwhiteway.com.
jacksonville.com.
kcl.ac.uk.
lakerlutznews.com.
law.cornell.edu.
macon.com.
loc.gov.
newspapers.com.
newspapers.library.in.gov (Hoosier State Chronicles).
nytimes.com.
smithsonian.com.
tampagov.net.
tampasbravest.com.
telegraph.co.uk.
theodorerooseveltcenter.org.
triposo.com.
webarchive.org

Index

End Notes

1   *Weekly Tribune*, March 30, 1905, p. 1.

2   Records of Evangelical Lutheran Church of St. Andreas, Bad Lauterberg, Germany.

3   German spas, germanculture.com.ua/daily/viel-spass-on-german-spas/.

4   Mugge, *My Memoirs*, p. 4, 39.

5   *Ibid.*

6   Franco-Prussian War, www.kcl.ac.uk/the-franco-prussian-war-150-years-on.

7   Prussian conscription, "German Military Records," genealoger.com.

8   "14th Amendment," law.cornel.edu/constitution/amendmentxiv.

9   Stiles, "Reinvented Freedom," *The New York Times*, July 26, 2018, nytimes.com/2018/07/26opinion/the-constitutional-amendment-that-reinvented-freedom.html.

10   Records of Evangelical Lutheran Church of St. Andreas.

11   Hartung Interview, Henderson County Public Library, pp. 2-3.

12   Kiefer family genealogy, Henderson County Public Library.

13   *Ibid.*

14   Hartung Interview, pp. 2-3.

15   Robert Mugge immigration, ancestry.com.

16   "A New Surge of Growth," *Immigration ... German*, Library of Congress, loc.gov/teachers/classroommaterials/presentationsandactivities/presentations/immigration/german4.html.

17   "Germans in America," *European Reading Room--Researchers*, The Library of Congress, loc.gov/rr/european/imde/germchro.html.

18   Rerick, *Memoirs of Florida*, pp. 630-31.

19   Wilhelm and Bertha Mahn immigration, ancestry.com.

20   Ludwig, Luise, Louis Mugge immigration, ancestry.com.

21   Terre Haute *City Directories*.

22   John McCullough Bible.

23   Terre Haute *City Directories*.

24   *Terre Haute Weekly Express*, April 21, 1869.

25   *Terre Haute Saturday Evening Mail*, April 20, 1872.

26   *Terre Haute Daily Gazette*, April 26, 1872.

27   Terre Haute *City Directories*, 1874-76.

28   Mugge, *Watchmakers & Jewelers Handbook*.

29   Terre Haute *City Directories*, 1874-76.

30   Mugge, p. 39.

31   *Terre Haute Saturday Evening Mail*, July 22, 1876, p. 8.

32   *Terre Haute Evening Gazette*, December 30, 1875.

33   *Ibid.*, March 8, 1876.

34   Indiana wedding license application, September 13-14, 1875.

35   John McCullough Bible.

36   *Terre Haute Express*, September 1875.

37   *Terre Haute Saturday Evening Mail*, October 21, 1876.

38   *Terre Haute Evening Gazette*, August 15, 1876.

39   John McCullough Bible.

40   Mugge, *My Memoirs*, p. 4.

41   *Ibid.*

42   Naturalization document, Mugge, *My Memoirs*.

43   *Tampa Morning Tribune*, May 25, 1913, p. 12.

44   Browne-Hazen, *The Blue Book*, p. 1-2.

45   Mugge, p. 4.

46   McCullough Bible.

47 *Sunland Tribune*, March 24, 1877, p. 3.

48 *Ibid.*, March 28, 1877, p. 3

49 *Ibid.*, May 5, 1877, p. 3.

50 Mugge, p. 16.

51 *Sunland Tribune*, June 30, 1877, p. 3.

52 *Ibid.*

53 *Ibid.*

54 *Ibid.*, July 7, 1877, p. 3.

55 *Ibid.*

56 *Ibid.*, August 25, 1877, p. 3.

57 *Ibid.*

58 *Ibid.*

59 *Ibid.*, September 22, 1877, p. 3.

60 *Ibid.*, October 6, 1877, p. 3.

61 Tampa Bay History Center document, November 13, 1877.

62 *Sunland Tribune*, April 6, 1878, p. 3.

63 *Ibid.*, April 27, 1878, p. 3.

64 *Morning Tribune*, May 25, 1913, p. 12.

65 *Sunland Tribune*, August 13, 1878, p. 13.

66 Rivers and Brown Jr., "Rejoicing in their Freedom," *Sunland Tribune* (academic version), p. 8.

67 "Growth of Tampa," *Weekly Tribune*, November 5, 1896, p. 4.

68 *Sunland Tribune*, August 17, 1878, p. 3.

69 *Ibid.*, September 21, 1878, p. 2.

70 *Ibid.*, February 15, 1879, p. 3.

71 McCullough Bible.

72 Naturalization document, Mugge, *My Memoirs*.

73 McCullough Bible.

74 *Ibid.*

75 Mugge, p. 4.

76 *Terre Haute Saturday Evening Ledger*, May 31, 1879, p. 8.

77 *Sunland Tribune*, January 29, 1880, p. 3.

78 *Terre Haute Weekly Gazette*, February 12, 1880, p. 3.

79 *Sunland Tribune*, January 29, 1980, p. 3.

80 *Ibid.*, February 12, 1880, p. 3.

81 *Ibid.*, April 15, 1880, p. 3.

82 *Ibid.*, April 22, 1880, p. 3.

83 *Ibid.*, August 12, 1880, p. 3.

84 *Ibid.*, April 15, 1880, p. 3.

85 October 2, 1880 ship records, ancestry.com.

86 *Sunland Tribune*, December 17, 1881, p. 3.

87 1882 Sanborn fire insurance map for Tampa.

88 Mugge, pp. 4, 193.

89 1880 Census records, ancestry.com.

90 Florida wills and probate records, ancestry.com.

91 Mugge, pp. 4, 12, 19, 40, 100.

92 *Ibid.*, 1990 Preface, p. x.

93 Author's 2018 interview with Gretchen Petri Harrington.

94 Florida wills and probate records, ancestry.com.

95 Mugge, p. 193.

96 "Tampa, Florida History," triposo.com.loc/Tampa2C_Florida/history/background.

97 Peeples, *Twenty-Four Years*, p. 89.

98 Mugge, *My Memoirs*, p. 5.

99 Peeples, pp. 100-01.

100 "Dr. Weightnovel," Mugge, pp. 10-11.

101 "Russian's exploits," *Tampa Tribune*, November 10, 1946, p. 7.

102 "The Rite of Spring 1913," May 16, 2013, telegraph.co.uk/culture/music/classicalmusic/10061574/The-Rite-of-Spring-1913-Why-did-it-provoke-a-riot.html.

103 "World's Medical Congress," *Sunday News* (Wilkes-Barre, Pennsylvania), September 18, 1887, p. 5.

104 "Pole or Negro?" *Springfield Daily Republic* (Springfield, Ohio), September 5, 1887, p. 1.

105 Mugge, p. 11.

106 Grismer, *Tampa*, p. 238.

107 1887 Sanborn fire map of Tampa, Florida.

108 Grismer, p. 193.

109 "Fire Department," *Tampa Tribune*, February 16, 1958, p.66.

110 Grismer, *Tampa*, p. 193.

111 Mugge, p. 193.

112 Rerick, *Memoirs of Florida*, p. 631.

113 Mugge, p. 6.

114 Author's 2018 interview with Gretchen Petri Harrington.

115 Mugge, p. 6.

116 *Tampa Journal*, September 29, 1887, p. 1.

117 *Weekly Journal*, May 26, 1988, p. 6.

118 Mugge, p. 193.

119 1889 Sanford fire map of Tampa.

120 "Tampa Doctor Battled Leprosy," *Tampa Tribune*, October 17, 1954, p. 69.

121 Interview with Gretchen Petri Harrington.

122 Records of Evangelical Lutheran Church of St. Andreas, Bad Lauterberg, Germany.

123 Mugge, p. 193.

124 *Ibid.*, p. 6.

125 Grismer, p. 238.

126   *Tampa Daily Journal*, March 26, 1890, p. 4.

127   *Ibid.*, April 30, 1890, p. 4.

128   *Tampa Journal*, October 16, 1890, p. 1.

129   Mugge, p. 6.

130   *Ibid.*

131   Letter in Tony Pizzo Collection, Special Collections of USF Libraries in Tampa.

132   "News Gleanings," *Jeweler's Circular and Horological Review*, May 6, 1891, p. 15.

133   1892 Sanborn fire map of Tampa, Florida.

134   Mugge, p. 13.

135   *Ibid.*, pp. 15-16.

136   "Rawlins Like A Mule," *Tampa Times*, September 6, 1912, p. 9.

137   Mugge, p. 15.

138   "Jim Crow Law," www.britannica.com/event/Jim-Crow/law.

139   Browne-Hazen, *The Blue Book*, p. 2.

140   "Here's the 'Jim Crow' Bill," *Weekly Tribune*, April 27, 1905, p. 2.

141   "Pertinent Remarks," *Morning Tribune*, May 6, 1906, p. 4.

142   Rivers and Brown Jr., "The Negroes are There to Stay," *Sunland Tribune* (academic version).

143   Mugge, p. 16.

144   "Peculiar Personality," *Tampa Tribune*, January 20, 1953, p. 54.

145   "Pioneer Florida," *Tampa Tribune*, May 31, 1959, p. 54.

146   "History of Beulah," bbictampa.org/history (via web.archive.org), pp. 1-2.

147   "Hello? Number?," *Morning Tribune*, Sunday, August 25, 1895, p. 3.

148   Mugge, *My Memoirs*, pp. 17, 193.

149   Author's 2018 interview with Gretchen Petri Mugge.

150   "Fraud! Taxes! Swindle!," 1893 circular.

151 *Tampa Tribune,* May 18, 1894, p. 1.

152 *Ibid.,* November 16, 1894, p. 1.

153 *Morning Tribune,* February 16, 1895, p. 1.

154 *Weekly Tribune,* March 14, 1895, p. 2.

155 "Ice for Everybody," *Morning Tribune,* May 24, 1895, p. 4.

156 *Ibid.,* October 3, 1895, p. 4.

157 *Ibid.,* February 5, 1895, p. 1.

158 "A Labor Case," *Weekly Tribune,* June 6, 1892, p. 1.

159 *Sunday Tribune,* February 24, 1895, p. 4.

160 *Morning Tribune,* March 13, 1895, p. 1

161 *Ibid.,* March 9, 1895, p. 4.

162 *Ibid.,* March 14, 1895, p. 1.

163 *Weekly Tribune,* March 14, 1895, p. 5.

164 "The Vaudeville Theatre," *Morning Tribune,* August 10, 1895, p. 1.

165 *Morning Tribune,* September 26, 1895, p. 2.

166 Mugge, p. 193.

167 "Ordinance No. 112," *Morning Tribune,* September 4, 1895, p. 3.

168 "Ordinance No. 175," *Ibid.,* August 7, 1896, p. 4.

169 "To Those That Drink Beer," *Weekly Tribune,* December 12, 1895, p. 7.

170 "Snarls to Unravel," *The Inter Ocean* (Chicago), November 8, 1893, p. 7.

171 *Wilkes-Barre Times Leader, The Evening News,* August 22, 1895, p. 7.

172 "A Corner on the Saloon Business," *Morning Tribune,* April 23, 1896, p. 1.

173 *Weekly Tribune,* March 5, 1896, p. 1.

174 "Medicine Men!" *Ibid.,* April 18, 1895, p. 6.

175 "Sick, Burgess Suicided," *Ibid.,* November 26, 1896, p. 1.

176 "Struck by a Scantling," *Ibid.,* November 5, 1896, p. 5.

177   "Russian's Exploits," *Tampa Tribune*, November 10, 1946, p. 7.

178   Mugge, p. 11.

179   "Election in Moscow," *Weekly Tribune*, April 22, 1897, p.7.

180   "Squatters Must Vacate," *Ibid.*, March 26, 1898, p. 1.

181   *Ibid.*, April 14, 1898, p. 8.

182   "In Litigation for 20 Years," *Morning Tribune*, January 4, 1905, p. 1.

183   "Pleasant DeSoto Park," *Weekly Tribune*, March 18, 1897, p. 7.

184   Mugge, p. 7.

185   "Fourteen Saloons Closed," *Weekly Tribune*, October 1, 1896, p. 1.

186   *Morning Tribune*, September 29, 1896, p. 1.

187   *Weekly Tribune*, October 16, 1896, p. 4.

188   *Ibid.*, December 16, 1896, p. 4.

189   *Morning Tribune*, November 7, 1896, p. 1.

190   *Ibid.*, November 10, 1896, p. 4.

191   *Ibid.*, February 26, 1897, p. 1.

192   *Ibid.*, March 3, 1897, p. 4.

193   *Ibid.*, March 16, 1897, p.4.

194   *Weekly Tribune*, April 1, 1897, p. 1.

195   *Ibid.*, June 3, 1897, p. 7.

196   *Ibid.*, p. 1.

197   *Weekly Tribune*, August 5, 1897, p. 4.

198   *Morning Tribune*, September 4, 1897, p. 4.

199   Mugge, p. 193.

200   Elaine Kent, "The Senior Years," Florida *Times-Union*, 1969 (date and page uncertain).

201   *Morning Tribune*, July 13, 1897, p. 4.

202   *Weekly Tribune*, July 22, 1897, p. 1.

203   *Morning Tribune*, October 29, 1897, p. 4.

204 Mugge, pp. 72-73.

205 *Morning Tribune*, September 25, 1897, p. 4.

206 Mugge, p. 72.

207 *Weekly Tribune*, December 30, 1897, p. 1.

208 Mugge, *My Memoirs*, pp. 16-17.

209 Grismer, *Tampa*, p. 238.

210 Herman J. Mankiewicz, Orson Welles, *Citizen Kane* screenplay (1941.

211 Mugge, pp. 8-9.

212 "Spanish-American War," britannia.com/event/Spanish-American-War.

213 Mugge, p. 8-9.

214 "Soldiers Wreck Saloons," *Morning Tribune*, June 8, 1898, p. 4.

215 "Inhuman Brutes," *Ibid.*, p. 1.

216 Canter and Rivers, "The Negroes are There to Stay," *Sunland Tribune* (academic version), 2018, pp. 63-64

217 *Morning Tribune*, September 8, 1898, p. 4.

218 Elaine Kent, "The Senior Years," *Florida Times-Union*, 1969 (date page uncertain).

219 "Midnight Blaze," *Weekly Tribune*, November 24, 1898, p. 3.

220 Mugge, p. 9.

221 *Morning Tribune*, January 5, 1899, p. 4.

222 "An Appreciated Present," *Ibid.*, February 3, 1899, p. 4.

223 "Fire Swept!" *Ibid.*, March 11, 1899, p. 1.

224 *Weekly Tribune*, March 16, 1899, p. 3.

225 *Ibid.*, June 1, 1899, p. 3.

226 *Morning Tribune*, August 12, 1899, p. 8.

227 *Tampa Times*, May 22, 1929 reprint, p. 4.

228 "Big Enterprise in Tampa," *Morning Tribune*, July 23 1899, p. 1.

229 *Ibid.*, February 6, 1900, p. 1

230 *Sunday Tribune*, October 22, 1899, p. 8.

231 *Morning Tribune*, August 29, 1899, p.1.

232 "How the Miscreants," *Ibid.*, August 31, 1899, p. 1.

233 *Ibid.*, October 31, 1899, p. 1.

234 "Robert Mugge had troubles," *Tampa Tribune*, January 7, 1990, p. 120.

235 Mugge, *My Memoirs*, p. 193.

236 *Morning Tribune*, January 18, 1900, p. 5.

237 *Ibid.*

238 *Ibid.*, February 17, 1900, p. 3.

239 *Weekly Tribune*, March 1, 1900, p. 5.

240 *Morning Tribune*, March 10, 1900, p. 8.

241 "Fire Wiped Out Several Saloons," *Ibid.*, April 19, 1900, p. 1.

242 "Whiskey Gauger in the City," *Ibid.*, April 27, 1900, p. 4.

243 "Distillery Begins Work," *Weekly Tribune*, May 24, 1900, p. 2.

244 "Enlarging His Plant," *Morning Tribune*, July 13, 1900, p. 7.

245 "Ordinance No. 175," *Ibid.*, July 14, 1900, p. 8.

246 "Kicking on Cows," *Ibid.*, July 1, 1900, p. 8.

247 "A New Cow Ordinance," *Ibid.*, August 18, 1900, p. 1.

248 "Cow Ordinance," *Ibid.*, August 25, 1900, p. 1.

249 Cemetery Lots for Negroes," *Ibid.*, August 18, 1900, p. 1.

250 *Ibid.*, September 22, 1900, p. 1.

251 "Beware, Ye Spitters," *Ibid.*, March 23, 1901, p. 1.

252 "Mayor to Veto Spitting Law," *Ibid.*, April 2, 1901, p. 1.

253 "Pull Down Your Signs," *Ibid.*, August 19, 1900, p. 1.

254 "His Sign Still Stays," *Weekly Tribune*, August 30, 1900, p. 8.

255 *Morning Tribune*, August 31, 1900, p. 3.

256 "Battle of the Centuries," loc.gov//rr/scitech/battle.

257 *Morning Tribune*, December 30, 1900, p. 2.

258 $25 Reward," *Ibid.*, January 1, 1901, p. 5.

259 "Goody-Goody," Ibid., February 26, 1901, p. 1.

260 "Mugge's Poles Criticised [sic]," *Weekly Tribune*, February 28, 1901, p.8.

261 "Robert Mugge had troubles," *Tampa Tribune*, January 7, 1990, p. 120.

262 "Mugge Buys a Brick Block," *Morning Tribune*, March 20, 1901, p. 1.

263 "Preacher and Saloonist," *Ibid.*, May 26, 1901, p. 9.

264 "Preacher Discussed Saloonist's Letters," *Ibid.*, May 28, 1901, p. 1.

265 "Tampa's Needs," *Ibid.*, June 18, 1901, p. 4.

266 *Weekly Tribune*, June 20, 1901, p. 4.

267 *Morning Tribune*, July 9, 1901, p. 7.

268 "General Strike is on Today," *Ibid.*, July 27, 1901, p. 1.

269 *Ibid.*, July 31, 1901, p. 4.

270 "Citizens' Group Kidnapped," *Tampa Tribune*, December 11, 1988, pp. 150-51.

271 "Ship Them to Distant Shores," *Morning Tribune*, August 7, 1901, p. 1.

272 *Ibid.*, August 10, 1901, p. 5.

273 "Marie Cooper Arrived Last Night ...," *Ibid.*, August 23, 1901, p. 1.

274 "Mercer Dies With Lie on His Lips," *Ibid.*, August 24, 1901, p. 1-2.

275 "The Mercer Hanging," Mugge, *My Memoirs*, p. 11.

276 *Morning Tribune*, September 17, 1901, p. 8.

277 "Long Cigar Strike Ended," *Ibid.*, November 24, 1901, p. 1.

278 "Robert Mugge, the Investor," Mugge, *My Memoirs*, p. 11.

279 "Going to the Old Country," *Morning Tribune*, April 24, 1901, p. 5.

280 "Sold to R. Mugge," *Ibid.*, May 8, 1901, p. 1.

281 "Saratoga to Move," *Ibid.*, September 20, 1901, p. 5.

282 "New Building," *Ibid.*, October 25, 1901, p. 2.

283 Mugge, p. 193.

284 "Sad Death," *Morning Tribune*, February 18, 1902, p. 6.

285 "Black Man at Dinner," *Ibid.*, October 20, 1901, p. 1.

286 "Alice Hathaway Lee Roosevelt," *Theodore Roosevelt Center at Dickinson State University*, theodorerooseveltcenter.org/Learn-About-TR/TR-Encyclopedia/Family-and-Friends/Alice-Hathaway-Lee-Roosevelt.aspx.

287 Rerick, *Memoirs of Florida*, pp. 630-31.

288 "Political Rumor," *Morning Tribune*, November 27, 1901, p. 7.

289 *Ibid.*, November 27, 1901, p. 4.

290 "Col. Mugge For Mayor," *Sanford Chronicle*, reprinted in *Morning Tribune*, December 7, 1901, p. 5.

291 "A Good Business Man," Tampa *Advance News*, reprinted in *Morning Tribune*, April 30, 1902, p. 4.

292 "More Campaign Lying," *Morning Tribune*, May 10, 1902, p. 4.

293 "Anent The Saloon Men," *Ibid.*, May 15, 1902, p. 4.

294 "Closed Sunday," *Ibid.*, May 18, p. 1.

295 "These are the Men" *Ibid.*, June 4, 1902, p. 1.

296 "Board of Public Works," Mugge, p. 8.

297 "Morgan's Printing Press," *St. Petersburg Times*, May 31, 1902, p. 1

298 "Electric and Ice Manufacturing Plant," Mugge, *My Memoirs*, p. 6.

299 "Oil Fuel Plant," *Weekly Tribune*, July 3, 1902, p. 7.

300 Johnson, *Sam Patch, the famous jumper*, pp. 132-34, 141.

301 "Temperance Meeting," *St. Petersburg Times*, July 19, 1902, p. 9.

302 *Morning Tribune*, July 1, 1902, p. 8.

303 "Defied the Mayor," *St. Petersburg Times*, July 26, 1902, p. 1.

304 *Ibid.*, July 26, 1902, p. 4.

305 "Pastors On Stand," *Weekly Tribune*, August 7, 1902, p. 7.

306 "Abortion battle," *Tampa Times*, December 14, 1971, p. 2.

307 "Fair Girl's Death," *Morning Tribune*, June 19, 1902, p. 1.

308 "Her Last Letters," *Ibid.*, June 20, 1902, p. 1.

309 "Prosecute Weightnovel," *Ibid.*, June 20, 1902, p. 4.

310 "Weightnovel Guilty," *Weekly Tribune*, January 29, 1903, p. 7.

311 "Supreme Court Grants," *Morning Tribune*, December 20, 1903, p. 1.

312 "Prison Doors at Last Open," *Ibid.*, January 22, 1904, p. 1.

313 "Doctor in Hospital," *Ibid.*, April 4, 1906, p. 1.

314 "Tampa's Most Unique Character," *Ibid.*, May 20, 1906, p. 8.

315 "Will Now Ship," *Ibid.*, November 3, 1907, p. 12.

316 *Ibid.*, August 31, 1902, p. 4.

317 "Proof of Charges," *Ibid.*, September 6, 1902, pp. 1, 5.

318 "Herald's Reply," *Ibid.*, September 7, 1902, pp. 6-7

319 "Proof Of Charges," *Weekly Tribune*, September 11, 1902, p. 7.

320 "The *Tribune's* Judgement," *Ibid.*, September 18, 1902, p. 2.

321 "Never Touched Me!" *St. Petersburg Times*, September 20, 1902, p. 1.

322 "Mugge Closes His Saloon," *Morning Tribune*, October 2, 1902, p. 4.

323 "Slot Machine," *Ibid.*, October 28, 1902, p. 5.

324 "Mayor is Missing," *Morning Tribune*, November 2, 1902, p. 1.

325 "Milian Sailed," *Ibid.*, November 4, 1902, p. 1.

326 "Merchants Protest," *Ibid.*, November 8, 1902, p. 1.

327 "Milian Wires," *Ibid.*, November 12, 1902, p. 8.

328 *Ibid.*, November 13, 1902, p. 4.

329 "Meeting Tonight," *Ibid.*, November 14, 1902, p. 1.

330 "Nickel In Slot," *Ibid.*, December 4, 1902, p. 1.

331 "Created Excitement," *Ibid.*, December 14, 1902, p. 5.

332 "The New Eureka," *Ibid.*, December 21, 1902, p. 6.

333 "20 Years Ago," *Tampa Times*, January 22, 1923, p. 4.

334 "Heroic Battle," *Morning Tribune*, January 27, 1903, p. 1.

335 "A Brief Interview," *Ibid.*, March 13, 1903, p. 3.

336 "Going to Europe," *Ibid.*, May 10, 1903, p. 1.

337 "Trip to Germany," Mugge, *My Memoirs*, p. 19.

338 Walden, "The Colorful History of Central State Hospital," *The Telegraph*, www.macon.com/living/liv-columns-blogs/article104958166.html.

339 Mugge, p. 19.

340 "To Sail on the Koln Today," *Baltimore Sun*, May 13, 1907, p. 6.

341 "Trip to Germany" and "Darmstadt," Mugge, pp. 19-22.

342 "Education in Germany," February 2, 2014, centenarynews.com.

343 Help for Horses," *Morning Tribune*, June 7, 1903, p. 2.

344 "Mugge Gives a Fountain," *Weekly Tribune*, June 25, 1903, p. 8.

345 "Victim of Mob," *Morning Tribune*, July 31, 1903, p. 1.

346 "Shot as He Fled," *Ibid.*, August 1, 1903, p. 1.

347 "Wadkins Departs," *Ibid.*, August 2, 1903, p. 1.

348 "Negro Outran Another Mob," *Ibid.*, August 2, 1903, p. 1.

349 "Hackmen Depart," *Ibid.*, August 2, 1903, p. 1.

350 "Robert Mugge is Threatened," *Ibid.*, August 4, 1903, p. 1.

351 "Mugge Now Carries a Gun," *Ibid.*, August 5, 1903, p. 1.

352 "The Tampa Plan Is the Best," *Ibid.*, August 8, 1903, p. 4.

353 "Mugge on Bonding," *Ibid.*, August 11, 1903, p. 7.

354 "On a Moonlight Drive," *Ibid.*, August 13, 1903, p. 6.

355 "Warning is Given," *Morning Tribune*, August 15, 1903, p. 1.

356 "Mugge Writes on Waterworks," *Ibid.*, August 18, 1903, p. 3.

357 "Why We Need Bonding," *Ibid.*, August 20, 1903, p. 1.

358 "War on Saloons," *Ibid.*, September 2, 1903, p. 1.

359 "Sabbath Sellers," *Ibid.*, September 4, 1903, p. 1.

360 "Make It General," *Ibid.*, September 5, 1903, p. 4.

361 "Mugge Asks for Fair Treatment," *Ibid.*, September 6, 1903, p. 5.

362 "Saloon Keepers Must Obey Law," *St. Petersburg Times*, September 12, 1903, p. 1.

363 "Sunday Liquor Stock," *Morning Tribune*, September 12, 1903, p. 1.

364 "Mugge Makes Affidavits," *Ibid.*, September 16, 1903, p. 6.

365 "The Art of Gathering," Rivers and Brown, *The Journal of African American History*.

366 "Buckingham Theatre Saloon," *Morning Tribune*, October 17, 1899, p. 3.

367 "Theatre Mascotte Saloon," *Ibid.*, December 8, 1899, p. 7.

368 "The Buckingham Theater," *Ibid.*, December 24, 1901, p. 1.

369 "Chappelle & Donaldson," *Ibid.*, January 14, 1900, p. 2.

370 "Buckingham Bijou," *Morning Tribune*, November 21, 1900, p. 2.

371 *Ibid.*

372 "Genuine Minstrel Show," *Ibid.*, February 6, 1903, p. 2.

373 "Only One Was Held," *Ibid.*, August 13, 1902, p. 2.

374 "Twenty-Seven Gamblers," *Ibid.*, February 15, 1903, p. 1.

375 "Sues for 'Coon' Cornetist," *Ibid.*, March 4, 1903, p. 2.

376 *Ibid.*, March 20, 1903, p. 1.

377 "Hurricane," *Ibid.*, September 13, 1903, p. 2.

378 "20 Years Ago," *Tampa Times*, as reprinted on September 15, 1923, p. 4.

379 "Schooner Lost," *Morning Tribune*, September 16, 1903, p. 1.

380 "That Buckingham Affair," *Ibid.*, September 19, 1903, p. 2.

381 "Sunday Seller," *Ibid.*, September 4, 1903, p. 1.

382 "Pardoning Board Work," *Ibid.*, April 6, 1905, p. 5.

383 "Tampa's Colored Organization," *Ibid*, January 7, 1908, p. 3.

384 "Mr. Mugge Departs," *Ibid.*, September 24, 1903, p. 6.

385 "Brandon," *Ibid.*, October 14, 1903, p. 7.

386 Mugge, *My Memoirs*, p. 72.

387 "Jackson's Dead Body," *Morning Tribune*, December 5, 1903, p. 1.

388 "Mugge Drunk?" *Ibid.*, December 9, 1903, p. 1.

389 "'Liars!' Roared Mugge," *Morning Tribune*, December 10, 1903, p. 1.

390 "Neighbors in Fatal Duel," *Ibid.*, January 16, 1904, p. 1.

391 "Took Bartender's Roll," *Ibid.*, January 22, 1904, p. 8.

392 "Mugge again swears off," *Ibid.*, January 26, 1904, p. 1.

393 "Bartender Was Killed," *Weekly Tribune*, February 4, 1904, p. 8.

394 "Beagles Free," *Morning Tribune*, February 9, 1904, p. 1.

395 "Survived Only a Few Days," *Ibid.*, February 10, 1904, p. 1.

396 "Light Infantry," *Ibid.*, February 23, 1904, p. 1.

397 "Patrolman Runs Amuck," *Ibid.*, February 23, 1908, p. 1.

398 "Beagles Is Discharged," *Ibid.*, February 26, 1908, p. 1.

399 "Geiger Hit," *Ibid.*, February 4, 1912, p. 10.

400 "Beagles on the Warpath," *Ibid.*, January 6, 1913, p.5.

401 Twain and Warner, *The Gilded Age: A Tale of Today*.

402 "For Sale," *Morning Tribune*, January 19, 1904, p. 1.

403 *Ibid.*, March 18, 1904, p. 5.

404 "Fire Sweeps Away," *Ibid.*, April 5, 1904, p. 1

405 "Mugge Was Quick," *Ibid.*, April 6, 1904, p. 1.

406 "In Four Days," *Ibid.*, April 7, 1904, p. 1.

407 Letter from Adolphus Busch to Robert Mugge, April 25, 1904.

408 "Notice," *Morning Tribune*, October 4, 1904, p. 1.

409 "Souvenirs," *Ibid.*, October 7, 1905, p. 1.

410 Letter from Adolphus Busch, April 25, 1904.

411 "Important Case," *Morning Tribune*, April 20, 1904, p. 1.

412 *Tampa Times*, as reprinted in *Miami News*, April 23, 1904, p. 3.

413 "'Not a Cent' Said Mugge ...," *Morning Tribune*, October 20, 1904, p. 1.

414 "30 Years Ago," *Tampa Times* of December 1901, as reprinted on December 12, 1931, p. 8.

415 Mugge, *My Memoirs*, pp. 64, 73.

416 "Mugge and the Fair," *Morning Tribune*, October 29, 1904, p. 4.

417 "Bonds Will Be Carried," *Ibid.*, November 3, 1904, p. 1.

418 "Full Election Returns," *Ibid.*, November 8, 1904, p. 4.

419 "A Great Crowd Watched," *Ibid.*, November 10, 1904, p. 6.

420 "Robert Mugge, the Man," Mugge, p. 14.

421 "Wholesale Liquors, Distiller," *Tampa, The Metropolis of South Florida*, p. 80.

422 "Born," *Morning Tribune*, January 25, 1905, p. 1.

423 "Injunction," *Ibid.*, March 26, 1905, p. 1.

424 "To Head Off the Sale," *Ocala Evening Star*, March 27, 1905, p. 1.

425 "Brewer Busch Loses," *Morning Tribune*, March 28, 1905, p. 1.

426 "Poor, Persecuted Mugge," *Ibid.*, March 29, 1905, p. 1.

427 "Frank Q. Brown," *Ibid.*, March 30, 1905, p. 8.

428 "Hotel Transaction," Mugge, *My Memoirs*, p. 13.

429 "Out For a Lark," *Morning Tribune*, April 11, 1905, p. 1.

430 "Neighbors Object," *Ibid.*, April 12, 1905, p. 8.

431 "Claim Ollie Has Reformed," *Ibid.*, April 13, 1905, p. 1.

432 "Mugge Fined Twenty-Five," *Ibid.*, April 14, 1905, p. 8.

433 "Officer Ahn Arrested," *Ibid.*, April 22, 1905, p. 2.

434 "Ahn's Checkered Career," *Ibid.*, May 6, 1905, p. 1.

435　"Mrs. Ahn No. 4," *Ibid.*, May 7, 1905, p. 1.

436　"Jim Ahn Again Wedded," *Ibid.*, June 16, 1906, p. 5.

437　"White Girl; Colored Boy," *Ibid.*, May 14, 1905, p. 1.

438　"Buys Eagle Saloon," *Kissimmee Valley Gazette*, March 10, 1905.

439　"Grants Mugge's Permit," *Ibid.*, May 5, 1905.

440　*Ibid.*, May 12, 1905.

441　"For Another's Sin," *Morning Tribune*, May 17, 1905, p. 1.

442　"Nickel in Slot," *Ibid.*, December 4, 1902, p. 1.

443　"Took Bartender's Roll," *Ibid.*, January 22, 1904, p. 8.

444　"Serious Fire," *Ibid.*, May 24, 1905, p. 1.

445　"To Build One-Story," *Ibid.*, May 25, 1905, p. 5.

446　"Saloon Man Complains," *Ibid.*, June 23, 1905, p. 1.

447　"Owns Tampa Bay Hotel," *Ibid.*, June 23, 1905, p. 12.

448　"A Good Piece of Work," *Ibid.*, July 15, 1905, p. 10.

449　"Leases the Tampa Bay," *Ibid.*, September 20, 1905, p. 1.

450　"Temperate Life," *Ibid.*, October 1, 1905, p. 12.

451　*Morning Tribune*, January 12, 1906, p. 4.

452　"From Mr. Mugge," *Ibid.*, January 13, 1906, p. 1.

453　*Ibid.*, January 14, 1906, p. 4.

454　"Wet and Dry Election," *Ibid.*, February 2, 1906, p. 1.

455　"Newsy Notes," *Ibid.*, February 13, 1906, p. 8.

456　"Cost of Paving," *Ibid.*, April 10, 1906, p. 1.

457　"Pertinent Remarks," *Ibid.*, May 6, 1906, p. 4.

458　"Board of Public Works," *Weekly Tribune*, May 10, 1906, p. 1.

459　*Ibid.*, May 10, 1906, p. 10.

460　"Board Public Works," *Morning Tribune*, June 6, 1906, p. 1.

461　"A Good Record," *Ibid.*, June 12, 1906, p. 4.

462　"Before Supreme Court," *Weekly Tribune*, June 7, 1906, p. 4.

463　"New Machine Shop," *Morning Tribune*, July 11, 1906, p. 6.

[464] "Serious Fire in Ybor City," *Ibid.*, July 13, 1906, p. 2.

[465] "Companies Must Furnish," *Pensacola Journal*, July 13, 1906, p. 1.

[466] "Decision On Mugge Suit," *Morning Tribune*, July 14, 1906, p. 1.

[467] "Card From Hubbard," *Ibid.*, July 18, 1906, p. 1.

[468] "Loses First 'Showdown,'" *Ibid.*, July 20, 1906, p. 1.

[469] "From German University," *Weekly Tribune*, July 26, 1906, p. 2.

[470] Mugge, *My Memoirs*, p. 27.

[471] "No More Seminole," *Morning Tribune*, September 5, 1906, p. 1.

[472] "New Building," *Ibid.*, October 12, 1906, p. 1.

[473] "Rehearing Refused," *Ibid.*, October 19, 1906, p. 1.

[474] "Mugge After Water Front," *Ibid.*, October 27, 1906, p. 1.

[475] "Business Briefs," *Ibid.*, November 3, 1906, p. 1.

[476] "Ice Plant Proposed," *Ibid.*, November 6, 1906, p. 1.

[477] "The Ice Contract," Mugge, p. 13.

[478] "New Steamship Company," *Morning Tribune*, November 10, 1906, p. 1.

[479] "Mugge's Saloon," *Ibid.*, November 8, 1906, p. 8.

[480] "No Booze for 28," *Ibid.*, November 10, 1906, 1.

[481] "Liquor Litigation," *Ibid.*, November 13, 1906, p. 1.

[482] "Saloon Men," *Ibid.*, December 1, 1906, p. 1

[483] "To be Rebuilt," *Ibid.*, December 30, 1906, p. 5.

[484] "Gasoline Lamp Plant," *Morning Tribune*, January 4, 1907, p. 1.

[485] "Robert Mugge, the Investor," Mugge, *My Memoirs*, p. 11.

[486] "Notice of Engagement," *Morning Tribune*, March 9, 1907, p. 5.

[487] "Eugene's Marriage," Mugge, p. 27.

[488] "Thoughtful Suggestions," *Morning Tribune*, March 10, 1907, p. 4.

[489] "A Suggestion," *Ibid.*, March 10, 1907, p. 16.

[490] "Million Dollar Steamship Co." *Ibid.*, April 7, 1907, p. 1.

[491] "On Cleanliness," *Ibid.*, June 5, 1907, p. 3.

492　"Trained Nurses," *Ibid.*, July 13, 1907, p. 6.

493　"Project Strongly Endorsed," *Ibid.*, April 10, 1907, p. 1.

494　*Ibid.*, April 13, 1907, p. 10.

495　"Mugge Wins," *Ibid.*, May 19, 1907, p. 1.

496　"1899 Act Constitutional," *Ibid.*, May 22, 1907, p. 1.

497　"Violation of Revenue Law," *Ibid.*, June 2, 1907, p. 1.

498　"Notice of Application," *Ibid.*, August 10, 1907, p. 7.

499　"Block Nearly Finished," *Ibid.*, June 20, 1907, p. 3.

500　"Full of Promise," *Ibid*, June 26, 1907, p. 2

501　"Fire Yesterday Causes Loss," *Ibid.*, November 1, 1907, p. 1.

502　"Steamship Morgan," *Ibid.*, November 21, 1907, p. 10.

503　*Ibid.*, December 6, 1907, p. 7.

504　"The Financial Panic of 1907," October 9, 2008, smithsonianmag.com/history/the-financial-panic-of-1907-running-from-history-82176328/.

505　"Would Overthrow Credit," *Morning Tribune*, January 26, 1908. p. 3.

506　"Another Reply to Mugge," *Ibid.*, February 4, 1908, p. 3.

507　"One More to Mugge," *Ibid.*

508　"More on Mugge's Letter," *Ibid.*, March 6, 1908, p. 7.

509　"Carry Nation.," *St. Petersburg Times*, January 29, 1908, p. 1.

510　"Carrie Nation To Call," *Morning Tribune*, February 2, 1908, p. 1.

511　"United Confederate Veterans," *Ibid.*, February 19, 1908, p. 1.

512　Leigh, "Who Burned Atlanta?" *The New York Times*, opinionator.blogs.nytimes.com/2014/11/13/who-burned-atlanta/.

513　"Ybor City Fire-Swept," *Morning Tribune*, March 1, 1908, p. 1.

514　"Tampa Realizes Fire Disaster," *Ibid.*, March 3, 1908, p. 1.

515　"Council Stops Rent," *Ibid.*, March 7, 1908, p. 1.

516　"Fire Chief Savage," *Ibid.*, March 12, 1908, p. 7.

517　Birth of Margarete Mugge, Oaklawn Cemetery Records.

[518] "Thrown Off Wheel," *Morning Tribune*, April 5, 1908, p. 1.

[519] "Loss and Suffering," *Ibid.*, April 28, 1908, p. 4.

[520] "Seek To Be Left Out," *Ibid.*, May 28, 1908, p. 1.

[521] "Mugge's Idea of 'Silliness,'" *Ibid.*, June 24, 1908, p. 2.

[522] "Caught Gaming," *Ibid.*, July 4, 1908, p. 1.

[523] Gibbon, "African American students," *Florida Times-Union*, November 1, 2016, www.jacksonville.com/opinion/2016-11-1/guest-column-upstart-private-orange-park-school-helped-pioneer-african-american.

[524] "Party Formed," *Morning Tribune*, July 24, 1908, p. 2.

[525] "No Faction Shall Secure," *Ibid.*, August 4, 1908, p. 3.

[526] "Seven Members of City Council," *Ibid.*, August 13, 1908, p. 3.

[527] "A 'Disturbing Element,'" *Ibid.*, August 15, 1908, p. 4.

[528] "Saloon Changes Hands," *Ibid.*, October 13, 1908, p. 8.

[529] "Rescind Them," *Ibid.*, November 13, 1908, p. 4.

[530] *Ibid.*, November 13, 1908, p. 4.

[531] "Death of Margarete Mugge," *Morning Tribune*, January 5, 1909, p. 8.

[532] Margarete Wilhelmine Eugenia Mugge, Oaklawn Cemetery Records.

[533] "Saloon Changes Hands," *Morning Tribune*, January 14, 1909, p. 7.

[534] "A Pleasant Surprise Party," *Ibid.*, June 17, 1909, p. 5.

[535] "Memphis Pays Little Heed," *Ibid.*, July 5, 1909, p. 1.

[536] "New Whiskey Law," *Ibid.*, *(Associated Press)*, July 11, 1909, p. 12.

[537] Mugge, *Practical Humanity*, pp. 59-62.

[538] Birth of Marie Mugge, *Morning Tribune*, July 7, 1909, p. 2.

[539] *Ibid.*, September 2, 1909, p. 5.

[540] Mugge, *My Memoirs*, p. 37.

[541] *Morning Tribune*, November 2, 1909, p. 7.

[542] "Eleven Attorneys," *Ibid.*, December 20, 1909, p. 10.

543   "Suit Opens in Court," *Ibid.*, December 29, 1909, p. 12.

544   "Pressure Feeble," *Morning Tribune*, January 2, 1910, p. 12.

545   "Plaintiff Side," *Ibid.*, January 4, 1910, p. 12.

546   "'One Squirt,' Lawyer Says," *Ibid.*, January 5, 1910, p. 12.

547   "Arguments On," *Ibid.*, January 6, 1910, p. 5.

548   "Water Company Motion Denied," *Ibid*, January 7, 1910, p. 12.

549   "Trial Will Drag into Next Week," *Ibid.*, January 8, 1910, p. 9.

550   "Sixty-Six Pounds Water Pressure," *Ibid.*, January 9, 1910, p. 12.

551   "Mugge Case Is Long Drawn Out," *Ibid.*, January 11, 1910, p. 9.

552   "Arguments Begin," *Ibid.*, January 12, 1910, p. 9.

553   "Knight Makes a Marathon Talk," *Ibid.*, January 14, 1910, p. 9.

554   "Mugge Is Given $16,000 Verdict," *Ibid*, January 15, 1910, p. 3.

555   *Ibid.*, January 26, 1910, p. 11.

556   "Loftis Opens Branch," *Ibid.*, May 18, 1910, p. 5.

557   *Weekly Tribune*, May 5, 1910, p. 8.

558   Mugge, *My Memoirs*, pp. 48-49.

559   "Officers Seize Whiskey," *Morning Tribune*, May 22, 1910, p. 21.

560   *Ibid.*, May 26, 1910, p. 9.

561   "Automobiles to be Built Here," *Weekly Tribune*, July 14, 1910, p. 10.

562   Bogdanovitch, "FILM; is that ticking?" *The New York Times*, April 11, 1999, nytimes.com1999/04/11/movies/film-is-that-ticking-pause-a-bomb.html.

563   "Crown Cap," *Craft Beer & Brewing*, beerandbrewing.com/dictionary/OgmlWvHjQc/.

564   *Morning Tribune*, August 11, 1910, p. 4.

565   "Giant Demonstration," *Morning Tribune*, August 12, 1910, p. 12.

566   "Cowardly Attack," *Ibid.*, September 15, 1910, p. 12.

567   "Two Men Taken," *Ibid.*, September 21, 1910, p. 1.

568   "Quiet Again Reigns," *Ibid.*, September 22, 1910, p. 16.

569 *Ibid.*, October 4, 1910, p. 7.

570 Martha Washington Mugge, *Tagebuch* (German for *Diary*), Summer 1910, pp. 1-3.

571 "Easterling Dies," *Morning Tribune*, September 29, 1910, p. 2.

572 "Saloons of Tampa Closed," *Ibid.*, October 5, 1910, p. 5.

573 "Inciting Murder," *Ibid.*, October 19, 1910, p. 1.

574 "Derry Taft Hanged," *Ibid.*

575 "Tampa is Isolated," *Ibid.*

576 "Waterworks Case Argues," *Ibid.*, November 18, 1910, p. 4.

577 "Peter O. Knight," Peeples, *Twenty Four Years*, pp. 164-66.

578 Bernanke, "Ending 'too big to fail,'" *Brookings*, May 13, 2016, brookings.edu/blog/ben-bernanke/2016/05/13/ending-too-big-to-fail-what's-the-right-approach/.

579 "Labor Agitators," *Morning Tribune*, November 24, 1910, p. 1.

580 "Reversal of Decision," *Ibid.*, December 21, 1910, p. 16.

581 "Court Decision," *Ibid.*, December 22, 1910, p. 12.

582 "No Indictments," *Ibid.*, December 23, 1910, p. 12.

583 "Five-Story Wholesale House," *Morning Tribune*, May 16, 1911, p. 12.

584 "Six Story Mugge Building," *Ibid.*, May 27, 1911, p. 12.

585 "As High as People Expect," *Ibid.*, June 22, 1911, p. 11.

586 "Eugene Mugge Injured," *Ibid.*, June 17, 1911, p. 8.

587 "Property Near Union Station," *Ibid.*, July 30, 1911, p. 4.

588 "Notice to Contractors," *Ibid.*, August 6, 1911, p. 18.

589 "Barroom Warmly Protested," *Ibid.*, September 6, 1911, p. 8.

590 "History of Anna Maria Island," annamaria.com/history-of-anna-maria-island/

591 Mugge, *My Memoirs*, p. 18.

592 *Ibid.*, pp. 49-50, 52-53, 54-56.

593 "Great White Way--the term," greatwhiteway.com/about.shtml.

594 "Alabama Great White Way," *Tampa Times*, January 30, 1912, p. 12

595 "Sunlight Lighting System," *Ibid.*, February 19, 1912, p. 7.

596 "Mugge to Build Brick Block," *Ibid.*, March 2, 1912, p. 19.

597 "Two Acres of Floors," *Ibid.*, May 11, 1912, p. 9.

598 "Robert Mugge Robbed," *Morning Tribune*, July 10, 1912, p. 3.

599 *Morning Tribune*, August 29, 1912, p. 2.

600 "$25.00 for Fighting," *Ibid.*, June 10, 1906, p. 1.

601 "Striking a Negress," *Ibid.*, November 2, 1907, p. 1.

602 "Here's Your Proof," *Ibid.*, May 6, 1902, p. 1.

603 "Attempted Blackmail," *Ibid.*, December 20, 1911, p. 3.

604 "Serious Charges," *Ibid.*, March 14, 1905, p. 1.

605 "Charges Against Officer Phillips," *Ibid.*, July 6, 1909, p. 8.

606 "Drunken Deputy Shoots Saloonist," *Ibid.*, April 3, 1911, p. 10.

607 "Rawlins Throws a Bomb," *Tampa Times*, September 3, 1912, p. 2.

608 "After Mugge's License," *Ibid.*, September 3, 1912, p. 2.

609 "Wants Higher Standard," *Ibid.*, September 4, 1912, p. 9.

610 "Mugge Given a Liquor Permit," *Ibid.*, September 4, 1912, p. 7.

611 "Mugge Gets Permits," *Morning Tribune*, September 5, 1912, p. 5.

612 "Rawlins Like a Mule," *Tampa Times*, September 6, 1912, p. 9.

613 "Mugge Fined in Police Court," *Ibid.*, September 21, 1012, p. 12.

614 "Great White Way," *Ibid.*, October 24, 1912, p. 14.

615 "Great White Way—the term," greatwhiteway.com/about.shtml.

616 "'Talkies' Will Replace 'Movies,'" *Morning Tribune*, January 19, 1913, p. 15.

617 "Pre-World War II Sound Era," Encyclopedia Britannica.com/art/history-of-the-motion—picture/The—pre-World-War-II-sound-era.

618 "New Mugge Building," *Morning Tribune*, February 10, 1913, p. 5.

619 "Mugge Takes a Peculiar Stand," *Tampa Times*, March 4, 1913, p. 19.

620 "Mugge Don't Want Gates," *Morning Tribune*, March 4, 1913, p. 7.

621 "Waiting on Mugge," *Weekly Tribune*, May 29, 1913, p. 9.

622 White, *Railroaded*, p. 509.

623 Twain and Warner, *The Gilded Age*.

624 White, *Railroaded*, pp. xxxiii-xxxiv, xxix.

625 "10-Story Hotel for this City," *Tampa Times*, March 18, 1913, p. 2.

626 "Plans Ten-Story Hotel," *Morning Tribune*, March 19, 1913, p. 10.

627 "Petition in Bankruptcy," *Tampa Times*, April 3, 1913, p. 2.

628 "Robert Mugge, the Investor," Mugge, *My Memoirs*, p. 11.

629 "Lawbreakers Are Against Charter," *Morning Tribune*, April 6, 1913, p. 8.

630 *Tampa Times*, April 7, 1913, p. 4.

631 "Ybor City Defeats Charter," *Morning Tribune*, April 1913, p. 8.

632 "The Mortal Triumvirate," *Tampa Times*, April 9, 1913, p. 1.

633 "An Appeal to Reason," *Morning Tribune*, April 11, 1913, p. 13.

634 "A Reply to Bolita," *Ibid.*, April 12, 1913, p. 13.

635 "To Deepen Hillsborough," *Morning Tribune*, April 17, 1913, p. 4.

636 "Hillsborough Deepening," *Ibid.*, April 23, 1913, p. 12.

637 "Not Acted on By Board," *Ibid.*, April 24, 1913, p. 5.

638 "Borrow Million for River," *Ibid.*, May 9, 1913, p. 5.

639 "To Have River Improved," *Ibid.*, May 10, 1913, p. 5.

640 "River Improvement," *Ibid.*, May 11, 1913, p. 8.

641 "Mugge Wants to Help," *Ibid.*, May 11, 1913, p. 11.

642 "Building Roads," *Ibid.*, May 22, 1913, p. 4.

643 "Ten Feet for a Street," *Ibid.*, July 6, 1913, p. 16.

644 "The Mugge Building," *Tampa Times*, April 19, 1913, p. 20.

645 "126-Room Hotel," *Ibid.*, May 31, 1913, p.9.

646 "Against River Improvement," *Morning Tribune*, June 7, 1913, p. 5.

647 "Will Operate Cars," *Ibid.*, June 14, 1913, p. 5."

648 "Mugge to Replace," *Tampa Times*, September 24, 1913, p. 9.

649 "Busch Made Big Gifts," *Morning Tribune*, October 19, 1913, p. 45.

650 *Kronprinzessin* Passenger List, ancestry.com.

651 *Morning Tribune*, December 2, 1913, p. 16.

652 Mugge, *My Memoirs*, pp. 58-60.

653 "New Steamer Line," *Morning Tribune*, December 9, 1913, p. 5.

654 "Hotel for Negroes," *Morning Tribune*, December 30, 1913, p. 4.

655 "Will Build $40,000 Apartments," *Ibid.*, January 4, 1914, p. 20.

656 "Hotel for Negroes," *Ibid.*, December 30, 1913, p. 4.

657 Mugge, early Black hotels, 2003 film *Last of the Mississippi Jukes* (MVD Visual).

658 *Morning Tribune*, January 29, 1914, p. 7.

659 "Mugge Hotel Will Open," *Ibid.*, March 24, 1914, p. 5.

660 "Central Hotel," Mugge, *My Memoirs*, P. 60.

661 "Banquet in Hall," *Morning Tribune*, May 13, 1914, p. 16.

662 "Work Going Ahead," *Weekly Tribune*, April 9, 1914, p. 8.

663 Mugge, p. 15.

664 "Whiskey With Water," *Morning Tribune*, May 26, 1914, p. 5.

665 "Verdict of Not Guilty," *Tampa Times*, May 26, 1914, p. 5.

666 *Morning Tribune*, July 21, 1914, p. 7.

667 Mugge, pp. 15, 66, 68.

668 "Tampa's Jewish History," *The Laker/Lutz News*, November 1, 2017, lakerlutznews.com.

669 "From Sublime to Ridiculous," *Tampa Times*, August 2, 1914, p. 8.

670 "Anxiety Felt Over Tampans," *Morning Tribune*, August 2, 1914, p. 3.

671 Royde-Smith, "World War I," *Encyclopedia Britannica*, britannica.com/event/World-War-I.

672 "Here's from Wife and Baby," *Morning Tribune*, August 29, 1914, p. 10.

673 "Council to Reduce Saloons," *Ibid.*, July 20, 1914, p. 5.

674 "Mugge Prefers to Open Hotel," *Tampa Times*, September 15, 1914, p. 14.

675 "May Be Opened First of Year," *Morning Tribune*, September 17, 1914, p. 14.

676 Mugge, p. 76.

677 *Ibid.*, p. 86.

678 "Metal Window," *Morning Tribune*, October 18, 1914, p. 13.

679 "Bay View is Promised Shortly," *Morning Tribune*, November 7, 1914, p. 9.

680 "Open Air Meeting," *Ibid.*, November 29, 1914, p. 1.

681 "Disturbers are Fined," *Ibid.*, December 1, 1914, p. 11.

682 "Mugge Building Finished," *Ibid.*, December 13, 1914, p. 10.

683 "Bowling Alley in Old Place," *Tampa Times*, January 9, 1915, p. 5.

684 "Mugge-Reiner," *Ibid.*, January 11, 1915, p. 6.

685 "Willing to Go Home to Fight," *Morning Tribune*, August 6, 1941, p. 11.

686 "Bay View Hotel Will Open," *Ibid.*, January 12, 1915, p. 13.

687 "Bayview Hotel Opens," *Ibid.*, January 19, 1915, p. 4.

688 "Bay View Hotel Open to Public," *Tampa Times*, January 19, 1915, p. 9.

689 "Bay View Hotel," Mugge, *My Memoirs*, pp. 62-63.

690 "Tampa's New Hotel," *Morning Tribune*, January 20, 1915, p. 6.

691 *Sunland Tribune*, August 25, 1877, p. 3.

692 *Tampa Times*, January 20, 1915, p. 5.

693 "Stanford Steps Down," *Morning Tribune*, January 31, 1915, p. 7.

694   "Stanford Out of Bay View," *Tampa Times*, February 1, 1915, p. 7.

695   "Bay View Hotel," Mugge, p. 63.

696   *Morning Tribune*, February 6, 1915, p. 16.

697   "E. S. Clauss," Mugge, pp. 63-64.

698   "Opening of Alleys," *Morning Tribune*, February 11, 1915, p. 6.

699   "Bowling Coming into Own," *Ibid.*, February 13, 1915, p. 14.

700   "Tried to Deceive Council?" *Tampa Times*, February 24, 1915, p. 10.

701   "Mugge Arrested," *Ibid.*, February 27, 1915, p. 5.

702   "A Plea for License," *Ibid.*, March 3, 1915, p. 9.

703   "Mugge Case Postponed," *Morning Tribune*, March 5, 1915, p. 5.

704   "Mugge Petition Returned," *Ibid.*, March 10, 1915, p. 7.

705   "Mugge Case Postponed," *Tampa Times*, March 11, 1915, p. 10.

706   "Mugge Secures a License," *Ibid.*, March 24, 1915, p. 6.

707   "Mugge Sentence Suspended," *Morning Tribune*, March 26, 1915, p. 14.

708   "Theft of Fans," *Ibid.*, April 16, 1915, p. 14.

709   "Photo Envelopes," *Ibid.*, April 23, 1915, p. 14.

710   Mugge, *My Memoirs*, p. 64.

711   "By the Bottle," *Morning Tribune*, April 30, 1915, p. 6.

712   Okrent, *Last Call*, pp. 83-86.

713   "Package Law Hits the City," *Morning Tribune*, September 14, 1915, p. 5.

714   "Local Dealers Will Not Fight," *Ibid.*, September 16, 1915, p. 5.

715   "Cancel policies," *Tampa Times*, September 21, 1915, p. 10.

716   "Denatured Saloon," *Morning Tribune*, September 30, 1915, p. 13.

717   "Social Club Files," *Ibid.*, September 29, 1915, p. 9.

718   "Saloon Fixtures," *Ibid.*, November 11, 1915, p. 10.

719   "City Council Uproot," *Ibid.*, October 1, 1915, p. 5.

[720] "John Barleycorn Back," *Ibid.*, October 1, 1915, p. 1, 11.

[721] "Adopted by the Sheriff," *Ibid.*, October 3, 1915, p. 9.

[722] "Size of Hip Pockets," *Ibid.*, October 4, 1915, p. 5.

[723] "Things are Different," *Ibid.*, October 14, 1915, p. 5.

[724] Mugge, p. 64.

[725] "Supreme Court Sustains," *Morning Tribune*, November 5, 1915, pp. 1, 4.

[726] "Folly of a Law," *Ibid.*, November 20, 1915, p. 6.

[727] "Farcical," *Ibid.*, December 2, 1915, p. 6.

[728] Stephens, "Why Edmund Burke," *The New York Times*, August 9, 2020, Section SR, p. 6.

[729] Mugge, p. 64, 65.

[730] "Munitions are Made," *Morning Tribune*, December 10, 1915, p. 5.

[731] "Liquor Law Violation," *Ibid.*, December 12, 1915, p. 21.

[732] "A Premonition" and "His Death," Mugge, *My Memoirs*, pp. 67-68,

[733] "Robert Mugge Dies," *Morning Tribune*, December 17, 1915, p. 1.

[734] "Robert Mugge Dead," *Ibid.*, December 18, 1915, p. 8.

[735] "Services Over Robert Mugge," *Ibid.*, p. 9.

[736] Mugge, pp. 68, 193.

[737] Mugge baptism records, Evangelical Lutheran Church of St. Andreas, (Bad) Lauterberg, Germany.

[738] "Mugge Funeral," *Morning Tribune*, December 20, 1915, p. 5

[739] "Card of Thanks," *Ibid.*, December 21, 1915, p. 5.

[740] "My Mother," Mugge, p. 100.

[741] "In Charge of Estate," *Morning Tribune*, December 24, 1915, p. 8.

[742] "Adjourns for the Term," *Ibid.*, p. 5.

[743] "Quiet New Year's Eve," *Ibid.*, December 31, 1915, p. 14.

[744] "How Could They Be?" *Miami Herald*, December 25, 1915, p. 4.

[745] "Great White Way," *Tampa Times*, April 3, 1916, p. 7.

[746] "Million Dollar Property," *Ibid.*, August 1, 1917, p. 1.

[747] "Board No. 1," *Morning Tribune*, June 16, 1918, p. 5.

[748] Mugge, p. 71.

[749] "One German's Opinion," *Tampa Times*, February 1, 1918, p. 4.

[750] Mugge, *Practical Humanity*, pp. 93-94.

[751] "Prohibition," *Encyclopedia Britannica*, www.britannica.com/event/Prohibition-United-States-history-1920-1933.

[752] "National Prohibition," *Morning Tribune*, January 16, 1920, p. 1.

[753] "Prohibition," *Encyclopedia Britannica*, www.britannica.com/.

About the Author

Since 1976, Robert Mugge has produced more than three dozen documentaries about various aspects of American culture, with particular emphasis on traditional forms of American music. In his 2023 book, *Notes from the Road: A Filmmaker's Journey through American Music*, Mugge described the making of what he considered to be his twenty-five key music films to date, from *Sun Ra: A Joyful Noise* and *Gospel According to Al Green* to *Deep Blues* and *New Orleans Music in Exile*. His 2024 book, *Saloon Man: A German Immigrant Battles the Limits of Liberty, 1870 to 1915*, is a biography of his highly accomplished great-grandfather, also named Robert Mugge. His 2024 film, unrelated to the book, is *Deep Roots: The Art and Music of Bill Steber and Friends*. In addition to his many years as an independent filmmaker, and more recent ones as an indie author, Mugge has served as Filmmaker in Residence for Mississippi Public Broadcasting and as an Endowed Chair Professor at Ball State University. For additional information, please explore www.robertmugge.com.

About the Publisher

The Sager Group was founded in 1984. In 2012 it was chartered as a multimedia content brand, with the intent of empowering those who create art—an umbrella beneath which makers can pursue, and profit from, their craft directly, without gatekeepers. TSG publishes books; ministers to artists and provides modest grants; and produces documentary, feature, and commercial films. By harnessing the means of production, The Sager Group helps artists help themselves. For more information, please see TheSagerGroup.net.

MORE BOOKS FROM THE SAGER GROUP

The Swamp: Deceit and Corruption in the CIA
An Elizabeth Petrov Thriller (Book 1)
by Jeff Grant

Chains of Nobility: Brotherhood of the Mamluks (Book 1-3)
by Brad Graft

Meeting Mozart: A Novel Drawn from the Secret Diaries of Lorenzo Da Ponte

by Howard Jay Smith

Death Came Swiftly: Novel About the Tay Bridge Disaster of 1879
by Bill Abrams

A Boy and His Dog in Hell: And Other Stories
by Mike Sager

Miss Havilland: A Novel
by Gay Daly

The Orphan's Daughter: A Novel
by Jan Cherubin

Lifeboat No. 8: Surviving the Titanic
by Elizabeth Kaye

Into the River of Angels: A Novel
by George R. Wolfe

See our entire library at TheSagerGroup.net

THE SAGER GROUP

Artifex Te Adiuva